D1570408

The Culture of Opera Buffa
in Mozart's Vienna

PRINCETON STUDIES IN OPERA

CAROLYN ABBATE AND ROGER PARKER,
SERIES EDITORS

Reading Opera edited by Arthur Groos and Roger Parker

Puccini's Turandot: *The End of the Great Tradition*
by William Ashbrook and Harold Powers

Unsung Voices: Opera and Musical Narrative in the Nineteenth Century
by Carolyn Abbate

Wagner Androgyne: A Study in Interpretation by Jean-Jacques Nattiez,
translated by Stewart Spencer

Music in the Theater: Essays on Verdi and Other Composers
by Pierluigi Petrobelli, with translations by Roger Parker

Leonora's Last Act: Essays in Verdian Discourse
by Roger Parker

*Richard Wagner, Fritz Lang, and the Nibelungen:
The Dramaturgy of Disavowal* by David J. Levin

Monstrous Opera: Rameau and the Tragic Tradition
by Charles Dill

*The Culture of Opera Buffa in Mozart's Vienna:
A Poetics of Entertainment* by Mary Hunter

The Culture of Opera Buffa in Mozart's Vienna

A POETICS OF ENTERTAINMENT

Mary Hunter

PRINCETON UNIVERSITY PRESS

PRINCETON, NEW JERSEY

Hunter, Mary Kathleen, 1951–
The culture of opera buffa in Mozart's Vienna : a poetics of
entertainment / Mary Hunter.
    p.   cm.
Includes bibliographical references and index.
ISBN 0-691-05812-1 (cl : alk. paper)
1. Opera—Austria—Vienna—18th century.   2. Mozart,
Wolfgang Amadeus, 1756–1791.   Operas.   I. Title.
ML1723.8.V6H86   1998
782.1′09436′1309033–dc21   98-12583

This book has been composed in Galliard

http://pup.princeton.edu

Printed in the United States of America

1   3   5   7   9   10   8   6   4   2

To My Parents

George and Shelagh Hunter

CONTENTS

Preface and Acknowledgments   xi

Editorial Policies   xv

Abbreviations   xvii

INTRODUCTION   3

  Theatrical Conversations   3

  Opera Buffa's Place in Viennese Entertainment   6

    German Theatre as a Context for Opera Buffa   7
    Audiences for Opera Buffa   13

  Viennese Opera Buffa as a Repertory   15

  The Poetics of Entertainment   18

    Opera Buffa as Pleasure   19
    Opera Buffa's Politics   20

  The Social Values of Closed Musical Numbers   22

  Mozart "in Context"   24

PART ONE: *Opera Buffa as Entertainment*

CHAPTER ONE
Opera Buffa as Sheer Pleasure   27

  Decontextualization: The Pleasures of the Ending   28

  The Pleasures of the Familiar   30

    Familiar Sources   31
    The Suggestion of Novelty   33
    Models and Archetypes: Familiarity and Convention   34
    Musical Familiarity and Predictability   36
    Plot Archetypes   40

  The Pleasures of Performance   42

    Performed Performances   46

CHAPTER TWO
Opera Buffa's Conservative Frameworks   52

  Realism and Distance   54

  Hierarchy in and around Opera Buffa   56

    The Reinforcement of Hierarchy as a Principle   58

  Affirming Stability   67

CHAPTER THREE
Opera Buffa's Social Reversals   71

    Challenging Hierarchy: Uncrowning the King   73
    Servants in Control: Emphasizing Entertainment   79
    Sentimental Heroines and the Power of Suffering   84

PART TWO: *The Closed Musical Numbers of Opera Buffa and Their Social Implications*

CHAPTER FOUR
Arias: Some Issues   95

    Type and Character   95
    Form and Character   102
    Arias and Individuality: Performance and Subjectivity
      in Aria-Endings   103

CHAPTER FIVE
Class and Gender in Arias: Five Aria Types   110

    The Buffa Aria   110
    The Serva/Contadina *Aria*   126
    Seria Arias: The Statement of Nobility   137
    Seria Arias: The Rage Aria   140
      Rage and Gender   144
    The Sentimental Statement   146
    Conclusion   155

CHAPTER SIX
Ensembles   156

    Some Issues   156
      Numbers   157
      Ensembles and Form   158
      Social Configurations   160
    Mid-Act Ensembles   161
      Smaller Ensembles: A Duet and a Trio   162
      Larger Ensembles: A Quartet   175

CHAPTER SEVEN
Beginning and Ending Together: *Introduzioni* and Finales   196

    Introduzioni   197
      The Ternary Structures of Introduzioni   198
      Functions of Introduzioni   209
    Finales   210
      Dramatic and Musical Structures in Finales   211

Social Structures in Finales   216
Finale Endings   223
Appendix A: Annotated Text of *I filosofi immaginari:*
   Second-Act Finale   227
Appendix B: Annotated Text of *Fra i due litiganti il terzo gode:*
   Second-Act Finale   234

PART THREE: Così Fan Tutte le Opere?
A Masterwork in Context

CHAPTER EIGHT
Così fan tutte in Conversation

                                             247

L'arbore di Diana *and* Così fan tutte   250
La grotta di Trofonio *and* Così fan tutte   257
Don Alfonso, Trofonio, and Flosofia   264
Text and Music in Trofonio and Così   269

CHAPTER NINE
Così fan tutte and Convention

                                             273

A Double-Edged Convention Embraced: Despina   274
Self-Conscious Conventions: Aria Types   278
Conventions Reconfigured: The Household and the Happy End   282
Così, Convention, and Comedy: Musical Beauty and the Relations
   between Text and Music   285
Conclusion   296

APPENDIX ONE
Operas Consulted

                                             299

APPENDIX TWO
Musical Forms in Opera Buffa Arias

                                             305

APPENDIX THREE
Plot Summaries for *I finti eredi, Le gare generose,*

   and *L'incognita perseguitata*   309

Works Cited   313

Index   323

PREFACE AND ACKNOWLEDGMENTS

THIS BOOK addresses a corner of the larger genre of opera buffa—namely a representative sample of the *opere buffe* performed in Vienna between about 1770 and 1790—and attempts to elucidate the habits, or conventions, of that repertory. I am interested in the ways these works iterate and reiterate their stories about class and gender, mobility and stability, rigidity and flexibility, cleverness and stupidity; and in their musical, textual, dramatic, and performative systems of signification. The "poetics" aspect of the book, then, lies in its attention to the qualities of the works themselves, and to the ways they re-enact the ancient habits of comedy. I am, however, also interested in the ways these works seem to have functioned in relation to the audience that went repeatedly to see and hear them. This repertory's undeniable capacity to entertain its audience lay partly in the extraordinary powers of its singers, partly in the social scene connected to going to the theatre, but surely also in the repertory's internal characteristics, habits, and values. Thus the "entertainment" aspect of the book—the attempt to figure out what was appealing about this repertory—is profoundly involved with the "poetics" aspect. This is, then, not a history of opera buffa in Vienna, nor is it a series of biographies of its chief protagonists. It is, rather, an exploration of the interaction between the works and their audiences' "horizons of expectations"[1]—horizons inevitably and powerfully shaped by the habits of the works themselves.

Although my approach is somewhat different from most who have gone before me in the study of opera buffa, the source work of Otto Michtner, Claudio Sartori, Otto Schindler, Taddeo Wiel, and Gustav Zechmeister has been my historical sine qua non[2] and the pioneering biographical and critical books and essays by Andrea Della Corte, Silke Leopold, Irène Mam-

---

[1] The term is Hans Robert Jauss's. See *Toward an Aesthetic of Reception,* trans. Timothy Bahti; introduction by Paul de Man (Minneapolis: University of Minnesota Press, 1982). In a more specifically eighteenth-century context, see Jauss, "Rousseau's *Nouvelle Héloise* and Goethe's *Werther* within the Shift of Horizons from the French Enlightenment to German Idealism," in *Question and Answer: Forms of Dialogic Understanding,* trans. Michael Hays (Minneapolis: University of Minnesota Press, 1988), pp. 151–97.

[2] Otto Michtner, *Das Alte Burgtheater als Opernbühne: Von der Einführung des Deutschen Singspiels (1778) bis zum Tod Kaiser Leopolds II (1792)* (Vienna: Böhlau, 1970); Otto Schindler, "Das Publikum des Burgtheaters in der Josephinischen Ära: Versuch einer Strukturbestimmung," in Dietrich, *Das Burgtheater und sein Publikum,* pp. 11–96; Taddeo Wiel, *I teatri musicali veneziani del settecento,* with afterword by Reinhard Strohm (Leipzig: Peters, 1979); Gustav Zechmeister, *Die Wiener Theater nächst der Burg und nächst dem Kärntnerthor von 1747 bis 1776* (Vienna: Böhlau, 1971); Claudio Sartori, *I libretti italiani a stampa dalle origini al 1800,* 7 vols. (Milan: Bertola & Locatelli, 1990–1994).

czarz, Wolfgang Osthoff, Michael F. Robinson, Reinhard Strohm, Charles E. Troy, Hellmuth Christian Wolff, and Roberto Zanetti[3] have all been fundamental to my work. Without their efforts, as well as the recently collected wisdom of *The New Grove Dictionary of Opera*,[4] it would be impossible to attempt a "poetics" of even this one corner of opera buffa. I can only hope that the hermeneutics I have performed on this repertory do not betray the solid foundations that have made them possible.

I am indebted to Bates College for sabbatical support, as well as for financial help in the production stages of the book; to the American Philosophical Society for a travel grant; to the National Endowment for the Humanities, who helped fund a year at the National Humanities Center in North Carolina, and to the Andrew Mellon fund of that institution for generous support as well as the provision of space, time, and library resources. I am grateful to the library staff at Bates College, especially Paula Matthews, Tom Hayward, and Elaine Ardia, who tracked down arcane sources and brought them to Lewiston when possible. The staff of the Musiksammlung of the Austrian National Library, and the music division of the Széchényi National Library in Budapest were generous with their help and materials, which are the sources for most of the music examples. These are many and occasionally long, in the hope that some readers might be moved to sing them through.

I am most grateful to friends and colleagues in eighteenth-century musical studies who have answered my questions promptly and generously: Bruce Alan Brown, Dexter Edge, Jennifer Griesbach, John A. Rice, and to Dorothea Link who found me copies of books otherwise available only via the xerox machine, and alerted me to several sources in the Musiksammlung of the Austrian National Library. Emanuele Senici was immensely kind in looking more than once at my translations from Italian; remaining faults and infelicities are entirely my own. Many colleagues have given generously of their time to read the manuscript in whole or in part, to offer suggestions, and to try to save me from myself. The book would be much the worse without the sage comments and encouragement of Thomas Bau-

[3] Andrea Della Corte, *L'opera comica italiana nel '700: Studi ed appunti* (Bari: Laterza, 1923); Irène Mamczarz, *Les Intermèdes comiques italiens au XVIIIe siècle* (Paris: Editions du Centre National de la Recherche Scientifique, 1972); Michael Robinson, *Naples and Neapolitan Opera* (Oxford: Clarendon Press, 1972); Wolfgang Osthoff, "Die Opera Buffa," in *Gattungen der Musik in Einzeldarstellungen. Gedenkschrift Leo Schrade,* ed. Wulf Arlt, Ernst Lichtenhahn, and Hans Oesch (Berlin and Munich: Francke, 1973), pp. 678–743; Roberto Zanetti, *La musica italiana nel settecento* (Busto Arsizio: Bramante, 1978); Reinhard Strohm, *Die italienische Oper im 18. Jahrhundert* (Wilhelmshaven: Heinrichshofen, 1979); Charles E. Troy, *The Comic Intermezzo: A Study in the History of Italian Opera* (Ann Arbor: UMI Research Press, 1979), Hellmuth Christian Wolff, *Geschichte der komischen Oper* (Wilhelmshaven: Heinrichshofen, [1981]). See also the relevant sections (by Silke Leopold) in Ludwig Finscher, *Die Musik des 18. Jahrhunderts* (Laaber: Laaber-Verlag, 1985).
[4] Ed. Stanley Sadie (London: Macmillan, 1992).

man, Bruce Alan Brown, David Ellis, Harold Powers, Elaine Sisman, Ann Scott, and Gretchen Wheelock. I have also benefited enormously from conversations with Edmund J. Goehring, Rebecca Green, Ronald Rabin, John A. Rice, and Jessica Waldoff. Three colleagues and friends—Wendy Allanbrook, John Platoff, and Jim Webster—deserve special mention for their extraordinary patience, interest, and encouragement: they have all taken time from their own projects to read the manuscript in whole or in part, sometimes more than once, and have made astute and encouraging comments. Every author should be lucky enough to have colleagues like these. Marta Steele and Jan Lilly at Princeton Press, Marc Mellits, who did the music examples, and Ethan Rowe all merit special thanks for their help in making the manuscript presentable.

I am blessed in my family. My older son has reminded me (often) of the importance of a mind open to music that may not on the face of it seem "good." My younger son's love of comedy keeps its importance fresh in mind. He was also invaluable in the final stages of preparing the manuscript. Both have been thoroughly good tempered about the sacrifices they have made to my work. My parents, to whom this book is dedicated, have encouraged and prodded in appropriate proportion; more importantly, they have shown me by example the sustaining value of intellectual work. To say that my husband, Jim Parakilas, has read much of the book several times, has cooked hundreds of dinners and engaged in probably thousands of hours of opera-buffa discussion, is to try to enumerate and thus to trivialize a debt that goes beyond my ability to express.

EDITORIAL POLICIES

Translations. I have provided the original language in the footnotes for all translations from eighteenth-century sources. Translations are mine except where otherwise noted. Punctuation and spelling in the texts from libretti have occasionally been corrected without comment. I have translated titles of rank where they correspond to a commonly used English word (*prince, baron, queen*). Where the English title is either less meaningful to most readers (e.g., *marchese*) or has no easy English equivalent (e.g., *contino*), I have left it in Italian. The only intentional exception to this concerns the roles of the Conte and Contessa in *Fra i due litiganti il terzo gode,* which I have left in Italian to avoid confusion with the Count and Countess in *Le nozze di Figaro.*

Operatic identification. The librettist and composer are indicated at the first mention of each opera. Thereafter I have normally used only the title, sometimes slightly abbreviated. Appendix 1 lists the main operas studied for this book, with the date of the first Viennese performance as well as the place and date of the premiere. The reader is referred to this appendix for details of names, authorships, and origins.

Plot summaries. Plot summaries for the majority of the most frequently or most elaborately discussed operas in this book (*L'amore artigiano, L'arbore di Diana, Il barbiere di Siviglia, Una cosa rara, Il curioso indiscreto, Fra i due litiganti il terzo gode, La fiera di Venezia, I filosofi immaginari, La grotta di Trofonio, La finta giardiniera, Le gelosie villane*) can be found in *The New Grove Dictionary of Opera.* Plot summaries for three operas discussed several times in this book but not included in *NGO—Le gare generose, I finti eredi,* and *L'incognita perseguitata*—can be found in Appendix 3.

ABBREVIATIONS

AfMw	*Archiv für Musikwissenschaft*
Brown, *Così*	Bruce Alan Brown, *W. A. Mozart: "Così fan tutte"* (Cambridge: Cambridge University Press, 1995)
COJ	*Cambridge Opera Journal*
DJbM	*Deutsches Jahrbuch der Musikwissenschaft*
EM	*Early Music*
JAMS	*Journal of the American Musicological Society*
JM	*Journal of Musicology*
M-Jb	*Mozart-Jahrbuch*
M&L	*Music and Letters*
Michtner, *DAB*	Otto Michtner, *Das Alte Burgtheater als Opernbühne* (Vienna: Böhlau, 1970)
Mozart, *Briefe*	*Mozart: Briefe und Aufzeichnungen. Gesamtausgabe,* collected and annotated by Wilhelm Bauer and Otto Erich Deutsch. 7 vols. (Kassel: Bärenreiter, 1962–75)
Mozart, *Letters*	*The Letters of Mozart and His Family,* ed. Emily Anderson, 2d ed. prepared by A. Hyatt King and Monica Carolan (New York: St. Martin's Press, 1966)
MT	*Musical Times*
NGO	*The New Grove Dictionary of Opera,* ed. Stanley Sadie (London: Macmillan, 1992)
NRMI	*Nuova Rivista Musicale Italiana*
OQ	*Opera Quarterly*
RIM	*Rivista Italiana di Musica*
SIMG	*Sammelbände der Internationalen Musikgesellschaft*
Warburton, *Libretti*	Ernest Warburton, ed., *The Libretti of Mozart's Operas,* 7 vols. (New York: Garland, 1992)
Zechmeister, *WT*	Gustav Zechmeister, *Die Wiener Theater nächst der Burg und nächst dem Kärntnerthor von 1747 bis 1776* (Vienna: Böhlau, 1971)

The Culture of Opera Buffa
in Mozart's Vienna

INTRODUCTION

THEATRICAL CONVERSATIONS

To the Burgtheater audience watching Da Ponte and Mozart's *Le nozze di Figaro* in the spring of 1786, the spectacle of Susanna fending off the unwelcome advances of the Count and finally achieving happiness with Figaro would have seemed quite familiar, notwithstanding the many and well-advertised novelties of the work.[1] Many, if not most, audience members would have known *Le mariage de Figaro*, the play by Pierre Augustin Caron de Beaumarchais on which the opera is based, as by the end of 1785 it had been published in German translation and was in any case something of a cause célèbre.[2] The audience could also have recognized Figaro himself and the Count and Countess Almaviva from Petrosellini and Paisiello's *Il barbiere di Siviglia*, a setting of the first play in Beaumarchais's trilogy, which had enjoyed its thirty-eighth performance at the Burgtheater only three months before the premiere of *Figaro*.[3] Regulars at the Burgtheater would also have recognized the more general theme of a virtuous lower-class woman importuned by a nobleman and eventually allowed to return to her proper lover. This theme was quite frequently played out on the Burgtheater stage; in May 1786 its most recent instantiations had been Bertati and Bianchi's *La villanella rapita*, for which Mozart wrote two insertion ensembles,[4] and Sarti's *Fra i due litiganti*, played only five days before *Figaro*. Three months after the premiere of *Figaro*, but before it had finished its first run,[5] the importuning-nobleman theme was replayed in Bertati and Sarti's *I finti eredi*, whose Viennese version included an inserted aria by Francesco Piticchio[6] in which the lower-class lover, Pierotto, ex-

---

[1] In the preamble to the 1786 libretto, Da Ponte describes *Le nozze di Figaro* as a "quasi nuovo genere di spettacolo." Warburton, *Libretti*, vol. 3, *The Mozart–Da Ponte Operas*, p. 6.

[2] Daniel Heartz, "From Beaumarchais to Da Ponte," in *Mozart's Operas*, edited, with contributing essays, by Thomas Bauman (Berkeley: University of California Press, 1990) p. 108, notes that Joseph II allowed a German translation of the play to be published even as he was forbidding a staged production by Schikaneder's troupe. See also Tim Carter, *W. A. Mozart: "Le nozze di Figaro"* (Cambridge: Cambridge University Press, 1987) p. 35.

[3] Michtner, *DAB*, p. 484, lists the most recent Burgtheater performance of Paisiello's opera before the May 1 premiere of *Figaro* as occurring on Feb. 1, 1786.

[4] It played between November 1785 and February 17, 1786. Dates are from Michtner, *DAB*, p. 484.

[5] *Figaro* premiered on May 1, 1786, and had eight more performances between then and November 18. *I finti eredi* premiered on August 1 and had seven more performances between then and December 8 (Michtner, *DAB*, pp. 485–89).

[6] Piticchio seems to have been resident in Vienna from 1786 to 1791. (s.v. "Piticchio" in *NGO*). Da Ponte wrote one complete libretto, *Il Bertoldo*, for him, which had eight performances in 1787. Da Ponte described him as "a man of little intelligence and imperceptible

presses his defiance of the importuning nobleman. This aria unambiguously and conspicuously quotes Mozart's "Se vuol ballare"—an aria that Figaro sings in defiance of the Count's designs on Susanna.[7] Later that season came Da Ponte and Martín y Soler's *Una cosa rara,* one of the great hits of the decade; it is another example of a story type using the same device of an importuned heroine. *Una cosa rara* does not literally quote *Figaro* (though it is also set in Spain), but its heroine, the excessively desired shepherdess Lilla, was played by Nancy Storace, Mozart's Susanna, who also played Giannina, the peasant heroine of Sarti's *I finti eredi,* as well as Rosina in *Il barbiere di Siviglia.* The great *basso buffo* Francesco Benucci was Mozart's first Figaro; he also played Pierotto in *I finti eredi* (which must have sharpened the effect of the quotation from "Se vuol ballare"), as well as Bartolo in *Il barbiere.*

Le nozze di Figaro, then, participated explicitly and publicly in an elaborate theatrical conversation involving composers, librettists, performers, and audiences; it included works written for Vienna alongside works imported there, and involved pieces that now form the cornerstones of Western high culture together with trivialities whose oblivion is well-deserved. It is a many-voiced, multilayered, immensely complex, and never completely recoverable conversation, of which a few still "audible" remnants endure. This book attempts to eavesdrop on that conversation, to report on its audible remnants and to put them into a broader cultural and intellectual context. These activities—eavesdropping, reportage, and contextualization—combine in an effort to portray the ways opera buffa functioned *as entertainment* in late-eighteenth-century Vienna, or, in other words, to suggest ways in which the social and aesthetic world of this genre interacted with the social and aesthetic world of its context. "Entertainment" for the purposes of this book means the general function of supplying pleasure and diversion of various sorts. It does not imply a value judgment in opposition to "art" or "great art." Mozart's *opere buffe* were as much a part of Vienna's entertainment culture as Paisiello's or Sarti's. To study them as entertainment in this sense does not deny or diminish their artistic value; rather it connects them with the context in which they were embedded and enriches our understanding of their claims on our attention.

ALTHOUGH I have described *Le nozze di Figaro* as part of *an* operatic conversation in Vienna, it was actually part of several, all occurring simultaneously in the same room, so to speak. The most obvious category of

---

(scarsissima) musical talent," a judgment contrasting sharply with Gerber's, who found his music "passionate" and interesting. The aria in question is competent but not passionate.

[7] Hunter, "'Se vuol ballare' Quoted: A Moment in the Reception History of *Figaro,*" *MT* 130 (1989) pp. 464–67.

conversation involves the interactions between particular composers, librettists, and singers. As they figure in this book, these interactions typically center on a given work (or a very small number of works) and are grounded in the circumstantial particulars of that work's creation and production. In the case of *Le nozze di Figaro,* for example, one can divine something about Mozart's professional relation to Paisiello from his absorption of elements of *Il barbiere* into *Le nozze di Figaro,*[8] something about the memorability of Mozart's music from Piticchio's quotation of it in *I finti eredi,* and something about Da Ponte's sense of himself as a librettist from his explicit and implicit treatment of Beaumarchais, not to mention his more local rival Casti.[9] In addition, in teasing out the threads of the web emanating from any given work, one learns about the ways a composer may have communicated with his audience by playing on the particular talents or proclivities of singers, and the ways in which those singers may have deflected attention from the "work itself" by engaging in other "conversations." In the first performances of *Il barbiere di Siviglia,* for example, Storace and Benucci imitated the German-speaking actor Friedrich Ludwig Schroeder and the singer Johann Valentin Adamberger, much to the delight of Joseph II; there is no reason to assume that these allusions did not also form some part of the audience's frame of reference for *Le nozze di Figaro,* given the continuities among the performers and the themes.[10]

My brief invocation of *Figaro*'s conversation with other particular works and performers also invokes other sorts, or levels, of operatic conversation. These other interactions are less immediately obvious than, and not (even) as concretely reconstructible as, the authorial jostling and performative games that formed part of the contingent life of opera buffa on the Viennese stage, but they may well be more significant in helping us understand how opera buffa in Vienna functioned both internally and as a form of entertainment. One less obvious category of conversation involves the relation of opera buffa to the other theatrical genres always simultaneously available in Vienna. Another such category is more abstract but nevertheless crucial to any understanding of opera buffa wherever it was performed. It involves the dialogue between individual operas and generic conventions of plot, character, dramatic function, musical "type," and vocal behavior. The idea that these operas "converse" with the conventions of the genre is, of course, related to the broader notion that eighteenth-century music—both vocal and instrumental—signifies in large

---

[8] Daniel Heartz, "Constructing *Le nozze di Figaro,*" in *Mozart's Operas,* 133–56.

[9] Daniela Goldin, *La vera fenice* (Turin: Einaudi, 1985), 102–3. See also Michael F. Robinson, "Paisiello, Mozart and Casti," in *Internationaler Musikwissenschaftlicher Kongress zum Mozartjahr 1991, Baden-Wien* (Tutzing: Schneider, 1993) pp. 71–79.

[10] Michtner, *DAB,* p. 158, quoting a letter from Joseph to Count Rosenberg.

part by means of a complex dialogic world of intra- and extra-musical references, or *topoi*.[11]

Although *opere buffe* were produced relatively regularly in Vienna by the 1760s, opera buffa as a genre enjoyed its greatest successes and played its most coherent aesthetic and ideological role in Vienna's entertainment offerings between about 1770, when Antonio Salieri composed his first opera buffa for the Burgtheater (this year marks the beginning of what Gustav Zechmeister calls the Viennese *Siegeszug* [victory march] of opera buffa)[12] and 1790, the year of Mozart's last collaboration with Da Ponte and also of Joseph II's death.[13] During this twenty-year period, at least 128 *opere buffe* were produced in Vienna, each receiving anything from a minimum of three or four to a maximum of fifty or more performances[14] over several years, often in two or more distinct productions.[15] However, opera buffa was never the sole or even the most important form of theatrical entertainment in Vienna; it was always set against, and was thus in implicit dialogue with, at least one other theatrical genre. The way it was understood in relation to that other genre, or those other genres, in part defines its function as entertainment.

Whereas in Italy opera buffa's primary (or sole) "counter-genre," or interlocutor, was opera seria, in Vienna that was not the case. In the 1760s, Gluck's presence made Vienna an important center of serious "reform opera," whose avant-garde aspects were carried on by Jean-Georges

[11] Wye J. Allanbrook's brilliant and influential readings of *Le nozze di Figaro* and *Don Giovanni* in *Rhythmic Gesture in Mozart: "Le nozze di Figaro" and "Don Giovanni"* (Chicago: University of Chicago Press, 1983) are the primary example of this sort of work in eighteenth-century operatic studies. Leonard Ratner, *Classic Music: Expression, Form, and Style* (New York: Schirmer, 1980) pp. 1–30, includes a more general exposition of the notion of *topoi*.

[12] Zechmeister, *WT,* pp. 345ff.

[13] See John A. Rice, "Emperor and Impresario: Leopold II and the Transformation of Viennese Musical Theater, 1790–92" (Ph.D. dissertation, University of California, Berkeley, 1987) for a discussion of the period immediately following.

[14] *Il barbiere di Siviglia* received 62 performances between its premiere in 1783 and the end of 1790; Da Ponte and Martín y Soler's *Una cosa rara* received nine performances in the three months of its first season, but 54 between the 1786 premiere and February 1791. See, however, Dexter Edge, "Mozart's Reception in Vienna, 1787–1791," in Stanley Sadie, ed., *Wolfgang Amadè Mozart: Essays on His Life and His Music* (Oxford: Clarendon Press, 1996) pp. 66–120, for a critique of the assumption that the number of performances of a work indicated its popularity.

[15] The chief basic sources for Viennese operatic history during this period are Zechmeister, *WT;* Michtner, *DAB;* and Franz Hadamowsky, *Die Wiener Hoftheater (Staatstheater) 1776–1966: Verzeichnis der aufgeführten Stücke mit Bestandnachweis und täglichem Spielplan,* Part I: 1776–1810 (Vienna: Prachner, 1966). Adding the *opere buffe* they list for this twenty-year period, and including several others for which libretti survive from productions during these years, one arrives at about 128 works.

Noverre and Gasparo Angiolini's ballets well into the 1770s. Opera seria, however, whether reformed or unreformed, was almost completely absent from the offerings in the 1770s; and apart from the trio of Gluck operas—*Iphigenie in Tauris, Alceste,* and *Orfeo ed Euridice*—staged in the autumn of 1781 for the visit of Grand Duke Paul of Russia and his wife—only one opera seria was given in the court theatres in the 1780s: Pietro Giovannini's and Sarti's *Giulio Sabino,* performed six times at the Kärntnerthortheater in 1785 as a special vehicle for the visiting castrato Luigi Marchesi.[16] The French theatre (spoken and sung), which had been at the center of aristocratic Viennese stage life for two decades, was dismissed in 1772; despite its brief reappearance in 1775–76, despite being a vivid mental presence for many members of opera buffa's audience between 1770 and 1790, and despite its pervasive influence on *opere buffe* written for Vienna, it is not the repertory against which opera buffa needs to be examined if the question is how that genre functioned as entertainment.[17]

German Theatre as a Context for Opera Buffa

The stage-genre with which opera buffa was in perpetual "dialogue" during the twenty years under consideration here was the German-language theatre, largely spoken but also sung. Before 1776, when Joseph II transformed the Burgtheater (the "French theatre") into a national theatre, opera buffa played about three times a week, mostly in the Burgtheater until 1774, thereafter more often in the Kärntnerthortheater, and German dramas seem to have alternated more or less loosely with them, as well as with the other available spectacles. The founding of the Nationaltheater involved dismissing the Italian troupe, and many of the singers went elsewhere.[18] The Kärntnerthortheater, however, was hired by a variety of *ad hoc* and traveling troupes, including some *opera buffa* players who also used the Burgtheater on Mondays and Wednesdays; thus opera buffa continued to be part of the scene, at least into 1779 (see Appendix 1, note 11). By 1783, however, the German-only operatic fare in the Burgtheater was judged to have been less than wholly successful, and a resident company of Italian singers was gathered to perform in the Burgtheater in daily alter-

[16] Michtner, *DAB,* p. 191. Hadamowsky also lists an *Armida* by "Giovanni Amadeo Neumann" (surely Johann Gottlieb Naumann) done in 1777. Naumann's name appears as "Neumann" on the Venice 1773 libretto of this opera.

[17] Zechmeister, *WT,* passim., gives a full account of the fortunes of the French companies in Vienna from 1747 until 1776. Bruce Alan Brown, *Gluck and the French Theatre in Vienna* (Oxford: Oxford University Press, 1991) provides the best and most detailed account of that repertory during Gluck's association with it. See also Bruce Alan Brown, "Lo Specchio Francese: Viennese Opera Buffa and the Legacy of French Theatre," in Hunter and Webster, *Opera Buffa in Mozart's Vienna* (Cambridge: Cambridge University Press, 1997) pp. 50–81, for an account of the effects of French theatre on Viennese opera buffa.

[18] Zechmeister, *WT,* p. 361.

nation with the German spoken drama; thus again, as in the earlier period, about three times per week.[19]

The German-language spoken repertory throughout our period ranged widely, from light comedies to the latest bourgeois dramas of Lessing and Beaumarchais, to translations of Shakespeare. Translations from French and English were standard throughout these years, as German material of the appropriate quality was not available in sufficient quantity. Singspiel was barely an issue before 1778, but from that year until 1783 forty-eight German-language works for the musical theatre were performed by the newly formed National Singspiel company (whose star soprano was an Italian—Caterina Cavalieri). There was, however, no "official" composer of Singspiel equivalent to Salieri in the Italian opera.[20] Although some of the works performed by the National Singspiel company were originally German-language pieces (among them Mozart's *Die Entführung aus dem Serail*), the vast majority—33 of 48—were translations of works originally in French or Italian; as Thomas Bauman notes, the Viennese showed "no interest in importing anything more than the texts of North or South German operas."[21] The seven-year trial of the National Singspiel company did not really allow the genre to get off the ground as an independent entity—indeed, Otto Michtner goes so far as to suggest that the francophile chancellor Kaunitz had some interest in reviving the French theatrical tradition in Vienna by encouraging German translations of opéras-comiques.[22] Be that as it may, the National Singspiel is probably best considered as a wing of the German-language theatrical enterprise in Vienna rather than as an independent "interlocutor" for opera buffa. Between 1785 and 1788 a number of Singspiels were again performed in the court-sponsored theatres, and the new works of Dittersdorf were particularly successful.[23] However, by this later period the indubitably bourgeois suburban theatres were the real home of German-language opera, and to the extent that they did not only translations of, but also glosses on the opera buffa repertory,[24]

[19] Ibid., pp. 352–53. See also Hadamowsky, *Die Wiener Hoftheater*, Part I, Spielplan, p. 3.

[20] See Franz von Heufeld's letter to Leopold Mozart, 23 Jan. 1778. Mozart: *Briefe* vol. 2, p. 235.

[21] Thomas Bauman, s.v. "Singspiel," *NGO*.

[22] Michtner, *DAB*, p. 43.

[23] Thomas Bauman, "German Opera from the National-Singspiel to *Die Zauberflöte*," in *The Oxford Illustrated History of Opera*, ed. Roger Parker (Oxford: Oxford University Press, 1994) p. 119. Many of the singers in the suburban theatres were members of the earlier National Singspiel troupe. See Michtner, *DAB*, pp. 214–15.

[24] See Dorothea Link, "*L'arbore di Diana*: A Model for *Così fan tutte*," in Sadie, *Wolfgang Amadè Mozart*, p. 373, on an 1813 travesty of Da Ponte's and Martín y Soler's *L'arbore di Diana*; see also Mozart's letter of 2 June 1790, in which he reports going to the "second part" of *Una cosa rara*, which was Schikaneder's and Benedikt Schack's *Der Fall ist noch weit seltener* (= *Una cosa molto più rara*) *Briefe*, iv, p. 110; *Letters*, p. 940.

opera buffa occasionally found itself in the complicated position of being the "courtly" target of the suburban theatres' parody while also functioning as German spoken drama's empty-headed "roommate."

It is beyond the scope of this book (not to mention the competence of its author) to describe the intrinsic qualities and conventions of the German-language dramas performed in Vienna at this time.[25] Nevertheless, a brief sketch of the debate surrounding the rise of "regular" (*regelmäßig*) vernacular theatre in Vienna at this time suggests the political and intellectual context that audience members may well have brought to opera buffa, and should thus serve to sharpen our sense of the sort of entertainment-function opera buffa may have performed for them.[26] Gustav Zechmeister reports that German theatre of the early 1770s was considered a perpetual investigation into the taste of the nation,[27] a succinct formulation that encloses several issues of relevance to the study of opera buffa in Vienna at this time. Among the most significant for opera buffa was the growth of a bourgeois, or partly bourgeois, administrative class devoted to the state (i.e., essentially the Habsburg court).[28] Members of this class, of whom Joseph von Sonnenfels and Tobias Philipp Gebler were particularly important representatives, saw the mission of the German theatre as intimately linked both to the encouragement of good morals and taste in significant portions of the population, and to a sense of nationhood that transcended the old feudal divisions. Calls for a theatrical school of bourgeois morals were part of a veritable flood of writing about the German theatre in the 1770s. Sonnenfels himself wrote at length about the state of the Viennese theatre in his *Briefe über die wienerische Schau-bühne*,[29] but in addition to such formal dissertations there were many more ephemeral publications, often of the season-souvenir sort, which listed the personnel performing on the stages of both court theatres, and the reper-

[25] Zechmeister considers this in some detail. See also the last chapter of Hilde Haider-Pregler, *Des sittlichen Bürgers Abendschule: Bildungsanspruch und Bildungsauftrag des Burgtheaters im 18. Jahrhundert* (Vienna and Munich: Jugend und Volk, 1980), which considers the move to a national theatre in some detail; and Monika Giller, "Die Sentimentalität im Spielplan und in der Darstellung des Burgtheaters am Ende des 18. Jahrhunderts (1776–1809)," doctoral dissertation, University of Vienna, 1966.

[26] "Regular" German drama is the term used to distinguish written-out plays (whether comedies, tragedies, or sentimental pieces) from the improvised comedy (*Stegreifspiel*), which the imperial theatre-administrators viewed with constant suspicion. See Heartz, *Haydn, Mozart, and the Viennese School 1740–1780* (New York: Norton, 1995) pp. 29–32.

[27] Zechmeister, *WT*, p. 363.

[28] Derek Beales, "Court, Government and Society in Mozart's Vienna," in Sadie, *Wolfgang Amadè Mozart*, pp. 3–20, is at pains to emphasize how "peculiar" the imperial court was during Joseph's reign. He is chiefly dealing with the period after 1780 when Joseph became sole ruler, but the twin tendencies toward bourgeoisification and increased imperial power were clearly well prepared during the regency.

[29] Vienna: Kurzböck, 1768; facsimile rpt. ed. Hilde Haider-Pregler (Graz: Akademische Druck- und Verlagsanstalt, 1988).

tory on both stages for a given season. They also sometimes include commentary—essays, opinions, reviews—that gives a vivid picture of the intellectual issues surrounding theatrical life in Vienna at this time.[30] Members of the Italian opera buffa company are listed in these records along with the members of the theatre company and the Singspiel; however, in contrast to the German repertory, the Italian operas themselves are neither described nor evaluated.[31] In addition, the various essays and anecdotes concern themselves almost entirely with the German spoken and sung theatre. Even before 1776, when there was no official national theatre, the Italian repertory received much less written attention than either the French or the German. Indeed, during the entire period under consideration, only one essay, in the *Theatralalmanach von Wien für das Jahr 1773*, treats opera buffa in a more or less theoretical manner, and it is not complimentary.[32]

This essay, probably by Christian Gottlob Klemm and/or Franz Heufeld (joint editors of the almanac) follows a long discussion of the rules of dramatic poetry, and opera buffa serves primarily as negative grist for the author's broader political and theoretical mill; the issues are both aesthetic and nationalistic:

> Generally the text to these pieces is beneath mention. The music, the singers and the decorations have to breathe life into them. It is unusual for a bearable example to come [directly] from the hands of the poet. Here the raw bad taste of previous centuries reigns. [The author has just criticized the "old fashioned" comic practice of stringing a series of gags together on a virtually nonexistent narrative thread.] One has to wonder that the Italians have not raised themselves at all above the old mess. Even when they manage this once in a while, there are [still]) contrived devices, stilted, artificial turns of phrase, and exaggerated things. The poetry of French comic operas is quite different; the Italians must know these [works]; and still we get nothing better from their poets, even if they are Arcadian.[33]

---

[30] There are, of course, private documents like the diary of Count Zinzendorf, occasional comments in the much later memoirs of Karoline Pichler, Michael Kelly, and Da Ponte, letters and other private writings by Mozart, Salieri, and others, as well as documents connected to Joseph II and his *Oberstkämmerer* Count Rosenberg. Interesting and indispensable as these are, they do not (or at least not reliably) document the tone and preoccupations of public theatrical life in the same way as the published almanacs and pocketbooks.

[31] Although evaluations of the German repertory were not an inevitable component of these almanacs, some comment on the pieces premiered during the previous season is not unusual.

[32] *Theatralalmanach von Wien für das Jahr 1773. Verfasset von einigen Liebhabern der deutschen Schaubühne* (Vienna: Kurzböck, 1773). The joint editors were Christian Gottlob Klemm and Franz Heufeld.

[33] Ibid., p. 114: Ueberhaupt verdienet die Poesie derselben keine Kritik. Die Musik, die Sänger, die Verzierungen müssen sie beleben. Selten, dass ein einziges nur aus den Hände des Poeten erträglich käme. Hier herrscht noch der rohe böse Geschmack der vorigen Jahrhunderte. Man muß sich über die Italiäner wundern, daß sie sich in diesem Fache gar nicht über den alten Wust erheben. Doch wenn sie es auch einmal thun, so sind es Concetti, geschraubte, gekünstelte Wendungen, und übertriebene Sachen. Da sind doch die komischen Opern der Franzosen in ihrer Poesie ganz anders; die Italiäner müssen sie doch kennen, und gleichwohl erhalten wir von ihren Poeten, und wenn es auch arkadische wären, nichts bessers.

There is a sense throughout this literature that opera buffa is both unofficial and irrelevant. No author is so crass as to say so in those terms, but an article in the 1777 *Taschenbuch des Wiener Theaters* comes close when, in the course of a history of the Viennese stage whose predictable culmination is Joseph's establishment of the national company and repertory at the Burgtheater, the author notes that after the departure of the dancer and choreographer Noverre in 1776, the German repertory had to compete with "nobody but an Italian opera buffa [company]."[34] This company, according to this author, did the German repertory more good than harm by comparison.

There is to my knowledge no surviving Viennese essay on opera buffa in general from the period between 1776 and 1790. However, in 1796, after years of performances of opera buffa mixed in with the German repertory, the *Wiennrischer [sic] Opernkalender* contains an essay on the "parts and basic principles of opera," which includes a considerable section on opera buffa. This is no more complimentary than the 1773 essay:

> The Italians know no other opera but seria and buffa. The French found that serious subjects could also be worked into little operas, and would arouse more interest. Every nation stuck with its model. . . . The opera buffa of the Italians is written purely for the music, but unfortunately made to certain conventional patterns which inevitably produce monotony, as does everything that groans undeviatingly under the iron foot of a pattern. The Italians care little about this; through the whole plot, as long as a situation is apt for music or the expression of wit, elegance or humor, they are easily pleased with it as drama. Before I go any further, some will make the objection that there is no more miserable form of theatre than this opera buffa, and they will name me a whole bunch of pieces that betray no hint of human understanding. Considered as comedy, and especially in the wretched productions we have seen on our stages, [these people] are right. The whole has no coherence, no interest, the people [characters] meet as if out of the clouds, grope around in the darkness in full light:[35] whatever they babble about is the stupidest stuff; in short, there is no absurdity that doesn't happen in these Italian operas.[36]

[34] *Taschenbuch des Wiener Theaters: Erstes Jahr.* (Vienna: Trattner, 1777) p. 70. The opera buffa company in question was a temporary company involving many of the singers who had recently been in the resident company. They rented the Kärntnerthortheater for a period under court license. The author lists the singers of the company, praises their voices, and sarcastically notes (p. 72) that "we are so fond of Italian opera that we are thoroughly delighted that in the capital city of Germany an Italian show is worth only a hundredth as much as a German one." [So sehr wir selbst Liebhaber der italienischen Oper sind, so sind wirs doch sehr wohlzufrieden, daß in der Hauptstadt Deutschlands ein welsches Spektakel nur den hundertsten Theil so viel gelt, als ein deutsches.]

[35] Here the author seems to refer to the many scenes in opera buffa which take place at night, but which were evidently not lit in such a way as to represent darkness.

[36] *Wiennrischer Opernkalender mit Scenen aus den neuesten und beliebtesten Opern auf das Jahr 1796* (Wien: Mathias Ludwig, 1796) p. 37: Die Italiener kennen keine andere Oper, als die Seria und Buffa. Die Franzosen fanden, dass auch ernsthafte Sujets sich zu kleinen Opern

This passage strikingly illustrates how little the terms of the debate between German and Italian theatre changed over more than twenty years.[37] The relation between the two genres did shift slightly between the earlier and later periods, however, as from 1783 until war and ill health diverted his attention, Joseph II, now emperor rather than co-regent, took a direct interest in (and exerted some personal control over) both the personnel and the repertory of the opera buffa company.[38] During the first few years of opera buffa's reappearance at the Burgtheater, Joseph visited opera houses in Italy and elsewhere, acted as a sort of talent scout for his own company, proudly reported on the successes of his own singers—particularly Benucci—when they made guest appearances away from Vienna, and sent Count Rosenberg-Orsini (the court official in charge of the Imperial theatres) scores and libretti of works that he thought might work in Vienna. In 1783 Joseph also established a standing order for opera buffa scores by Paisiello.[39] Some of this interest can be attributed to what we might now call a micromanaging temperament, and an effort not to let anyone else spend too much on this diversion, but some of it seems to have stemmed from a lively enjoyment of the genre itself. It is quite striking how much more comment he makes to Count Rosenberg about the opera company than he does about the German actors or other matters pertaining to the spoken stage.[40] It has been argued that Joseph reintroduced opera buffa onto the Burgtheater stage as a sop to the nobility,[41] but the extent and tone of his interest in the genre in the early years of his reign suggests that

---

arbeiten liessen, und mehr Interesse erwecken würden. Jede Nation blieb bey ihrem Muster. . . . Die Opera buffa der Italiener ist lediglich für die Tonkunst geschrieben, aber leider an gewisse konventionelle Muster gebracht worden, woraus nothwendig Monotonie entstehen muss, so wie aus allem, was unabweichlich unter dem eisernen Fuss eines Musters seufzt. Darauf achtet der Italiener wenig; wenn nun Situationen für Musik, Witz, Eleganz oder Laune im Ausdruck ist, über das Ganze der Handlung, als Drama, ist er leicht befriedigt. Ehe ich weiter gehe, wird man nur gleich den Einwurf machen, daß es kein elenderes Schauspiel gebe, als diese Opera buffa, und man wird mir eine ganze Menge daher nennen, die gar keinen Funken Menschenverstandes verrathen. Als Komödie betrachtet, und besonders so, wie sie auf unsern Bühnen jämmerlich zugerichtet gebracht werden, sey's zugegeben. Das Ganze hat keinen Zusammenhang, kein Interesse, die Leute kommen wie aus den Wolken zusammen, tappen bey hellem Lichte in der Finsterniß; was sie schwatzen ist albernes Zeug, kurz, es ist keine Absurdität, die nicht in diesen wälschen Opern vorkäme.

[37] Remarks about Weber and Rossini in the early nineteenth century continue many of the same tropes.
[38] Rudolf Payer von Thurn, *Joseph II als Theaterdirektor: Ungedruckte Briefe und Aktenstücke aus den Kinderjahren des Burgtheaters* (Vienna: Heidrich, 1920).
[39] Daniel Heartz, "Constructing *Le nozze di Figaro*" p. 138.
[40] Derek Beales, *Joseph II*, vol. 1 (Cambridge: Cambridge University Press, 1987) p. 235, however, notes that Joseph mentioned German-language productions "more frequently" when he was managing the national theatre than he had before he made the administrative change.
[41] Ernst Wangermann, *The Austrian Achievement 1700–1800* (London: Thames and Hudson, 1973) p. 124; Michtner, *DAB*, p. 148 suggests that the nobility was particularly pleased with the reintroduction of opera buffa.

there was more to it than simple appeasement. The combination of the conscious and effortful reintroduction of this foreign genre, and Joseph's publicly acknowledged interest in it had the odd effect of making opera buffa more "official" at the same time as it remained—at least outwardly— quite apart from his explicit political and social agenda.

In terms of public rhetoric, then, Vienna's opera buffa was starkly differentiated from the nation-building, proto-bourgeois, and generally edifying ideals of German drama. (That these ideals were not always met, however, even in this intense and focused context is suggested by Baron Riesbeck, who described the political function of theatre in Vienna in the late 1770s as "bread and circus."[42]) Foreign and anything but edifying, opera buffa can thus be understood as fulfilling the role of "mere entertainment"—mere, because it was not considered worth a theory or justification of its own, and entertainment because it was understood as primarily an occasion of pleasure. I elaborate below on the ways the theme of pleasure emerges from both opera buffa's context and its content, but first we must consider the question of who was being "merely entertained."

Audiences for Opera Buffa

Unfortunately this question can be answered only partially and indirectly. There are some clues to support the long-held notion that opera buffa counted as essentially aristocratic entertainment throughout this period: these include the Countess Mazelana's "time-share" subscription to a box in the Burgtheater in the early 1770s, in which she demanded entrance only to the opera buffa;[43] the comments in the *Wiener Realzeitung* in 1783 on the reintroduction of the Italian company, which suggest that the nobility would be particularly pleased to welcome back the (female) Italian singers;[44] the greater freedom given to those singers than to the German performers to frequent the parterre noble;[45] and the unbelievably assiduous attendance of Count Zinzendorf at opera buffa, compared to his apparently less frequent attendance at German drama.[46] There is no firm

[42] Johann Kaspar Riesbeck, *Briefe eines reisenden Franzosen über Deutschland*, ed. Jochen Golz (Berlin: Rütten & Loening, [1976]) p. 181.
[43] Otto G. Schindler, "Das Publikum des Burgtheaters in der Josephinischen Ära: Versuch einer Strukturbestimmung." In Margret Dietrich, ed., *Das Burgtheater und sein Publikum* (Vienna: Akademie der Wissenschaften, 1976) p. 73.
[44] Michtner, *DAB*, p. 148.
[45] Schindler, "Das Publikum," pp. 53–54. The freedom of the Italian singers—especially the women—to visit the parterre noble without paying (unlike their German counterparts) is not simply to be interpreted as a sign of the aristocratic aura of opera buffa: rather it also indicates a sort of salacious interest in these performers which would have been far less appropriate for actresses in a genre designed to refine the morals of a nation.
[46] Edge, "Mozart's Reception in Vienna," p. 81. Edge makes no blanket assertions about the nature of the audience for any genre.

evidence about the bourgeoisie's attendance at opera buffa, though Dexter Edge notes that at least at the end of the 1780s plays were better attended than operas, which could plausibly be understood as indicating a smaller bourgeois audience for opera.[47] Although there was price differentiation between the different sorts of seats, there seems to have been no difference in price between the opera buffa and the German drama when they were performed in the same theatre. Joseph's lowering of the ticket prices to the Burgtheater in 1776 may not have lasted long enough to benefit the audiences for opera buffa seven years later.[48]

Thus, while we might be able to support the notion of the "bourgeois" German drama distinct from the "aristocratic" opera buffa in terms of the contents of the works and the subtle implications of their reception, the verifiable evidence of actual attendance at the theatre on any given occasion neither reinforces nor negates such a notion. However, it is important to remember in this context that even with the most "progressive" interpretation of the evidence—namely that the increasingly various audiences for German drama also flocked to opera buffa—the Burgtheater audience (and that of the Kärntnerthortheater when it showed opera buffa) represented an incredibly small segment of the broader Viennese population. Otto Schindler estimates that 90 percent of the Burgtheater audience consisted of the top 7 percent of the population: first and second nobility, officials and prominent citizens, and the artistic community.[49] Johann Pezzl's comment in his indispensable *Skizze von Wien* about *Una cosa rara* is relevant here. He describes how this opera has taken the whole town by storm, each performance leaving between three and four hundred people still wanting a ticket, and continues, "One can go to no house, to no *fashionable* gathering (*Gesellschaft von gutem Ton*) without hearing a duet, a trio, or a finale [from *Una cosa rara*] sung or played on the piano."[50] In other words, the principal Viennese audience for opera buffa was high society, which included the landholding nobility and a few "layers" below that. I have assumed throughout the book that opera buffa's "ideal" audience—that is, the one it seems most actively to address—is not dissimilar to the actual Viennese spectatorship insofar as one can reconstruct that:

[47] Ibid.
[48] Schindler, "Das Publikum," pp. 41–42, describes the reduction of ticket prices in 1776. I do not know what the prices were in 1783, but according to the information in Edge, "Mozart's Reception in Vienna," Table 5:3, p. 77, the prices had risen considerably by 1789, and the cheapest seats (on the fourth floor) had almost tripled. According to a private communication from Dexter Edge, on the basis of ticket prices for concerts of the Tonkünstlersozietät in the 1770s and 1785 it seems possible that the "promotion price" for the Nationaltheater did not last long. The information is not definitive, however.
[49] Schindler, "Das Publikum," p. 92.
[50] Johann Pezzl, *Skizze von Wien* (Vienna 1786–90). Partially trans. in H. C. Robbins Landon, *Mozart and Vienna* (London: Thames & Hudson, 1991) pp. 54–191. This quotation, p. 137.

highly exclusive with respect to the broader population, but various and clearly stratified within its own confines.

VIENNESE OPERA BUFFA AS A REPERTORY

Although opera buffa's "ideal" audience is in part a critical construct derived from the values of the works themselves, the presence of an actual audience over this twenty-year period is crucial to understanding this group of works as a repertory—i.e., as a collection of operas given coherence and meaning as a group not only by virtue of their shared genre, but also by the fact that they were performed in a limited time period in a given place by resident performers for an audience that one can reasonably presume to be moderately continuous. This book is, then, a study of a local repertory rather than of a whole genre; though it must be noted that the habits of Viennese opera buffa seem in many ways to be continuous with those of the *opere buffe* produced from Naples to St. Petersburg, which omitted (or translated) regional dialect,[51] eschewed violent slapstick and gross obscenity, and often included a substantial dose of sentimentality. One obvious reason for this similarity is that most of the operas that passed through the Burgtheater were in fact the same ones that traveled across Europe; indeed, the majority of operas in the Viennese repertory were premiered in Florence, Naples, Rome,[52] other Italian cities, and, most importantly of all, Venice.[53] Over the twenty years the average ratio of newly composed to imported works remained about 1:2, though the proportions in any given season often differed from this.[54] Some of the conclusions of this book will, then, be relevant to the broader genre of opera buffa, but its "genre-study" aspects are in large part a by-product of its function as a repertory study.

The "repertory study" aspect of this book has a few significant consequences. One is the inextricable link between the notion of repertory and the question of entertainment: once a group of works is defined by the au-

---

[51] Some operas performed in Vienna did originally have sections of Neapolitan dialect: as late as 1786 the part of Bastiano in Paisiello's and Giuseppe Palomba's *Le gare generose* had to be translated into Tuscan for export.

[52] Federico Pirani, "*Il curioso indiscreto:* Un'opera buffa tra Roma e la Vienna di Mozart," in *Mozart: Gli orientamenti della critica moderna. Atti del convegno internazionale, Cremona . . . 1991* (Lucca: Libreria Musicale Italiana Editrice, 1994) p. 49, notes the strong connection between Rome and Vienna at this time. In his "Operatic Links between Rome and Vienna, 1776–1790," in Sadie, *Wolfgang Amadè Mozart*, pp. 395–402, he emphasizes the many links between the singers of the Viennese troupe and the Teatro Valle in Rome.

[53] However, cf. John A. Rice on the "Neapolitanization" of the Viennese repertory during Leopold II's reign (1790–92), in "Emperor and Impresario," pp. 139ff.

[54] Between 1770 and 1772 no imported works were performed; between 1783 and January 1784 there were no new works. Michtner erroneously identifies Mazzolà and Salieri's *La scuola dei gelosi* as a newly composed work; in fact it was written for Venice in 1778.

dience that witnessed them, it becomes important to think about what happened (or could plausibly have happened) between those works and their spectators and listeners. This issue permeates the book. Another consequence of studying a repertory rather than a genre is that the definitions of "work" and "context" change. To study a repertory of opera buffa in the late eighteenth century is to study the works as they were performed in that place and time, to the extent that that is recoverable. Thus one must abandon the notion that the integral, complete, and final original work—the *Fassung letzter Hand* or its equivalent—should always be the first object of study, and replace it with the notion that the main object of consideration is what a given audience might have witnessed in a particular place during a given period of time.[55] The notion of "the work" then becomes not the final thoughts of a single creator, or even the final thoughts of two "authors" (composer and librettist), but rather an ongoing collaboration between those authors and what might otherwise be thought to be its "context"—the performers, set designers, censors, and other figures vital to establishing what played on any given evening.

One witness to the friability of "the work" in this situation is the relatively rare publication of the scores of these works as wholes, though arrangements of excerpts evidently for domestic performance were common. (Salieri's *La grotta di Trofonio,* published in a beautiful edition by Artaria, is a rare exception outside France.) Most of these works survive as published librettos, which quite frequently do not correspond in every detail to the scores of the works claiming to represent the same production; as autographs, which have no particular authority with respect to individual productions; and, most vitally, as manuscript scores copied by professional copyists. Sometimes these are integrally copied manuscripts: the opera scores (mostly) numbered in the seventeen-thousands in the music collection of the Austrian National Library are typically of this sort; they are often in remarkably good condition and may have served as exempla from which the practical scores were copied. These practical scores, on the other hand (many of them identified with a call number beginning with KT), form a testament to the rigors and complications of ongoing opera

---

[55] It is in fact just as impossible to know exactly what an audience would have witnessed as it is in some instances to determine the final intentions of a composer. This is true of any score, of course, though it seems more true of opera than of, say, a piano piece because of the greater number of integral variables: stage set, costume, gesture, etc. (It is significant that those authors who have concerned themselves most deeply with the ontological status of the musical work have dealt exclusively with instrumental music.) See, e.g., Roman Ingarden, *The Work of Music and the Problem of Its Identity,* trans. Adam Czerniawsky, ed. Jean Harrell (Berkeley: University of California Press, 1986); Lydia Goehr, *The Imaginary Museum of Musical Works* (Oxford: Clarendon Press, 1992); Francis Sparshott, "Aesthetics of Music: Limits and Grounds," in *What Is Music,* ed. Philip Alperson (University Park, PA: Pennsylvania State University Press, 1987) pp. 33–100.

production.[56] They often consist of gatherings by various hands crudely stitched together with little concern for consistency or beauty. Pages have been folded together and then unfolded, pasted over, sewn together, and crossed out; the texts are often translated, presumably for German-language productions in the suburbs in the 1780s, and the notes are sometimes altered. Singers are sometimes mentioned in the scores, and occasionally the composers of substitution or insertion numbers are also named. It is essentially impossible to tease out distinct or internally consistent "layers" of performance history from these sources.

Operas imported from elsewhere were almost always changed in some way from the original (or at least from the version of the score that made its way to Vienna), and operas written for Vienna were also altered both within and between production runs. Cast changes often meant changes in the scores, but it is rarely possible to deduce and untangle the successive or alternate versions of a single production. Very little is known about cast changes once an opera was launched. Joseph II explicitly forbad the advertisement of such changes except in exceptional circumstances, as when Adriana Ferrarese del Bene took over the role of Diana in *L'arbore di Diana* in October 1788. However, the generalized evidence of the scores shows that the most common alteration (apart from cuts) was aria substitution or insertion. Some arias (like the Piticchio piece mentioned above, or Mozart's various substitute arias) seem to have been newly composed, but others were lifted from other operas.[57] Aria substitutions could lend individual roles a rather different aspect from one production to another— a difference suggested most accessibly today in the change from Nancy Storace's Susanna (who sang "Deh vieni non tardar" in the original 1786 production) to Adriana Ferrarese's Susanna (who sang the large-scale rondò "Al desio di chi t'adora" in the 1789 revival). It was less common for ensembles to be substituted or inserted,[58] though both practices became more usual in Vienna over the twenty-year period; and it was almost

---

[56] The KT call number indicates that they were in a collection at the Kärntnerthortheater before they found their way into the Austrian National Library. The "presentation" or "exemplum" copies (with call numbers in the 17000s) of many of these works often do not match the KT scores, and the 17000 scores often represent what seems to be an earlier layer of the work. See Ronald Rabin, "Mozart, Da Ponte, and the Dramaturgy of Opera Buffa" (Ph. D. dissertation, Cornell University, 1996) pp. 416–18.

[57] For example, "Ben lo dicea mio padre," a bass aria originally written for Livigni and Paisiello's *L'innocente fortunata* is to be found in three Viennese scores; and the rage aria for the Contessa, "Vorrei punirti indegno," in Sarti's *Fra i due litiganti il terzo gode* is lifted from Anfossi's setting of *La finta giardiniera*. Other arias are dismissed from (literally torn out of) one opera in favor of a substitute but then reappear pasted into another.

[58] Sarti's and Tommaso Grandi's *Le gelosie villane* is unusual in having four ensembles (all trios) inserted or substituted; this appears to reflect a growing Viennese taste for ensemble singing in opera buffa. Mozart's ensemble additions to Bianchi's *La villanella rapita* are another example of this relatively unusual practice.

unheard-of for a finale to be changed by substitution, though cuts, both major and minor, were common.[59] On the whole, though, the shape and trajectory of the plots in most operas performed in Vienna during this period were essentially the same as the originals, even where large numbers of substitutions were made.

My primary material for this study, then, has been the Viennese librettos and the scores that correlate (at least to some extent) with those librettos. It is important to remember, however, that the surviving written and printed sources are the merest shadows of the actual stage-life of these works, and that the notion of "a" (single) Viennese version of an opera is a gross simplification. I have not examined all ca. 128 *opere buffe* performed in Vienna during this period. Rather, I have looked at a representative sample, spread relatively evenly over the twenty years, and including some works performed by the temporary companies in the Kärntnerthortheater in the earliest years of the Nationaltheater. Appendix 1 lists the sample of 79 works used to represent this repertory.[60] For reasons of comprehensibility, however, I have concentrated my discussions on a relatively small number of operas, some with a palpable connection to Mozart, others because they seem to me particularly interesting or representative, and others because they are available in either a modern edition or recording.

The Poetics of Entertainment

The evidence about how opera buffa entertained its audiences is almost as elusive as the evidence about who those audiences were. Like the evidence about the class structure of the Burgtheater audience, the "entertainment value" of this repertory is defined as much by what is omitted or ignored as by what is said. However, in contrast to the frustrating lack of evidence about who sat in the theatre seats, the lack of testimony about the social and aesthetic functions of this opera buffa repertory is paradoxically quite helpful—and not (only) because it allows the scholar's imagination to roam. One of the most interesting aspects of the literature is that at the same time as opera buffa as a compositional enterprise was dismissed as "nothing-but" silliness, the vocal (and sometimes other) charms of the singers were regularly discussed, and there is a sense throughout the contextual literature that the genre was the source of considerable pleasure. Sonnenfels's description of the tenor Giacomo Caribaldi in his *Briefe über*

---

[59] An interesting but possibly post-1790 exception to this rule occurs in the finale to Bertati and Bianchi's *La villanella rapita*. In the Viennese score (KT 467) the entire finale was a substitution by Joseph Weigl and an unknown librettist. See below, Ch. 3, p. 75.

[60] Ten of these—nine by Haydn and one (*La finta giardiniera*) by Mozart—were not performed in Vienna but are included in the sample for reasons of accessibility and closeness to the Viennese repertory.

die wienerische Schaubühne, with its mixture of censoriousness and swooning delight, can stand for the uneasy mixture of pleasure and opprobrium which the whole genre inspired in Vienna's cultural avant-garde in the 1770s: "Caribaldi has only learned the superficial stuff (Ueberladungen) from his predecessors, and gives back a failed copy of what he has seen. His acting is forced and monotonous. . . . However, this mediocre actor has a throat that delights; a tenor voice that has something sweet and touching about it, and over which he is sufficiently the master to be able to give it, in its place, the proper slackening and tension that forms the chiaroscuro of singing and is thus the soul of expression, just as [vocal] modulation is in oratory."[61]

Opera Buffa as Pleasure

My argument proper, and thus Part I of the book, begins with the notion that opera buffa not only provided pleasure, but that its function as first and foremost a pleasure-giving entity was crucial to its meaning in Vienna. The context alone gives some inkling of this: even the most disapproving critics admitted that the music (as written and as performed) could redeem the stupidity of the other dimensions of the occasion, and the genre's ability to hold and then retake the stage in the face of the juggernaut of vernacular drama certainly suggests that the audience valued the enjoyment it provided. However, not only does the context confirm opera buffa's pleasurable nature, but the texts of the works themselves thematize pleasure in various ways—by dissolving the action into explicit celebration at the ends of many works, by engaging in multilayered cross-references made possible by the highly conventional nature of the genre, and by foregrounding the act of performance both within the dramatic narrative and outside it. Chapter 1 elaborates the thematics of pleasure in opera buffa.

The music of opera buffa also suggests that the genre's occasion is a devotion to pleasure. Not only is most of it easily apprehensible and pleasant, but—despite the frenetic surface pace of many ensembles—its unfolding is quite leisurely, at least by the standards of Mozart's or Haydn's instrumental music. Solo statements at the beginning of ensembles are often surprisingly long (see, e.g., the opening of Carlo Goldoni's and Florian

---

[61] Joseph von Sonnenfels, *Briefe über die wienerische Schaubühne* no. 13 (Vienna, March 13, 1768) p. 72: "Caribaldi hat seinem Vorgänger nur die Ueberladungen abgelernet, und giebt das, was er gesehen, als eine verunglückte Kopie, schlecht wieder. Sein Spiel ist gezwungen, und einförmig: . . .

Aber, der mittelmässige Schauspieler hat eine Kehle, die entzückt; eine Tenorstimme, die etwas gewisses Rührendes, und Süsses an sich hat, und darüber er so ziemlich Meister ist, um ihr an seinem Orte die schickliche Nachlassung und Anspannung zu geben, die im Gesange das Helldunkle ausmachet, und so die Seele des Ausdrucks ist, wie in der Deklamation der Modulation."

Leopold Gassmann's *L'amore artigiano*—Example 7-2), and cadential phrases in various places in the musical structures are almost always repeated. Indeed, the music of opera buffa is in general quite repetitive, perhaps to ensure that audiences paying intermittent attention could "get" everything. This combination of leisureliness and repetitiveness creates an aesthetic that permits a diffused attention to the various pleasures—on and off stage—of the event. In addition, despite the relatively restricted harmonic vocabulary of much of this music, the scores betray an extraordinary attention to easily apprehensible, immediately effective, and uncomplicatedly pleasurable aspects of the music—aspects we now tend to think of as superficial, secondary, and nonstructural. Dynamic markings in particular are complex and detailed, changing frequently to underscore both the declamation and the meaning of the text (see, e.g., Paisiello's buffa aria "A voi darla in matrimonio" given in its entirety as Example 5-1). In addition, details of articulation and texture are also carefully and pleasurably variegated in many of these works, drawing attention to the sonorous surface and to the text rather than to the underlying structure.

Opera Buffa's Politics

Opera buffa's staying power in Vienna attests not only to the sweetness of its pleasures, but also to the ways in which they may have supported the ideals of the prevailing power structure. Indeed, the emperor's willingness to stage *Le nozze di Figaro* has been understood as a clever move in his war against aristocratic privilege, as the work showed the aristocracy in the audience the futility of insisting on outdated and inappropriate "rights."[62] This cannot, of course, be proved; it seems to me at least as likely that Joseph's interest in the project had to do with his concern to represent himself as tolerant as that it represented his understanding of the Count as an Austrian aristocrat.[63] Be that as it may, *Le nozze di Figaro* is by no means unique among Vienna's *opere buffe* in addressing urgent questions of life in society, particularly the relations between the classes and the proper behavior of the genders. I argue that many if not all of these operas are profoundly political in the broadest sense of the term, though only a minority seem as elaborately linked to the external political situation as *Figaro*. Within the secure framework of their cultural position as "mere entertainment"—a position that in itself has political import—these works commu-

---

[62] Volkmar Braunbehrens, *Mozart in Vienna 1781–1791,* trans. Timothy Bell (New York: Grove Weidenfeld, 1989) p. 213, calls this opera "a contribution to Josephine domestic policy."

[63] Wangermann, *The Austrian Achievement,* p.160: "As late as 1787 . . . [Joseph] could not conceive that hostile political literature could represent a danger to his government or to his objectives."

nicate complex and in some ways contradictory sets of social values. On the one hand, as I describe in Chapter 2, as a group they strongly valorize the conservative notions of a clear and immutable hierarchy and an unchanging and familiar social order. On the other hand, as Chapter 3 illustrates, opera buffa routinely represents reversals of this conservative order: patriarchs are trounced, servants take control, and women move out of the narrative frame to exercise a moral and sentimental power at odds with their powerlessness in the action. These reversals can, of course, be explained with reference to the longstanding norms of comedy and carnival, whose principles assert that an overturning is always contained and thus politically (if not psychologically) neutralized, either by plot trajectories that marry off the foundling or put the impostor in his place, or by another "frame" or "rule" inside or outside the work. These theoretical principles certainly operate in opera buffa, and the frame of "sheer pleasure" acts as a further buffer between the operatic reversals of power and their potential for real-world disruption. At the same time, however, the "performed" nature of many of opera buffa's reversals—the virtuosic performance of rhetorical collapse by the buffoon, the servant's temporary control of the auditorium (as well as the stage) in the course of organizing the lives of his or her betters, and the suffering woman's powerful appeal to the sentiments of the audience—allows them all to one degree or another to escape the controlling frames of comedy and mere pleasure. Thus the "progressive" or at least change-oriented social content of works in this genre often leaves a residue of irritation in relation to its "conservative" frames. This residue of irritation was surely present in any repertory of opera buffa, but in Vienna it makes particular sense in relation to the unstable and in some ways incoherent "potpourri of . . . traditional and progressive" ways of thinking characteristic of the Josephine period in that city.[64]

In describing this repertory of opera buffa as "profoundly political," I am not claiming that individual operas routinely responded to particular political circumstances or events. The social and political—and even ideological—content of these operas is rarely explicit. I have, for example, never read a libretto that literally says, "Stratification is necessary to society," or "Women should exercise a particular sort of power in a separate domain from men." Rather, the notions that stratification is inevitable and beneficial, that some women have a moral and emotional power quite different from that of most men, and other comparably general ideas about how society works, are enacted in essentially every opera, and repeated on many different levels of individual works. Redundancy is crucial to the patterns of meaning both in individual operas and across the repertory. The often-noted aesthetic conventions of the genre—the disguises, deceits, and

[64] Beales, "Court, Government and Society in Mozart's Vienna," p. 20.

fallings-in-love, the aria types, the character types, the finale-structures, the predictable harmonic language—are, then, matched by (and often connected to) social conventions—almost no marriages across class lines, clear differentiation between the genders below the aristocracy, marriage the outcome for almost all women, and the capacity for sensibility given to only a few. In other words the poetics of the repertory—its internal habits and devices—are intimately linked to its function as entertainment. Thus, in looking for political and social content, I am interested less in the particularities of individual works than in the repertorial profile provided by the topics and issues iterated and reiterated in opera after opera. This repertorial profile may or may not resemble the political profile of the whole pan-European genre: indeed, further study could relatively easily determine to what extent any venue's choice of repertory (e.g., a preference for escapist pastorals or antiauthoritarian comedies) might indicate the particular political function of opera buffa in that place at that time. However, it is also the case that the social and political values of any segment of the genre might be understood differently in London's mercantile world than in the isolated castle of Eszterháza or the imperial city of St. Petersburg and thus that the choice of repertory could not be understood as descriptive of the political culture or ideology of that place. The pleasures and the politics of opera buffa often crystallize in the space between the work and the audience; to describe at least the shape of that space, if not its contents, is one aim of this book.

THE SOCIAL VALUES OF CLOSED MUSICAL NUMBERS

Part II of the book is a detailed discussion of various sorts of closed musical numbers (arias and ensembles). The assumption behind these detailed discussions is that it is in the musical working out of expressions of individuality, of the relations of individuals to groups, and of the ways in which social groups are represented, that some of the most important social "work" of opera buffa is done. Examination of the relations between class and gender in some conventional aria-types, for example, demonstrates that these works typically represent the differences between lower-class men and women as greater than the differences between men and women of the aristocracy; also that social mobility seems to mean something rather different for men than for women. Different sorts of arias evoke different relations between character and performer. In a culture where, increasingly, the dissolution of the actor into the role was considered the height of naturalism and the most desirable sort of artistic communication,[65] the ways

[65] The Heufeld/Klemm essay quoted above from the 1773 *Theatralalmanach von Wien* (p. 74) also includes the following, which is by no means unique: "The spectator at every dramatic performance must forget that he is watching something staged by art; only then, if he

in which some arias also encouraged the *performer's* self-presentation surely played into live concerns about verisimilitude and the representation of subjectivity. Ensembles, in representing groups of characters engaged together in a common dramatic and musical task, raise questions about life in society: who can or should be represented engaged in activity with whom? Are gender and class relevant to the group dynamics of the occasion? Perhaps more significant than the raw stage picture of who can be seen doing what with whom is the question of how ensembles typically identify individuals in relation to the groups of which they are part. One of the striking aspects of the majority of larger ensembles in this repertory is that they quite clearly define individuality as the result of social processes rather than as something stemming from a unique and fully expressed selfhood.

I do not, of course, claim that the social world of these operas directly reflects that of its audience, and the examination of these closed musical numbers is certainly the place in the book where the reconstruction of the conversation between repertory and audience is most one-sided. What I would claim, however, is that in a situation where at least part of the audience went repeatedly to these often-repeated reiterations of a remarkably consistent social world, it is reasonable to assume that some elements of that world were found to be satisfying or meaningful.

Considering the closed musical numbers of these operas in terms of their social values does not mean ignoring their formal and dramaturgical qualities. Indeed, it is very often in the manipulation of formal elements that a character defines him- or herself as a type or an individual. One formal element meaningful at every level of these works is the process of ending. As comedy, opera buffa is defined—at least in part—by its ending, which characteristically brings a quick stop to the imbroglio that has reigned through most of the work, patches up misunderstandings, and asserts both the possibility and the desirability of a strongly controlled social order. The endings of *opere buffe,* as of many comedies, are simultaneously inevitable-and-satisfying, and arbitrary-and-unsettling—Mozart's Da Ponte operas (even *Figaro*) counting as no exception here.[66] But even on a smaller level, endings—of phrases, of arias, of ensembles, and of scenes—are extraordinarily strongly articulated throughout this repertory, and they often embody the tensions and ambiguities of the genre as a whole. The end of an aria, for example, is often the place where the relative dominance of the

---

has no concept either of the author, or of the actor *qua* actor, does he fully enjoy the air of the performance." [Der Zuschauer muß bey jeder dramatischen Vorstellung vergessen, daß er etwas durch Kunst veranstalteten sehe; nur dann, wenn er gar keinen Begriff, weder von dem Dichter, noch von dem Schauspieler als Schauspieler, hat, genießt er die Luft der Vorstellung ganz.]

[66] Most modern students of these operas have something to say about their endings, but particularly relevant here is Bernard Williams, "Mozart's Comedies and the Sense of an Ending," *MT* 122 (1981) pp. 451–54.

character and the singer is most uncertain, and the ends of ensembles—as of first-act finales and second-act finales in three-act operas—often lock the participants in cheerful musical unanimity at the same time as they express conflict, despair, or confusion. What these endings typically embody is not so much ambiguity in the sense of uncertainty, as a double perspective through which the observer is always aware of two (or more) "pictures" but can only fully appreciate one at a time. The constant possibility of double or multiple perspectives, some contradicting others, but some simply alternative, may have given the performers room to act out either collectivity or anomie. It may also have given the spectator (as it certainly does the scholar) an opportunity to play within the genre's constantly shifting nexus of meanings.

Mozart "in Context"

Despite its opening discussion of *Le nozze di Figaro,* this book is not about Mozart, though he is an inevitable and pervasive presence, and his Da Ponte settings serve as familiar touchstones throughout the book. It is a study of a repertory, and its focus on the habits of that repertory is inevitably and intentionally leveling. It is in part a study in asking the same questions of the transcendent and the trivial, not in an effort to debunk the value of the transcendent or to valorize the trivial by joining it to the transcendent, but rather to problematize the easy binary oppositions (Mozart vs. "the others," universal vs. contingent, art vs. entertainment) that those terms imply. But it is also in part a study in Mozart's context: like most readers (I suppose), I came to this subject through Mozart, and one of the things I wanted to know was how Mozart's comic masterpieces fit into the world of this repertory. Thus the last two chapters are a study of *Così fan tutte,* both in terms of how it converses with particular "colleagues" (much as *Le nozze di Figaro* converses with *Il barbiere di Siviglia, La villanella rapita,* and *I finti eredi*), and in terms of its conversation with the genre as a whole. *Così* is particularly appropriate for this question, because it not only seems to be conventional, as many critics have noted, but it is crucially and profoundly about the meaning of convention. I argue that in this work Mozart "takes on" both Martín y Soler and (especially) Salieri; in doing so, as well as in making convention the principle aesthetic and moral *topos* of the work, he connects his immediate and contingent context—the repertory in which he and Da Ponte were so deeply embroiled, and some of whose habits this book tries to recreate—with the largest and most urgent questions about life and art. The profundity and delicacy with which Da Ponte and Mozart raise and partially answer these questions far exceed any attempt to explain their achievement; nevertheless, that achievement, I argue, depends absolutely on the particular context of Viennese opera buffa.

PART I

Opera Buffa as Entertainment

Chapter One

OPERA BUFFA AS SHEER
PLEASURE

IF THE INTELLECTUAL context of opera buffa in Vienna suggests that its occasion was understood as being "about" pleasure, the theatrical context of operatic performance did not gainsay this.[1] The Viennese theatres, like opera theatres all over Europe, provided a variety of pleasures in addition to the show: cards were played,[2] with card tables and lights rentable;[3] snacks and drinks were sold during the performance itself by roving vendors, or *Numeri*;[4] and especially for the first aristocracy, whose box-subscriptions allowed them to go night after night to repeat-performances of operas, those boxes functioned as publicly visible salons, where social life could be conducted much as it might have been at home. Indeed, Count Johann Joseph Khevenhüller reported that Joseph II's surprising avoidance of the theatre was due in part to its unsavory social goings-on.[5] Premieres evidently attracted more focused attention than reruns; nevertheless, the impression given by the sources is that the show (whether opera buffa or spoken drama) was often only one of the pleasures of the occasion. Unlike the German spoken drama, however (at least in its most serious guise), opera buffa by and large played into, and was understood as congruent with this ethos of multivalent delight. Not only did those who wrote about the repertory locate it among the mindless pleasures, but the works present themselves in various ways as "about" pleasure for its own sake—decon-

---

[1] Vienna was, of course, not unique in configuring the theatre as a site of more-than-theatrical pleasure. Numerous accounts of visits to Italian theatres, large and small, for opera seria and opera buffa, indicate that conversation, card-playing, and flirtation were as much the focus of the occasion as the show itself.

[2] See Peter Beckford, *Familiar Letters from Italy, to a Friend in England* (Salisbury: J. Easton, 1805) p. 86: "The new theatre [La Scala in Milan] is said to be a good one: the boxes are large; and it is not unusual to play at cards and sup in them. I can never reconcile myself to card playing at an opera. . . . It can only be of advantage to a deaf man, who probably would win all the money." Beckford's visit took place in 1787. Burney also noted the card and pharo tables at La Scala, in *The Present State of Music in France and Italy* (1773; rpt. New York: Broude Brothers, 1969) p. 84.

[3] The *Theaterzetteln* (posters) for the Burgtheater sometimes include the following sentence: "Ein ordinari Spieltisch sammt Licht und Karten zahlt jedesmal wie gewöhnlich 2 fl." (A regular card table with light and cards costs 2 fl. per time, as usual.)

[4] Gerhard Tanzer, *Spectacle müssen seyn: Die Freizeit der Wiener im 18. Jahrhundert* (Vienna: Böhlau, 1992) p. 175, shows a print of a "Numero" selling snacks in the Parterre of the Burgtheater.

[5] Quoted in Tanzer, *Spectacle müssen seyn,* pp. 169–70.

textualized, comforting, atavistic, easy, and sensual. They do this in part by their ending-habits, in part by relying on the familiar, and in part by emphasizing the act of performance.

DECONTEXTUALIZATION: THE PLEASURES OF THE ENDING

Opere buffe, like many comedies, often assert from within the *merely* pleasurable nature of the occasion, its function as escape or diversion from, rather than model for, daily life. Christopher Herbert has observed that comedy typically pursues and celebrates pleasure with great energy and tenacity. He describes it as "dominated by the will to pleasure"[6] and points to the "ritualized happy ending" as the locus classicus of the pleasure principle as it is played out in comedy. Opera buffa fits this model exactly. The parting words of many operas—those heard as the audience is preparing to re-enter the "real world"—contain their most explicit references to pleasure for its own sake and (typically) without moral justification. The following endings are characteristic of the wider repertory:

FRA I DUE LITIGANTI *Adapted Goldoni/Sarti*

Più fra noi non si contenda	There'll be no more arguments;
Ma cantiam con lieto cor:	Rather, we'll sing happily:
Viva sempre, e qui discenda	Long live, and descend here
Bella pace, e dolce amor.	Lovely peace and sweet love.

LA FRASCATANA *Livigni/Paisiello*

Non si parli più d'affanni,	No more talk of misery,
Non si parli di dolor;	No more talk of grief,
Non si parli più d'inganni,	No more talk of deception,
Ma si parli sol d'Amor.	But let's talk only of love.

LA VEDOVA SCALTRA *Goldoni/Righini*
(also found in I CONTRATEMPI by *Porta/Sarti*)

Sù beviamo, cantiamo, balliamo,	Come on, let's drink, sing, dance,
Ci ritorni la pace nel core;	Let peace return to our hearts,
Scenda Imeneo congiunto	Let Hymen joined to Cupid descend,
ad Amore,	
E ci faccia vieppiù giubilar.	And let's have celebration on
	celebration.

These final moments mention various reasons for celebration: the relief of the happy ending itself after the toils and confusions of the plot, the satisfaction of defeating a vice, the delight of drink (and often food), and, sig-

---

[6] Christopher Herbert, "Comedy: The World of Pleasure," *Genre* 17 (1984) pp. 401–16.

nificantly, the pleasure of music itself. Some opera buffa endings do suggest a moral—the end of *Don Giovanni* is a famous example—but these tend to occur in works whose plots center on the behavior or essential nature of a single individual—villain, buffoon, or a faithful and constant woman—rather than on a less focused untangling of an imbroglio. And where a moral is stated (or hinted at), it typically dissolves into a call to celebration. Thus, at the end of *La finta giardiniera,* the well-tested fidelity of Sandrina/Violante is duly praised but is then absorbed into a more general celebration of love and happiness:

Viva pur la Giardiniera	Long live the gardener-girl
Che serbò fedele il core;	Who remained faithful;
Viva il Conte, viva amore,	Long live the Count, long live love,
Che fa tutti rallegrar.	Which makes everyone rejoice.

In Bertati (or Petrosellini) and Anfossi's *Il curioso indiscreto* (which turns on the stupidity of the buffoon rather than the virtue of the heroine) the final recitative ends (like the final chorus of *Don Giovanni*), with "D'un curioso indiscreto il fine è questo" ("This is what becomes of those who meddle"); however, at this point the company sings a refrain almost identical to that in *La finta giardiniera:* "Viva sempre, viva amore/ Che fa tutti rallegrar."

Music is both an explicit and implicit component of the celebratory endings of *opere buffe;* many works end with references to singing and dancing or to parties with musical accompaniments, and all *opere buffe* end with choruses in which the words—usually highly formulaic and repetitive—take a back seat to the act of singing. Wye Allanbrook has interpreted the resort to music at the end of many *opere buffe* as in part an appeal to community—a dissolving of the divisive word into the healing power of music,[7] and Zvi Jagendorf has taken the opera buffa ending as described by Lorenzo Da Ponte as the ideal toward which all comic endings strive:

> It is clear why the stretta is so desirable at the end of comic opera. The joyful noisy climax is comic riot tamed by music. Something that without music would be close to confusion or absurdity is through music given a shape. It is the sound of release, the closest perhaps the modern stage can get to the licensed riot of Aristophanes' endings. . . . Because it is a musical imitation of riot, Da Ponte's stretta is the opera's way of turning to the audience for applause. The happy noise on stage is the signal for an equivalent outburst from the audience.[8]

---

[7] Wye J. Allanbrook, "Mozart's Happy Endings: A New Look at the 'Convention' of the 'Lieto Fine,'" *M-Jb* 1984/85, pp. 1–5. She mentions not only examples in which there is an explicit verbal appeal to music in the very last chorus but also moments like the *seghidiglia* in the second-act finale of *Una cosa rara,* where the recourse to music is enacted but not mentioned as such.

[8] Zvi Jagendorf, *The Happy End of Comedy: Jonson, Molière and Shakespeare* (Newark: University of Delaware Press, 1984) p. 34.

These readings see the musicality of the opera buffa ending as an appeal to community, either in the abstract or in relation to a particular gathering of people at a particular occasion. It is also true that the insouciance or "clapped on" aspect of many of these endings[9] assert the *merely* pleasurable nature of the whole occasion; such endings imagine the audience to which they appeal as a group gathered in the spirit of pleasure. Jagendorf notes that the endings of spoken comedies typically turn back on themselves, referring to past events in the work rather than to the future.[10] The invocations of music (and love and food) at the ends of many *opere buffe* do not literally recapitulate the events of the plot, but on an abstract level they do reiterate and thus remind the audience of the self-containedly and sheerly pleasurable nature of the occasion.

THE PLEASURES OF THE FAMILIAR

This repertory of opera buffa also serves the notion of pleasure for its own sake in ways less literal than the self-reflexive invitation to party. One aspect of the repertory's more oblique emphasis on pleasure is its extreme and pervasive dependence on the known and the conventional. This has, I think, two pleasure-giving effects. One is the easy or atavistic retreat into an utterly predictable realm;[11] the other is the way in which that realm presents itself as "about" its own rules. The constant presence of intertextual references (both general and specific) in all these works on every level creates a self-contained world, one of whose primary pleasures is the game of cross-identification. Mozart's self-conscious quotations from *Fra i due litiganti il terzo gode* and *Una cosa rara* in the second-act finale of *Don Giovanni* invoke this game, as does the above-mentioned Piticchio quotation of "Se vuol ballare."[12] This game is not limited to quotations of tunes, however; texts, characters, singers, and larger dramatic and musical devices and conventions—even whole genres—are routinely and constantly co-opted into opera buffa's "play of signifiers," or conversation with its repertory and genre.[13]

---

[9] I take this phrase from Allanbrook, "Mozart's Happy Endings," p. 5.

[10] Jagendorf, *The Happy End of Comedy*, p. 42.

[11] On the psychologically regressive nature of some comic opera, see Ilaria Crotti, "Percorsi della farsa tra romanzo e teatro," in *I vicini di Mozart*, ed. Maria Teresa Muraro and David Bryant, vol. 2 (Florence: Olschki, 1989) pp. 489–549. Crotti suggests that the *farsa* as it developed in Venice in the 1790s was much less shimmering intertextual than opera buffa, and much more likely to reproduce its sources literally. She relates this to the bourgeois/popular character of its audiences, and their regressive desires to have their collective knowledge reinforced.

[12] Introduction, pp. 3–4.

[13] Opera seria is a standard import in opera buffa: it serves as a target for ridicule but also as a model of emotional seriousness. See Hunter, "Some Representations of Opera Seria in Opera Buffa," *COJ* 3 (1991) pp. 89–108.

In a study of Verdi's librettos, Mario Lavagetto gives a psychological explanation of the pleasures of pervasive conventionality. He divides all texts
into two sorts—those that constantly problematize their own structural
conventions, and those that "obstinately" follow them. Counting libretti
among the second sort, he writes:

> It could be that one might find this constraining, but I don't think it wise to value
> it in that way. It is, rather, worth the trouble to emphasize that . . . the pleasure of
> the text seems to coincide perfectly with the pleasure of repetition illustrated by
> Freud [in *Beyond the Pleasure Principle*]; desire is fulfilled [by] representing itself
> or recognizing itself in the representation offered to it.[14]

The repetition described by Freud involves both the reconfiguration of
real-life events into a simpler and more manageable pattern (the transformation of a mother's temporary absences into the hiding and subsequent
rediscovery of toys), and the reiteration of the pattern (the child's repeated
playing of the hide-and-seek game), which gives pleasure by confirming
and reconfirming the child's sense of mastery over the game. Like the
child's game, opera buffa as we will see "abstracts" complicated social
structures and behaviors into rigid and predictable patterns, and its conventionality also offers the pleasure of mastery to those familiar with the
rules (and it would have been near-impossible for its contemporary audiences not to be familiar with them).

Familiar Sources

Beyond the simple facts that all *opere buffe* were performed and attended
multiple times and were thus literally familiar after the first hearing or
two, and also that many works were given second productions during the
twenty years under consideration,[15] the fact that many libretti were based
on works already known to the majority of literate or theatre-going audience members must have reinforced the sense that opera buffa typically
dealt in the known. Some of the models were plays; both the relevant
Beaumarchais Figaro plays (*Le Barbier de Séville* and *Le Mariage de Figaro*),
for example, were known in Vienna before the introduction of Paisiello's

---

[14] Mario Lavagetto, *Quei più modesti romanzi* (Milan: Garzanti, 1979) p. 174. The relevant passage of Freud can be found in part II of *Beyond the Pleasure Principle,* tr. James Strachey (New York: Norton, 1961) pp. 8–11.

[15] These include *La contadina in corte* (1767, 1770, and 1782), *La fiera di Venezia* (1772
and 1785), *La locandiera* (1772 and 1782), *Metilde ritrovata* (1772 and 1778), *La frascatana* (1775 and 1783), *Le due contesse* (1776 and 1787), *Le gelosie villane* (1777 and 1783),
La vendemmia a.k.a *La dama incognita* (1779 and 1784), *Il falegname* (1783 and 1789), *Il
re Teodoro in Venezia* (1784 and 1790), *Le nozze di Figaro* (1786 and 1789), *Il burbero di
buon core* (1786 and 1789), and *Gli equivoci* (1786 and 1790). There was a noticeable tendency at the end of the period, perhaps for financial reasons, to bring back works that had
premiered only three or four years earlier.

and Mozart's operas,[16] while Martín y Soler and Da Ponte's *Il burbero
di buon cuore* (1786) was a reworking of the Goldoni play of the same
title, performed in French in Vienna in 1772.[17] Da Ponte and Stephen
Storace's *Gli equivoci* (1786) was based (via M. Letourneau's translation
as *Les méprises*) on Shakespeare's *Comedy of Errors*. Although this play
was not performed in Vienna, the libretto relied on local enthusiasm for
its author.[18] Bertati and Paisiello's *I filosofi immaginari* (1783) was preceded not only by its own German translation, first presented in 1781,
but by Gennaro Astarita's setting of the same libretto, first presented in
1774. Novels (or excerpts therefrom) were a frequently used source: *Il
curioso indiscreto* (1785), for example, was based on an episode from
Cervantes' *Don Quixote,* which was also used in two earlier operas,
Lorenzi and Paisiello's *Don Chisciotte della Mancia* (1771) and Boccherini and Salieri's *Don Chisciotte alle nozze di Gamace* (1770). Sometimes the familiar material was available in several quite different versions
or media. The Don Giovanni story is a good example of this; in Vienna
in particular it had before the 1788 performance of Da Ponte and
Mozart's work been represented not only in Porta and Righini's *Il convitato di pietra* (1777), but also in Gluck's ballet *Don Juan* (1761). The
principle of familiarity was so pervasive that even a self-consciously "different" or original libretto like Casti's *La grotta di Trofonio* (set by Salieri
in 1785) appealed to familiar Classical authority to justify its subject.[19]
The use of familiar material in the Viennese opera buffa repertory differs from the frequent use of translations from English and French in the
German repertory. Whereas the German-language companies used translations as a way of creating more or less from scratch a large and varied
repertory in the vernacular, the Italian repertory of opera buffa—which
had no need of building up—seems to have used familiarity as an end in
itself.

[16] See Introduction, p. 3.

[17] Zechmeister, *WT,* p. 532. See also Brown, "Lo Specchio Francese," in Hunter and Webster, *Opera Buffa in Mozart's Vienna* (Cambridge: Cambridge University Press, 1977) pp.
61–63, for discussion of the relations between the play and the opera.

[18] See, among other sources dealing with Shakespeare's popularity in Vienna, Elaine Sisman, "Haydn's Theatre Symphonies," *JAMS* 43 (1990) pp. 292–352.

[19] The preface to the libretto reads, in part: "Fra le bizzarre stravaganze immaginate da'
Greci Mitologi singolarissima certamente è quella dell'antro di Trofonio. . . . Unico per altro
non è nella Mitologia l'antro di Trofonio, . . . poichè oltre a quegli, che riportati sono dai
Poeti greci, e latini, e particolarmente da Ovidio nel lib. XV. delle sue metamorfosi, notis-
sima, e celebre resa fu dai nostri Epici la fontana d'Ardenna, le di cui acque cangiavano
l'Amore in odio, e l'odio in amore." (Among the bizarre fantasies imagined by Greek mythology, certainly the strangest is that of the cave of Trophonius. . . . The cave of Trophonius, besides, is not unique in mythology . . . as besides those reported by the Greek and Latin poets,
and particularly by Ovid in Book XV of the *Metamorphoses,* the most noted and famous of
these epics is the fountain of Ardenna, whose waters changed love into hate, and hate into
love.)

The Suggestion of Novelty

Despite its habitual reliance on familiar material, opera buffa, unlike opera seria, did not generate dozens of settings of the same "canonic" libretto, advertised with the same title every time, regardless of the often substantial changes to the text itself.[20] There is, for example, no opera buffa equivalent to the throng of *Olimpiades* or *Demetrios* set in the course of the eighteenth century. Indeed, it was common buffa practice to change the title of a piece as it migrated from city to city (or sometimes between one production run and the next in the same city). Anfossi's setting of Petrosellini's *L'incognita perseguitata,* for example, was also performed in various places as *La Giannetta, La Giannetta perseguitata,* and *Metilde ritrovata.* In Vienna in 1773, and again in 1778 it seems to have been performed as *Metilde ritrovata,* probably to distinguish it—at least in the first instance—from Piccinni's setting of *L'incognita perseguitata,* performed in Vienna in 1772.[21] If in the opera seria repertory there are more operas than titles, the works of Metastasio in particular forming a canon to which composers seem to have wanted to attach themselves, among *opere buffe* there are more titles than operas—novelty being the initial attraction rather than the substance of the work. Indeed, it is not unusual to find an indication like "la musica tutta nuova" attached to a work shamelessly cobbled together from recognizably old parts. In other words the paradigmatic opera buffa practice with respect to novelty seems to have been precisely the inverse of the paradigmatic seria practice: while in the former genre audiences were promised novelty and served largely familiar fare, in the latter they were promised familiarity (or perhaps reliable quality) and served with at least a portion of new material. Some opera buffa librettos were set two or three times by different composers (Haydn's *opere buffe,* for example, are almost all second or third settings), but in contrast to the Metastasian canon, it is rare to find more than two or three settings of a single text. Even the best-loved of Goldoni's libretti were typically set no more than five or six times. In addition to the novelty promised by the quick turnover of libretti and the variety of titles for single works, the delicate balance between comfort and surprise was perpetuated when (as often) apparently new librettos turned out to be minor reworkings of earlier pieces under new titles; not surprisingly, Goldoni's works seem to have been particularly subject to this

[20] See Helga Lühning, *Titus-Vertonungen im 18. Jahrhundert: Untersuchungen zur Tradition der Opera Seria von Hasse bis Mozart* (Cologne: Arno-Volk Laaber-Verlag, 1983) for a description of the vagaries of at least one libretto in the course of the century. See also Reinhard Wiesend, "Le revisioni di Metastasio di alcuni suoi drammi e la situazione della musica per melodramma negli anni '50 del settecento," in *Metastasio e il mondo musicale,* ed. Maria Teresa Muraro (Florence: Olschki, 1986) pp. 171–97.

[21] Zechmeister, *WT,* pp. 540 and 545.

sort of treatment. The anonymous libretto to *Fra i due litiganti,* for example, is a lightly altered reworking of Goldoni's *Le nozze,* and Bertati's *Il geloso in cimento* is a version of Goldoni's play *La vedova scaltra.* It is impossible to know the extent to which audiences might have understood opera buffa's familiarity-disguised-as-novelty as part of the genre's intertextual game, or simply as its comfortable backdrop.

Models and Archetypes: Familiarity and Convention

The "game" and the "comfortable backdrop" are not, of course, mutually exclusive. However, insofar as there is a distinction between them, it has to do with the difference between the quotation of something specifically identifiable and the reuse of a well-known convention. The "game" aspect of these works is probably most relevant to the network of particular associations that a single work might have triggered in a specific audience. However, the poetics of the repertory as a whole are more fully explained by reference to the larger archetypes in general circulation in that repertory than to local intertextualities. Opera buffa cannot be understood without reference to archetypes on every level—including plot, character, and musical devices both large and small. The works also play up their implicitly conventional nature by explicitly announcing their predictability. For example, the basic plot structures of these works are often announced in the first couple of pages of the libretto (i.e., before the text proper begins), so that even at a premiere the audience could tell at a glance what sort of story to expect. The cast list for Petrosellini and Cimarosa's *Il pittore parigino,* for example, is typical in presenting not only the names of the characters, but also brief descriptions of rank or occupation and the familial, affective, or economic relation of each character to at least one other. This information often suggests the likely final alliances :

MLLE. EURILLA   Rich young woman, dedicated to poetry, in love with
       Mons. di Crotignac
BARON CRICCA   Betrothed to Eurilla; choleric and jealous man
MONS. DI CROTIGNAC   French painter, in love with Eurilla
CINTIA   Eurilla's cousin; lively girl (*ragazza di spirito*), in love with the
       Baron
BROCCARDO   Eurilla's agent

Here we have a present bad match, between the ill-tempered Baron and the artistic Eurilla, and a potential good one, between Eurilla and the equally artistic Monsieur di Crotignac (a tenor). Although tenor parts were not as rigidly associated with primary lovers in this repertory as they became in the nineteenth century, in this configuration of characters the fact that Monsieur Crotignac is a tenor certainly advances his claim to Eurilla's hand. The cast list also suggests the final attachment of the Baron to Cintia, since Cintia is already enamored of the Baron, and there is no social obstacle to their union. Some librettos, particularly those for first productions, also provide an *argomento*—a summary of the prehistory of the plot which usually prefigures the end.

The character-descriptions at the beginnings of librettos often announce the singer type as well as the character type. Although in many libretti from Italian opera houses the characters are specifically divided into rank and type—e.g., *prima buffa* (principal female comic singer or singing actress), *prima donna* (usually the principal female singer), *primo buffo caricato* (principal comic bass)—and although this was in Vienna a well-understood way of thinking about singers and roles,[22] Viennese librettos do not typically print these singer-oriented descriptions. Nevertheless, the combination of rank and brief description in the cast list often suffice to "fix" a character in social status, in likely trajectory, and in emotional or expressive type. Names also contribute to this fixing of character types: serving girls called Serpetta, Serpina (both meaning "little snake"), or Vespina ("little wasp") are without exception scheming, worldly wise, and witty characters in what we now think of as soubrette roles. Whatever their character (sentimental or scheming), female servants and country girls are essentially without exception marked by diminutive name-endings (Nannina, Lisetta, Angiolina, Zerlina, Despina). Male servants and country boys below the rank of land-agent or valet also typically have diminutive endings to their names (Pippetto, Cecchino, Pasquino, Leporello, Masetto), and occasionally augmentative ones (Mengone, Pierotto). These names often indicate not only relative powerlessness in the hierarchy of characters, but also a sort of boorish stupidity. (Even Lepor*ello,* who is by no means stupid, is bound to his bodily needs in characteristically unrefined ways.) Men announced in the cast list as misers, false philosophers, and old heads of households, and who are dignified (or mocked) with the title Don are usually dupes and sung by comic bass singers. Roman, Classical, or Ariostan names (Irene, Aurora, Clarice, Lucinda, Flavia, Angelica, etc. for women, and Lindoro, Ottavio, Orlando, Rinaldo, Ruggiero, Ernesto, etc., for men) indicate both high rank and seria-like musical type; one can expect male singers with such names to be tenors rather than basses, and both men and women of this type to have at least one virtuosic aria in the course of the opera.

By suggesting that many aspects of an opera buffa were either immediately familiar, or predictable on the basis of the front matter of the libretto, I do not mean to suggest that all operas and characters perfectly exemplify the types I have described. Obviously some works labor more obviously

---

[22] See, for example, Mozart's famous letter to his father of 7 May 1783, in which he expresses a desire to write an opera with three equally important female roles, one seria, one *di mezzo carattere,* and one buffa. Mozart, *Letters* II, p. 848; *Briefe,* iii, p. 268.

under the "iron foot of a pattern," some manipulate the various levels of convention more complexly and subtly, and some strike out in bolder new directions than others. Originality in relation to these archetypes is, however, not prima facie a criterion of value. For example, Bertati and Paisiello's *I filosofi immaginari* plays out very straightforwardly the plot-type of the father-duped-to-allow-his-daughter-to-marry, and the characters are fully comprehensible in terms of well-established singer- and role-types. But despite its lack of structural originality, the details of the characterization and the generally high quality of the music make it (as far as one can tell from the score alone) extremely attractive entertainment. Its (brief) revival in the repertory of the Italian troupe in 1783 after its success in German several years earlier may be some indication of its popularity. Mozart's variations on Giuliano's aria (I, 8) "Salve tu domine," (K.398/416e) may also indicate the work's popular success. Zinzendorf found the music "very beautiful, the play a bit indecent, very short, strongly applauded; the duets and finales charming, but I prefer the *litiganti*."[23] Zinzendorf preferred "the *litiganti*" to almost every other opera, so this does not much diminish the impression that *I filosofi immaginari*—however conventional—pleased him.

Musical Familiarity and Predictability

Just as the opening pages of most librettos suggest the general direction and outcome of the plots and the types and relationships of the characters, so the beginnings of most arias—the majority of numbers in most operas—suggest, by means of the character singing, the lexicon he or she uses, the dramatic circumstances, and the choice of musical *topos,* what is likely to come. The easy comprehensibility of most aria-beginnings plays into the notion of the comforts of the familiar, but it also sets the game of prediction in motion. For example, when the noble lover Ramiro in Anfossi's setting of *La finta giardiniera* begins an aria *Allegro,* in common time, in C major, with a triadic melody over a *trommel* bass, all set to a nature metaphor—in "seria" style, in other words—the educated listener would expect, and does in fact get, a "sonata-like" or truncated da capo form (this expectation will be heightened if one has the libretto and notes the two-quatrain form of the text) with coloratura placed close to the cadence in the secondary key (occasionally at the beginning of the secondary key area) and also in a comparable place later in the aria. (Mozart's setting of the same text uses the same basic conventions; see Example 1-1.)

Eurilla's first aria in Cimarosa's *Il pittore parigino* begins in a manner similar to this, both in its musical style and in its linguistic register. But unlike the arias mentioned above, whose primary tone is eloquence and power, Eurilla's dissolves into more or less free-form raving; the exposition

---

[23] Michtner, *DAB,* p. 162.

1-1: Anfossi, *La finta giardiniera* I,1
Ramiro, "Se l'augellin sen fugge," mm. 20–34

Translation: Should the little bird flee from its prison one day, [it will no] longer go joking around

is followed by a *Largo* section admitting her love for Monsieur Crotignac, and a fast final section expressing delirium: the arpeggiated flourish up to high A is particularly unusual at this point in a phrase in this sort of section and seems especially "delirious." The fact that this raving comes after such a conventionally poised expository paragraph makes it all the more effective as a depiction of losing control:

1-2: Cimarosa, *Il pittore parigino*, I,10
Eurilla, "Sul mio core invan presume," mm. 21–27; 45–50; 83–90;
100–106

1-2: *(Continued)*

so ben i - o l'ar-dor che sen - to, l'ar-dor che sen - to nel mio

sen bell' i - dol mi - o, nel mio sen bell' i - dol mi - o

cru - de stel-le a-mor ti - ran-no, quan-te sma-nie al co-re io sen-to, quan-te sma-nie al co-re io sen-to

Translation: You presume in vain on my heart...
             I will not allow myself [to be commanded by love]...
             I know well the ardor that I feel in my breast, my love...
             Cruel stars, tyrannical love; I feel such delirium in my heart

Plot Archetypes

Among the most important arenas for the display and manipulation of conventional archetypes in opera buffa are the plots. In the following paragraphs I describe some of the most common archetypes, not with a view to exhaustive cataloguing of all possible models and combinations, or in any attempt to elucidate any particular work in any detail, but rather with the aim of demonstrating how these structures could create a well-understood network of expectations about plot shape and trajectory, such that any given work could on the one hand stay close enough to the pattern to be familiar, and on the other, find sufficient room for variation or for recombination of related elements to provide a measure of pleasurable uncertainty.[24] There are of course connections between the various archetypes, as well as many works that draw on elements of several archetypes. But in general it is characteristic of this repertory that the basic plot-model is easily evident, or that the various conventional riffs and devices that make up the plot are presented in a relatively straightforward or wholesale manner.

The triumph of young love over rigidity, lust, or greed in the form of a father, uncle, or guardian who tries to prevent his daughter, niece, or ward from marrying the young man of her choice, is one of the most common basic plots in this repertory. The lovers, often aided and abetted by servants or other household members, devise a plot or series of plots that either force the older man to sign a real wedding contract in a fictitious situation, or that humiliate him into agreeing to the wedding. Two trajectories intersect in this plot; the "ascent" of the couple, and the "descent" of the dupe, who inevitably fails to achieve his own desires and falls from a position of some authority to a risible subordination to or dependence on his juniors. Paisiello's *Il barbiere di Siviglia* follows this model exactly, as, of course, does Rossini's more familiar setting. This plot-archetype offers several levels of pleasure beyond the simple fact of its familiarity. Plots of this sort almost always involve several moments of purely performative delight, including the split-second timing of the imbroglio at moments of deceit and discovery and at least one virtuosic vocal and gestural performance of frenzy and collapse by the dupe. They also evoke (in rather genteel fashion, to be sure) the carnivalesque social/political delight of seeing an authority figure outwitted and beaten; at the same time, the replacement of

---

[24] Ronald Rabin, "Mozart, Da Ponte, and the Dramaturgy of Opera Buffa," (Ph.D. dissertation, Cornell University, 1996), pp. 60–70, lists several earlier attempts at categorizing Goldoni's librettos according to conventional structures. Rabin himself lays out a complex system of more or less hierarchical categories (moral, theme, plot, motive, character-type) whose variously conventionalized instantiations interact in any given work. Thus works with the same theme may have quite different plots, and vice versa. My list of plot archetypes takes account only of the sequence of events in the story, and of the relations of the characters insofar as that affects the sequence of events.

the first authority figure with a new young master assures the audience that the fundamental order underlying the plot has not been undermined.

A related archetype involves elopement or abduction. Here an already-married or betrothed couple find themselves in a foreign environment, with the heroine about to be wed to the local ruler or patriarch; sometimes (as in Mozart's *Die Entführung* and Haydn's *L'incontro improvviso*) the heroine spends some time alone in the exotic location before the hero finds her. The happy outcome in this case always depends on the generosity of the ruler or head of household;[25] in that sense these operas stand between those in which outwitting a dupe is the central action, and those in which a previously importunate and inappropriately amorous nobleman finally allows the country girl or serving maid to marry her proper beloved (see below). Viennese *opere buffe* on the abduction model include Chiari and Guglielmi's *La sposa fedele,* Palomba and Paisiello's *Le gare generose,* and Act II of Bertati and Anfossi's *Isabella e Rodrigo.* One of the "sensual" pleasures of these operas is their exotic color; their endorsement of familiar European manners and values combines the generalized notion of the pleasure of the familiar with the more political satisfaction arising from the restoration of social (and ethnic) stability.

Some plot archetypes revolve around the situation of a single character, and one of the most significant in this repertory is the sentimental heroine. Her inevitable trajectory is toward a socially fitting and emotionally desired betrothal or wedding. Her primary function is to engage the audience's sympathies and stimulate their capacity for sensibility, which she may do in a variety of ways, all of which to some degree or other involve her persecution or victimization. Although the figure of the sentimental heroine appears in a number of different operatic stories, two plot subtypes are paradigmatic for this character type. In the first she is besieged by the unwelcome and inappropriate attentions of a man of much higher social rank, but she ultimately marries her socially appropriate suitor. The nobleman is typically portrayed as evil, the young woman is always attached to someone else, and the sympathies of the audience are engaged by this alone. It is always clear very early in the piece that the heroine will not be forced into a socially inappropriate match, and her mixture of sentimentalism, naïveté, and a certain pertness verify the correctness of her placement among the lower social orders. *La villanella rapita* and *I finti eredi* both exemplify this type.

[25] Comic operas in which the ruler/head of household dispenses generosity can be related to seria plots in which a virtuous ruler closes the action with a final merciful dispensation. Daniel Heartz, "La Clemenza di Sarastro: Masonic Beneficence in the Last Operas," in *Mozart's Operas,* (Berkeley: University of California Press, 1990) pp. 255–76, has already pointed out the relation between the Singspiel's Sarastro and the opera seria's Tito; similar relations between serious and comic (or semi-comic) characters obtain throughout the repertory.

The second plot type revolving around the sentimental heroine is exemplified by Goldoni and Piccinni's influential *La buona figliuola*. Here and in comparable operas the attentions of the nobleman are reciprocated by the young woman, and the outcome is a happy union between the lovers, permitted by the discovery that the heroine is in fact of noble birth (or more rarely, simply of noble character). The heroine in this plot type is victimized by the jealousy and spite of other women—either sisters or cousins of the amorous nobleman, whose amour-propre is injured by his interest in a nobody, or serving-girls or peasants who are envious of the likely elevation of their apparent peer. In Vienna this plot was echoed in *L'incognita perseguitata,* as well as in Livigni and Paisiello's *L'innocente fortunata,* in Puttini and Anfossi's *La vera costanza,* and (to some degree) in *La finta giardiniera.*[26] The "noble foundling" aspect of these plots provides both the dramatic motor of destabilization (she may, after all, be truly lowborn), and the usual reassurance of stability (she is usually not stable).

The final plot-archetype I would mention, and the one most accommodating of variation, involves the unraveling of wrongly constituted alliances. *Così fan tutte* is the most famous example of a libretto based on the premise of wrongly allied couples. Casti and Salieri's *La grotta di Trofonio* is another example of the same archetype,[27] as are Porta and Sarti's *I contratempi* and Livigni and Anfossi's *Le gelosie fortunate.* Lorenzi and Haydn's *La fedeltà premiata* also refers to it. One might think that most *opere buffe* deal in some way with mixed-up couples, and of course they do. But what distinguishes this archetype from the others I have mentioned is that there is neither a dupe who forms the primary obstacle to happiness nor a central character whose emotional life controls the work; and nor, indeed, is there the combination of capture and exoticism found in the abduction/elopement operas. Because this is the plot-archetype most susceptible to variation, it may be that the "game" element of the pleasure it provides—i.e., predicting likely outcomes—is more compelling than the reassurance of familiarity offered by the other plot archetypes mentioned above.

THE PLEASURES OF PERFORMANCE

As the introduction to this book suggests, eighteenth-century Viennese commentary on opera buffa more or less begins and ends with questions of performers and performance. Among Joseph II's many comments on the opera buffa company and repertory in his correspondence with Count Rosenberg, for example,[28] he makes more than passing comment on only

[26] Daniel Heartz, *Haydn, Mozart, and the Viennese School 1740–1780* (New York: Norton, 1995) p. 394, notes this connection.
[27] I compare these two operas in more detail in Chapter 8.
[28] Rudolf Payer von Thurn, *Joseph II als Theaterdirektor* (Vienna: Heidrich, 1920).

five actual works: Paisiello's *Il barbiere di Siviglia,* in which he tells Rosenberg to get on with the casting, then (later) comments on Benucci's, Storace's, and Mandini's performances;[29] Neri and Guglielmi's *Le vicende d'amore,* in which he saw Benucci sing in Caserta in 1783;[30] Palomba and Cimarosa's *Chi dell'altrui si veste,* which he also saw in Caserta but found too "Neapolitan" for Vienna, though good for Celeste Coltellini;[31] Da Ponte and Martín y Soler's *L'arbore di Diana,* in which he recommended reassigning the part of Diana to Caterina Cavalieri;[32] and Giovannini and Sarti's opera seria *Giulio Sabino,* which he had chosen as the proper vehicle for the castrato Luigi Marchesi.[33] It is perhaps not surprising that as head of the imperial theatrical enterprise, Joseph should be more concerned with personnel than aesthetics. But his emphases are also entirely typical of all sorts of contemporary commentary on the genre. Thus, in an amusing skit comparing the merits of Singspiel and opera buffa, essayist Joseph Richter has his supporter of the Singspiel praise the capacity of the German performers to convey verbal and dramatic meaning in their singing (in other words, their capacity to give a dramatically integrated performance); his supporter of opera buffa, on the other hand, pooh-poohs all that and talks about vocal qualities:

> MUSIKKENNER: "What is all this about feelings and action? The throat of a German is simply not as adapted to high notes as that of Italian women. . . .
> HERR VON Z.: "Surely you don't mean trills and warbles, do you?"
> MUSIKKENNER: "Warbles! Warbles! Excuse me, Herr von Z—, but you have no right to judge music, since, as you told me yesterday, you know nothing about it.[34]

The author of the 1773 essay excerpted in the Introduction (p. 10) puts performance among the things that redeem the typically miserable buffa libretto, and redemption by performance is also a theme in Charles Burney's comments on a Viennese performance of Petrosellini and Salieri's *Il barone di Rocca antica:* "I did not receive much pleasure from the overture, or the

---

[29] Letters of June 19, 1783, in ibid., p. 33, and August 14, 1783, ibid., p. 35.
[30] Letter of December 31, 1783, written on a trip to Caserta, ibid., p. 39.
[31] Ibid.
[32] Letter of 11 June, 1788, ibid., p. 78. The part was eventually given to Adriana Ferrarese del Bene.
[33] Letter of 23 July, 1785, ibid., p. 64.
[34] J. Richter, *Der Zuschauer in Wien,* 3d ed., vol. 5 (Vienna: Hochenleitter, 1790) pp. 13–22:

> MUSIKKENNER: Was wollen Sie mit Ihrem Gefühl, mit Ihrer Acktion? [*sic*] Schon die Kehle einer Deutschen ist zu den hohen Tönen nicht so geschicket, als bei den Italiänerinnen. . . .
> HERR V. Z: Sie meinen doch nicht Triller und Gurgeleyen?
> MUSIKKENNER: Gurgeleyen! Gurgeleyen! Verzeihen Sie mir, Herr von Z—, aber von der Musik können Sie unmöglich urtheilen, da Sie, wie Sie mir erst gestern gestanden [*sic*], nicht eine Note kennen.

two first airs; the music was languid, and the singing but indifferent. There were only four characters in the piece, and the principal woman did not appear til the third scene; but then she gave a glow to every thing around her; it was one of the Baglioni [Costanza], of Bologna, whom I had heard both at Milan and at Florence, during my tour through Italy."[35] Goethe's comments after a 1786 visit to San Moisè (the Venetian theatre most devoted to opera buffa and the source of a noticeable proportion of Vienna's *opere buffe*) are entirely comparable: "Yesterday evening, opera at [St. Moisè] . . . ; not very good! The libretto, the music, the singers—everything lacked that certain inner energy which is the only thing that can lend excitement to such a presentation. No one part of it could be called poor, but only the two women made an effort both to act well and project themselves agreeably. That is at least something. The two have beautiful figures and good voices and are charming, sprightly, appealing little persons. As for the men, however, not a trace of inner strength or any desire to create an illusion for the audience, and no particularly fine voices."[36] (He does not mention the title, librettist, or composer of the work in question, but the best candidate is Bertati and Gazzaniga's *Le donne fanatiche,* which includes two "prima buffa" roles and was played this season.)[37]

Goethe's comment about the sprightly and appealing women with good figures also echoes a couple of connected themes in the literature about opera buffa—sex and sensory delight. A striking example is the *Realzeitung*'s 1784 comment about the reinstatement of a resident buffa troupe: "Blessed are they who have hungered and thirsted after Italian divas, for they shall be satisfied for a good price."[38] The composers, librettists, and even male singers of opera buffa are conspicuously absent from this sketch; female singers represent the genre as a whole, and not only that, but the pleasures they promise seem to extend beyond their vocal capacities. The analogy between professional singing or acting and prostitution was commonplace all across Europe both in and before the eighteenth century, and it was on the whole less pronounced in Vienna than in some other places. Nevertheless, commentary about particular performances often mentions the physical attributes of the female performers,

---

[35] Charles Burney, *The Present State of Music in Germany, The Netherlands, and United Provinces* (1775; facsimile rpt., New York: Broude Brothers, 1969) p. 245.

[36] Johann Wolfgang von Goethe, *Italian Journey,* trans. Robert R. Heitner. Goethe Edition, vol. 6 (New York: Suhrkamp, [1989]) p. 64. The date of this entry is October 3, 1786.

[37] Irene Tomeoni Dutilleu and Giulia Gasparini were the singers. Taddeo Wiel, *I teatri musicali veneziani del settecento,* with afterword by Reinhard Strohm (Leipzig: Peters, 1979) p. 398.

[38] "Selig sind die hungern und dürsten nach welschen Operistinnen, denn sie werden für gute Bezahlung ersättiget werden." Michtner, *DAB,* p. 148, from the *Wiener Realzeitung* of 1784. See also John Rosselli, *Singers of Italian Opera: The History of a Profession* (Cambridge: Cambridge University Press, 1992). Chapter 3, "Women," notes the beginnings of improved status for women singers of opera seria in the mid-eighteenth century.

and occasionally even the music seems to have aroused some sexual interest. Zinzendorf's 1783 comments about Nancy Storace as Dorina in *Fra
i due litiganti* seem astonishingly unguarded: "Storace played [the role]
like an angel. Her beautiful eyes, her white neck, her beautiful throat, her
fresh mouth, made a charming effect."[39] His 1787 comments on the duet,
"Pace, caro mio sposo," in *Una cosa rara* suggest comparable enthusiasm
for the music that Storace sang: "I find the duo between Mandini and
Storace so tender and so expressive that it poses a danger to the young
members of the audience. One needs to have had some experience in order
to see it with a cool head."[40] Zinzendorf's extreme susceptibility to this
music (surely aided and abetted by the acting of Storace and Mandini)
echoes in a specifically sexual framework Sonnenfels's helplessness (quoted
above, p. 19) in the face of the sheer sound of Giacomo Caribaldi's voice.

It is inadequate to consider performance, a mere side-effect of the score,
whose vitality has left its traces in the contextual information of the period.
Rather, the act of performing is also thematized and highlighted in the
works themselves. As with any opera, opera buffa includes moments where
attention is implicitly drawn to the singer's skill, whether "accidentally," as
in a line that exhibits a particular beauty of tone, or "on purpose," as in
coloratura or other obviously difficult passages. And as in spoken comedy,
the gags, confusions, disguises, and tricks of opera buffa implicitly call attention to the acting skills that bring them off (timing, declamation, gesture, imitative ability, etc.). However, one thing that links opera buffa more
closely to spoken comedy than to opera seria in terms of performativity is
the frequency of opportunities for characters explicitly to enact a performance on stage, often, but not always, for the benefit of an onstage audience as well as for the auditorium spectators.[41] These performances invite
both audiences to take pleasure in the demonstration of a skill, which may
be vocal pyrotechnics, physical gesture, or something more connected to
the forward motion of the story, like persuasiveness or witty solipsism.
They typically direct the auditorium audience's attention to the moment
and to the performer rather than to the larger dramatic context or to the
role, and thus "break the frame" of the dramatic illusion. Such self-reflexive performances alter the relation between the performer and the role and
force a layering of the audience's attention. In repeatedly refocusing attention on the moment and on the act of performance, and particularly in
making that shift in focus explicit, opera buffa enacts the typically comedic

[39] Michtner, *DAB*, p. 387: "La Storace y joua comme un ange. Ses beaux yeux, son cou
blanc, sa belle gorge, sa bouche fraiche faisent un charmant effet."
[40] Quoted in John Platoff, "A New History for Martín's *Una cosa rara*," *JM* 12 (1994)
p. 101.
[41] Zvi Jagendorf notes the generally performative nature of comedy. *The Happy Ending
of Comedy*, p. 12.

strategy of inducing in the audience a critical distance from the narrative. The explicit focus on the pleasures of the moment, however, is also part of the general tendency of opera buffa to "decontextualize" itself—to assert that its occasion is about itself rather than about life beyond the theatre.

Performed Performances

The stage song is the most obvious subcategory of performed-performance;[42] Cherubino's "Voi che sapete" is a well-known example, as is Rosina's music-lesson aria "Deh riede la primavera" from Paisiello's *Il barbiere di Siviglia;* both of these songs use the singer's status as learner as an excuse. The serenade is another common occasion for an operatic song: Don Giovanni's "Deh vieni alla finestra" is the best-known example in this repertory. Characters who either are or pretend to be opera singers also "perform" on stage: the two arias of the *prima* and *seconda donne* Eleonora and Tonina in Casti and Salieri's *Prima la musica e poi le parole* function in this way, as do Calloandra and Falsirena's duet, "Aci, ben mio" and Falsirena's "Rabbia, bile, affanno, e gelosia" from the same composer's *La fiera di Venezia.* There is a delicate and complex relation between the character and the performer in all such staged performances. To the other characters on stage, the character they "know" has suddenly become a performer—someone to be valued (or mocked) for his or her executive skill (or lack thereof). To the auditorium audience, there is a sudden invitation to consider a performance as a performance. Of course this enjoyment of the performance per se is always tempered by a consideration of how well the *actual* performer acts the *role* of performer, and in the best examples of the stage song, how well the music suggests not only the act of performance but something about the character. Cherubino's "Voi che sapete," for example, is justly famous for its momentary but intense evocation of adolescent pangs of desire which animate the character more than the singer; the lyric concentration of Rosina's lesson-song tells us something about her feelings for her "music teacher" (who is really the Count in dis-

---

[42] And the one most discussed in Edward Cone's "The World of Opera and Its Inhabitants," in *Music: A View from Delft: Selected Essays,* ed. Robert P. Morgan (Chicago: Chicago University Press, 1989) 125–38. "Voi che sapete" is Cone's starting point. Singing and "singing" in opera are also debated by Peter Kivy in "Opera Talk: A Philosophical Phantasie," *COJ* 3 (1991) 63–77; David Rosen, "Cone's and Kivy's World of Opera," *COJ* 4 (1992) 61–74; and Ellen Rosand, "Operatic Ambiguities and the Power of Music," *COJ* 4 (1992) 75–80. Kivy made a final response to Rosen in the same journal, vol. 4, 179–86. My argument in what follows includes the distinction between singing and "singing" (that is, singing we perceive as something like heightened speech and singing we perceive as a representation of singing), but it also addresses gesture and other nonsung modes of performance. I would also suggest that it is possible for an aria to fade in and out of a mode where performance qua performance is foregrounded, and that the self-conciously performed quality of a given piece depends on more than its explicit rhetoric or circumstances.

guise),[43] and in *Una cosa rara* the Prince's clumsy syllabification in his serenade "Non farmi più languire" can be read as a humorous comment on his generally unsuccessful attempts to seduce the shepherdess Lilla:

1-3: Martín y Soler, *Una cosa rara*, II, no. 12
Prince, "Non farmi più languir," mm. 3–9

Translation: *(from outside)* Don't make me languish further, my life; let me see that lovely face a bit.

Although staged singing of various sorts is common in opera buffa, it is by no means the only sort of performed-performance. Another common example is the (male) comic character's acting-out of an imagined situation, which allows him literally to step out of character and to take on various personae or voices in the course of the aria, or to act out various phases of a situation. Basilio's often-cut aria, "In quegl'anni" from the fourth act of *Le nozze di Figaro,* is a familiar but relatively mild example of this. In Anfossi's *Il curioso indiscreto,* the Marchese sings a similar sort of aria to the Contino as he imagines how to recapture an errant mate: his alternative persona is feline.

Figuriamo, ch'io fossi or un gatto;	Let's imagine I'm a cat
E all'incontro tu fossi un sorcetto;	And, as we meet, you're a mouse;
Io mi metto così quatto quatto	I crouch here like this,
Quì in un canto, e tu fermo di là.	Here in one corner; and you're over there.
Io sto cheto, ed al varco ti attendo,	I quietly wait in the passage for you,
Disinvolto fo lesto due giri,	I make two easy turns,

[43] This aria is fascinatingly related to Susanna's "Deh vieni non tardar" in *Le nozze di Figaro*—not only musically, in its melodic style and use of obbligato winds, and textually, in its abundance of pastoral imagery, but also in its function as performance with an ambiguous audience. Rosina is ostensibly singing to her teacher and to Bartolo (who has fallen asleep) but is "really" singing to Almaviva. Susanna is ostensibly singing to Almaviva but "really" to Figaro, whom she knows is listening. Nancy Storace sang both these roles, which would no doubt have strengthened the connection for a Viennese audience. Musically, Rosina's piece has also been compared to the Countess's "Porgi amor"—see, for example, Daniel Heartz, "Constructing *Le nozze di Figaro*," pp. 140–42.

Tu mi guardi, e pian pian ti ritiri:	You see me and retreat slowly,
Senti poi, che cosa si fa;	Listen now to what happens.
Chiudo gli occhi, t'alletto, e lusingo,	I close my eyes, charm, and deceive;
Partir fingo, ma sol cangio loco,	I pretend to leave but only move,
E tu allora ti avanzi per poco	And you, then, come forward a bit,
Per di là ti rivolti, e di quà.	Turning here and there.
Ma io presto spiccando un gran salto	But I suddenly make a great leap
Colle granfe ti prendo d'assalto,	And grab you with my claws,
E contento sbuffando, soffiando,	And happily puffing and panting
Gnaolando così me ne vò.	And miaowing, thus, I go.
Che ti pare del bel paragone?	What do you think of this lovely comparison?
So pensarla da vero Marchese.	It takes a real Marquis to think of it.
E l'ingurie, li torti, l'offese	This is the way I'll punish
Con quest'arte in colei punirò.	[Her] injuries, wrongs, and offenses.

Like most such arias, this one has some relevance to the drama despite its new persona; in this case the "cat's" pursuit and roughing-up of the "mouse" emphasizes the Marchese's misplaced self-confidence about his hunting abilities. It could also (especially given the right production) suggest a threat to the Contino himself (who has, after all, fallen in love with the Marchese's betrothed under his very nose), and tinge the subsequent meetings of the Contino and the betrothed with a sense of risk. However, despite the announced pretext for all these arias, they are all separable enough both from the normal forward flow of the action and from the normal persona of the character singing as to constitute self-conscious performances, enjoyable on their own terms; and their emphasis on re-enactment or graphic imagining reinforces their performative dimension. In addition, the patter climax of such arias (analogous to the coloratura climax of the seria-style aria) focuses attention on the skills of the performer and away from the aria's dramatic context or pretext.

The final example of performance that explicitly draws attention to itself is the situation where the character turns to and addresses the audience, either momentarily or for a whole aria. A famous Mozartean example of such a turn to the audience is Guglielmo's "Donne mie, la fate a tanti," in *Così fan tutte,* in which he tells the ladies of the audience how badly they treat their lovers. Figaro, in contrast, addresses the men in the audience in "Aprite un po' quegli occhi," though the subject is once again the horrors of the female sex. This frequent scenario in opera buffa is usually consigned to the comic characters. Unlike the comic re-enactment discussed above, however, which is an almost exclusively male phenomenon, both sexes equally make the frame-breaking turn to the audience. Such moments remind everyone of the presence of the footlights and of the artifice (in this case the "performed" quality) of the work in question. Sometimes the ar-

tifice works more than one way, as in the following aria of the clever country girl Ninetta who is trying to blackmail her old and unappealing suitor
Crisanto into letting her have the officer who has charmed her. She threatens to commit suicide if she cannot have her way (see Example 1-4):

(Un poco adagio $\frac{4}{4}$)

In quegl' ultimi momenti,	In those last moments,
Fatta gelida e spirante,	Cold and dying,
Rivolgendo a voi gli accenti,	Pleading with you, I'll say,
"Moro, ingrato, io vi dirò:	"I die, wretch.
Tu crudel cagion ne sei	You, cruel man, are the reason
Che sul fior degli anni miei	That, in the flower of youth,
In fra l'ombre io mè ne vò."	I depart for the underworld."

[*al soldato*] · [*to the soldier*]

Non credete quel ch'io dico,	Don't believe what I say;
Ch'io lo faccio per burlar;	I'm playing a joke;
State cheto che l'amico	Stay calm so the old man
Si comincia a conturbar.	Begins to worry.

a Crisanto: · *to Crisanto:*

Voi tacete? Voi piangete?	You're silent? You're crying?
Deh quegli occhi a me volgete,	Oh, turn your face toward me;
Quell'occhietto pietosetto.	That compassionate little eye.

Crisanto, a poco a poco commosso se la accosta, e le porge la mano. · *Crisanto, gradually moved, approaches her and offers her his hand.*

Questa mano, quel risetto	This hand, that little smile
Mi fa in vita ritornar.	Brings me back to life.

(Allegro $\frac{6}{8}$)

Imparate, Donne care,	Now, my dear ladies, learn
Questi vecchi a corbellar.	How to bamboozle these old men.

The aria begins with a relatively simple melody with the trademark sentimental characteristics of "sighing" pairs of eighth notes, and the rising
arpeggio figure (in measure 12) also often found in sentimental pieces.[44]
When Ninetta (warming to her theme) rehearses her deathbed speech, the
accompaniment warms up as well, assuming the sentimental characteristic
of violin ripples under a slower-moving melody. The turn to the audience

[44] This rising figure (often followed, as here, by a suspension on the top note of the arpeggio) occurs prominently in the paradigmatic sentimental piece of the later eighteenth century,
Gluck's "Che farò senza Euridice" from *Orfeo ed Euridice* and is found in many comparable
utterances throughout the buffa repertory as well as in opera seria. Cecchina's opening aria
in Piccinni's *La buona figliuola* also includes this motive (see Example 3–2, mm. 29–30).

1-4: Naumann, *Le nozze disturbate*, II,7
Ninetta, "In quegl'ultimi momenti," mm. 8–14; 17–21; 36–40

1-4: *(Continued)*

Im - pa - ra - te Don - ne   ca - re   que - sti   vec - chi a cor - bel - lar

at "Imparate, Donne care" coincides with the striking change of tempo; this text returns many times in the course of the final section of the aria, and, indeed, these two lines end the piece. In this aria (effective in part because of the great beauty of the sentimental section), Ninetta performs for the old man, announces to the soldier that she is faking it, and tells the women in the audience that, in effect, you have to be able to perform to get your way with men. The *character* thus draws retrospective attention to the skills of the *singer* in the opening slow section. Although the multiple levels of performance in this aria are relatively unusual, its techniques of comic distancing are utterly normal for the comic characters in opera buffa. Although the *parti serie* sing arias requiring, and drawing attention to, vocal virtuosity, they almost never announce their utterances as performances, preferring to stay within the frame of the action.

In breaking the narrative frame, or demolishing the "fourth wall," the comic turn to the audience disturbs the progress of dramatic time and, like other sorts of "performativity" in opera buffa, focuses audience attention on the felt qualities of the moment—the surprise at being suddenly addressed, the comedy of being part of the cast without being really part of the story, perhaps the embarrassment of having one's presence acknowledged (though that may be an exclusively modern reaction), and so on. The felt qualities of this sort of moment are of course not the same as the felt qualities of admiration for vocal or theatrical skill or the bodily pleasures of attending to a particularly lovely voice; nevertheless, the process of instigating, and then directing the audience's attention to, an immediate and almost involuntary response is a crucial part of opera buffa's rhetoric of pleasure.

Chapter Two

OPERA BUFFA'S CONSERVATIVE FRAMEWORKS

ALTHOUGH opera buffa clearly asserts that sheer pleasure is its function, and although its context seems to support the genre's self-representation, these works do in fact regularly address some of the social and ideological changes working their way through Europe during the eighteenth century. Questions of social mobility, pretension, inner and "outer" nobility, the limits, benefits, and obligations of power, and the changing relations between the genders are all integral to these operas. One could reasonably argue that the strength of the repertory's frame as mere entertainment and sheer pleasure contains and neutralizes the potentially problematic representations of socially sensitive subjects—after all, "what is not permitted to be said in our time is sung," as the writer for the *Realzeitung* noted right after the premiere of *Le nozze di Figaro*.[1] And if Mario Lavagetto's Freudian argument is taken seriously, then one could also argue that opera buffa's reconfiguration of these real social tensions as a series of stock dramatic formulae allows them to be absorbed into the comforting domain of the familiar and controllable.[2]

But entertainment is, after all, a political category, as imperial adviser Tobias Philipp Gebler may have recognized in a 1775 document, "A Most Humble Suggestion for the Improvement of the National Stage and Theatre in General," attributed to him: "Every subject who can give joy and pleasure in alternation keeps his spirits up and bears work and ill fortune patiently. Public dance-places, concerts, walks, [and] especially good plays are the means to make the public cheerful. He who tries to keep his fellow citizen in a good humor lightens the burden of government for the Regent, since it will be easier to rule his subjects in this cheerful condition

---

[1] Michtner, *DAB,* p. 208.

[2] *Quei più modesti romanzi* (Milan: Garzanti, 1979) chapter 1, n. 14. The repetitious child's game described by Freud confirms the child's mastery not only over the game itself, but also over the troubling circumstances that gave rise to it. In a more sociological mode, Richard Dyer, "Entertainment and Utopia," *Movie* 24 (1977) pp. 2–13; reprinted in Rick Altman, ed., *Genre: The Musical* (London and New York: Routledge & Kegan Paul, 1981) pp. 175–89, suggests that one function of entertainment is to enact Utopia by compensating for the tensions or absences in the society that spawns it. Thus, according to this model, one utopian component of opera buffa would be the clarity and predictability of the social order it projects, in the face of increasing fluidity and disorder in late-eighteenth-century society.

than [it would be] if they were discontented."[3] Gebler is worrying here
about the pliability of the bourgeois and thinking at least in part about the
vernacular theatre as a school for national morals, but his larger point is
that adequate and pleasurable diversion renders a citizenry in general less
likely to revolt. There is no reason to believe that something like this rea-
soning was not in place when Joseph reintroduced the opera buffa in 1783,
or that it was not at least part of the earlier dynamics of keeping the opera
buffa troupe when other forms of stage life were dropping by the wayside.
If we accept that entertainment is a political category—the "mereness" of
the medium doing nothing to diminish the political value of its social
place—then it becomes necessary to ask what political or social purpose the
materials of entertainment serve. Is it education, as the German-language
theatre was intended to be? Pacification, as Gebler suggests about all entertainment? Utopian model?[4] Rabble-rousing, as Joseph feared about *Le
mariage de Figaro*? Carnival, as some modern theorists claim about various forms of entertainment?[5] Some combination of these, or something
else altogether? Having asked these questions, I have to admit that I cannot answer them definitively about opera buffa. However, an examination
of the repertory's habits in dealing with questions of social structures and
individual morality within those structures can help us recreate its social
and political values, which can then be located in relation to some of the
circumstances in which the works played.

In the late eighteenth century, Vienna—and the Habsburg Empire more
generally—was a place of many contradictions, particularly with respect to
rank and class. In his magisterial social history of Austria, Ernst Bruckmüller identifies the court as one of the primary engines of social change
between the sixteenth and the eighteenth centuries, as it cobbled together
a bourgeoisie to satisfy its own needs both for competent advisers and for
a critical mass of subjects loyal solely to the Habsburg court.[6] The Habsburgs did this in part by creating an increasingly large and socially varied
bureaucratic class to do the necessary work of sustaining the court, and in
part by offering increasing numbers of patents of nobility to members of
the merchant class.[7] Thus, by the Josephine years, Vienna embodied the

---

[3] Zechmeister, *WT,* p. 52: "Jeder Unterthan, der abwechselnd Freude und Vergnügen
spenden darf, wird beim Muthe erhalten und erträgt Arbeit und Unfälle geduldig. Öffentliche
Tanzplätze, Concerte, Spaziergänge, besonders gute Schauspiele sind die Mittel, das Volk
aufgeräumt zu machen. Derjenige, der sich nun bestrebt, seine Mitbürger bei guter Laune
zu erhalten, erleichtert dem Regenten die Regierungslast, denn es wird leichter sein, seine
Unterthanen in dieser Gemütsverfassung zu beherrschen als wenn sie unzufrieden wären."
Gebler's authorship is not confirmed.
[4] See Richard Dyer, "Entertainment and Utopia."
[5] See Chapter 3 for more discussion of the carnivalesque.
[6] Bruckmüller, *Sozialgeschichte Österreichs* (Vienna and Munich: Herold, 1985) pp.
276–82.
[7] Ibid., pp. 253–54.

contradictory situation of an almost nonexistent court[8] whose plain-spoken and modestly dressed emperor had managed to concentrate un-precedented amounts of power in his own hands, who encouraged the growth of public opinion, which naturally included dissent,[9] but ruled es-sentially by fiat, and (closer to home) who was passionate about the seri-ous moral task of the theatre but loved opera buffa. Rather than encour-aging a more flexible sense of social class, however, the combination of a bourgeois style court and resistant landholding aristocrats, plus the con-comitant flux between the upper bourgeoisie and the second aristocracy actually created, according to Bruckmüller, a hyper-awareness of and sen-sitivity about status.[10] Moreover, the apparently sturdy bourgeois culture that supported the imperial establisment was actually relatively weak, inso-far as it drew its power from the court rather than from the establishment of its own institutions.[11]

Bruckmüller observes that the end of the feudal period saw a mismatch between the aristocracy's sense of itself as immutable and static, and the ac-tuality of constant change as noble status became available to more peo-ple. This conjunction of an assertion of stability and historical continuity with the reality of change and instability is exactly congruent with the in-ternally contradictory values of opera buffa, as well as with its contradic-tory place on the Viennese cultural scene. The present chapter discusses the aspects of opera buffa that most closely reflect Bruckmüller's assess-ment of the aristocracy's self-perception; the following chapter treats some aspects in tension with these.

REALISM AND DISTANCE

Although opera buffa is political in a general sense and clearly communi-cates "social values," it makes relatively few explicit references to particu-lar political events or personages. For example, apart from the allegory of the closing of the monasteries said by Da Ponte to be an aspect of *L'arbore di Diana,* this repertory gives no indication that freedom of religion and the relative powers of church and state were burning issues;[12] and despite the pervasive concern with class and rank in these works, even the ones written for Vienna do not obviously indicate that changes in the tax struc-ture were reorganizing the relations between peasants, landholding aristo-crats, and the central government. Even the general political representa-

---

[8] Derek Beales, "Court, Government and Society in Mozart's Vienna," in Stanley Sadie, ed., *Wolfgang Amadè Mozart* (Oxford: Clarendon Press, 1996) pp. 3–5.
[9] Wangermann, *The Austrian Achievement* (London: Thames and Hudson, 1973) pp. 130–47.
[10] Bruckmüller, *Sozialgeschichte Österreichs,* pp. 240–41.
[11] Ibid., p. 286.
[12] Da Ponte, *Memorie,* 2d ed., ed. Giuseppe Armani (Milan: Garzanti, 1980) p. 127.

tions of opera buffa are oblique, operating by means of the implicit affirmation of general principles rather than by the explicit rallying of audience opinion on behalf of a particular structure or situation. This obliqueness arises in part from the genre's complicated relation to contemporary reality. On the one hand, the characters of opera buffa hold ranks and occupations familiar to every member of the audience, they express emotions familiar to all, almost all are set in the present, and many take place in real locations—Venice,[13] "around Genoa,"[14] Velletri,[15] etc. On the other hand, the events of most operas are thoroughly unrealistic, depending on a combination of improbable coincidence and implausible disguise, expressed in modifications of traditional *lazzi* (commedia dell'arte routines); some involve an element of the fantastic that seems to remove the action even further from reality.[16] Even in the majority of operas without a fantastic aspect, the pervasive use of well-trodden conventions lends their ostensible realism a sense of distance from the real world. The geographic locations given in many libretti serve as a convenient synecdoche for the relation between literal realism and more abstract representation. Venice, Genoa, and Velletri, etc. are, indeed, all real and contemporary places, giving the illusion of actuality; however, they almost never correspond with the actual locations where the opera was first produced, let alone where it traveled. The operas set in these places thus appear to all their audiences to be taking place somewhere "like here but not here." This contrasts sharply with comic opera practices earlier in the century when recognizable Neapolitan and Venetian streets and squares turned up in many Neapolitan and Venetian comic operas, and local dialect was used not only to distinguish the risible bumpkins from the sympathetic centers of attention, but also to express the heartfelt emotion of central characters, lending the works "an air of unadorned reality," as Piero Weiss notes about early Neapolitan comic opera.[17] The later eighteenth-century practice of putting an opera's geographic location at one or two removes from immediate reality ensures some glimmers of recognition; at the same time, the distance from the immediate location of the performance allows the events of the opera both the comforts of separation (this is not about me) and the potential discomforts of generality (this is about many people like me).

The notion that aspects of contemporary life are represented at one remove, or as abstracted versions of reality, carries over from the locations of operas to their configurations of characters and even to some aspects of the

---

[13] E.g., Boccherini and Salieri's *La fiera di Venezia.*
[14] Petrosellini and Piccinni's *L'astratto.*
[15] Porta and Sarti's *I contratempi.*
[16] Casti and Salieri's *La grotta di Trofonio* is among the clearest examples of this.
[17] Piero Weiss, s.v. "Opera buffa" in *NGO.* See also David Kimbell, *Italian Opera* (Cambridge: Cambridge University Press, 1991) p. 316.

plots. The assemblages of people on the stages of opera buffa rarely reproduce the normal social configurations of late-eighteenth-century society,
and the vicissitudes of the plots are, as I mentioned above, almost never realistic. Nevertheless, with remarkable uniformity the abstract configurations of characters (whose relative rank and status are emphasized by the
music) and the trajectories of the plots in these works repeatedly affirm two
important and socially relevant conservative principles: that hierarchy is inevitable and necessary, and that social stability is always to be desired.

HIERARCHY IN AND AROUND OPERA BUFFA

As I mentioned above, the increased fluidity of rank and status in
eighteenth-century Europe, including Vienna, did not lead to a lessening
of the preoccupation with hierarchy. Johann Pezzl's self-consciously
bourgeois *Skizze von Wien,* for example, describes a society in flux, where
merchants and other deserving types could assume many if not all of the
privileges of high rank. At the same time, his essay is almost obsessively
concerned with the rights, privileges, and obligations of people of different classes in a variety of situations.[18] And Ernst Bruckmüller seizes on one
of Lady Mary Wortley Montagu's anecdotes from a visit to Vienna earlier
in the century, about the intransigence of two ladies in coaches in a one-
lane alley—neither willing to cede rank by giving way to the other—as another piece of evidence for the increasing anxiousness about status.[19] This
anxiety—and its absence in societies whose class boundaries were less negotiable—was perhaps best described by Dr. Johnson's friend Hester
Lynch (Thrale) Piozzi, in the account of her travels through France and
Italy in the mid-1780s. Her account of a visit to a household in Milan describes with a touch of nostalgia the positive effects of total and uncompromised social stratification:

> I have a notion there is much less of those distinctions at Milan than at London,
> where birth does so little for a man, that if he depends on *that,* and forbears other
> methods of distinguishing himself from his footman, he will stand a chance of
> being treated no better than him by the world. *Here* a person's rank is ascertained,
> and his society settled, at his immediate entrance into life; a gentleman and lady
> will always be regarded as such, let what will be their behavior. . . . The strange fa-
> miliarity this class of people [i.e., liveried servants] think proper to assume, half
> joining in the conversation, and crying *oibò,* when the master affirms something
> they do not quite assent to, is apt to shock one at beginning, the more when one
> reflects upon the equally offensive humility they show upon being first accepted

---

[18] Johann Pezzl, *Skizze von Wien* (Vienna 1786–90). Partially trans. in H. C. Robbins Landon, *Mozart and Vienna* (London: Thames and Hudson, 1991) pp. 54–191.
[19] Bruckmüller, *Sozialgeschichte Österreichs,* pp. 240–41. Pezzl also recounts this anecdote
(*Skizze von Wien,* p. 80).

into the family. . . . This obsequiousness, however, vanishes completely upon ac-
quaintance, and the footman, if not very seriously admonished indeed, yawns,
spits, and displays what one of our travel-writers emphatically terms his flag of
abomination behind the chair of a woman of quality, without the slightest sensation of its impropriety.[20]

The familial intimacy of masters and servants in this picture is reminiscent of many *opere buffe,* which also represent the unquestioned hierarchy
that is its basis.

The theatres in which opera buffa played conveyed similarly double-
edged meanings. On the one hand they permitted a display of inclusive-
ness—anyone who could pay was permitted in the auditorium, and aristocrats attending the Burgtheater mingled with a variety of others in the
parterre noble. On the other hand, both imperial theatres not only effectively excluded the majority of society by means of the ticket prices[21] but
also enforced traditional social distinctions even among those who could
afford the theatre, by reserving the boxes—both by price and by custom—
for the first aristocracy, who could subscribe for an entire season. Other
areas of the theatre were comparably associated with particular social strata.
Otto Schindler points out that until 1776 (when the difference widened
to 13 kreutzers), there was only a 4-kreutzer price difference between the
fourth floor and the second Parterre; that minimal price difference, however, was attached to a perceptible social/psychological distinction between the two areas.[22] Margret Dietrich describes the social geography of
the Burgtheater in 1790 as follows:

> In Mozart's time, one looked directly from the 3rd and 4th side boxes, which be-
> longed to the Court, directly into the orchestra; from here one could survey both
> the stage and the auditorium. Then there was the front—the parterre noble, that
> was visited primarily but not exclusively by the nobility, and also by officers, gov-
> ernment officials, and artists (authors, composers, architects, painters, but above
> all by the premier theatre-artists, Italian singers and dancers). . . . Behind the
> parterre noble was the second parterre, extending to the back wall of the hall. In
> other theatres for which there is documentation, Otto G. Schindler finds this area
> devoted to "civil servants (Beamten) and bourgeois." Above the "ordinary
> parterre" rose the middle boxes of the first and second level, next to which there
> were 13 or 14 smaller boxes along the side of the hall up to the front of the stage.
> They were rented on a seasonal basis almost exclusively by the court aristocracy
> and the high nobility. . . . The third level was reconstructed around 1790 entirely

[20] Hester Lynch Piozzi, *Observations and Reflections Made in the Course of a Journey
through France, Italy and Germany,* ed. Herbert Barrows (Ann Arbor: University of Michigan Press, 1967) p. 37.

[21] See above, p. 14.

[22] Schindler, "Das Publikum des Burgtheaters . . . ," in Dietrich, *Das Burgtheater und sein
Publikum* (Vienna: Akademie der Wissenschaften, 1976) pp. 51–52.

as a gallery. . . . Here there were reserved seats rented by the upper bourgeoisie, manufacturers, merchants, bankers and so on, but there were also free seats for theatre personnel. . . . On the fourth level, in the Mathieselgalerie, in the "Clouds" or "Paradise" stood the strata of the public who could afford to pay the least.[23]

Opera buffa participated in both the communal and the hierarchical aspects of its theatres. From the beginning the genre had represented characters of various social strata engaged in the same imbroglio and partaking of the same resolution. *Parti serie* (whether so identified or not) had been involved in opera buffa since the beginning of the century; in the course of the century they progressed from aloof figures who sang next to but not with the comic roles to figures involved in many or most aspects of the plot and equal participants in concerted numbers. As in the inclusive-yet-layered disposition of the theatre, however, the closely woven network of characters almost never involved the dissolution of social boundaries and was always balanced against other ways in which the principle of hierarchy was reinforced.

The Reinforcement of Hierarchy as a Principle

One way opera buffa reinforced the value of hierarchy even as it enacted the pleasures of community was simply by asserting repeatedly and with crystal clarity the fact of social stratification. This is evident even on the opening pages of the librettos of this repertory. Different works include different sorts of characters and designate different amounts of social space between the layers, but it is always clear how the characters are ranked.[24] Indeed, both Viennese and Italian libretti typically announce the ranks or occupations of the characters; noble characters are given titles, people in the middle ranks of society are either given an occupational title (e.g., mayor), or their position in the social structure is clear; and lower-ranked characters are either given occupations (e.g., servant) or their family origins (e.g., "son of a cook") are stated. The title page of Da Ponte and Martín y Soler's *Una cosa rara* exemplifies this clarity:

---

[23] Margret Dietrich, "Dokumentation zur Uraufführung," in Susanne Vill, ed., *Così fan tutte: Beiträge zur Wirkungsgeschichte von Mozarts Oper* (Bayreuth: Mühl'scher Universitätsverlag, 1978) pp. 24–25.

[24] Only once in this repertory (in Salieri's 1774 setting of *La calamità de' cuori*) do we find characters designated by temperament or behavior rather than by class:

    ARMIDORO   Costante (faithful lover)
    ALBINA   Amorosa (amorous)
    GIACINTO   Vezzoso (charmer)
    BELLAROSA DETTA CALAMITA DE' CUORI   (a.k.a. Hearts' Magnet)
    BELINDA   Stizzosa (whiner)
    SARACCA   Bravaccio (bigmouth)
    PIGNONE   Avaro (miser)

ISABELLA   Queen of Spain
GIOVANNI   Prince of Spain
CORRADO   Master of the Horse
LILLA   Shepherdess/mountain girl
GHITA   Shepherdess/mountain girl
LUBINO   Shepherd/mountain boy ⎫
TITA   Shepherd/mountain boy ⎬ Lovers of Lilla and Ghita
LISARGO   Village mayor (Podestà) ⎭

The principle of clearly defined rank even on occasion takes precedence
over dramatic surprise; in a number of libretti where the denouement consists in the discovery that someone thought to be lowly is really of noble
origins, the initial "misranking" is advertised in the cast list. Thus, in the
1779 Viennese libretto of Bertati and Gazzaniga's *La vendemmia*,[25] we
find the following listing:

DON ACHILLE   Marquis of Poggio antico
CONTE ZEFFIRO   Flatterer and sponger
D[ONNA] ARTEMISIA   Supposed lady
AGATINA   Supposed shepherdess
CARDONE   Village landlord; jealously in love with Agatina
PANCOTTO   Agatina's father ⎫
AGRESTONE   Agatina's uncle ⎬ mute roles

One function of this listing and others like it[26] is to establish the proper
range of responses to these characters. In the Vienna version of *La vendemmia,* for example, Agatina is a simple, rather sentimental girl loved, apparently inappropriately, by the Marchese. Her music is marked by long
melodic lines and an unusual amount of melodic chromaticism, presumably intended to signify a certain depth of feeling. To announce in the cast
list that this character is really of noble birth lends veracity to her musical
demonstration of sensibility, particularly at the beginning of the opera
when she has had little other opportunity to engage the audience's sympathies:[27]

[25] This libretto differs in its cast list from the score in the Österreichische Nationalbiblio-
thek (KT 459, presumably from the 1783 revival of this work), and from the Italian score in
the Eszterháza collection, both of which include two additional characters, Lauretta and Don
Fausto. The version performed in Venice in 1778 includes Lauretta but not Don Fausto. In
any case, the point about Agatina's announced rank is not affected by these changes.
[26] See also, for example, the self-explanatory title *La finta giardiniera,* the description of
Giannetta in *L'incognita perseguitata* as "young girl of unknown origins living in the Baron's
house; later discovered to be [the Count] Ernesto's sister"; or (in reverse), from Neri and
Guglielmi's *Le vicende d'amore,* the Baronessa Doralice, the "capricious and fickle young
woman who turns out not to be a lady"; the "dissonance" between Laurina's occupation as
"gardener" and her brother's high military rank in Petrosellini and Piccinni's *L'astratto;* and
the character Marcotondo, who is "pretending to be the Conte Caramella" in Anelli and
Cimarosa's *I due supposti conti.*
[27] The whole text of this aria is given in Chapter 3, p. 87.

2-1: Gazzaniga, *La vendemmia, ossia la dama incognita*, I,8
Agatina, "Del destin invan mi lagno," mm. 12–24

Translation: I complain in vain about my fate, [I am] miserable, afflicted and alone.
For heaven's sake, who will comfort me? Who will help me, for heaven's sake?

In addition to clearly advertising the prevailing hierarchy of the characters in the opening pages of any given libretto, opera buffa also relies on
social configurations whose structure of authority can be taken for granted.
The cast list of *Una cosa rara,* for example, leaves no doubt that natural
authority resides with the Queen; there is no need for explanation or justification of her right to adjudicate the disputes of the other characters beyond the recognition that this configuration of characters represents a kingdom in miniature. There are relatively few actual kingdoms in this
repertory, however; the typical opera buffa "realm" is considerably more
modest, if no less clearly hierarchical. The rural fief is a not-unusual miniaturization of the kingdom: here the lord of the manor rules over assorted
women, administrators, and peasants. In Bertati and Sarti's *I finti eredi,* for
example, the Marchese di Belpoggio (an absentee landlord for the first half

of the opera) has jurisdiction over the local administrator (*vicario*), his daughter, and three peasants. A further miniaturization of the fief is the noble household: a self-contained little "kingdom" with a patriarch at its head, under whom all the other characters are arranged as subordinate family or dependent employees, and which functions as a synecdoche for feudal power relations. The Almaviva household in *Le nozze di Figaro* is obviously of this sort; although the Count is finally thwarted and defeated, the drama of the opera depends to a large extent on a fully projected sense of his power in the household. The closest match to Beaumarchais's and Da Ponte's version of the household in *Le nozze di Figaro* is Sarti's *Fra i due litiganti il terzo gode,* based on Goldoni's libretto *Le nozze;* this household includes the Count, his wife, his land agent, the Countess's chambermaid, another female servant, a male servant, and a gardener. Other noble households with slightly different structures include the Marchese's household in *La buona figliuola,* which includes the Marchese, his sister and her betrothed, the gardener-girl Cecchina, and three other servants or farmhands. (The German soldier Tagliaferro who eventually unravels Cecchina's identity is from outside the household.) The Marchese Calandrino's establishment in *Il curioso indiscreto* includes his betrothed, Clorinda, his niece Emilia and her betrothed Aurelio, and two servants. His friend the Contino is a constant visitor.

Much more common in the repertory than households or fiefs headed by the middle and high aristocracy are households somewhat lower down the social scale. Like the noble households just described, however, these establishments are typically headed by single men and represent a clear line of authority from the patriarch to his daughters, nieces, or wards, and on down to the servants and gardeners. A frequent title for such heads of household is the somewhat ambiguous "Don."[28] *Il barbiere di Siviglia* uses this household structure (though Bartolo is not "Don.") Other operas using this configuration of characters include Bertati and Paisiello's *I filosofi immaginari,* Goldoni and Haydn's (and Paisiello's) *Il mondo della luna,* and Bertati and Anfossi's *Lo sposo disperato,* among many others. Bertati and Cimarosa's well-known *Il matrimonio segreto* is also based on this model.

The household (noble or middle-class) has a number of advantages as a social formation in comedy. It is theatrically convenient, since it provides both a location and a ready-made set of relationships ripe for comedic manipulation. A glance through the early evening network TV listings suggest

---

[28] M. L. Bush, *Noble Privilege,* vol. 1 of *The European Nobility* (New York: Holmes and Meier, 1983) p. 142, describes "Don" as a designation of noble *status* (i.e., the capacity to become a Cavaliere) rather than *rank:* "In the course of time . . . it came to embrace the whole of the non-titled nobility in the Iberian and Italian peninsulas."

that even today the household formula has not lost its appeal. For the eighteenth century, certainly, and perhaps also today, the household is also a
convenient way of presenting a "natural" hierarchy: an arrangement of
characters whose structure of authority seems entirely comfortable and
which therefore does not need to be explained in the course of the drama.
Interestingly, though, the households of opera buffa almost never contain
(even as a core) a two-parent-plus-offspring unit. Fathers are often replaced
by uncles or guardians; wives are rare, especially among the aristocracy; and
mothers almost entirely absent.[29] *Le nozze di Figaro* and *Fra i due litiganti*
are quite unusual in their inclusion of aristocratic wives. Where there is a
married couple there are almost never offspring—Figaro and his newly discovered parents are in fact the only complete biological family unit among
the operas I have examined, and their biological connection is presented as
a useful—if also touching—cog in the machinery of the plot rather than as
the primary center of emotional energy.

The absence of wives and mothers is partly a practical matter, the relatively small casts of opera buffa—between four and eight characters[30]—
allowing no duplication of dramatic function. Thus insofar as a wife's
role would be "about" submission to her husband (and this is the case
for all the opera buffa wives I have seen), it could be elided with the role
of daughter, and insofar as a mother's role would be to exercise authority over the young people, that could be elided with the role of paterfamilias. The characteristic absence of a female figure with any real claim
to authority also allows the image of an "ideal" male-headed hierarchy
to appear unimpeded. The "manipulated" or "abstracted" household
has been characteristic of comedy since its inception, and the absent
mother is not uncommon in eighteenth-century bourgeois dramas and

---

[29] Among the librettos surveyed, each with an average of six to seven characters (thus
among ca. 450–500 characters), there are only nineteen married couples. Six of these
are couples who are either estranged from each other or who are in disguise as unrelated,
and whose plot entanglements therefore resemble those of unmarried people. Seven are
subsidiary characters from the lower classes, whose trajectories in relation to each other do
not matter very much, and only six are major characters in their respective operas. Two
operas—Salieri and Mazzolà's *La scuola dei gelosi* and Livigni and Anfossi's *I viaggiatori felici*—include two couples each. Only four operas in this repertory include mothers.
Puttini and Anfossi's *La vera costanza* (also set by Haydn) is the only one to use mother-
hood as a sentimental device. Calzabigi's libretto *L'opera seria*, set by Gassmann, and *La
canterina*, set by Piccinni as well as Haydn, include comic stage mothers (the former including no fewer than three of the species). In Da Ponte and Martín y Soler's *Una cosa rara*,
the Queen is the mother of the Prince, but the regal aspect of this role far outweighs the
maternal.

[30] Works originally labeled *intermezzo* typically have fewer characters (four or five) than
works originally labeled *dramma giocoso* or *commedia per musica*, whose average number of
characters is seven or eight. Other designations, such as *farsetta*, are less helpful as to the likely
number of characters, and an individual work could also be given various designations in its
travels around Europe. Occasionally a work appears in different versions with different numbers of characters.

novels.[31] However, the households in opera buffa seem less bound by either biological or marital ties than households in comparable contemporary genres; opéra comique, for example, has more instances of complete, biologically connected families than opera buffa, and uses the family both as a locus of sentiment and as a model of behavior. And about one-third of the Burgtheater's German-language spoken dramas as described by Monika Giller include mothers or stepmothers, though the nuclear family as a center of attention is nowhere near as frequent as this, and the mother-figures are almost as often wicked stepmothers as nurturing parents.[32] In addition, while plays and novels with absent mothers have often killed them off before the action begins, thus creating a palpable gap in the drama, in opera buffa their absence is usually unremarked.[33] The household in opera buffa is thus more nearly "about" authority than it is about affection or even duty, and its prevalence as a dramatic setup mirrors the generic interest in hierarchy rather than the increasingly important cultural deployment of the bourgeois nuclear family.[34] It is not clear why this should be so; one possible explanation, which fits with the notion that opera buffa typically established strongly conservative social frameworks, is that the household "about" hierarchy rather than affection represents the aristocratic family's concern with lineage and proper continuation through a male line rather than the ideal bourgeois family's concern with the "feel" of the home. Thus, even when the households of opera buffa do not literally represent the landowning aristocracy, their structures recall those of feudal society.

The other characteristic arrangement of characters in opera buffa is a rep-

[31] Susan E. Gustafson, *Absent Mothers and Orphaned Fathers: Narcissism and Abjection in Lessing's Aesthetic and Dramatic Production* (Detroit: Wayne State University Press, c1995); Gail K. Hart, "Voyeuristic Star-Gazing: Authority, Instinct and the Women's World of Goethe's *Stella*," *Monatshefte* 82 (1990) 408–20, argues that the removal of women from the fictional families of German bourgeois drama is a response to the fragility of male authority.

[32] Of the 45 plays for which Monika Giller gives plot summaries in "Das Sentimentalität im Spielplan und in der Darstellung des Burgtheaters" (doctoral dissertation, University of Vienna, 1966), 17 include mothers or stepmothers.

[33] The preference for male-headed household hierarchies is by no means dead. Even though television is beginning to catch up with contemporary demographics and is building comedies around single-parent families, many of them are still headed by fathers; this hardly reflects real life.

[34] It is particularly interesting to compare the cast lists of this repertory of opera buffa with those of Goldoni's plays, since the two repertories are related in both themes and origins. The first striking difference is that the casts of the plays are typically very much larger than—often twice as large as—the casts of opera buffa. This difference is no doubt as much a matter of practicality as of aesthetic principle. Following from this, one finds relatively few plays in which the household is the primary organizing unit; it is much more usual for a household to be part of a larger and more various arrangement of characters. When households are presented, though, they are more often genuinely familial groupings than they are in opera buffa. Even though the relative size of the typical cast for each genre is shaped by practical considerations, one can see that the choices for opera buffa made in the pragmatic process of concentration focus interest more on questions of authority and potential sources of friction than on pleasant obligation and potential loci of affection.

resentative range of characters bound together by accident of location or other loose connection. As with household arrangements, these gatherings usually present a selection of characters whose pecking order is obvious even before the beginning of the work. Such social microcosms are found in slightly fewer than half the operas in this repertory, and divide almost evenly between works representing two social levels and those represent- ing three. The cast list of Livigni and Paisiello's *La frascatana* clearly shows the three layers of its social setup, even though the characters are not listed quite in order of social rank:

VIOLANTE   Daughter of a rich deceased gardener from Frascati
DONNA STELLA   Daughter of a captain living in Velletri, betrothed to the
   Cavaliere Giocondo of Rome
CAVALIERE GIOCONDO   Secret admirer of Violante
NARDONE   Son of a Roman artisan, who works as a fisherman in Marino
DON FABRIZIO   Violante's tutor, jealously in love with her
LISETTA   Servant at the inn
PAGNOTTA   The Cavaliere's servant.

Here, Violante, Nardone, and Don Fabrizio represent the middle ranks of society, Donna Stella and the Cavaliere Giocondo the lower aristocracy, and Lisetta and Pagnotta the serving classes. Although the intrigue of the drama involves some mixing up of the layers, the trajectory of the drama is toward clear distinction, and the treatment of the characters is commen- surate with that trajectory; although the Cavaliere is desperately in love with Violante, he is forced by Pagnotta, as well as by Violante's love for Nardone, to keep his proper, if loveless, arrangement with Donna Stella.

Two-level collections of characters may include either aristocrats or lower nobility and peasants or servants, or more or less middle-class people and their servants. The sprawling cast of Porta and Righini's *Il convitato di pietra,* for example, clearly divides the aristocracy from the peasantry:

DON GIOVANNI TENORIO   Neapolitan nobleman
DON ALFONSO   Minister to the King of Castille
IL COMMENDATORE DI LOIOA   Castillian
DONNA ANNA   The Commendatore's daughter
DONN' ISABELLA   Daughter of the Duke of Altomonte

———————

ELISA   Fisherwoman
OMBRINO   Fisherman
CORALLINA   Innkeeper
TIBURZIO   Servant at the inn
LISETTA   Donna Anna's chambermaid
ARLECCHINO   Don Giovanni's servant

Da Ponte and Mozart's version of the same story (the libretto based on Bertati's 1787 book for Venice) illustrates the potential complexities of mapping social categories onto musical and dramatic "registers" of expression. The cast list in the libretto divides the characters fairly clearly into two strata—an aristocratic, or at least gentle-born upper layer (Don Giovanni is a "cavaliere"; Donna Anna and Donna Elvira are both described as "dama," even though we know Donna Anna's parentage and we are not told that of Donna Elvira), and a peasant and servant-class lower stratum. It is, however, a truism of the literature on this opera that the music represents three strata: seria (aristocratic), buffa (peasant and servant), and *mezzo carattere* (Donna Elvira and Don Giovanni). But these are dramatic and musical distinctions carved from a bipartite social structure, which is, of course, part of the point of the opera. The dramatic and musical middle in *Don Giovanni* is the space occupied by those who either fail to live up to aristocratic ideals or are denied the privileges of aristocratic life, rather than by those who occupy the *socially* middling positions of merchants, administrators, and citizen widows; the power of this aesthetically but not socially middle stratum comes in part from the way it is tensely balanced between two unambiguous social poles.[35]

Not all two-level casts involve aristocrats and peasants or servants; some include middle-ranked characters and their servants. These casts normally involve a more or less equal group of middle-ranked characters, and one or two characters in obviously dependent relation to them, usually servants. *Così fan tutte* uses this model (though it also calls upon the household model). Casts with only aristocrats and middling characters (i.e., no servants or peasants) are barely represented in this repertory of opera buffa, in contrast to Goldoni's plays.[36] It is not altogether clear why opera buffa should avoid this sort of social structure; one possibility is that the genre had always represented servants or peasants, had singers who specialized in such roles, and simply continued out of inertia. Another related possibility is that peasants and servants had easily recognizable musical vocabularies, unlike the middle stratum of society.[37]

One *effect* of opera buffa's characteristic social structures, however, is that members of the lower orders are almost always represented as dependent on the members of the upper ranks of society, and, with rare excep-

---

[35] In their *Don Giovanni* (Venice 1787), Bertati and Gazzaniga make Donna Elvira a more straightforwardly buffa character with sentimental aspects (see her aria "Povere femmine"); she has none of the emotional power and nobility of Da Ponte and Mozart's character.

[36] One possible exception to this general rule is Petrosellini and Cimarosa's *L'italiana in Londra*. Whether the social structure of this opera, which includes an English lord, a Dutch merchant, a Genoese lady, and an innkeeper, as well as a foolish traveler, was influenced by its English setting is hard to say.

[37] Thanks to Wye Allanbrook for this observation.

tions, likely to remain so. Figaro's picaresque and economically various past, described in "Scorsi già molti paesi," in *Il barbiere di Siviglia,* and still in the memories of the audiences for *Le nozze di Figaro,* is rare in this repertory. Leporello's threats to leave Don Giovanni do not materialize until the latter dies, which is, of course, convenient for the opera, but it may also testify to the almost familial strength of the bond between employers and servants, and the concomitant expectation that a serving position in a family was to be a lifetime commitment. Dependence of this sort is manifested in opera buffa not only through household servitude but also through the feudal subordination of peasants to their lord, and through the economic dependence of lower-class artisans and producers (milliners, shoemakers, etc.) on aristocratic or high-bourgeois consumers. This last is usually demonstrated by the making of individual items for particular consumers.[38] Even in operas that represent households below the aristocracy, the relations between the servants and masters are typically closer to feudal allegiance than to the notion of a free labor market. Perhaps the most striking example of this is in Palomba and Paisiello's *Le gare generose,* where, within the Boston household of the merchant Mr. Dull, the eloped (merchant-class) couple from Naples who serve as the center of interest in the drama are slaves, whose fortunes depend entirely on Mr. Dull's good will.[39] The description of the couple as slaves may well have been a comment on American society, but their manifest position in the household is indistinguishable from that of dozens of servants in nonexotic households.

These structures of dependence surely represented something recognizable to Viennese audiences in the 1770s and 1780s: Johann Pezzl, for example, describes the way ladies' maids were provided with husbands if they reached a certain age without marrying, almost as if they were offspring in the household.[40] And the increasing numbers of factories in the region, despite employing (in some cases) hundreds of people, still more often than not operated under an imperial privilege, and thus, at least in principle, at imperial whim.[41] However, at the same time, the profound alterations in the relation of the peasant to the landholder after the abolition of serfdom in 1781, the growth of direct taxation, the loosening of the bond between

[38] Goldoni's libretto *L'amore artigiano* illustrates this particularly clearly.

[39] Bruce Alan Brown has kindly pointed out to me that this libretto seems to be based on Ranieri de' Calzabigi's *Amiti e Ontario, o I selvaggi,* set by Giuseppe Scarlatti according to *NGO* (s.v. "Calzabigi" and "Scarlatti, Giuseppe"), and premiered at the Burgtheater in 1772. The full text of this *argomento* is presented in translation in Hunter, "Bourgeois Values and Opera Buffa in 1780s Vienna," in Hunter and Webster, *Opera Buffa in Mozart's Vienna* (Cambridge: Cambridge University Press, 1997) pp. 171–72. Appendix 3 includes a plot summary of the opera.

[40] Pezzl, *Skizze von Wien,* trans. in Landon, *Mozart and Vienna,* pp. 147–48.

[41] See Bruckmüller, *Sozialgeschichte Österreichs,* pp. 252–53; 256–58. See also Pezzl, *Skizze von Wien,* Part VI (1790), trans. Landon, p.184.

producer and consumer that was an inevitable consequence of factory work, and the increasing employment options for members of the working and serving classes (no doubt enhanced by Maria Theresia and Joseph's establishment of universal primary schooling) must have made the rigidly stratified, apparently immutable, and repeatedly justified world of opera buffa seem (at least in part) like the sort of atavistic retreat that Mrs. Piozzi found in her Milanese household—a world whose certainty about itself seemed appealing in some ways but which was in reality no place for an Enlightened soul.

Affirming Stability

One of the most important features of opera buffa's representation of social hierarchy is that it appears to be immutable. This is true partly because strong, persistent, and pervasive generic conventions such as character types, plot archetypes, and musical types on various levels create a world that remains very much the same from opera to opera. The overdetermined predictability of the plot-outcomes also reinforces the notion of immutability; to be able to predict the relationships at the end of the opera from the cast list on the first or second page of the libretto (see above, pp. 34–35) gives the impression that there is no significant alternative to the social order there represented. In addition to the forms of predictability and the conventions I have already discussed above, some *opere buffe* also use the stability of the comic tradition more broadly construed to reinforce the notion of immutable social norms or ideals. Northrop Frye remarks of comedy that it typically involves the movement from one society to another, from "a society controlled by habit, ritual bondage, arbitrary law and the older characters to a society controlled by youth and pragmatic freedom."[42] At the same time, he notes, the new society presented at the end of a comedy is an echo of "a golden age which existed in the past before the main action of the play begins. Thus we have a stable and harmonious order disrupted by folly, obsession, forgetfulness, 'pride and prejudice,' or events not understood by the characters themselves, and then restored."[43] Many *opere buffe* make explicit the implicit or putative stable and harmonious order described by Frye, and enact not once but twice the stabilizing ternary form of classic comedy. It is not uncommon, for example, for an opera to begin with a chorus celebrating the pleasures of life—often in pastoral terms, but also in the form of drinking or dancing choruses. Such choruses anticipate the celebratory final choruses of most *opere buffe*. I *finti eredi*, for example, opens with the following choral stanza:

[42] Northrop Frye, "The Mythos of Spring: Comedy," in his *Anatomy of Criticism* (Princeton: Princeton University Press, 1957) p. 169.
[43] Ibid., p. 171.

Quanto è bella la campagna;	How beautiful is the countryside,
Come dolce, e come è grata!	How sweet and lovely!
Qui si gode ognor l'amata,	Here one can always enjoy
La felice libertà.	Beloved and happy liberty.

The opera ends:

Che tutti godano	Let all enjoy
Con lieto giubilo:	With happy rejoicing.
Viva si sentino	Let us hear cheers
Di quà e di là.	From here and there.

Dunque balliamo:	So let's dance;
Tutti godiamo	Everyone enjoy
Di questa vera	This true
Felicità.	Happiness.

Thus, as Frye remarks, the Edenic good cheer of the beginning is restored at the end, completing the stabilizing arc of comedy. But some *introduzioni* encapsulate this comedic ternary form in themselves, thus reiterating in miniature the form of the whole and doubling the opportunity to perceive it. In *La finta giardiniera,* for example, the *introduzione* begins:

Che lieto giorno, che contentezza;	What a happy day! What contentment!
Qui d'ogni intorno spira allegrezza.	Here one breathes happiness all around.
Amor qui giubila brillando va.	Here love triumphs and shines.

After this opening chorus each of the characters sings a self-introductory stanza describing his or her prevailing emotion: these statements accumulate to define the principal dramatic tensions of the work:

RAMIRO:
Fra cento affanni sospiro, e peno;	I sigh and suffer with a hundred miseries.
Per me non splende mai di sereno;	For me the sun never shines;
Per me non trovasi felicità.	For me there is no happiness.

PODESTÀ:
Il cor mi balza per il piacere;	My heart is jumping for joy.
Fra suoni, e canti; devo godere;	I ought to have a great time amidst playing and singing
Sandrina amabile pur mia sarà.	[Because] lovely Sandrina will be mine.

SANDRINA:
Sono infelice, son sventurata;	I am unhappy, I am destitute;
Mi vuole oppressa la sorte ingrata;	Unkind fate wishes me oppressed.
Di me più misera no, non si dà.	There is no-one more miserable than me.

NARDO:
| Neppur mi guarda, neppur m'ascolta; | She will neither look at me nor listen to me; |

Farà costei darmi di volta.	That one will drive me crazy.
Che donna barbara senza pietà.	What a cruel lady without mercy.

SERPETTA:

Con quella scimmia già s'è incantato;	He's already besotted with that baboon;
Fa il cascamorto lo spasimato.	He's swooning and languishing.
Ma se mi stuzzica la pagherà.	But if he plays with me he'll pay for it.

RAMIRO:

Celar conviene la pena ria.	I should hide my dreadful pain.

PODESTÀ:

Via sollevatevi Sandrina mia.	Come on, get up, Sandrina love.

SANDRINA:

Son troppa grazie, troppa bontà.	You are too generous, too kind.

RAMIRO:

Vedrò placata l'iniqua stella?	Shall I see the iniquitous heavens placated?

NARDO:

Non so lasciarla ch'è troppa bella.	I don't know how to ignore her—she's too beautiful.

SERPETTA:

Son pieni gl'uomini di falsità.	Men are full of deceit.

The opening chorus then returns unchanged.[44] Daniel Heartz notes with regard to Mozart's setting of this text that "we can only recoil at the falsity of their communal "Che lieto giorno" on its return."[45] If one reads this ternary structure as having to do with individual psychology, then the unmotivated good cheer of the ending does seem "false," as Heartz suggests. If, however, one understands the sudden snap into good cheer and the reintegration of individuals into society as having to do with the nature of the action to come, and about that action's larger social place, then it seems somewhat less jarring, and even appropriate. In projecting even temporary agreement, resolution, and social calm after some tension or disquiet, *introduzioni* predict the resolutions of their operas, laying to rest any possibility of anxiety on that account. They also set the basic societal terms on which they operate. Kenneth Reckford describes one of the functions of Aristophanic (and by extension, much other) comedy as "the recovery of good temper," not only among the characters but also in the audience.[46] And G. K. Hunter writes, "Our response to comedies is governed by a de-

---

[44] Chapter 7 treats *introduzioni* at some length; although the literal ternary form of the two *introduzioni* mentioned here is not in fact very common, the movement from collective harmony through dissent back to collective harmony is quite normal.

[45] Daniel Heartz, *Haydn, Mozart and the Viennese School 1740–1780* (New York: Norton, 1995) p. 597.

[46] Kenneth Reckford, *Aristophanes' Old-and-New Comedy* (Chapel Hill: University of North Carolina Press, 1987) p. 11.

veloping generosity of spirit, an eventually indulgent regard for error and folly. . . . The *telos* or purposive end of comedy seems normally to be one which invites us to catch up these emotions in an eventual act of forgiveness or an act of oblivion."[47] *Introduzione*-endings that suddenly turn niggling into a picnic, or individual misery into collective merriment give neither the characters nor the audience time (or much of an occasion) to forgive, but they do enable audience and characters to exercise an indulgence for folly born of the sense that it cannot harm the solid social structures containing it.

If Reckford's and Hunter's arguments about comedy are persuasive with respect to opera buffa, then the conservative fames and structures of this repertory can be read as having served at least two social functions. The first is the regressively comforting retreat into a fantasy version of an older social order—something like the role played by the rhetorical trope of the "normal American family" in the modern debate about "family values." We might also understand these works' assurance of immutable hierarchy as having provided a familiar and pleasurable occasion for the development of "indulgence" not only toward individual folly, but also toward larger disruptions of an apparently fixed order. These disruptions are the subject of the next chapter.

---

[47] G. K. Hunter, "The Idea of Comedy in Some Seventeenth-Century Comedies," in *Poetry and Drama in the English Renaissance: Essays in Honor of Jiro Ozu,* ed. Koshi Nakanori and Yasuo Tamaizumi (Tokyo: Kinokuniya, 1980) pp. 71–91.

Chapter Three

OPERA BUFFA'S SOCIAL REVERSALS

IF THE OUTERMOST framework of opera buffa is its reception and self-presentation as sheer pleasure, the inner frame, so to speak, is its representation of immutable hierarchy as the social fundament of the genre. However, opera buffa would not be comedy if it did not routinely test and stress those conservative frames with a variety of disruptive elements. Appealing alternatives to the framing order arise (in *Così fan tutte,* for example, the "wrong" lovers might marry); normally subordinate characters occupy the center of attention and sympathy for considerable stretches of time (Susanna is a classic example); structurally powerful characters are made to look foolish or even wicked (Count Almaviva serves as the obvious case here); and problems of power are continually in the air (*Don Giovanni* can be read—at least in part—as a disquisition on the obligations and limits of aristocratic privilege). One could argue that opera buffa's explicit function as mere entertainment reduces its social reversals and disruptions to the status of decontextualized titillation, and surely that is how some spectators would have understood them. At the same time, the fact that these endlessly reiterated reversals all concern then-recognizable—and negotiable—social relations suggests that one should not ignore their potential for effects beyond easy titillation.

There are at least two complementary ways of understanding the social dimension of opera buffa's comic reversals: we can call them the "direct" and the "carnivalesque" modes of understanding. Reinhard Strohm's acute observations about mid-century opera buffa can represent the former. He writes: "Opera buffa does not simply represent different relationships between the various strata like a broad panorama; rather, the problems of upward social mobility, of socially unequal marriages between the nobility and the bourgeois, of unworthy or ignorant behavior of nobility, of the mistaking and switching of high and low origins, and of social fraud, are among the central themes of the genre. [These are], then, themes that call into question and ironize socially embedded distinctions."[1] Basing his argument in part on a reading of Goldoni's stage plays, Strohm argues that the primary social aim of opera buffa was to effect some sort of reconciliation

---

[1] Reinhard Strohm, *Die italienische Oper im 18. Jahrhundert* (Wilhelmshaven: Heinrichshofen, 1979) pp. 249–50.

between the classes.[2] This reading partly depends on the assumption that the various social reversals and upsets characteristic of the genre are to be understood as reflecting fairly directly a variety of currently unresolved social issues. This reading makes sense in the context of a repertory in which the realism of local settings and dialect quite literally "brings the issues home." With respect to the Viennese repertory of the last third of the century this reading works best when the issues addressed by the reversals seem to have specific relevance to the situation, as in the case of the little rash of "apologetic patriarchs" in the 1785–86 season (see below). However, the plethora of distancing mechanisms in the Viennese repertory make Strohm's optimistic picture of opera buffa's social engagement only intermittently relevant.

The carnivalesque represents another framework for understanding the display of social reversals and upsets. Socially, carnival is said to work by a sort of reverse psychology; the permission to exceed all the usual boundaries—by eating and drinking enormously, ritually debunking authority, challenging and reversing the normal social and sexual distinctions—discharges disruptive energies and ultimately serves to reinforce the order it seems to challenge.[3] Since the rediscovery of Mikhail Bakhtin's work on Rabelais in the last few decades, carnival has also become a common literary-critical, as well as an anthropological-semiological trope.[4] The way the carnivalesque works through paradox, eventually effecting the opposite of what it represents, makes it particularly attractive as a way of understanding comedy, which also, according to classical theory, corrects by encouraging critical distance rather than emulation. Thus the elements of opera buffa that Strohm and others might understand as participating quite straightforwardly in the process of social change could, then, through the lens of carnival, also be understood paradoxically as stones in the edifice shoring up the outmoded values of a disappearing social order.

The point of this discussion is not to pit "literalist" or "progressive" readings of opera buffa against "carnivalesque" or "conservative" ones. Indeed, if it is difficult to know in modern culture whether the ubiquitous

---

[2] Ibid., p. 253.

[3] See Monica Rector, "The Code and Message of Carnival: 'Escolas-de-Samba,'" in Thomas Sebeok, ed., *Carnival!* (Berlin: Mouton, 1984) p. 42: Rector describes carnival as a response to "the . . . need to release [people's] instincts, reaching a catharsis that will ease the frustrations of their daily lives. That is to say, the catharsis leads the 'folião' into a symbolic social balance. This balance represents the transition from what is forbidden to what is permitted."

[4] Bakhtin, *Rabelais and His World,* trans. Helen Iswolsky (Bloomington: Indiana University Press, 1984). See also Jacques Attali, *Noise: The Political Economy of Music,* trans. Brian Massumi (Minneapolis: University of Minnesota Press, 1985). Recent critical operatic studies, like Martha Feldman, "Magic Mirrors and the *Seria* Stage: Thoughts towards a Ritual View," *JAMS* 48 (1995) pp. 423–84, and Rebecca Lee Green, "Power and Patriarchy in the Goldoni Operas of Joseph Haydn" (Ph.D. dissertation, University of Toronto, 1995), also make use of carnival as an interpretive device.

sex and gratuitous violence in popular entertainment translate literally into bad behavior in the real world, or whether they serve the carnivalesque function of discharging socially destructive energies, it is even less possible to know whether the various social reversals and unsympathetic representations of opera buffa served to encourage or stall social change. Moreover, these two modes of understanding are not necessarily mutually exclusive. In any given opera, and in any particular circumstances, one pleasurable reversal may seem like the licensed excess of carnival, and another like constructive social criticism. Thus, rather than trying to place the disruptive elements I have chosen to discuss in particular camps, I want to use a set of questions posed by Umberto Eco in his essay "The Frames of Comic 'Freedom'"[5] to tease out some of the possible functions and implications of the most classically comic aspects of opera buffa. In this essay Umberto Eco asks whether and how particular "rules" about life in society are violated and then restated. Eco's main purpose is to distinguish between carnival, where the rule is by definition reinforced but not restated, and "humor," where the rule may be restated but can also be criticized. He uses the overly made-up old woman as one example; in the carnivalesque mode we may laugh at the smeared-on lipstick from a position of superiority, thus implicitly restating a rule about cosmetic propriety, but in the context of "humor," we criticize the rule requiring old women to minimize their age at the same time as we smile at her.

Eco's analysis is valuable not because it provides perfect pigeonholes for this repertory of opera buffa, which it obviously does not, but because it suggests some questions that bring its complex social functions to the surface; that is, his analysis allows us to ask both of the repertory as a whole and of any given work or element within a work: "What rule is violated? What is the function of the violation? What is this rule about? (How) is it restated elsewhere in the work? In the following pages I examine the repertory's three most characteristic violations or reversals: the overthrow of a patriarch in a hierarchical society, the rule of the servant in the master's house, and the power and centrality of the suffering woman in a system designed to maximize male authority. Each of these provides a different set of answers to Eco's questions; each fulfills a different function, both in the frame of the work and in the context of late-eighteenth-century Viennese society.

CHALLENGING HIERARCHY: UNCROWNING THE KING

One of the most classically carnivalesque devices in this repertory is the displacement of a patriarch, or as Bakhtin calls it, "uncrowning the king."[6] As Bakhtin explains it, carnival time, or a literary version thereof, provides a

---

[5] In Sebeok, ed., *Carnival!* pp. 1–10.
[6] Bakhtin, *Rabelais,* ch. 3.

socially sanctioned opportunity for the forces of popular culture, freedom, youth, or disorder (or any combination of these) fictitiously to remove an authority figure from his privileged position, often accompanying the removal with beating and even burning-in-effigy. The "rule" here is the obedience of the ruled to the rulers and the inviolability of the power of the latter over the former; the violation involves exposing the rulers as vulnerable to whatever force (brain or brawn) the ruled care to apply. There are few drubbings and no burnings in this repertory of opera buffa,[7] but there are many instances where the initial authority figure is deposed or in some way demoted. The most common version of this is exemplified by the well-known story of *Il barbiere di Siviglia*, where the guardian (standing in for the father) is tricked into giving up his ward to a younger man. The archetype of father figure challenged by young lover is as old as comedy itself and has, as Northrop Frye points out, associations with the "mythos of spring," the endless cycle of the seasons and of the generations.[8] The reversal of authority in these operas serves the classic comic function of teaching by ridicule: those who fail to recognize the importance of true love (within acceptable limits) and the necessity of generational change will inevitably turn out to be fools.

In many *opere buffe* based on this archetype, the psychological rightness of the generational challenge is reinforced by the social correctness of the end result, despite the deposition of the current authority-figure. That is, the young lover in most of these operas is of a social rank equal to, or higher than, the father figure, and the end thus maintains the fixity of social strata even in displacing the generations. This is of course the case in *Il barbiere di Siviglia*, with the Count Almaviva as the challenging lover and the indubitably middle class Dr. Bartolo the defeated paterfamilias. In operas on these plots, then, the disruptive dethroning of an authority figure, with its explicit valuing of the "bourgeois" values of cleverness and effort over the "aristocratic" values of institutionalized authority and social paralysis, and its implicit potential to suggest social revolution, is immediately contained by the reestablishment of a well-understood social hierarchy. Thus, although one might read the comedy of the uncrowned patriarch in opera buffa as a sort of safety valve, whose "rule" is so clear that it needs no restatement, this genre is in fact normally careful to "restate the rule," thus reducing the device to localized and socially innocuous fun. Where the pa-

---

[7] This sort of Punch and Judy violence had been, however, quite characteristic of the semi-improvised Hanswurstiads officially banned in 1770, and still available in a variety of other nontheatrical entertainments. See Gerhard Tanzer, *Spectacle müssen seyn* (Vienna: Böhlau, 1992) p. 163; also pp. 137ff. on the increasing differentiation between "high" and "low" culture in the latter part of the century.

[8] Frye, "Comedy: The Mythos of Spring," in *Anatomy of Criticism* (Princeton: Princeton University Press, 1957) pp. 163–65.

triarch is also the main buffoon of the plot, which is quite often the case, the comic performativity of the role of increasingly implausible authority figure also helps, as I mentioned above, to contain any potential social disruptions of this reversal.

Perhaps the most brutal example of an "uncrowned patriarch" in this repertory is Bertati and Bianchi's *La villanella rapita,* first performed in Venice in 1783. In this opera the heroine, Mandina, is tempted and abducted, though not evidently raped, by the local count. The opera ends with Mandina's peasant lover and father recapturing her from the Count's palace and bringing her back to the village, where her marriage to her peasant lover Pippo is legalized. The Count pursues them with a posse of armed men but is defeated by the already-legalized arrangements. The peasants celebrate and the Count grumbles—a thoroughly carnivalesque dethroning, which implicitly reinforces the rule about the impermeability of social strata. However, the Viennese score of the opera contains a whole substitute finale for the second act, with music by Joseph Weigl; here the Count (not unlike the Count in *Le nozze di Figaro*) apologizes for his errant desires and offers the peasants money in restitution. It is not clear when this finale was inserted, since the 1785 Vienna libretto contains the original ending, and the opera was performed only eight times in 1785–86. (However, the 1785 libretto also contains the texts of Mozart's inserted ensembles; it is not just a reprint of the 1783 book.) Hadamowsky lists a couple of performances of this opera ("neuinszeniert") in 1794, when Weigl was the official composer to the court theatres, and it is plausible—even likely— that the substitution was made then.[9] (Weigl was a nineteen-year-old student of Salieri in 1785 and made one bad attempt at composing an *opera buffa* around that time; he also spent many hours making himself generally useful to the opera buffa company, and getting to know the repertory; it is unlikely but not out of the question that he could have produced a substitute finale on order during this earlier period.)[10]

It is worth noting that whether this change was made in the 1780s or in the 1790s, the Count's final apology changes the purview of "the rule" from the absolute social propriety of certain couplings to the obligations of the powerful with respect to those couplings; in that sense this ending is politically much closer to *Le nozze di Figaro* than is Bertati's original trouncing. The obligations of rulers in relation to the rules is also the subject of *Una cosa rara,* the collaboration between Da Ponte and Vicente Martín y Soler that took Vienna by storm six months after the premiere of

[9] Franz Hadamowsky, *Die Wiener Hoftheater (Staatstheater) 1776–1966: Verzeichnis der aufgeführten Stücke mit Bestandnachweis und täglichem Spielplan,* Part I: 1776–1810 (Vienna: Prachner, 1966).

[10] Rudolph Angermüller, "Zwei Selbstbiographien von Joseph Weigl (1766–1846)," *DJbM* 16 (1972) p. 54.

Figaro. Lilla, the shepherdess heroine of the piece (and the "rare thing," being both beautiful and chaste) gains the sympathy and protection of the Queen because her brother wants to marry her off to the old and boorish mayor, when she is happily in love with the shepherd Lubino. The Queen, moved by the girl's innocence, beauty, and unfortunate plight, orders Corrado, the master of the horse, to take Lilla under his protection. Meanwhile, the Prince (son of the Queen and heir to the throne) falls in love with Lilla and engages Corrado's help in trying to seduce her. Corrado himself is greatly taken with Lilla and also attempts to seduce her, double-crossing the Prince in the process. Various complications ensue, of course, but the crux comes in the second-act finale when the Queen hears of money being passed in the attempt on Lilla's virtue, and demands an explanation. The Prince asks Corrado not to betray him to his mother; Corrado accepts all the blame and is banished.

QUEEN:	Chi è l'iniquo?	Who's the criminal?
PRINCE (*to Corrado*):	Non scoprirmi	Don't betray me.
CORRADO:	Io no certo	Not me.
MAYOR:	Nemmen io	Nor me.
CORRADO:	Ah Signora il fallo è mio	Ah my Lady, the crime is mine
	E la pena io pagherò.	And I will take the punishment.

Despite his inappropriate desires, however, the Prince is at least as much an inept and lovesick youth as a persistent or seasoned seducer; his expressive mode is lyric and pastoral as much as arrogantly or virtuosically aristocratic. His eventual escape from punishment, then, is validated by a self-presentation and music calculated to engage the listener's sympathy as much as his or her admiration. The Prince's most high-flown music is his aria "Seguir degg'io chi fugge," in which he complains that someone of his status shouldn't have to go to so much trouble to seduce a mere peasant. Even here, though, he lapses into a lyrical triple meter description of his amorous miseries. Corrado, on the other hand, never waxes lyrical, and his one aria, a deceitful description of the inability of old men to make love, is a classic buffa aria, with characteristically sudden changes of declamation pattern and affect.[11] His true villainy is exposed in the recitatives, but he is allowed no solo music that might encourage sympathetic identification.

Una cosa rara demonstrates a complex balance between the usual comic pattern in which the ending explicitly reinforces a presumably fair and generous social order, and a more socially critical model, in which misdeeds at the highest level are represented as unpunishable. The pastoral aspects of this opera further complicate this balance. On the one hand, explicitly pas-

---

[11] See John Platoff, "The Buffa Aria in Mozart's Vienna," *COJ* 2 (1990) pp. 99–120, for a description of the conventions of this sort of aria.

3-1: Martín y Soler, *Una cosa rara*, II, no. 7
Prince, "Seguir degg'io chi fugge," mm. 1–7 and 99–105

Translation: Should I chase her, who flees? who disdains to love me?
But meanwhile, my heart languishes in grief.

toral settings and subjects in opera buffa were strongly associated with sentimentalism and escapism, as is clearly the case with *Una cosa rara*:[12] the
Queen explicitly praises the simple and virtuous life of the peasants, and
Lilla betrays neither Mandina's temporary capacity to be tempted by rank
and wealth (in *La villanella rapita*), nor Susanna's cleverness; she is essentially only beautiful and good, despite her occasional snappishness with
Ghita, the other shepherdess. That sentimentalism lends the opera a rather
saccharine quality, insulating the Prince from direct criticism. (The rural
setting of *La villanella rapita* and its explicit praise of country values also
diminish the likelihood that the apologizing Count is not really sincere.)
However, the pastoral had also long served as a haven from which to launch
social criticism: in the case of *Una cosa rara,* the much-praised simplicity
and honesty of the shepherds and shepherdesses is an implicit criticism of
the Prince's duplicity.[13]

It is impossible to gauge the way in which the forgiveness of princely pec-
cadilloes and the punishment of the sins of court employees was either intended or understood literally to reflect Viennese society, but the similarity of the configuration of an impeccably virtuous female sovereign, a
prince unfortunate in love, and an unforgivably corrupt courtier, to the late
Maria Theresia, Joseph himself, and the aristocracy, is striking, particularly
since the repertory includes no other actual monarchs.[14] The fact that the
libretto is based on a play by Luis Vélez de Guevara does not diminish the
potential political significance of Da Ponte's choice to retain the original
configuration of ranks. (It would, for example, have been perfectly within
the bounds of the genre to transform the Queen into a sister of the Prince,
and the Prince into a lower noble.)

The years 1785 and 1786, then, saw the premieres of three operas (two
composed for Vienna), which solved the carnivalesque problem of the uncrowned patriarch in ways different from the norm of having him replaced
with a younger but socially equal equivalent; and in a sense the abruptness
of the original ending of *La villanella rapita* is "balanced" by the politically

[12] See Dorothea Link, "The Da Ponte Operas of Martín y Soler" (Ph. D. dissertation, University of Toronto, 1991) pp. 199–200, on the musical aspects of pastoral in *Una cosa rara*;
Rabin, "Mozart, Da Ponte, and the Dramaturgy of Opera Buffa" (Ph.D. dissertation, Cornell University, 1996) pp. 135–40, on the stasis of Da Ponte's verse for this opera; Platoff,
"A New History for Martín's *Una cosa rara*," *JM* 12 (1994) p. 93 on the pastoral qualities
of this libretto. See also Edmund J. Goehring, "Despina, Cupid and the Pastoral Mode of
'Così fan tutte,'" *COJ* 7 (1995) pp. 107–33, on sentimentalism and the pastoral.

[13] The intersection of pastoral, sentimentality, and social commentary in this repertory deserve further research, especially in light of Wye Allanbrook's persuasive reading of *Le nozze
di Figaro* as a utopian pastoral.

[14] I do not mean that Joseph was notorious for socially unacceptable sexual exploits; indeed, Derek Beales (*Joseph II*, vol. I: *In the Shadow of Maria Theresia* [Cambridge: Cambridge
University Press, 1987] p. 335) suggests that frustration and loneliness for female company
were Joseph's principal sexual characteristics after the early death of his first wife, whom he
evidently loved devotedly (ibid., pp. 76–77). If *Una cosa rara's* Prince is figured as a lovesick
youth, his resemblance to Joseph is perhaps more striking.

more complicated apologies in *Una cosa rara* and *Le nozze di Figaro*. *Una cosa rara* is indubitably a more "conservative" work than *Le nozze di Figaro*: in the latter the Count apologizes, whereas in the former his most explicit admission of guilt takes the form of passing it on to someone else.[15] After his scapegoating of Corrado, however, the Prince admits that Lilla is an "esempio di onestà," thus implicitly according her higher moral status than himself—surely an apology of sorts. Thus both these operas (and the altered version of *La villanella rapita*) share the spectacle of an errant ruler being reintegrated into the social order by means of some sort of admission of wrongdoing, however ambiguous. It is not clear whether the pair of apologetic noblemen has a particular political referent; nevertheless, it is generally agreed that the middle of the 1780s is the point at which Joseph's reforms began to go sour, and Joseph himself began a process of retrenchment, particularly with respect to the free political expression of his subjects. For example, already by 1783 Joseph's more conservative advisors were beginning to be able to persuade him to reverse some of the Baron van Swieten's liberal decisions as censor, particularly with respect to works dealing with religious questions;[16] in December 1785 came the Freemasonry Act, which brought Masonic lodges under the control of the state and was intended to control their proliferation in the provinces,[17] and in 1786 he issued the "Secret Instruction" to the Viennese Chief of Police, Count Pergen; this document essentially permitted internal spying.[18] Neither the Viennese Freemasons nor Josephine apologists (not mutually exclusive groups) seem to have suffered inordinately in the immediate aftermath of these edicts, but it is clear that the demise of the climate of boundless possibility and Enlightenment optimism began around the time that this pair of penitent patriarchs appeared on the buffa stage. Whether the spectacle of a self-confessedly fallible ruler was in some sense intended to absorb the potential dissent of the relevant sectors of the Burgtheater audience may never be known, but these unusual reconfigurations of comic convention are worth noting for their capacity to move beyond mere topical reference to something like pointed political commentary.

Servants in Control: Emphasizing Entertainment

In the accompanied recitative before "Dove sono," Mozart and Da Ponte's Countess Almaviva implies that it is a servant's place to be publicly and continuously involved in the imbroglio, with all its disguises, tricks, deceptions,

---

[15] Platoff, "A New History for Martín's *Una cosa rara*," p. 92.

[16] Wangermann, *The Austrian Achievement* (London: Thames and Hudson, 1973), pp. 159–62.

[17] Volkmar Braunbehrens, *Mozart in Vienna, 1781–1791*, trans. Timothy Bell (New York: Grove Weidenfeld, 1989) pp. 242–49.

[18] Wangermann, *The Austrian Achievement*, p. 165.

and other *lazzi,* while characters from the upper social strata, particularly the "parti serie," should stay somewhat apart from these goings-on:[19]

> But what evil is this, changing my clothes with Susanna's, and hers with mine, under the cover of night? O heavens, to what a degraded state am I reduced by a cruel husband, who having first loved, then offended, and then betrayed me, [now] with an unheard-of combination of infidelity, jealousies, and rages, makes me turn to a servant for help.[20]

The Countess's feeling of indignity is entirely justified in the context of this repertory; it is in fact the case that servants and peasants provide the stage activity that keeps the action moving, and the works alive and entertaining, while the *parti serie* behave in a more dignified—or at least a less antic—manner. Within this broad context of more public involvement in the imbroglio, servants and peasants exhibit a continuum of behavior ranging from essentially diversionary stage gesture or performance to the invention and execution of tricks or stratagems that substantially affect the progress of the drama. In other words servants move from mere activity at one end of the spectrum to something more like dramatic action at the other. In the context of one familiar opera, one could represent this continuum as the space between Susanna's and Marcellina's duet "Via resti servita," which is a relatively isolated (even dispensable) moment of comic activity, and Susanna stepping out of the closet in the second-act finale, which, in addition to being a great comic moment, also moves the plot to another stage.

For the purposes of my larger argument I am more interested in the instances of comic behavior that more nearly approach dramatic action—which are, incidentally, much less common than local displays of "mere" activity. The exercise of action by a character in the lower orders of society almost always involves the topsy-turvy spectacle of superiors being subjected to the rule of the servant, or forced to play along with events as arranged by that servant, and one is led to ask both what function is served by the temporarily upside-down world and how (or whether) this topsy turvy is set right or contained. Only about half the operas in this repertory

---

[19] Not all characters with aristocratic titles are *parti serie,* of course. Some characters of noble birth are frankly comic, like Count Perucchetto in Haydn's *La fedeltà premiata;* and of course part of their comedy is the incongruence between their rank and their behavior. Such characters engage in considerable stage activity, usually of a sort that draws attention to their clumsiness or stupidity, and that does not contribute significantly to the forward movement of the plot. Other high-born characters may occupy the more flexible dramatic role of *mezzo carattere,* and while perhaps not as physically active as the buffoon noble, may contribute more directly to the forward motion of the plot.

[20] Ma che mal c'è? cangiando i miei vestiti / Con quelli di Susanna, e i suoi co' miei . . . / Al favor de la notte . . . oh cielo a quale / Umil stato io son ridotta / Da un consorte crudel, che dopo avermi / con un misto inaudito / D'infedeltà, di gelosie, di sdegni, / Prima amata, indi offesa e alfin tradita / Fammi or cercar da una serva aita. *Le nozze di Figaro* III, 7.

include lower-class characters who engage in action in the restricted sense I mean, and among these there is considerable variety both in the sorts of action engaged in and in its rationale. This action, regardless of its content, may be on the servant's own behalf, as Figaro's various machinations in *Le nozze di Figaro*, or (at least in part) on a superior's behalf, if not directly on his orders, as Figaro's tricks and stratagems in *Il barbiere di Siviglia* or Despina's various pieces of business in *Così fan tutte*. Nevertheless, whatever the action, whatever the extent of its effect, and however wise or clear-eyed the servant, it is always the case that both what Frye calls the "blocking" motion that triggers the need for the action, and the permission or decision that allows it to stop, are initiated by the upper-class members of the cast.[21] Servant control of the action is always framed by the desires and decisions of the "betters." Thus, in *Le nozze di Figaro*, for example, it is the Count's desire for Susanna which sets off Figaro's series of stratagems, and at the end it is the reconciliation between the Count and Countess that permits the formal (though not the emotional) union between Figaro and Susanna.

Sarti's *Fra i due litiganti il terzo gode* very clearly exemplifies both the power of the servant and the limits of his influence. In this opera the land-agent Masotto is the third *litigante*, or contender, for the hand of the maid Dorina. The first two are the servant Titta, favored by the Count (evidently because he will not object to that nobleman's desire to dally with Dorina), and the gardener Mingone, favored by the Countess (perhaps because his situation will remove Dorina from the Count's clutches). Masotto reveals his interest in Dorina relatively early on in the opera and from then on tries a number of strategies to attain his ends. (She acquiesces in his interest, and their eventual marriage is clearly a happy outcome; at the same time she does not express much overt desire for him.) In the second act (scenes 8 and 9) Masotto tells the Count that Dorina will not marry Mingone, and the Countess that she will not marry Titta; he tries to persuade them that they are closer to agreement than they might think. He then attempts to manoeuvre the Count and Countess into a more affectionate relationship, presumably thinking that if they were not at loggerheads they would be more inclined to support his own claim to Dorina's hand. The following aria represents the crucial portion of his manipulation of his superiors:

Servo umilissimo	[I am] a servant most humble
Osequiosissimo;	And respectful.
Quando mi chiamano	When you call me
Sarò prontissimo;	I'm there on the double.
Restino restino	Feel free to stay
Con libertà.	Where you are.

---

[21] Frye, *Anatomy of Criticism*, p. 165.

Un passettino in là,	**Step a little there,**
Volti quel viso in quà.	**Turn your face this way.**
Ah che contento amabile	Ah what lovely happiness
Quando due sposi s'amano.	When husband and wife love each other.
Il cor che d'ira è torbido	The heart that is clouded with anger
In pace tornerà.	Will return to peacefulness.
È fatta la pace,	You've made peace,
Già siete contenti.	You're already happy.
Che cari momenti,	What precious moments,
Che lieto goder.	What happy enjoyment.
Tenermi non posso,	I can't restrain myself,
Si salti si rida,	I'm jumping and grinning.
Evviva la face	Hurray for the flame of
D'amor che s'annida;	Love nestling there.
Vi venghino addosso	Let happiness and pleasure
La gioja, il piacer.	Be upon you.[22]

The lines given above in bold, where Masotto physically positions the warring couple, and which the anonymous librettist has distinguished metrically from the preceding and following passages, are repeated numerous times in the first section of this through-composed aria: indeed, they serve as its cadence and set up the beginning of the second section ("È fatta la pace"). The repetitions also give the actors a wonderful opportunity for comic display. In the event, Masotto's scheme works too well. The Count and the Countess defer to each other to the extent that they quarrel about who should be the one to give way. In the second-act finale, Dorina flees to the garden and refuses all suits, and Masotto wins his bride not by scheming or strategizing, but simply by announcing his desire to the Count and Countess, who are by this point sufficiently worn down to agree.

Masotto is very close to Da Ponte and Mozart's Figaro, not only in his situation but also in his structural role. He projects himself as resourceful and wily and clearly sees himself as in control of the situation. At the same time, although his machinations change the local course of the plot, and thus qualify as "action," his plots and stratagems do not in fact get him very much closer to his aims; it is rather Dorina's removal of herself from the imbroglio that precipitates the end, just as in *Le nozze di Figaro* it is the scheme cooked up by Susanna and the Countess that brings down the Count and allows both the aristocrats' reconciliation and the servants' wedding. Masotto and Figaro both exert power over the action, but in both cases that power is limited not only by being triggered and contained by the decisions and actions of the upper-class characters, but also by its own inappropriately grandiose sense of itself.

The second example of an instance in which the servant takes—or ap-

---

[22] Text from the score in the Austrian National Library: Mus. Hs. 17888.

pears to take—control of the action is not a single work, but rather the plot type often considered the paradigm of the genre, that is, the *serva padrona* model in which the machinations of a serving girl permit her to catch and marry a man considerably superior to her in social status. The defining characteristic of this model is the servant's enactment of a series of tricks or stratagems to achieve a socially advantageous marriage. The "fully fledged" version of this plot was relatively rare in the Viennese repertory of the 1770s and 1780s, despite its popularity earlier in the century.[23] Nevertheless its echoes were still very much alive in the twenty years under consideration here. In particular, indulgence in disguise and trickery was a common aspect of manipulative minxes even if they did not rise in social station as a result thereof; Despina's appearances as doctor and notary are very much in this tradition, for example. In Boccherini and Salieri's *La fiera di Venezia,* the middle-class minx Falsirena spends most of the opera pretending to seduce the Duke Ostrogoto, who is betrothed to a lady of his own class, despite his infatuation with Falsirena. In the course of the "seduction," Falsirena makes successive appearances as an unemployed opera singer, a French soap vendor, and a German baroness, using the appropriate languages in all cases. Like other teasing women in this repertory, Falsirena stays in her social place at the end, and the motivation for the trickery appears to be a desire to play games, perhaps related to the carnival setting of the opera, as well as a need to project her unsentimental and cynical view of social relations.[24] Neither of these motivations has the dramatic clarity or power of the true *serva padrona*'s ambition, however, and it is generally the case that the lower- and middle-class women who engage in these tricks without a consequent rise in station have only local structural

[23] Charles E. Troy, *The Comic Intermezzo* (Ann Arbor: University of Michigan Press, 1979) pp. 81–82, finds this plot type in about half the early eighteenth-century intermezzi he studied. It is, however, much rarer in this later repertory. The few works played in Vienna with *serva padrona* plots include three operas by Paisiello—*Le due contesse* (Petrosellini), *La contadina di spirito o sia Il matrimonio inaspettato* (based on Chiari), and his setting of Federico's *La serva padrona;* also the original intermezzo version of Sacchini's *La contadina in corte*, and Borghi's *L'amore in campagna*. Like the transformations of the Pamela story, *serva padrona* operas that modify the class implications of the plot are more frequent than operas that simply have the maid marry the master. In Petrosellini and Piccinni's *L'astratto*, for example, the servant Giocondo marries the middle-class daughter Angelica, but before this takes place, Giocondo discovers that he is the son of a banker from Livorno.

[24] The succession of performances designed to confuse and bamboozle is also characteristic of the "marriage à la mode" plot type in which a lively young wife manages to live the carefree life of her choice despite the attempts of her bumbling husband to contain her. This plot is most familiar today as Donizetti's *Don Pasquale;* it was also a common plot in the early and mid-century intermezzi. See Irène Mamczarz, *Les intermèdes comiques italiens* (Paris: Editions du Centre National de la Recherche Scientifique, 1972) pp. 73–76. It is not, however, found much in the repertory performed in Vienna in the last third of the eighteenth century. Bertati and Anfossi's *Lo sposo disperato* is a sort of "prequel" to this plot, as the aristocratic heroine is forced to marry the bourgeois boor, but the plot does not involve her subsequent intrigues to deceive him.

control of the action; the delight they cause is more focused on their per-formance skills than on the frisson of topsy-turvy social structures.

Thus the question, "How is the rule restated?" with respect to servants who exercise power incommensurate with their status is answered on the level of the plot in the way their actions are typically contained by the de-cisions and dispositions of their superiors. But the question, "What is the function of the violation?" is answered ontologically, or in terms of the sort of experience offered to the audience by moments of "servant power": such moments are often couched explicitly as performances. Masotto's "Servo umilissimo," played in Vienna by Michael Kelly, is a wonderful opportu-nity for a virtuoso moment of comedy. Don Alfonso and Despina's pup-peteering of the paralyzed not-yet-lovers in "La mano a me date" in *Così* is a comparably performative moment, which, characteristically for this opera, both relies on the convention of the manipulative servant, and changes it with the inclusion of Don Alfonso.[25] Even when servant-engi-neered imbroglios do not involve the physical manipulation of stiff and un-willing superiors, there is often a performative element in the disguises, de-ceits, and sudden discoveries that are part and parcel of most schemes, including those of the *serva padrona* descendants mentioned above. Just as explicitly performative moments normally reinforce the "merely plea-surable" function of opera buffa, so moments when the servants are in con-trol are "trivialized" politically by being couched as occasions to focus on the skill of the executant. On the other hand it is also the case that the top echelon of the Burgtheater company played the very servants whose pow-ers I claim were "contained" by being performative.[26] Thus it is at least possible that while on one level the sheer pleasure of witnessing these mo-ments pushed their political import into the background, on another level the importance of the singers who performed them served to validate, or at least to make more palatable, the rearrangements of power they enacted.

SENTIMENTAL HEROINES AND THE POWER OF SUFFERING

If the machinations of the *serva padrona* in this repertory merge with other servant activities in the form of performative gags with little long-range

---

[25] This moment is often played with sassy comedy, but Peter Sellars's production takes the moment as an opportunity for Despina and Don Alfonso (who are intermittently a couple) safely to play out a private reconciliation. In addition to participating in the "psychologizing" of Despina, this moment also helps downplay the class differences between the lovers and the servant.

[26] Kelly played Masotto in *Fra i due litiganti;* Bussani played Pagnotta in *La frascatana.* Both these singers counted as stars in the company, according to Michtner (*DAB*, p. 148). Celeste Coltellini (described by Joseph II in 1784 as a "first-class singer," if not quite Storace) played Vespina and Falsirena.

dramatic relevance, her *goal*—to move up in the world by means of marriage—is taken over by versions of the *buona figliuola* story, in which the young woman loves someone who is her apparent superior, looks likely to lose him because of the difference in status, and then discovers that she is in fact his social equal. Horst Weber sees the *buona figliuola* plot type as an extension of the *serva padrona* type, but in fact they differ in at least two crucial ways.[27] The first involves the obvious point that there is no real class distinction between a Cecchina-like heroine and her eventual husband, and the second is the associated fact that the sentimental heroine is essentially passive with regard to the action. She engineers nothing; indeed, it is in large part her sweet passivity that marks her as noble.[28] The dramatic mechanisms in this plot archetype are completely different from those in the serva padrona archetype, depending as they do on the arousal of sympathy for the heroine and evoking a moral world quite foreign to the deceit and bamboozlement so riotously enjoyed by the "maid-mistress" and her descendants.

Within the context of the dramatic action, sentimental heroines actually reinforce several rules about women of a certain class. The first is that their identity is entirely relational. Women are most frequently listed in the cast lists as someone else's sister, wife, betrothed, cousin, daughter, or servant, but the sentimental heroine takes this relational identity one step further, as her nature is defined as much by the effect she has on others as by the efforts she makes on her own behalf. Her passivity is thus an integral part of her relational identity. She herself engineers no action, but she is the focal point of almost everything engineered by the other characters. She is usually desired by essentially every male in the cast and is therefore the focus of every female's jealous concern, although she has made advances to no-one. When she flees, the other characters all hunt her down; when she is courted by importunate noblemen, she produces jealousy and spite in everyone from her proper lover to servants who think they themselves should have been the objects of the nobleman's desires. Thus she occupies only the space imagined for her by the other characters; she is in a sense the blank eye of the dramatic storm. Connected to the rule about relational identity is a rule about dependence: according to this rule a woman's chief interest in life is marriage. Although the female characters in opera buffa treat marriage in a variety of different ways—as a means of reinforcing their status, as an almost hopeless but much-desired outcome, as a comfortable certainty, as a right, and occasionally as a missed opportunity—it is indubitably the main purpose in life for most of them. Sentimental heroines who

---

[27] Horst Weber, "Der Serva-padrona-Topos in der Oper: Komik als Spiel mit musikalischen und sozialen Normen," *AfMw* 65 (1988) pp. 87–110.

[28] See Chapter 1, pp. 41–42 for a description of the plot types involving the sentimental heroine.

suffer on account of love, whether by choice or chance, are no exception. The third rule supported by the figure of the sentimental heroine is that the maltreatment of women is unexceptional, if also unfortunate; that women in some sense need to be kept in their place by threats and abuse. Most sentimental heroines endure persecution without active resistance, in effect complying with the genre's habit of not shaming or punishing characters (especially men) who engage in activities ranging from unjustified mistrust and ostracism to actual physical violence, though this is never shown on stage. In *La finta giardiniera,* for example, the reason that Violante/Sandrina is in disguise in the first place is that she hopes to get a secret glance (and then possibly to regain the affections of) the man who stabbed her in a fit of jealousy and left her for dead a year before the start of the opera. Porta and Righini's *L'incontro inaspettato* involves comparable pre-opera violence. In Anelli and Piccinni's *Griselda,* whose Viennese performance in 1794 is slightly outside our period, but whose story was well-known throughout the eighteenth century (and is echoed in Puttini's *La vera costanza*), the heroine's husband Gualtiero humiliates her to the extent of having her make up the marriage bed for his supposed new wife (actually Griselda's long-lost daughter) before he reveals that this was all to test her fitness as his wife.[29] The end of the opera praises her patience and humility, enjoining other wives to take note. The sentimental heroine's characteristic response to this treatment is not to confront or accuse her persecutors, but rather to escape to a garden or copse (or occasionally to more threatening surroundings) and lament her plight, and then in some cases to fall asleep, which, of course, allows her to be found and restored to happiness with no hint of her own will or activity.[30]

Sentimental heroines do not overturn the rules for female behavior. Rather, they sidestep them, developing a power that is paradoxically both separate from and dependent on the abovementioned notions of relationality and passivity. Like overthrown patriarchs and controlling servants, however, they raise questions about the nature, distribution, and exercise of power. And as with the overthrown patriarchs and the controlling servants, performance is inextricably related to the social implications of this role. The musical and performative power of the sentimental heroine was widely acknowledged in the eighteenth century: Piccinni's friend and biographer Pierre-Louis Ginguené, for example, wrote of *La buona figliuola:* ". . . and in the middle of all the persecutions, [is] Cecchina, always protest-

[29] This ancient story regained popularity at the end of the eighteenth century. In addition to Piccinni's setting mentioned above, there were also settings of the story by Pietro Alessandro Guglielmi and Ferdinando Paer in the 1790s, Guglielmi's to a text by Sertor for Florence in 1796, and Paer's to Anelli's text for Parma in 1798.

[30] See Hunter, "Landscapes, Gardens and Gothic Settings in the *Opere Buffe* of Mozart and His Contemporaries," *CM* 51 (1993) pp. 94–105.

ing her innocence . . . *The accents of grief;* this is what ravished the Roman audience."[31] (Emphasis mine.) In other words, it was not only Piccinni's music that "ravished" the audience, but the embodied performance of that music, the act of singing, that brought it to life.

Although sentimental heroines sing a variety of sorts of aria in various situations, the song-like entrance aria, unpreceded by dialogue or participation in an ensemble, epitomizes the performative and emotional power of this character type. Goldoni and Piccinni use this sort of aria to good effect at the very beginning of *La buona figliuola,* as Cecchina sings:

Che piacer, che bel diletto	What pleasure and delight
È il vedere, in sul mattino,	In the morning to see
Colla rosa il gelsomino	The jasmine competing
In bellezza gareggiar!	With the rose in beauty!
E potere all'erbe ai fiori	And to be able to say
Dir son io coi freschi umori,	To the grass and flowers that
Che vi vengo ad inaffiar.	It is I who comes with fresh dews to water you.

3-2: Piccinni, *La buona figliuola,* I,1
Cecchina, "Che piacer, che bel diletto," mm. 25–32

The beauties of nature are a fairly common theme for sentimental heroines, their affinities with nature working literally and figuratively to naturalize their unassertive sweetness. The other common theme for the entrance aria is the self-pitying lament: Nina's famous entrance aria "Il mio ben, quando verrà" in Paisiello's opera of the same name is a famous example. Agatina's "Del destin invan mi lagno," which occurs close to the beginning of Bertati's and Gazzaniga's *La vendemmia* (see Example 2-1) is another:

Del destin invan mi lagno,	I complain of my fate in vain,
Meschinella afflitta, e sola:	Miserable, lonely wretch that I am.
Per pietà chi mi consola,	For heaven's sake, who will console me,
Chi m'ajuta per pietà?	Who will help me?
Dover prendere per forza	I am forced to take a husband

[31] Andrea Della Corte, *Piccinni (Settecento Italiano): Con Frammenti Musicali Inediti e Due Ritratti* (Bari: G. Laterza, 1928) p. 36.

Uno sposo, che non piace.	Who does not please me.
Ah dov'è quel cor capace	Ah, where is the heart
Di poterlo sopportar?	Capable of bearing this?
Pastorelle innamorate,	Amorous shepherdesses,
Dite voi, se lo provate,	Tell me, if you feel it too,
Quanto è grave il mio penar.	How serious my suffering is.

The Countess's "Porgi amor" in *Le nozze di Figaro* also falls into this category of opening lament.

Whether the textual content of the entrance aria is admiration of nature or a lament, however, the women who sing them all appear without first having been seen in interaction or in concert with other characters, without an onstage audience consciously to address (even though there may be a hidden listener), and in a state of total self-absorption. This absorption is in some ways analogous to the absorption of the figures in paintings by Chardin, Greuze, and others that form the partial subject of Michael Fried's book *Absorption and Theatricality: Painting and Beholder in the Age of Diderot*.[32] Fried argues, with Diderot, that the power of a representation of absorption is exactly the arresting power of a subject's apparent unawareness of an audience—in other words the image's "negation of the beholder" or its *anti-theatricality*.[33] What we have in Cecchina's "Che piacer" and in other comparable moments is, paradoxically, a performance of absorption or antitheatricality; it is effective as a performance precisely because it does not directly address the audience. However, it cannot exist without being performed, and in fact the "eavesdropping" presence of the auditorium audience is what gives it meaning. (Fried's absorbed figures are of both genders, whereas the self-absorbed entrance lament or pastoral is a largely female phenomenon.)[34]

The tension inherent in the notion of the performance of absorption is reflected in the ways these entrance arias all evoke and embody "song." Here I mean not stage song of the "Voi che sapete" sort, but song as something performed almost absentmindedly as a sign of separation from the mundane world. These entrance pieces are all in cantabile style—that is, they eschew both elaborate virtuosity and speechlike declamation patterns in favor of smooth lines in more or less regular phrases. In addition, they may emphasize their song-likeness by using a strophic form, by dwelling on a pastoral or song-like subject, or (like "Porgi amor") they may have ac-

---

[32] Berkeley: University of California Press, 1980.

[33] See David Marshall, *The Figure of Theater: Shaftesbury, Defoe, Adam Smith and George Eliot* (New York: Columbia University Press, 1986) for an extended discussion of the inherent theatricality of literary evocations of sympathy, which stands in implicit contradiction to Fried's argument.

[34] Two male exceptions to this largely female type are Filiberto's "Questo grato ruscelletto" in Porta's and Sarti's *I contratempi* (this aria is in fact by Giacomo Rust and appears to be an early substitution), and Lubino's "Lilla bella" in *Una cosa rara*.

companiments whose more or less constant surface rhythm is significantly faster than the rhythm of declamation in the voice, thus drawing attention to its "singing" quality. Song in this sense in opera buffa is almost always used to suggest a separation from immediate circumstances; pert serving girls sing songs (though not at their initial entrances) when they want their lovers to think they aren't paying attention to them, bumpkin boys sing songs as they bumble into situations they aren't going to be able to cope with, and so on. The sentimental heroine's invocation of song at the moment of her entrance, then, is a marker of her distance from the mechanics of the intrigue, and also an indicator of her willed ignoring of the auditorium audience.

I have argued elsewhere that the sentimental sympathies of the auditorium audience form a domain analogous to the emerging bourgeois household, in which, despite the framework of male financial and material control, the wife and mother holds uncontested sway over the sentimental and moral development of the children and the servants—even, to some extent, over her husband.[35] The sentimental heroine, recognizing, as it were, her incapacity to affect the progress of the plot through the normal means of stratagems, trickery, or simple insistence, escapes, not only to the natural world within the drama, but to a domain outside the frame of the action, where power consists of the ability to compel sympathetic attention and to persuade by demonstrating incontestable virtue.

The sentimental heroine garners sympathetic attention in part by the beauty of her music; not only entrance arias, but moments of escape and lament more generally are often marked by touching cantabile lines that float above rhythmically active (and often carefully orchestrated) accompaniments. Dorina's moment of solo desperation in the second-act finale of *Fra i due litiganti* is a case in point; note the clarinet line in counterpoint with the voice. (See Example 3-3.) This type of music draws attention to its own beauty, in part by being divorced from the stage action, in part by emphasizing the singing (rather than the declamatory) qualities of the voice, and in part by displaying an unusually sensuous surface in the accompaniment. It is particularly effective in a finale, where the stage is usually filled with participants, and the normal mode of solo vocal delivery is short phrases emphasizing dialogic interaction with the other characters. (Dorina's touching misery is followed by comparable moments for Masotto and Titta; despite their equally pitiable states, the tone of this segment is established by her.)

---

[35] See Hunter, "Rousseau, the Countess, and the Female Domain," in *Mozart Studies 2*, ed. Cliff Eisen (Oxford: Oxford University Press, 1997) pp. 1–26, which replicates much of the argument of these pages. Rebecca Lee Green, "Power and Patriarchy," pp. 372ff. also discusses the tensions in opera buffa between the patriarchal model of male determination and control and the emerging bourgeois model of the household.

3-3: Sarti, *Fra i due litiganti il terzo gode*, II, finale, mm. 204–8; 213–17

Translation: Oh, what horror, what fear! What am I, poor thing, to do?

The effect of these "performances of absorption," then, is that they *demand* sympathy and identification by enacting a pretty or pitiable scene, and by virtue of the music's beauty. But just as the power of the "performance of absorption" paradoxically depends both on the presence of an audience and on the illusion that it is not there, the permissibility of that power depends on its exercise in the service of a demonstration of powerlessness; sentimental heroines make their strongest appeals to the audience when they have least control of the stage action. In one sense, then, they do embody the carnivalesque principle of reversal—their control of the auditorium delights and entertains at the same time as the narrative frame reminds the audience of the propriety of female passivity and dependence on the decisions of others. But on the broader level of social meaning, as I suggested above, the rules of passivity and relational identity are modified or stretched rather than reversed and then restated. In terms of the rule of passivity, the sentimental heroine exercises a "performative power" out of proportion to her capacity to affect the action of the drama. That power, however, is confined to situations where she is essentially pleading for sympathy. In terms of the rule of dependence, her power to enlist the audience's sympathy when she is derided or rebuffed by everyone in the cast rests on the audience's willingness to react appropriately; there is nothing immutable or structural about it.

The social context for the demonstration of female power in a domain separate from that of most other characters in the opera is not specifically Viennese but is, rather, part of the pan-European reconfiguring of gender relations that went along with the general bourgeoisification of society. This was a reconfiguration in which women increasingly became understood as the soul of the bourgeois home whose primary task was to unite beauty and virtue in ruling a domain that provided moral education to children and solace to men.[36] One would not believe from reading Johann Pezzl's 1786 description "concerning love" in Vienna that these ideals were met in his city:

> People from the middle class, from the lesser nobility and the families of councillors, seek from love and the ensuing marriage either a position, or capital, which will enable them to live comfortably. Since these intentions are quite open, and the bride fully realizes that the matter turns not on her person, but on an important matter of secondary interest, she entertains no illusions about her husband's true

---

[36] Joan B. Landes, *Women and the Public Sphere in the Age of the French Revolution* (Ithaca: Cornell University Press, 1988) argues that the exclusion of women from the bourgeois public sphere marginalized them in their homes. Daniel Gordon, "Philosophy, Sociology and Gender in the Enlightenment Conception of Public Opinion," *French Historical Studies* 17 (1992) pp. 899–903 takes issue with this line, arguing that the female-headed salon, analogous to the bourgeois home, and perhaps in some ways closer to the operatic stage, was a source of the eminently public virtue of sociability.

affections and is in no wise disappointed in her expectations. She marries him because in doing so she can become a matron, live more easily, and be mistress of the
house."[37]

The sarcastic tone of this excerpt, however, does suggest that even in the
upper layers of society (if only in its bourgeoisifying quarters), the ideals of
marriage for love and a home centered on moral and sentimental, rather
than material, values did in fact exist in Vienna, if only in the breach. Thus,
to the extent that opera buffa's sentimental heroines managed the task of
making vocal and musical (and preferably physical) beauty seem like a
demonstration of virtue and thus a justification for a female "domain" and
a certain sort of domestic morality, they posed a more serious challenge to
the trivializing and atavistic frames of the genre than did either the uncrowned patriarchs or the controlling servants. The figure of the sentimental heroine suggests that performance—one of the elements that contain and neutralize the other two reversals—could also be enlisted in the
service of endorsing a social order different from the one hammered home
in other aspects of the genre. But it had to be performance on what, in a
Viennese context, we might call the "German" model, namely an occasion
when the singer was totally absorbed into the role,[38] when the audience
was as unaware of the "art" of the occasion as possible, and when a moral
lesson could be inculcated—the more effectively when the occasion was
thoroughly pleasurable.

[37] Pezzl, *Skizze von Wien,* trans. in Landon, *Mozart and Vienna* (London: Thames and
Hudson, 1991) p. 111.
[38] Cf. the comment in the 1773 *Theatralalmanach,* quoted in the Introduction, p. 65.

PART II

The Closed Musical Numbers
of Opera Buffa and
Their Social Implications

Chapter Four

ARIAS: SOME ISSUES

THERE ARE several reasons for looking closely at arias in the course of a study of opera buffa as entertainment. The crudest is that the aria is by far the most common closed musical number in opera buffa, and any consideration of how the genre presents its meanings has to take the aria—the basis of the dramaturgy—into account. Every character with any part in the plot gets at least one aria, and anyone of significance gets two or three or more. The numbers of arias in individual operas decrease somewhat between 1770 and 1790, partly because of the lengthening of arias, partly because of increasing numbers of ensembles, and occasionally as a result of more fluid relations between recitative and aria or between aria and ensemble, such that "aria" is no longer such an unambiguous category.[1] Nevertheless, even by the end of the period, most operas include between fourteen and eighteen arias, and even those with fewer typically include more arias than ensembles. More important than sheer weight of numbers, however, is the aria's function as the chief carrier of meaning about individual characters. To be sure, ensembles (especially the larger ones) can create a pressure to act which reveals aspects of characters inaccessible to solo numbers, but on the whole the "essence" of a character is most clearly expressed in the series of arias he or she sings in the course of an opera. Arias, then, are among the most important clues to "character type," a concept of primary importance in understanding the social profile of this repertory.

TYPE AND CHARACTER

The main vehicle for these meanings is the "aria type," a concept much in use since the eighteenth century but quite variable in meaning. In the late eighteenth century, the concept of aria type (derived more from opera seria than opera buffa) was most closely related to generally expressive qualities manifested primarily in the melodic and declamatory qualities of the vocal line. John Brown, for example, in his *Letters upon the Poetry and Music of the Italian Opera* (1789), lists five basic types: the *aria cantabile*, the *aria di portamento*, the *aria di mezzo carattere*, the *aria parlante*, and the *aria*

---

[1] Trofonio's big aria "Spirti invisibili," in Salieri's *La grotta di Trofonio*, I,10, for example, segues directly into a chorus, while Plistene's exit from the grotto in II,6 is set as a *scena*. The influence of Salieri's "French connection" on these pieces is obvious.

di bravura, these being associated, respectively, with tenderness, dignity, seriousness, agitation, and any affect requiring dazzling display.[2] Johann Christmann, in his *Elementarbuch der Tonkunst* (1782–89),[3] describes three primary types: like Brown, he includes the *aria di bravura;* his *aria di strepito* is quite like Brown's *aria parlante* in stressing syllabic declamation and an agitated manner; and he also includes the *aria d'espressione,* in which a variety of affects are expressed, each with its own tempo. Vincenzo Manfredini's *Difesa della musica moderna* (1788) also mentions the *aria cantabile,* in which vocal and expressive considerations are primary, and has the *aria di bravura* in common with most other writers on the subject.[4]

More modern writing about aria types is less consistent than its eighteenth-century counterpart. Commonly noted modern types include the buffa and seria arias, which rely on a conjunction of character and expression,[5] the rondò, which is defined by its form (see Appendix 2), but which writers also associate with seriousness of expression, dramatic importance, and the nobility (inner and outer)of the character,[6] and the cavatina, also thought of as a combination of formal and dramatic elements.[7] However, because opera buffa is conventional in so many dimensions, it is possible to define types in an almost infinite number of ways, from categories as vague as "sentimental statement," or "lament," or "seria parody," to types as specific as "aria in which the tenor lover sends a regretful (often indecisive) message to an absent beloved," (e.g., Don Ottavio's "Il mio tesoro").[8] As James Webster notes, any given aria lies at the center of an indefinitely large network of connections and associa-

---

[2] *Letters upon the Poetry and Music of the Italian Opera: Addressed to a Friend. By the Late Mr. John Brown, Painter* (Edinburgh: Bell and Bradfute, 1789) pp. 36–40 and *passim.*

[3] Both the Brown and the Christmann excerpts are quoted in Leonard Ratner, *Classic Music,* pp. 280–81.

[4] Vincenzo Manfredini, *Difesa della musica moderna e' suoi celebri esecutori* (Bologna: Trenti, 1788; Facsimile rpt. Bologna: Forni, 1972) p. 195.

[5] Platoff, "The Buffa Aria in Mozart's Vienna" (*COJ* 2 [1990] 99–120).

[6] John A. Rice, "Rondò vocali di Salieri e Mozart per Adriana Ferrarese," in Muraro and Bryant, *I vicini di Mozart* (Florence: Olschki, 1989) vol. 1, pp. 185–209.

[7] Wolfgang Osthoff, "Mozarts Cavatinen und ihrer Tradition," in *Frankfurter musikhistorische Studien: Helmuth Osthoff zu seinem siebzigsten Geburtstag* (Tutzing: Schneider, 1969) pp. 139–77, identifies an association between the term "cavatina" and a textual content involving the deathly aspects or consequences of love, or hallucination. He also, however, notes that this is one subtype of the larger and more amorphous notion of the cavatina. Gerhard Allroggen, "Die Cavatine in der italienischen Oper des 18. Jahrhunderts," in *Festschrift Arno Forschert zum 60. Geburtstag am 29 Dezember 1985,* ed. G. Allroggen and Detlef Altenburg (Kassel: Bärenreiter, 1986) pp. 142–49, describes the complex eighteenth-century history of this aria type, establishing the formal principle of varied repetition as a way in which the cavatina distinguished itself from the da capo aria, and noting that by the end of the century "cavatina" no longer had the associations with "cavata" (carved out) that it had earlier in the century.

[8] This type does not originate with "Se cerca, se dice," from Metastasio's *Olimpiade,* but it is certainly related to it.

tions.[9] Some of these networks are unrecoverable today (e.g., the arias in which Nancy Storace imitated other performers—surely a "live" type in the Burgtheater at the time), but many are accessible from the scores. Because I am primarily interested in the social structures created by these operas, I am most concerned to describe aria types that address or manipulate the class and gender of their singers in ways that contribute to the overall social or ideological profile of the repertory. Thus in the next chapter I examine five aria types in which the musical and textual elements convey something consistent about the sorts of characters who sing them. These are the buffa aria already widely recognized as a standard type,[10] the "*serva/contadina* aria" sung by some female peasants and serving girls,[11] the seria statement of pride or rank,[12] the aristocratic rage aria, and the aria of [amorous] sentiment. The first two types of aria might be included among Brown's *arie parlanti,* though the *serva/contadina* aria can tend toward the *cantabile;* the seria statement could belong either with Brown's *aria di portamento* or with his *aria di bravura,* and the sentimental statement would often count as an *aria cantabile,* or as another common eighteenth-century type, the *aria d'affetto.* The first four of my "sociodramatic" aria types operate at the social and dramatic polarities of these operas and suggest a more or less rigid framework of behaviors for and attitudes to certain sorts of characters. The last aria type—the aria of sentiment—is sung by both genders and more than one rank of character; in some ways it mediates between the polarities established by the other aria types, but in others it is equally, if differently, tied to rank and gender. These aria types and their social implications are the subjects of the next chapter.

These types do not cover every aria in opera buffa, of course, and their terms of definition are not entirely consistent with one another. Nevertheless, each type is defined and articulated by a well-defined set of conventions, differently weighted in each case. The rank, gender, and dramatic function of the characters is the obvious starting point for all the types except the aria of sentiment. Each type also has a characteristic lexicon, both textual and musical. The speech of characters below the aristocracy is char-

[9] James Webster, "The Analysis of Mozart's Arias," in *Mozart Studies,* ed. Cliff Eisen (Oxford: Clarendon Press, 1991) pp. 107–8, includes a discussion of the concept of aria type. He lists five presumably "primary" types: the *aria d'affetto,* the noble or heroic aria, the female buffa aria, the male buffa aria, and the rondò.

[10] Platoff, "The Buffa Aria in Mozart's Vienna," and "Catalogue Arias and the 'Catalogue Aria,'" in Sadie, *Wolfgang Amadè Mozart* (Oxford: Clarendon Press, 1996) pp. 296–311; Ronald Rabin, "Figaro as Misogynist," in Hunter and Webster, *Opera Buffa in Mozart's Vienna* (Cambridge: Cambridge University Press, 1997) pp. 232–60.

[11] Webster's "female buffa aria," in Webster, "Analysis," pp. 107–8, corresponds in part to my *serva/contadina* aria but is probably more comprehensive, since my definition of this type would not include "Venite inginocchiatevi."

[12] This is similar to Webster's "heroic" aria type. Webster, "Analysis," p. 107.

acteristically more concrete and more given to enumeration and listing than the paradigmatic speech of aristocratic characters; the seria speech of aristocratic characters tends toward the metaphorical and abstract. This distinction between concrete and abstract is mirrored, if obliquely, in the paradigmatic vocal differences between high- and low-ranked characters: whereas aristocratic characters tend to dissolve the referentiality of their utterances in coloratura—the extension of a single syllable over many notes—comic lower-class characters tend to clutter the syllables together in passages of patter. The general expressive quality of an aria—whether elevated, galant, or comic, to use the eighteenth century's tripartite division of styles—also contributes to the identification of type.

Close in importance to the rank and gender of the character and the general expressive quality of text and music in an aria's instantiation of its type is the dramatic situation in which it occurs, though this may be as likely to suggest a subtype (e.g., the entrance lament, or the statement of amorous expectation, both of which fit within the general category of the sentimental statement[13]) as a type as a whole. The category "dramatic situation" obviously includes the nature of the events that led up to the aria and its dramaturgical positioning, but it may also include the presence (or absence) of an interlocutor, and the aria's construction of the relationship between singer and interlocutor. Thus, just as seria-like arias for aristocrats tend to "abstract" the words of their arias into vocalizing, so aristocrats are more likely than lower-ranked characters either to abstract the interlocutor into an apostrophized absentee, or to be so caught up in the expression of feeling (whatever its nature) that the actual interlocutor seems irrelevant. Lower-ranked characters expressing comic or at least nonelevated sentiments tend to be much more specifically involved with one or several onstage characters (or with the audience they directly address), even if they do not gauge their involvement very tactfully. Indeed, the comic mismatch between the rhetorical intent of the singer and the effect of his utterance on his audience is a staple device in the buffa aria, as the discussion in the next chapter shows.

These and other highly conventional devices can, as I have been suggesting, serve to reinforce the typological definition of an aria and its associations with particular sorts of characters; they can also complicate or deepen an aria's category. For example, when a comic character from the middle or lower ranks of society suddenly engages in long-breathed and rather plain melody over a rhythmically active accompaniment, without obvious parodistic or pretentious intent, the association of that musical type with the "noble simplicity" of certain serious (sometimes seria) characters

---

[13] The Countess's "Porgi amor," in *Le nozze di Figaro* and Ferrando's "Un'aura amorosa," in *Così* exemplify these two subtypes.

can suggest a sympathetic aspect to a previously risible character. Thus in Petrosellini and Piccinni's *L'astratto,* the gambling-obsessed hero, Leandro, is introduced in the act of playing cards, oblivious to the sniping of his sisters about how they'll be married before him. He, however, is also nursing what seems to be a hopeless affection for the gardener Laurina, and expresses his feelings about her in a comic mixture of extravagant metaphor and all-too literal physical description:

Io mi sento in mezzo al core	I feel right in my heart
La fucina di vulcano.	The volcano's fire.
Va soffiando il foco amore,	Love kindles the fire,
E l'incendio piano piano	And the burning bit by bit
Nel mio sen crescendo va.	Grows in my breast.
Sol potrebbe la mia bella	Only my beloved could
Queste fiamme, oh Dio, temprare;	Moderate these flames, oh God;
Pur mi vede consumare,	Yet I am consumed,
Pur le chiedo, oh Dio, pietà.	And so I ask her for mercy, oh God.
Ahi che caldo . . . che gran fuoco,	Ouch, what heat . . . what a great burning,
Ardo tutto, vado in cenere,	I'm all aflame, I'm going to burn up.
Ah meschin non trovo loco,	Ah wretch, I find no [peace];
Ah di me che mai sarà?	Ah, what will become of me?

Like many seria arias, this aria uses metaphor (passion as volcano), and some rather grand words (*consumare, incenere*) as well as invoking divine assistance (or at least mercy). But like many comic arias, this one descends to quite specific description of physical effects and sensations—the burning gradually increases in his breast, the heat hurts, and so on. On the face of it, one could read this aria as a simple parody, but Piccinni's music complicates that reading. The aria opens with a gentle tune over an active accompaniment, very much like any serious aria beginning, "Io mi sento . . . nel core." (See Example 4-1.) The rising figures that appear in lines 3–4 (see Example 4-2) begin to suggest that perhaps the feelings are not to be wept for, and by the end of the aria ("Ah meschin,"), his desperation is expressed as classically comic patter. This aria is mostly comic, but the sentimental associations of the opening music linger and suggest that perhaps this character is worth a little sympathy. (And sure enough, Laurina turns out to be of gentle birth, and Leandro is shown to be worthy of her.) One could argue on this basis that the opening music merely anticipates the resolution of the *plot* rather than the essence of the *character,* and of course it does, but the musical impression of a confused young man with a good heart is still strong. (Indeed, the young man is so confused that the music does not modulate back to the tonic from the dominant until the final ritornello.)

4-1: Piccinni, *L'astratto,* I,3
Leandro, "Io mi sento in mezzo al core," mm. 8–11

Individuality in the opera buffa aria, then, is normally constructed not in opposition to the conventions of the genre, but rather by means of the manipulation of a dizzying array of conventional possibilities, some of which are apprehensible as such, others of which operate subtextually and subconsciously. Conventions work in at least two ways to develop a character's individuality: on the one hand the use of one archetype rather than another may assert his or her distinctness from other characters in the same opera, and on the other, a particular combination and layering of conventional associations can contribute to a sense of a character's depth and psychological plausibility. Indeed, it is true not only of Piccinni's Leandro but also of Mozart's famously "human" Countess that "humanity" and "individuality" emerge from a complex interweaving of dramatic, musical, and textual conventions—many but by no means all of them integral to opera buffa. Until relatively recently writers on Mozart's operas have not taken seriously the profundity and virtuosity with which he used the languages

4-2: Piccinni, *L'astratto,* I,3
Leandro, "Io mi sento in mezzo al core," mm. 16–20

of the repertory in which his Da Ponte settings appeared,[14] partly because
of an understandable ignorance about that repertory, partly because of the

[14] Among the most important recent work on this subject is Heartz, *Mozart's Operas*
(Berkeley: University of California Press, 1990) *passim;* Brown, *Così;* and "Beaumarchais,
Paisiello and the Genesis of *Così fan tutte*" in Sadie, *Wolfgang Amadè Mozart,* pp. 312–38;
Link, *L'arbore di Diana:* A Model for *Così fan tutte,*" in Sadie, *Wolfgang Amadè Mozart,*
pp. 362–73; Platoff, "The Buffa Aria in Mozart's Vienna"; Platoff, "How Original Was
Mozart? The Evidence from Opera Buffa," *EM* 20 (1992) 105–17; Rabin, "Mozart, Da
Ponte and the Dramaturgy of Opera Buffa" (Ph.D. dissertation, Cornell University, 1996),
and "Figaro as Misogynist." However, the notion that Mozart's Da Ponte settings connect
to musical and generic conventions is increasingly common in the literature. The entire argument of Allanbrook, *Rhythmic Gesture in Mozart* (Chicago: University of Chicago Press,
1983), for example, depends on the notion that Mozart's operatic music is rooted in the
musical conventions of his age, and particularly in the pervasive deployment of *topoi,* whose
conventional associations invoke a wide range of social and aesthetic meanings. See also
Stefan Kunze, *Don Giovanni vor Mozart: Die Tradition der Don-Giovanni-Opern im italienischen buffa-Theater des 18. Jahrhunderts* (Munich: Fink, 1972), and Sabine Henze-
Döhring, *Opera Seria, Opera Buffa und Mozarts "Don Giovanni"* (Laaber: Laaber-Verlag,
1986).

romantic ideology of originality and transcendence, and partly, of course, because of the extraordinary richness and complexity and beauty of the music. It is, nevertheless, important to point out here that one of the paradoxes of convention, fully exploited by Mozart, is that the more virtuosically a composer manipulates and combines conventional devices, and the wider the variety of their origins, the more "natural" the depiction of humanity may seem to be.

FORM AND CHARACTER

The musical forms of arias can also contribute to the construction of individuality by means of the layering of conventional devices. (Appendix 2 tabulates the formal outlines characteristic of the repertory.) A few whole forms have clear conventional dramatic associations: these include the compressed da capo and (to a lesser extent) the rondò, which are characteristic of, respectively, the most elevated of seria statements, and of intense statements of sentiment by aristocratic and other central female characters. Clearly "meaningful" forms also include ternary form, which is (with the exception of Martín y Soler's general penchant for it) generally associated with pastoral moments; and strophic forms, which always denote putatively preexistent songs and tend to be associated with lower-ranked characters. All four of these forms are defined by clear articulation of sections and (strophic form aside) typically involve thematic contrast between paragraphs. In other words they are forms whose salient characteristics are immediately apprehensible, and which can thus be used to make a dramatic point. Most arias, however, do not manifest any of these forms; the repertory encompasses a variety of binary, "sonata-like," additive (e.g., rondo) and through-composed structures dependent on the form of the text and the needs of the drama. Thus in most arias there is no pre-existent conventional association between the whole form of the piece, the character type singing, the expressive qualities of the text, and the dramatic situation.[15] Nevertheless, some elements or aspects of musical form do have conventional associations, and what we might term the "rhetoric" of form can contribute significantly to the meaning of an aria.[16] The "rhetorical"

[15] There are a couple of instances where certain dramatic or typological features are statistically over-represented in a given aria form; the fact that 63 percent of arias in ABAC form and 60 percent of rondos (in the modern formal sense) are sung by women, who constitute only 44 percent of all characters, are cases in point. These statistical anomalies are quite suggestive, but they do not establish hard and fast meanings for, or expectations of, these forms, such that it would be possible to remark, for example, that Mozart's use of a rondo form for Guglielmo's "Donne mie" marks him as "effeminate."

[16] Ronald Rabin, "Mozart, Da Ponte, and the Dramaturgy of Opera Buffa," pp. 146–61. Rabin defines rhetoric as a combination of form and expression, using the eighteenth-century division of all music into "high, middle, and low" styles as an organizing principle.

aspects of form—that is, the aspects that seem most consistently and meaningfully tied to character, expression, and means of persuasion—include the mutual relations of tonal, thematic, and textual structures and the resultant clarity or confusion of formal articulation; the capacity of thematic return to indicate eloquence or ineloquence, and the internal coherence or contrast in the musical material, which can suggest mental or psychological progress, stasis, or even collapse.[17] The next chapter describes how certain paradigmatic aria types employ characteristic sorts of formal rhetoric; it is important to remember in the abstract, however, that none of the formal devices I mention here are dramatically (or socially) meaningful independent of the texts they set and the situations they represent.

Tonal structure per se can of course be an aspect of formal rhetoric, but it is not the one most typically constitutive of character in this repertory. The vast majority of arias begin with an opening paragraph that moves from tonic to dominant (whose cadence is more or less strongly articulated) and return to the tonic without much intervening modulation, remaining there (with the occasional brief excursion to the minor or the flat side) until the end. The universality of the basic tonal structure on the one hand, and the infinite diversity with which it is treated on the other make dramatically meaningful classifications of aria forms essentially impossible. That is not, of course, to deny that in any given case a composer might not manipulate a tonal structure or tonal expectations for dramatic ends, as Piccinni does in Leandro's aria described above; it is merely to say that beyond the general expectations that there will be a move to the dominant and that the piece will spend the vast majority of its second half (or last section) in the tonic, dramatically meaningful manipulations of tonal structures usually depend more on the particularities of the relations between text and music than on the conventional associations of particular tonal habits.

ARIAS AND INDIVIDUALITY: PERFORMANCE AND SUBJECTIVITY IN ARIA-ENDINGS

In this book as a whole I am less concerned with the ways particular characters emerge as plausible or unique individuals than with the ideological significance of the categories into which most characters more or less unproblematically fall. However, before moving to a discussion of socially salient types, I want to address from a different perspective—namely, the ways arias end—the nature of individuality as constructed by the arias in this repertory. If the *dramatic* function of an aria is to place the character in the action, and to elaborate on his or her essence, the *theatrical* function of this sort of number is to exact a response from onstage interlocu-

[17] Rabin, "Figaro as Misogynist," *passim,* but esp. pp. 236–37.

tors, from the auditorium audience, or both. The process of ending an aria brings both these functions into relief; their relations to each other, however, vary considerably and profoundly affect the meanings of these solo utterances. Opera buffa arias often expend considerable time on ending materials, with much repetition and significant amounts of raw time given to the announcement and enactment of the end. Arias for basso buffo are particularly clear in this regard; among Mozart's arias of this type one might mention Figaro's obsessive repetition of "già ognuno lo sa" in "Aprite un po' quegli occhi," or Guglielmo's fivefold cadence using the words "un gran perchè" in "Donne mie la fate a tanti." Indeed, in this latter aria the cadential motive first set to the words "li comincio a compatir" is one of the crucial building blocks of the piece; one could argue that in some sense this whole piece is "about" cadence. Wye Allanbrook has pointed out that arias with little or no structurally significant thematic return often employ an emphatic and repetitive ending strategy in lieu of more literally symmetrical musical rhymes.[18] In other words the very blurring of boundaries and fluidity of material that can give the impression of spontaneous thought or thoughtless confusion can also create a formal need for emphatic and indubitable closure. This is clearly true of "Aprite un po'." It is also true of "Donne mie," despite the many occurrences of the transitional "ma la fate a tanti . . . " and the cadential refrain. The rondo-like form of this aria begins to seem endlessly extensible once the whole text has been exposed and the *minore* episode has been grounded with an emphatic (major mode) cadence of its own (mm. 108–14). The aria therefore needs its multiple cadences to validate and emphasize the end. Buffa arias are not alone in their "quantitative" emphasis on ending, however. In seria arias with coloratura passages, the coloratura in the recapitulation is often longer than it is in the exposition and is often followed by a series of repeated cadential phrases, either absent or presented in short form in the exposition.

In both these cases the sheer quantity of ending material is often prepared by, or emphasized with, a "performative climax," either an ecstasy of patter in the buffa aria, or a passage of coloratura display in the seria aria. Here the performer takes precedence over the character: coloratura or melisma in seria arias focusing attention on the quality and agility of the voice, and the patter passages in buffa arias focusing attention on the performance, testing the performer's ability to spit the syllables out with speed and accuracy. Even here, however, the eruption of patter and the emergence of coloratura are prompted either by a specific occasion, or by the character's need to demonstrate the eloquence, pretension, confusion, or vituperation of his or her type.[19] I would rarely be tempted by this reper-

---

[18] Wye J. Allanbrook, "When the Fat Lady Sings," unpublished typescript, pp. 10–11.

[19] It is curious that comic characters demonstrate rhetorical failure by uttering many words, and seria characters demonstrate eloquence by getting stuck on a single syllable.

tory to argue that the character is (totally) obliterated in the primal sonic experience of the voice, as Carolyn Abbate does about Mozart's Queen of the Night,[20] even though the act of performance in both these cases surely competes with the dramatic illusion, and the individuality of the character fades into both the conventions of the aria type and the expectations associated with the *vocal* type of the basso buffo or the coloratura soprano. Thus while performative climaxes may—and did[21]—emphasize the individuality of the *singer*, thus reinforcing at least the vocal distinctness of a given character, they de-emphasize that *character's* psychological plausibility.

In some arias whose endings are not characterized by performative exuberance, the end is nevertheless given significant weight by a developmental or "progressive" form. Formal fluidity tends to focus attention on the "forward motion" or linear progress of an aria; and when the musical processes of change and development can be correlated with a character's progress through a text, the end of an aria can be seen as representing a new state of consciousness pointing, as it were, forward to the rest of the drama rather than backward to the earlier stages of the aria. Characters shown in the process of changing or making up their minds often give the impression of an inner life, or a psyche, in ways unavailable to characters who do not so "expose" themselves;[22] thus the end-orientation of formal "progressivity" often seems to stand for or embody the psychological movement of a self-determined, plausible human character. Giannetta's through-composed cavatina[23] "Deh se ti guida onore," a substitution by Salieri in Anfossi's setting of *L'incognita perseguitata*,[24] is a simple example of this. The aria is reproduced in full in Example 4-3 (text on p. 108).

At this point in the opera, the apparently low-born heroine Giannetta has decided that it creates too much social disturbance and misery for her to continue her amorous attachment to the nobleman Asdrubale and pleads with him to abandon her. The four lines of the text alternate be-

[20] Carolyn Abbate, *Unsung Voices: Opera and Musical Narrative in the Nineteenth Century* (Princeton: Princeton University Press, 1991) pp. 10–11.

[21] See below, Examples 8-2 and 8-3 for Luigi Tarchi's virtuosic writing for Adriana Ferrarese, which shows remarkable similarities to Mozart's. See Gidwitz, "Mozart's first Fiordiligi," *COJ* 8 (1996): 199–214, on the particular qualities of Ferrarese's voice and the way composers adapted themselves to it. See also Rice, "Rondò vocali."

[22] The psychological aspect of Webster's analysis of "Porgi amor" in Webster, "Analysis" grows out of his analysis of the "progressivity" of the form. See also Jessica Waldoff's analysis of Haydn's music for Rosina (in *La vera costanza*) in "Sentiment and Sensibility in *La vera costanza*," in Dean Sutcliffe, ed., *Haydn Studies* (Oxford: Oxford University Press, forthcoming).

[23] So designated in the Library of Congress manuscript (Mus. 1919, Item 7), evidently of Italian origin.

[24] The Vienna 1773 libretto includes this text, and in the Austrian National Library manuscript, Mus. Hs. 17946, this aria is headed "Del Sigr. Salieri." I have not seen the original libretto for this opera, but the Milan 1773 version has in this place a more galant and playful text: "Ah Contino, mio carino / Vieni pur, non dubitar," etc.

4-3: Salieri, insertion aria in Anfossi, *L'incognita perseguitata*, I,11
Giannetta, "Deh, se ti guida onore" [entire]

4-3: *(Continued)*

tween admonishments to him ("do the right thing," "it isn't the end of the world") and indications of her own feelings ("leave me alone," "don't forget me.") The text as a whole moves from an appeal to morality to an unabashed appeal to sentiment; one could read this as a move from taking a brave stance to expressing the truth of her dependence on Asdrubale. From her point of view, perhaps, it could be represented as a decision not to pretend indifference. In any case, despite not embodying a particularly admirable self-presentation by late-twentieth-century standards of female self-sufficiency, this text nevertheless represents psychological movement propelled by the inner life of the singer.

Deh, se ti guida onore,	Ah, if honour guides you,
Lasciami in pace, o Dio,	Leave me in peace, for God's sake;
Consola il tuo dolore,	Console yourself,
Ricordati di me.	And remember me.

Salieri's music is decidedly end-weighted. The second couplet occupies twelve measures with two more for an orchestral cadence, in contrast to the eight measures of the opening couplet. More importantly, the second half begins with a cadential phrase (mm. 9–13), and the piece's principal formal task thereafter is to complete the cadence not quite achieved in measure 13. Unlike the text, however, whose last line immediately represents the real truth of the matter, the music de-emphasizes "ricordati di me" in mm. 12–13, as it simply completes the melody in a not very striking vocal register and with utterly unremarkable material. The setting of "consola il tuo dolore" to the most memorable (and most repeated) motive in the aria suggests that, unlike the text alone, the aria as a whole is really about Giannetta's generosity to Asdrubale. However, on the second cadential diversion (m. 18)—all the more prominent precisely because it is the *second* failure to finish—the cadential E is shoved up an octave, on the word "me" no less, and Giannetta gets to repeat "ricordati di me" a third time. Salieri's setting suggests more tension between self-sacrifice and self-interest than does the text alone, and Giannetta's sudden decision to point out that separation would cost her something is comparably more dramatic when sung than when simply read. The power of this moment of decision comes precisely from its function as an ending, and from the weight it bears as the final (and successful) attempt to complete a process begun more than half the aria earlier. The strength of this ending is validated immediately after the aria, when Giannetta agrees to entertain Asdrubale's suit.

The idea of emotional or psychological progress through an aria is, of course, standard in discussions of Mozart's Da Ponte operas, and the extent to which Mozart embodies psychologically plausible and dramatically pertinent progress in the musical processes of his arias is taken to be a measure of his greatness as a dramatist. James Webster's detailed analyses of the

Countess's "Porgi amor" and Susanna's "Deh vieni non tardar" demonstrate both the coherence and the continuous movement of these arias; the psychological distance of the ends of both arias from their beginnings is one of the principal results of Webster's analyses.[25] As he says, "The chief structural feature . . . is that of developing towards a culmination or changed state of being . . . such end-orientation is not restricted to *Figaro* or to a few privileged arias; it is a fundamental principle of organization in late Mozart."[26] "Porgi amor," and "Deh vieni non tardar," along with other short sentimental statements in the Da Ponte operas, are extraordinary in the repertory in the extent of their thematic development in the context of single-tempo key-area forms, but the principles of fluidity, change, and resultant end-orientation so movingly and effectively deployed by Mozart are basic to the larger repertory of opera buffa arias.

There are thus two ending-paradigms in opera buffa arias, one related to the notion of aria as performance, the other related to the notion of aria as speech, or thought. They seem to have contradictory, or at least partially contradictory effects. Some arias, in their formal fluidity and blurring of boundaries, and in the manifest distance of the end from the beginning, give the impression of being "motivated" by the text and character, of being moments of self-determination, or plausible individuality, in an otherwise rather predictable or static dramatic structure. Other arias, however, in their finalizing emphasis on performance, also explicitly remind us of the artificiality of that illusion, of the conventions of performance, and of the fragility of the notion of plausible character in a medium that emphasized performance in as many ways as did opera buffa. Probably the majority of arias, however, end in ways that are neither fully "psychological" and individualizing, nor fully performative and typological but rather balance elements of these poles in a variety of ways. Aria endings in this repertory all juxtapose a dramatic context against a theatrical one, a character against a singer, and an individual against a type. Those juxtapositions, which raise questions of realism vs. artifice, sympathy vs. critical distance, education vs. pleasure, and self-determination vs. conformity, can, like so many aspects of opera buffa, have wide-ranging social implications at the same time as they divert and entertain.

[25] Webster, "Analysis," pp. 151–69 and 181–83. However, see his warning in "Understanding Opera Buffa: Analysis = Interpretation," in Hunter and Webster, *Opera Buffa in Mozart's Vienna*, pp. 370–74, that analysis does not necessarily reveal value.
[26] Ibid., p. 196.

Chapter Five

CLASS AND GENDER IN ARIAS:
FIVE ARIA TYPES

ALTHOUGH this chapter covers the social and dramatic range of arias in this repertory, from the most comic to the most sentimental, from the lowest to the highest, it does justice neither to the incredible variety of arias nor to the virtuosity with which stereotypes and conventions are combined and reconfigured. Rather, it attempts, in examining the most characteristic sorts of utterances for the most conventional sorts of characters, to give a sense of the framework within which authors, singers, and audiences could have worked. This framework is dramatic, in the sense that certain characters tend to function in particular ways in the narrative of the opera; social, in the sense that certain character types tend to embody (whether negatively or positively or ambiguously) some of the ideologies projected by these operas; and, of course, musical and textual, in the sense that it is in the concrete workings-out of vocabularies, themes, and structures that characters most clearly reveal what they are about.

THE BUFFA ARIA

This aria type—the frantic comic piece for the *primo buffo* singer—is perhaps the paradigmatic aria type for the whole genre of opera buffa. It is most often sung by the one voice type never used in opera seria—the bass[1]—and it emphasizes the genre's preference for stage gesture and action over sheer vocal skills.[2] It clearly demonstrates the formal fluidity of opera buffa arias and is often a moment of hilarity resulting from the character's confusion or ineptitude. As an aria type sung exclusively by men, usually from the middle ranks of society, it also forms part of the genre's ideology about non-noble masculinity.[3] Arias of this type are almost with-

---

[1] Occasionally buffa arias are sung by tenors, as the Contino Belfiore's self-introductory piece "Dal scirocco al tramontano" in *La finta giardiniera,* or Prince Ali's spectacular "Ecco un splendido banchetto" in Friberth and Haydn's *L'incontro improvviso.*

[2] Platoff, "The Buffa Aria in Mozart's Vienna," *COJ* 2 (1990) p. 101, describes this aria type as "afford[ing] a talented singer and actor an extended opportunity for comic expression."

[3] The obvious exception to this is the fairly significant representation of parvenu noblemen who demonstrate the flimsiness of their claims to nobility in part by singing buffa arias; there are also instances where circumstances compel a genuinely noble character to engage in buffa shenanigans (Prince Ali's "Ecco un splendido banchetto," in Frieberth and Haydn's

out exception "about" pretension in some way or other; the paradigmatic singer of the buffa aria is a man of bourgeois or barely noble origins exercising inappropriate power, unearned authority, or demonstrating a certainty later shown to be misplaced. (Figaro's "Aprite un po'," the most famous example of this aria type in Mozart's Da Ponte settings, falls into this last category, though Figaro also exercises a sort of false authority as an expert on women.) Almost all such arias allude to something higher, in their text content, lexicon, address, or musical *topoi*: even the $\frac{4}{4}$ meter with the characteristic dotted-quarter, eighth pattern with which the vast majority of these arias begin ("Aprite un po'" exemplifies this) can be heard as a gloss on a more elevated style, whether the march or the seria aria.[4] Although these numbers are almost never focused enough on a specific seria device to count as full parodies, the pervasive aura of some never-quite-achieved—and thus by implication never-achievable—higher idiom emphasizes the character's ambitions. At the same time, his inevitable collapse into sputtering inanity ensures that those ambitions come across as unrealizable. Excess and inarticulateness are the other implicit topics of buffa arias; excess suggesting that boundaries (including but not limited to those of social place) have been violated, and inarticulateness often emphasizing the character's inability to maintain even the boundaries of acceptable speech. Of all the aria types in this repertory, the buffa aria is one of the two that prescribe a clear response. (The sentimental lament is the other.)

Petronio's "A voi darla in matrimonio" from Bertati and Paisiello's *I filosofi immaginari* exemplifies a number of the most important characteristics of this sort of aria. Example 5-1 gives it in its entirety. In the opera as a whole, the old "philosopher" Petronio refuses to let his daughter Clarice marry her beloved Giuliano; the match is eventually achieved by means of Giuliano disguising himself as the ancient and world-famous philosopher Argatifontidas, who takes a fancy to Clarice—a match that Petronio fully approves, as it appears to bring him closer to fame. "A voi darla," however, occurs in the first act (scene 3) before Giuliano has become Argatifontidas; it explains Petronio's reasons for his refusal:

A voi darla in matrimonio	I could not in all conscience
Per coscienza io non potrei,	Give her to you in marriage;

L'incontro improvviso is a case in point; it is also one of the few buffa arias that is not about pretension); and there is the occasional instance where a noble character—though never a *parte seria*—engages in a buffa aria for no very clear reason. For example, the marchese's alternative arias in *I finti eredi* (II,10): "Nel mirar la bella dama" (by Marcello da Capua, in KT 160), and "Staremo allegramente," (in the Austrian National Library manuscript Mus. Hs. 17848) both count as buffa pieces.

[4] Allanbrook, *Rhythmic Gesture in Mozart* (Chicago: University of Chicago Press, 1983) p. 169, notes that "Aprite un po'" begins as an "exalted march"; she also suggests (pp. 168–70) that the "high style" of Figaro's whole *scena* has already been "debased" by Basilio (in "In quegl'anni") as well as by the Count (in "Vedrò mentr'io sospiro").

Ignoranti, voi, e lei,	Both of you ignoramuses;
Bella unione in verità.	What a match that would be.
Nascerian degli ignoranti;	You would produce ignoramuses . . .
Ma pazienza, andiamo avanti.	But never mind, let's continue.
Tornan questi a maritarsi,	These in turn get married,
E vedere a procrearsi	And are sure to produce
D'ignoranti bambinelli	Enormous numbers
Una grande quantità.	Of ignorant babies.
(ridendolo in faccia)	*(laughing in [Giuliano's] face)*
Cosa nasce? che nel giro	What is the result? that
Di tre secoli in sostanza:	In essence, in three hundred years
Tutto il mondo già rimiro	I see the whole world
Pieno solo d'ignoranza,	Full of nothing but ignorance,
E la colpa saria mia	And such dreadful lack of civilization
Per si ria bestialità.	Would all be my fault.

The sixteen-line text, divided into a quatrain and two six-line units, with rhyming *tronco* lines at the end of each unit and irregularly distributed rhymes in the bodies of the verses, is a typical, if relatively modest example of the species; unlike some such texts it does not change to a shorter line-length toward the end, though Paisiello "compensates" for this by speeding up the declamation, in measures 34–36, 71–75, 95–98, and finally in the climactic eleven measures of almost uninterrupted sixteenth-notes (mm. 108–18), complete with characteristic *basso buffo* octave leaps. This aria demonstrates Petronio's pretension in several ways. As with most such figures, his plans for his daughter's marriage have much more to do with his own worldly ambitions than with her desires. In addition, his notion that in a mere three centuries the entire population of the world would result from his permission to let Clarice and Giuliano marry is characteristically lacking in a sense of proportion. The opening melody of the aria reflects the bombast of his central conceit, in its sturdy dotted rhythms, triadic outline, and the emphasis on the main beats in the first violin and bass. (One might hear the second violins' accompaniment as undercutting this pomp.) The strong cadences at measures 16–20, 37–39, 76–78, and 125–133 also emphasize Petronio's over-grand sense of himself and the extent of his authority.

The grandeur of his conception of himself as responsible for the state of the world in three hundred years is put in its place by his obsession with procreation. In line 6 ("Ma pazienza . . . ") he tries to focus on the large social consequences of the results of Clarice's and Giuliano's marriage but finds himself inevitably back at procreation, as he imagines their descendants producing more offspring. At this point he gives in to his obsession, which Paisiello emphasizes by repeating "bambinelli" in measures 35–37, 73–76, and 111–13. Petronio's incapacity to control his obsession is a ver-

5-1: Paisiello, *I filosofi immaginari*, I,3
Petronio, "A voi darla in matrimonio" [entire]

5-1: *(Continued)*

5-1: *(Continued)*

5-1: *(Continued)*

5-1: *(Continued)*

5-1: *(Continued)*

5-1: *(Continued)*

5-1: *(Continued)*

5-1: *(Continued)*

5-1: *(Continued)*

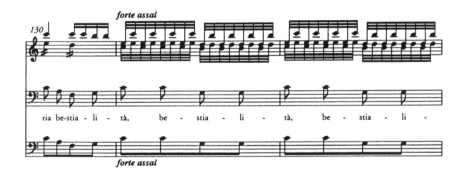

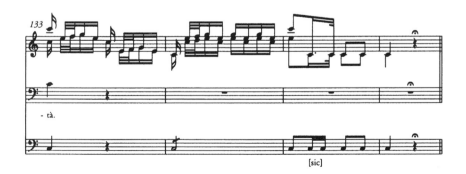

sion of the rhetorical "degeneration" crucial to this aria type.[5] As buffa arias go, this is not a particularly extreme example of rhetorical incapacity, but it does illustrate the general point quite well, especially since, as a philosopher, Petronio prides himself on his learning. Paisiello's setting of this text further emphasizes Petronio's lack of eloquence by fragmenting and recombining sections of text; the practice of emphasizing rhetorical incompetence with incongruous juxtapositions of phrases is another of the hallmarks of this aria type. Thus, in measures 78–82, he starts the whole text ("A voi darla . . .), but after his initial refusal to give Clarice away, skips immediately to the far future implications of the marriage ("Cosa nasce?").

Paisiello's setting of "A voi darla in matrimonio" is not in the multiple-tempo through-composed form perhaps most characteristic of the buffa aria,[6] but its formal rhetoric is exemplary with respect to this aria type. The most important rhetorical element here is the underarticulation of tonal and thematic boundaries, resulting in a sense of formal fluidity—even of incoherence or a lack of direction.[7] The text is set through essentially three times, but text units tend not to be very clearly identified with musical motives, so that the return of previously heard text is not heard as a significant structural juncture. Similarly, although certain thematic figures recur, the recurrences are not always coordinated with significant tonal events. The single most important recurring figure is the accompanimental motive found first in mm. 8–10, and then repeated (with variations) in 23–25, 42–44, 53–54, 64–69, 76–77, 79–81, and so on.[8] The most significant repeated material in the vocal line is the sequential scalar figure first found in measures 44–52 in the first section after the close of the exposition, and then repeated in mm. 119–27, as a sort of thematic anchor before the end. Despite the strong cadence in the dominant (m. 39) preceded by the predictable crescendo of patter, and even a recitative-like little retransition back to the tonic (mm. 39–41), that tonal return is marked neither by the presence of the original thematic material nor by a return to the opening words. The aria is not exactly through-composed, in the sense of not

[5] Rabin, "Figaro as Misogynist," in Hunter and Webster, *Opera Buffa in Mozart's Vienna* (Cambridge: Cambridge University Press, 1997) p. 246.

[6] See Platoff, "The Buffa Aria in Mozart's Vienna," pp. 117–19, on the characteristic formal flexibility and variety of these arias. The musical forms of buffa arias are extremely varied, ranging from sonata-like forms with triple return, to multiple-tempo through-composed forms, to a wide variety of structures based on a key-area tonal plan. There is no indisputably "buffa" aria form; however, it is worth pointing out that more than three-quarters of the multiple-tempo (= more than two-tempo) through-composed arias in this repertory are sung by men, and most of these are buffa arias. There are no rondòs, no simple ternary forms, and no "compressed da capo" forms among buffa arias.

[7] Platoff, "The Buffa Aria in Mozart's Vienna," p. 107; Rabin, "Figaro as Misogynist," p. 246.

[8] This use of an accompanimental motive to "hold a piece together" in the face of either thematically rather indefinite vocal lines (as Petronio's patter) or constant mutation of thematic material, is a basic technique of opera buffa writing particularly important in ensembles.

repeating material on a long-range basis; at the same time, unless one calls it a "loose rondo," it fits into no clear or well-established set of formal expectations. As John Platoff notes about buffa arias in general, this one is end-weighted, with more emphasis on the closing than the opening material. The repeated attempts to close on the one hand demonstrate both incoherence and excess, but on the other, can be read as compensating for the absence of a formal or well-articulated "grounding" of second-group material in the tonic.

Buffa arias also typically demonstrate a "mismatch" between form and content: they either exhibit remarkable poverty of invention over stretches of musical time, or they juxtapose contrasting ideas in places and ways that do not assist the communication of tonal or textual structures. Paisiello's setting, particularly in the exposition, uses the latter technique. The first group, for example, consists of five different motives, each with its own accompanimental figure (mm. 1–4, 5–10, 10–12, 12–16, 16–20). Thus, although there is a strong cadence in the tonic in measure 20, and new material moving to the dominant in measures 21–22, the fact that "new" material is no novelty de-emphasizes the formal importance of this move. In addition, the transition to the dominant (mm. 22–28) is characterized by thematic incoherence. This technique allows for—even encourages—an apparently disorganized variety of gesture quite in keeping with the comic actor's art, and it emphasizes the incoherence of the speaker.

In addition to demonstrating pretension and a certain sort of inarticulateness, "A voi darla in matrimonio" also manifests the *primo buffo's* characteristic overinvolvement with the content of his speech and the consequent misjudging of his interlocutor(s). Petronio's obsessive repetition of "bambinelli" is one example of this (and it is easy to imagine that it is not the babies but the way they come into being that is the focus of his real concern), but his extension of the idea of procreation into the next several centuries is typical of the way the singers of buffa arias project either their situations or their metaphors into absurdity. The Marchese's re-enactment of the cat and mouse chase in *Il curioso indiscreto* (quoted in Chapter 1) also exemplifies a characteristic literalization of a metaphor, as well as adding to the comedy by boasting of his hunting prowess to the man who has already caught the prey originally destined for the Marchese.

Another way in which the singers of buffa arias demonstrate their overinvolvement with their subject matter is in their construction of lists, or catalogues. Favorite subjects for listing include countries visited or conquered, family trees, weapons owned and used, foods eaten, and other pleasures enjoyed. These catalogues provide many opportunities for lively and comically unselfconscious re-enactment; they are also often "too long" both for their topic and for their context. As in Leporello's "Catalogue" aria in *Don Giovanni,* the actual list is typically only a part of the text; it may be in a shorter meter than what precedes it, and it is typically sung in patter fashion. Such a list often takes over the aria, and obliterates its raison d'être, often stunning (or boring) its onstage listeners, and demonstrating yet again the inability of the buffa aria singer to judge his audience.

An important occasion for the buffa aria which may include all of the postures and gestures noted above is the antifemale diatribe. Figaro's "Aprite un po'" is the locus classicus of this sort of utterance; Guglielmo's "Donne mie" also exemplifies it, if more genially.[9] The normal conceit of such arias is that women hide a series of horrors or evils under a deceptive veil of sweetness and delight. Figaro's description of "thorny roses, charming wolves, benign she-bears, malign doves," is exactly of this sort. The jealous Leandro's diatribe in Petrosellini and Paisiello's *Le due contesse* (II,13) makes the same point more prosaically:

Son le donne quasi tutte	Almost all women are
Capricciose lusinghiere,	Deceitful and capricious,
Seduttrici menzognere,	Lying seductresses,
Piene sol di falsità.	They're nothing but false.
E noi siamo poverini,	And we, poor things,
Quasi tutti di buon core;	Are almost all well-meaning;
Siam sinceri nell'amore,	We are sincere in love,
Siam l'istessa fedeltà.	We are fidelity itself.
So ben io se dico il vero,	I know I'm speaking the truth,
La contessa ancor lo sa.	And the Countess knows it too.
Ah Tiranna, mi dispero	Ah, tyrant, I despair
A si nera crudeltà.	At such horrible cruelty.
Donne, donne dispietate,	Ladies, cruel ladies,
Quant'è pazzo chi vi crede	Whoever believes you is crazy;
Sempre sempre siete state	You have always been
Il tormento d'ogni età.	The torment of every age.

Here the first four lines are set to a couple of patter motives, and while the self-justifying lines in the middle are set to more ingratiating melodic material, the patter motives dominate the aria, the predominant tone is vituperation, and the usual buffa topic of rhetorical lack of control pertains here as elsewhere.

By the eighteenth century it had long been a staple of comic theory that comedy corrected by ridicule.[10] The buffa aria, with its overdetermined

[9] Brown, "Beaumarchais, Paisiello and the Genesis of *Così fan tutte*," in Sadie, *Wolfgang Amadè Mozart* (Oxford: Clarendon Press, 1996) p. 324, remarks that this aria type goes back to canto 20 of Ariosto's *Orlando Furioso*.

[10] Goldoni, for example, took as one of his prime directives that the purpose of comedy was to correct vice and to put bad habits up to ridicule. In his remarks about *Pamela nubile* in his memoirs, for example, he writes: "Comedy, which is, or ought to be, a school for propriety, should only expose human weaknesses for the sake of correcting them"; Goldoni, *Memoirs of Carlo Goldoni, Written by Himself*, trans. John Black., edited with a preface by William A. Drake (1926; rpt. Westport: Greenwood, 1976) p. 255.

combination of pretension, ineloquence, and excess, is a prime example of this. The actual social significance attached to making fun of pretension and excess would, however, surely have varied from location to location. In Vienna, where certain sorts of bourgeois ambition were encouraged, at least by the court and its circle, it is hard to believe that these arias served as a serious lesson to the good burgers of the city. On the other hand, both Pezzl and Riesbeck mention with disapproval the extravagant display of certain members of the first aristocracy, particularly when the display was not matched or earned by industry and prudence;[11] and Pezzl, in some ways uncharacteristically, but also tellingly, criticizes the way liveried lackeys would dress up like fashionable cavaliers, frequent places not accessible to liveried servants, and attract the attentions of nice bourgeois girls.[12] Thus, if the buffa aria served a function beyond the delivery of comic pleasure, it was perhaps more a socially generalized criticism of groundless pretension than an attempt to contain a particular class of man. In other words, this may have been an instance where the pleasure clearly provided by *buffo* singers like Benucci encouraged the audience to understand the socially rather pointed message of many buffa arias in broadly moral or comic terms.

THE *SERVA/CONTADINA* ARIA

There is no direct female equivalent to the buffa aria, perhaps partly because there is no direct female equivalent to the buffoon who is the paradigmatic (though by no means the only) singer of the buffa aria. Nevertheless, female characters of the peasant or serving classes—especially those of secondary importance in the plot—have a recognizable aria type quite distinct from the buffa aria. The *serva/contadina* aria is by no means the only sort of aria sung by lower-ranked women, any more than the buffa aria is the only sort of aria sung by buffoons; nor is it the almost compulsory item for its character type that buffa arias are. However, this female aria type both articulates a dramatic location for, and raises some social issues about certain sorts of lower-ranked women. Unlike the buffa aria, which makes its social or moral point by means of unmistakable ridicule, the *serva/contadina* aria has a more ambiguous tone.

---

[11] Pezzl, *Skizze von Wien,* trans. in Landon, *Mozart and Vienna* (London: Thames and Hudson, 1991) pp. 168–69. Johann Kaspar Riesbeck, *Briefe eines reisenden Franzosen,* ed. Jochen Golz (Berlin: Rütten & Loening, [1976]) pp. 148–49, on the difference between the ways the Emperor and Prince Lichtenstein appeared in public.

[12] Pezzl, *Skizze von Wien,* trans. Landon, p. 169. Landon condensed the following passage: "So übermütig diese müssige Bengel in den Häusern und Vorzimmern sich gebärden, wo sie anzumelden haben, so verachtet sind sie doch im bürgerlichen Leben." [These idle rascals bear themselves so insolently in the houses and anterooms where they are required, that they are despised in bourgeois life.] See Pezzl, *Skizze von Wien: Ein Kultur- und Sittenbild aus der josefinischen Zeit,* ed. Gustav Gugitz and Anton Schlossar (Graz: Leykam, 1923) p. 205.

The main defining attributes of this aria type are its association with peasant or serving-class characters, its attitude, and its focus on men (pro and con). While the characteristic attitude of the singer of the male buffa aria is overinvolvement with what he says, often coupled with a comic misjudging of, and a sort of oblivion about, his stage audience, the characteristic stance of the singer of the *serva/contadina* aria is insouciance, coupled with both an acute awareness and an astute summing-up of her audience (often with the intention of teasing, deceiving, or manipulating them). Pretension is not unknown among lower-ranked female characters but is not as characteristic a posture of even the most ambitious serving or peasant girl as it is of the *primo buffo,* and there is often a sort of self-consciousness about it—a consciousness of "to-be-looked-at" status[13]—quite absent from most buffa arias. Part of the characteristic consciousness of the audience in *serva/contadina* arias is that they tend to rely much more heavily on the explicit identification of female characteristics *as female* than buffa arias do on the identification of male characteristics *as male.* The singers of these arias often take it upon themselves to explain the nature of womanhood to audiences both on and off stage, especially in arias complaining about men; the burden of such pieces is usually that men shouldn't be so cruel to women because women are, after all, entirely agreeable. Whereas men spend most of their misogynist diatribes listing female faults, women spend most of their anti-male statements defending themselves rather than attacking men. Serving-class femininity, then, is presented as an "other" to masculinity; it is an "otherness" of which its possessors are fully conscious, and which they are delighted to manipulate in their own interests, which almost without exception have to do with men, as sources of comfort, providers of goods, or thorns in the side.

Most of the characters who sing *serva/contadina* arias in this repertory end up marrying—usually not the man they have long sighed after, but someone of appropriate status who has either loved them all along but been rebuffed, or who has failed to get the heroine. (Despina is an exception in this respect.) Most serving girls and peasants desire the condition of marriage as much as, if not more than, a particular man; indeed, part of the characteristic insouciance of their paradigmatic aria type seems to come from the sense that men are all pretty much the same, that women as sweet pliable things should be desirable to almost any male of the species, and that if women are to offer their sweet pliability to men, those men should be prepared to pay—often, but not always, in material goods. The self-denial and passivity of the sentimental heroine are not for these characters—at least not when they sing these arias. The servant Serpina in *Il curioso indiscreto,* for example, is quite clear about what she wants:

[13] Laura Mulvey coined this phrase in "Visual Pleasure and Narrative Cinema," which first appeared in *Screen* 16 (1975): 9–16, but which has been widely reprinted since.

Eh ci vuol altro	It takes more,
Padron mio caro	My dear master,
Che motti e chiacchiere	Than pleasantries and chatter,
Parole, e inchini:	Words and bows:
Ci von regali,	It takes gifts,
Ci von zecchini	It takes money
Per farci subito	To make us
Innamorar.	Fall in love right away.
Una mantiglia	A mantilla
Di raso vero:	Of real satin;
Di drappo un'abito	A suit of cloth—
Da forastiero:	But foreign (of course):
Bella una scuffia	A beautiful hat
All'Ollandese.	In the Dutch manner.
O fatto a pizzo,	Or made of lace,
O alla francese.	Or in the French style.
Con fiori e penne	With flowers and feathers
In quantità.	In large amounts.
Voi già capite,	You understand already,
Voi m'intendete:	You hear me;
Oro, ed argento	Gold and silver
Solo ci vuole.	Are all that's required.
Che di gran ciarle,	Because today a lady
E vezzi e parole,	Has had enough of
Oggi la Donna	Chatter and charm
Più ne sa far.	And speechifying.

The maid Livietta's second aria in *Fra i due litiganti* illustrates a number of these characteristics and serves as our primary example of the *serva/contadina* aria. Example 5-2 gives it in its entirety. At this point in the plot, Livietta (who is wildly envious of the maid Dorina's many suitors) has overheard the land-agent Masotto's plan to marry Dorina despite the wishes of the Count and Countess. She uses this dangerous knowledge to persuade Masotto to find her a mate (preferably Titta):

Sono una fanciullina	I am a girl
Si docile e buonina,	So sweet and complaisant;
Che di me più giovevole	There is no-one in the world
Nel mondo non si dà.	More pleasant than I.
La convenienza poi	And *politesse* dictates
Vuol che egualmente facciasi;	That things be done equally;
Che ottengasi di voi	That what is gotten for you
Quelche da me si fà.	Is also gotten for me.
Ah se un sposo voi me date,	Ah, if you find me a husband,
E se avete ciò che amate,	And if you have what you love,
Che duetti giocosetti,	What cheerful duets and
Che balletti vedo già.	Dances I can already imagine.

5-2: Sarti, *Fra i due litiganti il terzo gode,* II,4
Livietta, "Sono una fanciullina" [entire]

5-2: *(Continued)*

5-2: *(Continued)*

5-2: *(Continued)*

5-2: *(Continued)*

5-2: *(Continued)*

Like many such arias, Livietta's begins with a description of her sweetness, a strategy no doubt intended to lend her credibility as she begins to manipulate her interlocutor. Her use of diminutives (*fanciullina, buonina, giocosetti*) to describe herself and her activities is one of the most characteristic lexical aspects of these arias, going along with the diminutive names of their singers. Livietta is, like Serpina quoted above, out to get something (though not material goods) and is comparably shameless—at least by the standards of well-bred womanhood—in asking for what she wants.

Perhaps partly because the singers of *serva/contadina* arias often want something from their interlocutors, they tend to gauge them quite acutely; certainly more so than the typical *primo buffo* character. And because their arias have purposes that require manipulating the desires or affections or fears of their various interlocutors, their rhetorical strategies as manifested in the forms of their arias tend to be more various than those of their male counterparts. There is, for example, no musical form that could be considered characteristic of the *serva/contadina* aria in the way that the multi-tempo through-composed aria could be considered characteristic of the buffa aria. However, just as formal under-articulation and various sorts of prolixity are characteristic of the paradigmatic utterance of the *primo buffo,* regardless of its overall form, so the opposites of these features—ultra-clear formal articulation and compactness—are the characteristic formal-rhetorical features of *serva/contadina* arias. These arias are typically more "coherent" than buffa arias in the sense that they tend not to leap from one expressive topic to another within the space of a period, and they have a slightly greater tendency to repeat material both more literally and in a way that reinforces other aspects of musical structure. They project a formal clarity that gives the impression, if not of high-flown eloquence, then at least of rhetorical competence and an ability to frame and contain an utterance.[14]

This "impression of coherence" is certainly projected by the text of Livietta's "Sono una fanciullina." It is in a compact three-quatrain form (two of *settenari,* one of *ottonari*) with rhyming *tronco* lines at the end of each stanza, and its use of rhyming couplets at crucial junctures (the beginning, and lines 9–10, where she cuts to the chase and specifies her request), give a prominent impression of orderliness. These structural regularities in the text actually contain striking irregularities in accentual patterns, but to the extent that these are disguised by the music, the relevant structural quality

---

[14] Despina's "Una donna a quindici anni" belongs exactly to this formal-expressive type. Although the form of this aria exactly fits no well-established model, the topical coherence of the periods, the repetition of the same order of events in the second part of the faster section (mm. 51–74) as in the first part (mm. 21–51), and Mozart's retention of essentially the same melody for the same words lends the aria as a whole a clarity and coherence very much part of the typological tradition I have just described.

of the text-as-sung is its impression of predictability and regularity. The music of Livietta's aria is, like so many of these pieces, in $\frac{2}{4}$ meter (the other favorite meter for such pieces is $\frac{3}{8}$), and in G major, which is, again, a common key for this aria type (F major is the other favorite key). Formally, it is a textbook rondò (though it is not at all a textbook example of the normal dramatic associations of the form, and as such is testimony to the flexibility with which opera buffa composers often treated the relation between form and drama). It begins with a coherent first group (mm. 15–28) unified by the repetition of the melodic pattern of the opening measure, a slightly contrasting second group (mm. 31–38) introduced by an orchestral modulation to the dominant, an opportunity for a cadenza before the return of the first group (m. 38), and a literal repetition of that first group. The faster tonal return section involves an opening period (mm. 57–64), a little cadential extension built on that period's closing motive (mm. 65–68), and a cadential phrase in two parts, the first a coloratura triplet passage quite typical of this sort of aria, and the second a conventional closing motive. This whole section is then repeated without alteration, and a short ritornello closes the aria. The vocal line of this aria is characterized by unbroken use of two- and occasionally four-measure phrases, with one elision (m. 68), repeated at m. 84. (The orchestral music is both motivically more disjunct and phraseologically somewhat less regular). The vocal range of the aria is a mere octave (g' to g''), and with one small exception the accompaniment takes a back seat to, and doubles, the voice.[15] The exception is mm. 64ff., where the declamatory vocal line turns out to be the end of the instrumental motive first introduced at the end of the opening ritornello. Thus even a local "surprise" ties up a motivic loose end.

Unlike the messy excess of the typical buffa aria, then, the tidy outlines and diminutive-filled lexicon of the *serva/contadina* aria defines its singers as charming and clever, if also manipulative and not always straightforward, "cutely" comic—even Despina has to dress up as a man to be really funny—and small.[16] The performative aspects of these arias also differ from buffa arias: the melismas that often occur toward the end are normally quite short and not conspicuously virtuosic, but they may have given the singer an opportunity to show off her pretty throat and flirt with the on- and offstage audiences. Indeed, one of the most significant aspects of these arias is their undercurrent of sexual experience or availability; the forwardness of many

[15] Compare the relative independence and strongly gestural aspects of the accompaniment in Petronio's aria quoted above.

[16] Perhaps interestingly related to this is the modern practice of casting such roles (Despina, Zerlina, and Susanna are the obvious Mozartean examples) with singers who are physically smaller (shorter and almost always thinner) than those who sing the more serious or dramatic roles.

serving girls suggests that sex is a natural and pleasant, but not particularly intense part of life, and that for many of them it is part of a system of exchange rather than a result of romantic feeling. Pezzl's paragraphs on chambermaids fit with the theatrical representation of the characters who sing *serva/contadina* arias. His remarks on the subject are essentially all about sex—first he describes the Viennese chambermaids as "young, pretty, plump, and lively creatures," and then spends the rest of the passage on the question of whom they had affairs with, and whether they were, in the end, "decent" (*honetten*).[17] The evident and matter-of-fact sexuality of the *serva/contadina* aria contrasts not only with romantic fulminations of the Dorabella sort, but also with the sensitivity and apparent purity of the sentimental heroine. It would be wrong, however, to imagine this aria type as the place where sexuality ran amok in opera buffa. Rather, the clarity and tidiness of the serving girl's rhetoric seem to contain the potential dangers of staged licentiousness by diminishing and trivializing it.

Seria Arias: The Statement of Nobility

Like buffa arias and *serva/contadina* arias, seria arias are defined first by the characters who sing them. These are typically the *parti serie*—the most elevated (though not necessarily the most dramatically important) in their operas; and the texts typically reflect the elevation of the characters, either in the use of pervasive simile or metaphor, moralizing impersonal language, or in the expression of noble personal sentiments. These arias often occur quite close to the beginnings of operas; approximately half of them are their singer's first arias, and in this position they serve to establish the character's rank and type. *Parti serie* of both genders sing these arias; unlike buffa arias and *serva/contadina* arias, which divide by gender, seria statements of nobility do not distinguish consistently or clearly between male and female characters. This lack of gender distinction in the most elevated arias may relate—at least on a pragmatic level—to the older practice of using castrati or even women for the male *parte serie,* resulting in little or no vocal difference between the male and female seria roles.[18]

The nobleman Ramiro's opening aria in *La finta giardiniera* exemplifies the more metaphorical sort of text, while the goddess Diana's second aria in *L'arbore di Diana* exemplifies the more self-descriptive sort.

[17] Pezzl, *Skizze von Wien*, trans. Landon, pp. 148–49.

[18] For example, the part of Ramiro in both Mozart's and Anfossi's *La finta giardiniera* was written for a castrato, as was Ernesto in Anfossi's *L'incognita perseguitata* (though this role was also played by a tenor). Ernesto in Haydn's *Il mondo della luna* was also sung by a castrato, Pietro Gherardi. The original casts of many operas with libretti by Goldoni used women in the male *parte seria* roles. See the cast lists in *Tutte le Opere di Carlo Goldoni*, vols. X and XI, ed. Giuseppe Ortolani (Milan: Mondadori, 1952).

RAMIRO:
Se l'augellin sen fugge
Dalla prigione un giorno,
Al cacciatore intorno
Non più scherzando va.

Libero uscito appena
Da un amoroso impaccio,
L'idea d'un altro laccio,
Ah che tremar mi fa.

DIANA:
Sento che Dea son io,
Sento che ho regno e soglio,
E dall'usato orgoglio
Mi sento rinfiammar.

E se promette calma
Il placido sembiante,
Ho i fulmini nell'alma,
Fo terra, e ciel tremar.

If the little bird flees
From its prison one day,
It will no longer go
Playing around the hunter.

At the moment of release
From an amorous entanglement,
The idea of another noose,
Ah, it makes me tremble.

I feel myself to be a goddess,
I have a kingdom and a throne,
And I feel myself inflamed
With my customary pride.

And [even] if my placid face
Promises calm,
I have lightning in my soul
And [can] make heaven and earth
    tremble.

5-3: Martín y Soler, *L'arbore di Diana*, I,9
Diana, "Sento che Dea son io," mm. 27–36

The incipit of Diana's aria is shown in Example 5-3; Example 1-1 shows the incipit of Anfossi's setting of Ramiro's aria.[19] These arias are both in

---

[19] See Volker Mattern, *Das Dramma Giocoso: La finta giardiniera* (Laaber: Laaber-Verlag, 1989) pp. 204–13, for a detailed comparison between the Anfossi and the Mozart settings of "Se l'augellin sen fugge."

compressed da capo form,[20] which is a hallmark of this sort of aria. Occasionally, comparable sentiments will be expressed in multiple tempo form (as they are in Fiordiligi's "Come scoglio,"[21]) but the compressed da capo "stands for" nobility in a way that no other form does. The examples above, both in $\frac{4}{4}$ or cut time, open with a stately melody over a pulsating bass line with slow harmonic rhythm. Their melodic character suggests John Brown's *aria di portamento*. Arias of this type usually include at least two passages of coloratura, one in the second paragraph of the opening section and one in the parallel place in the "recapitulation."

These arias are more consistent—even rigid—in their rhetorical and formal habits than any other category of aria. And those rhetorical habits in themselves tend to emphasize clear contrast between formal sections, consistent relations between text, tonal structure, and thematic material, and eloquence of a rather prepackaged nature. In a genre that tends (at least on a local level) to value quick-wittedness, flexibility, and the power of sentiment, the rigidity and predictability of these statements of nobility seems to mark the position of the characters who sing them as irrelevant—a judgment implicitly endorsed by the operas in which these arias function as the point from which the characters who sing them move toward greater fallibility and "humanity."[22] However, the often stunning displays of vocal power in these arias also, I think, stand for the Baroque aristocratic tradition of representing power through sheer display, which may not have been—at least for the Viennese aristocracy—a simple matter for derision.[23] Martha Feldman has pointed out the "magic" aspects of the virtuoso singing characteristic of opera seria[24]—a magic acknowledged in Vienna in 1785 when the Kärntnerthortheater was reopened especially for the arrival of the castrato Luigi Marchesi. This magical, or irrational, power of the voice—especially when engaging in extreme coloratura—can be understood as analogous to the "irrational" hereditary power of the rulers in a

[20] Ratner, *Classic Music* (New York: Schirmer, 1980) pp. 276–79. Charles Rosen *Sonata Forms* (New York: Norton, 1980) p. 56, describes this as the "sonata form with trio" (also deriving it from the da capo form); but to my mind the term "compressed da capo form" more clearly reflects the origins of this form and its associations with dramatic type.

[21] "Come scoglio" is a complex mixture of formal elements. To the extent that we hear it as A (1–22) B (22–53) . . . A (58–78) C (Più Allegro), it resembles a rondò; to the extent that we hear 1–53 as an expository paragraph, and 58–78 as a retransition and recapitulatory segment, it may invoke sonata-like procedures.

[22] *L'arbore di Diana* is among the most spectacular cases of this. Fiordiligi's progress in *Così* is comparable, even though "Come scoglio" is not a compressed da capo aria. In *La finta giardiniera* Ramiro remains apart from the central action of the drama; his opening aria thus sets his type for the opera.

[23] Norbert Elias, *The Court Society,* trans. Edmund Jephcott (New York: Pantheon Books, 1983) p. 67, notes the aristocratic "obligation to spend on a scale befitting one's rank." Pezzl, *Skizze von Wien,* trans. Landon, p. 105 describes expenditures of upward of 200,000 gulden per year in the princely houses of Vienna; and Riesbeck (pp. 183–85) comments that the high aristocracy in Vienna were as lavish as any he had seen in his travels.

[24] Feldman, "Magic Mirrors and the *Seria* Stage," *JAMS* 48 (1995) pp. 469–71.

feudal system and is in any case given a social dimension in opera buffa by means of its contrasting juxtaposition with the more textually grounded (less irrationally vocal) singing of characters with no pretension to, or history of, God-given power over others. Whether the vocal power of the seria singer in opera buffa was understood in the context of nostalgia for less negotiable social relations or as a debunking of absolutism must have depended on the particulars of the operas in which it occurred, and on the political "imaginary" of the individual audience members. It is, however, likely that an ingrained respect for the "presentational" power of the seria singer played in unstable counterpoint against the comic distance induced by the debunkings and marginalizations accorded many of the *parti serie* who stayed "in place" through the opera.

SERIA ARIAS: THE RAGE ARIA

Although rage arias (variously called *aria agitata, aria di strepito, aria di smania, aria infuriata* in eighteenth-century sources) are a clear and frequent category in opera seria, they all but disappear in the opera buffa of the 1770s and 1780s. There is a very small number of "pure" rage arias, sung mainly by female *parti serie*,[25] but in general rage as an undiluted and serious noble posture is not part of the buffa lexicon. Even the few examples of real rage in this repertory do not match the vituperative intensity of their texts with a comparable musical focus; Anfossi's music to Arminda's "Vorrei punirti indegno," in *La finta giardiniera,* for example, seems positively flaccid in comparison to, say, Elettra's "D'Oreste, d'Ajace," or, indeed, to Mozart's G minor setting of Arminda's words; and while one might simply attribute this to differences in compositional capacity, it also accurately reflects larger tendencies of the genre. (See Example 5-4.)

In most operas in this repertory, rage turns into something else, and the arias that express rage can often be assimilated into other aria types. Noble rage shades into expressions of pride, nobility, haughtiness, or a demand for sympathy, while the rage expressed by comic characters turns into spluttering buffa display. The concentrated Sturm und Drang demonstration of fury in which Mozart's Elettra or Haydn's Armida indulge either disappears from or is transformed in this repertory. Two arias demonstrate the fate of concentrated rage.

The first is in Bertati and Gazzaniga's *L'isola di Alcina,* a buffa version of the Ariostan story of the seductive witch Alcina and her enchanted island. This aria comes at the point where Alcina realizes that she is likely to be defeated (by the bumbling Baron who has stuffed his ears and covered his eyes to protect himself from her charms).

---

[25] A paradigmatic example of this type is the Marchesa Lucinda's "Furie di donna irata," in *La buona figliuola.* See also Diana's "Impudica indarno fuggi," in *L'arbore di Diana,* and Calloandra's "Troppo l'offesa è grande," in Salieri's *La fiera di Venezia.*

5-4: Anfossi, *La finta giardiniera*, II,1
Arminda, "Vorrei punirti, indegno," mm. 19–27

Translation: I want to punish you, wretch; I want to break your heart.

Sento un affanno in petto;	I feel anguish in my breast,
Ma affanno pur non è . . .	But then it isn't anguish . . .
Tutto mi da sospetto;	Everything makes me suspicious,
Ma non so già il perchè . . .	But I don't know why.
Ah da una donna irata . . .	Ah, flee, flee
Fuggite, sì, fuggite . . .	From a furious woman . . .
Ah no; restate . . . udite . . .	Ah no; stay . . . listen . . .
Ma cosa dir non sò.	But I don't know what to say.
Confusa,[26] agitata,	Confused, agitated,
Con sdegno vi miro;	I look at you with disdain,
Ma dopo sospiro . . .	But then I sigh . . .
Confuso il cervello,	My mind is confused,
L'affanno novello	I don't know how to understand
Intender non può.	This new misery.

Textually and musically this starts out like the rage aria one might expect from an Alcina, but after this grand beginning she simply cannot keep it up, and the entire aria becomes a disquisition on the impossibility of rage. Not only does the text indicate her vacillation between disdain and desire, but the topical variety of the music, even at the very beginning, moves the aria away from the characteristic single focus of the true rage aria:[27]

[26] "Confusa" is the word in the Vienna score; other sources have "sorpresa."
[27] Emanuele Senici, "'Col suono orribile de' miei sospir': Rage Arias in Viennese Opera Buffa of the 1780's," unpublished paper, Cornell University, 1994.

5-5: Gazzaniga, *L'isola di Alcina,* II,10
Alcina, "Sento un affanno in petto," mm. 1–10

Although the whole opera is clearly a spoof on a tried and true seria story, this aria is not exactly parody, insofar as Alcina is neither the wrong sort of character to be singing a rage aria nor is she consciously assuming a posture of greater elevation than she can sustain. The issue here is perhaps the *generic* inappropriateness of rage.

The other fate of the rage aria in opera buffa is pure parody; here rage is an assumable and ridiculous posture performed for comic effect. At the end of *Il curioso indiscreto,* the heroine Clorinda, having despaired of both her former fiancé the Marchese and her true love the Contino, decides to confuse them both and feign insanity. She sings a lovely little pastoral ditty, identifies the Marchese and the Contino as Timante and Olinto (characters in Metastasio's *Demofoonte* and *Demetrio,* respectively), and launches into a typical seria raging tirade, with running scales and high B♭'s:

5-6: Anfossi, *Il curioso indiscreto,* II,7
Clorinda, "Son Regina disperata," mm. 13–19; 20–26

Son Regina disperata,	I am a queen in desperation,
Siete voi Vassalli indegni;	You are my unworthy subjects;
Tanto ardire ne' miei Regni,	My rage will not permit
Non lo soffre il mio furor.	Such audacity in my domain.

As quickly and easily as she has assumed this posture, Clorinda moves to a cosy buffa idiom with diminutive nouns, and, in a lilting *Andantino* triple metre, woos them both:

Volgi a me quei begl'occhietti,	Turn your lovely little eyes to me
(ad Marchese)	*(to the Marchese)*
Stendi pur la tua manina,	Hold out your little hand, then,
(ad Contino)	*(to the Contino)*
Cari occhietti, bei labbretti,	Dear little eyes, lovely little lips,
Tutto vostro è questo cor.	My heart is all yours.

5-7: Anfossi, *Il curioso indiscreto*, II,7
Clorinda, "Son Regina disperata," mm. 59–65

Having completely confused the men with this simultaneous seduction, Clorinda claims to be delirious and calls them liars and madmen in a final *Presto* $\frac{4}{4}$ envoi. Clorinda's aria is characteristic of buffa rage in that it is associated not only with opera seria (or with the parody thereof) but also with the act of performance.[28]

Rage and Gender

There are also gender implications in the fate of the rage aria. Apart from the obvious parodies, in which the character is not in fact angry, female rage is not mocked but domesticated, either by softening its musical expression, as in Anfossi's "Vorrei punirti indegno" mentioned above, or by failing to sustain it, as in Alcina's aria. One implication of these changes is that the unselfconscious excess required of the true raging woman is outside the ideology of womanhood conveyed by these works. Buffa women may perform in various ways, they may indicate anger in a larger plea for sympathy, and they may indulge in vocal display in demonstrations of pride and desperation, but they may not lose themselves in dark "irrational" fury. This contrast between seria and buffa rage is symptomatic of a gradual shift in thought about women from a pre-Enlightenment notion that the primary attributes of womanhood are excessive and barely controllable lust

---

[28] See also Falsirena's extravagant rage aria "Rabbia, bile, affanno, e stizza," in *La fiera di Venezia,* which is preceded by her announcement that she is going to sing a buffa aria. Hunter, "Some Representations of Opera Seria in Opera Buffa," *COJ* 3 (1991) pp. 89–108.

and passion (and thus that the primary job of men with respect to women is to control and punish them) to a quintessentially Enlightenment view that womanhood was defined by dependence, nurturing instincts, and a gift for domesticity. These two views of womanhood are not, of course, mutually exclusive; nor was there any sudden or decisive shift from one to another in the late eighteenth century.[29] Nevertheless the striking containment of female rage in opera buffa does suggest that in works where some version of "real life" was ostensibly presented, where an increasingly sentimental aesthetic reigned, and where sympathy and identification were as desirable from the audience as comic distance or alienation, it was increasingly difficult to represent women out of control.

Most male rage in this repertory is converted into the category of the buffa aria; men do not sing parodies of rage arias as much as they knock furiously around the stage expressing a considerably lower form of anger, often mixed with panic or other affects. There is, however, a very small number of noncomic male rage arias, among which are the Count's "Vedrò mentr'io sospiro" in *Le nozze di Figaro* and Lubino's "Vo' dall'infami viscere" in *Una cosa rara*. Although neither of these pieces is parody and neither is weakened or softened in the manner I have described for female rage arias, both are undercut by suggestions of the comic. The nobility of Lubino's aria is lessened in obvious ways, first by being sung by a bumpkin, albeit a generally sympathetic one, and by a linguistic excess that veers toward rodomontade rather than impressive fury. There is a specificity about the physical results of his vengeance that also connects him with the buffa world in which he belongs rather than with true seria *sdegno*:

(LINES 3–5)

Vo' farli a brani a brani;	I'll cut them up into lots of pieces
E dar per cibo ai cani	And give their bones and flesh
L'ossa, e le carni lor.	To the dogs for dinner.

The ways in which the seriousness of the Count's aria is undercut are less obvious: Wye Allanbrook notes that Bartolo's previous use of a similar

---

[29] There is an enormous literature on the emergence of the cult of domesticity. A particularly useful survey is to be found in Michelle Crampe-Casnabet, "A Sampling of Eighteenth-Century Philosophy," in Natalie Zemon Davis and Arlette Farge, eds., *Renaissance and Enlightenment Paradoxes,* vol. 3 of Georges Duby and Michelle Perrot, eds., *A History of Women in the West* (Cambridge: Harvard University Press, Belknap Press, 1992–94), 315–48. See also Jean-Louis Flandrin, *Families in Former Times: Kinship, Household and Sexuality,* trans. Richard Southern (Cambridge: Cambridge University Press, 1979). Felicity Nussbaum, *Torrid Zones: Maternity, Sexuality, and Empire in Eighteenth-Century English Narratives* (Baltimore: The Johns Hopkins University Press, 1995) places the cult of domesticity in a broader context of class, race, and nationality. Rebecca Lee Green, "Power and Patriarchy in the Goldoni Operas of Joseph Haydn" (Ph.D. dissertation, University of Toronto, 1995) discusses the emerging notion of separate spheres as it applies to both the music and the words of some of Haydn's operas.

idiom (and key and instrumentation) in "La vendetta" has already con-
taminated the Count's use of it; one might also note, as Koch does, that
beyond the confines of *Le nozze di Figaro* the rage and vendetta idioms are
already undercut by their comic associations in the genre at large: "Ever
since they began to dress up buffoon ariettas in the form of broad-scale
arias, the serious arias have necessarily declined more and more in value;
for as soon as the humorous masters the form of the serious, the serious
takes on the features of the humorous."[30] Allanbrook also notes the air of
hysteria that pervades this aria, noting that it subverts the power of the
Count's rage. She notes in particular the topical variety of his music as evidence of this hysteria; whereas "true" rage arias maintain a single affect
with rigorous intensity, *buffo* fulminations tend to leap from one topic to
another.[31] The Count's aria is by no means a buffa aria, but its generic associations with other bass-voiced fulminations, and its internal assemblage
of affects, do prevent it from being the uncompromised visitor from the
seria realm that the Count would clearly like it to be. Thus, whereas gender is irrelevant to the seria statement of nobility, subordinating the differences between men and women to the assertion of rank, it becomes relevant again in rage arias, whose intensity of passion is ill-suited both to the
aesthetic and to the gender ideology of opera buffa. Here the generic norm
of sputtering men and domesticated women comes to the fore, in part to
tailor the "splendor, heroism, [and] passion" of opera seria to opera buffa's
more modest dimensions, and in part perhaps to control and rationalize
the potentially dangerous power of fury.[32]

THE SENTIMENTAL STATEMENT

If expressions of comic pretension, sly flirtatiousness, noble pride, and
noble rage divide opera buffa characters by rank and gender, expressions
of sentiment seem—at least on the face of it—to offer an occasion for the
breaching of social barriers, and for the creation of a middle space that characters of both genders and various stations can occupy "on the merits" of
their sentiments rather than on the basis of their social place. Expressions
of sentiment are occasions for the Countess and Susanna, as well as the
Queen and the two shepherdesses in *Una cosa rara* to meet as equals; for

---

[30] Johann Christoph Koch, *Journal der Tonkunst* (Erfurt, 1795) vol. II, p. 102. Quoted
in Allanbrook, *Rhythmic Gesture,* p. 144.

[31] Ibid., p. 145.

[32] Christoph Friedrich Daniel Schubart, *Ideen zu einer Aesthetik der Tonkunst,* ed. Ludwig
Schubart (Stuttgart: Scheible, 1839) p. 352: "Opera [seria] is an invention of the highest
imagination; [with] **splendor, heroism, passion,** the marvelous, fantasies and ideals from Ariosto's worlds or from Ovid's *Metamorphoses*... ("... die Oper eine Erfindung der üppigsten
Phantasie ist; ... **Pracht, Heroismus, Leidenschaft,** Wunderbares, Imaginationsgeburten
und Ideale, aus Ariostens Welten, oder aus Ovids Verwandlungen ... ").

Don Ottavio and Masotto[33] to express equally heartfelt feelings; and for Zerlina and Lilla[34] to captivate the upper-class audience as well as their bumpkin lovers. The subject of sentimental statements is invariably love, whether desired, achieved, or denied. First-person descriptions of the character's emotions (often couched in pastoral similes and metaphors), and affectionate or pleading addresses to the beloved are the most characteristic dramatic occasions for such arias.

However, a closer examination of the various categories of sentimental aria suggests that they do not—or at least not simply—define a fluid democratic realm between stiffly stratified buffa and seria extremes. Rather, the sentimental statement helps to redefine the relation between gender and class, linking the expression of sentiment with women, with naturalness, and with an upper-class sensibility. The deployment of the rondò—the paradigmatic sentimental utterance—provides the most obvious support for this hypothesis. About three quarters of rondòs are sung by women; many of them by women from the upper strata of society. When the singers of rondòs are not from the upper social strata, they are often the sentimental centers of their operas, which confers upon them a sort of inner nobility and an aura of "naturalness." Rondòs in opera buffa typically express deeply felt sentiments (the Countess's "Dove sono" and Fiordiligi's "Per pietà" are the obvious Mozartean examples), and the moment of the rondò is often the dramatic crux.[35] Indeed, most operas that include a rondò include only one. Rondòs proper, however, comprise only about 3 percent of the arias in this repertory—other sentimental arias being in "pseudo-rondò" two-tempo form[36] and a variety of one-tempo forms, some designated "cavatina."[37] Thus, although the deployment of rondòs is symptomatic of the social import of sentimental statements, the larger ramifications of this deployment—particularly with regard to the subtle denaturalizing of male expressions of sentiment—must be sought elsewhere.

In the earlier phase of these twenty years, sentimentalism among the lower classes is quite often undercut for both genders, though perhaps more obviously for men than for women. In *L'amore artigiano*, for example, the hero Giannino (sung in Vienna by Sonnenfels's favorite, Caribaldi) sings a lovely song, "Occhietti cari," praising his beloved Rosina, which dissolves into a vituperative contrasting section; the dramatic effect of this undercutting of his expressivity, however, is mitigated, to the extent that

---

[33] The land-agent in *Fra i due litiganti*.

[34] The heroine of *Una cosa rara*.

[35] Rice, "Rondò vocali," in Muraro, *I vicini di Mozart* (Florence: Olschki, 1989) vol. 1, p. 187.

[36] See Manfredini, *Difesa della musica moderna* (1788; rpt. Bologna: Forni, 1972) p. 195.

[37] Late-eighteenth-century sources typically agree that formally the cavatina consists of "only" one (textual) part. These sources are, however, contradicted by some musical sources, in which large two-part arias are described as "cavatina."

5-8: Sarti, *Fra i due litiganti il terzo gode*, II,2
Masotto, "L'onda placida," mm. 8–14

Rosina has no fully sentimental piece, and the tone of the whole opera is more comic than romantic.[38] In *Fra i due litiganti,* however, in which the heroine, Dorina, has some thoroughly sentimental moments, the undercutting of male sentiment is both more subtle and more meaningful. At the beginning of the second act, the land agent Masotto, whose chief expression of love for Dorina to this point has been a willingness to wheel and deal to get her, stops dead in his tracks and sings a pretty pastoral aria (Ex. 5-8):

L'onda placida, e tranquilla	The calm and tranquil brook
Col suo grato mormorio,	With its sweet murmuring
Par ch'arrida al piacer mio,	Seems to smile on my pleasure,
E più lieto il cor mi fa.	And rejoices my heart.

[38] Cf. Heartz, *Haydn, Mozart and the Viennese School 1740–1780* (New York: Norton, 1995) p. 416.

The aria begins with a gentle tune in cantabile style, and its lack of significant thematic contrast links it with other expressions of sentiment in this repertory. However several things subtly undercut its capacity to tug at the heartstrings. One is the overused metaphor of the murmuring stream: Masotto seems to have no more spontaneous means of expressing his amorous feelings. Another is the resort to coloratura at the end of the aria, which seems out of proportion with the sweetness of the sentiment expressed:

5-9: Sarti, *Fra i due litiganti il terzo gode*, II,2
Masotto, "L'onda placida," mm. 30–35

e più lie - to il cor mi fà, e più lie - - - to il cor mi fà

Finally, and most importantly, this aria seems like a rehearsal of his own earlier comic admonition to the bumpkin suitors: "In amor ci vuol finezza" ("We need to be refined in matters of love") rather than a natural outgrowth of the circumstances or his feelings. Thus, although Masotto's love for Dorina is not in question, his status as a servant characterized more by activity than feeling is, I think, reinforced rather than complicated by this aria.

The slightly forced quality of Masotto's sentiment in this aria, however, is not solely related to his rank. Aristocratic men who sing love songs also tend to rely on tired metaphors, and their language is often more flowery than that of their female counterparts—especially those apparently from the lower strata of society. Asdrubale's first love song to Giannetta in *L'incognita perseguitata*, which serves as an example here, can fruitfully be compared to Giannetta's sentimental aria to him later in the act. (This was reproduced in full as Example 4-3.) Asdrubale sings (see Example 5-10):

Due pupillette amabili	Two lovely little eyes
M'hanno piagato il cor.	Have wounded my heart.
E se pietà non chiedo	And if I do not ask
A quelle luci belle,	These lovely eyes for mercy,
Per quelle, sì, per quelle	I will die of love
Io morirò d'amor.	For them.

Like most sentimental males, Asdrubale describes a happily if impersonally amorous condition; women, however, are more likely to use the sentimental occasion as a naked and immediately personal plea for sympathy, either from the audience or from another onstage character. The difference in lexicon may also be related to this difference in rhetorical function. Both

5-10: Anfossi, *L'incognita perseguitata*, I,4
Asdrubale, "Due pupillette amabili," mm. 9–14; 22–26

arias are cantabile, use a single slow tempo, and are through-composed: Asdrubale's is in three motivically distinct sections with ritornellos in between and an occasionally ornate vocal line; Giannetta's is extraordinarily continuous, with almost no instrumental punctuation, and a comparatively plain vocal line. (Salieri does not, to be sure, manage Gluck's—or even Martín y Soler's—stunning simplicity.) The combination of satisfaction and ornate language in the male sentimental aria, then, presents the capacity for fine feeling essentially as an accomplishment—as something instilled, achieved, and then produced more or less on order.[39] The greater tendency of women to present sentiment as lament, and the often less decorative musical and textual language of female sentimental arias, suggest, in contrast, that indulgence in sentiment is a less tutored and more natural female activity—at least for women from (or apparently from) the more "natural" social strata. It is, however, crucial to remember that women who sing in Giannetta's strikingly direct and compelling manner almost always earn the affections of an upper-class lover. Love among the respectable classes, then, is increasingly defined as a complementary pairing: whereas

[39] Even in arias where the actual expression of sentiment seems fairly straightforward, there is often something artificial, or forced, about the occasion on which this sentiment is produced. One could argue this about "Un'aura amorosa." It is certainly true about the Cavaliere Ernesto's lovely aria "Begli occhi vezzosi" in Haydn's *Il mondo della luna*. This aria concerns his beloved Flaminia, but it is also a self-justification in response to a servant's accusation that Ecclitico, his partner in bamboozling the old fool Buonafede, is driven more by greed than love.

the woman's guarantee of pedigree is her capacity to express her sentiments directly and movingly, the man's is his capacity to be moved rather
than to demonstrate comparable expressive power.

Not all men are happy in love, of course, and male characters in opera
buffa do bewail their lot. But even here it is not unusual for something to
be slightly askew in the lament. In Goldoni/Poggi's and Salieri's *La locandiera,* for example, the Cavaliere di Ripafratta is stirred by the first pangs
of love—an emotion to which he has loudly claimed to be immune, and
which the innkeeper Mirandolina has, as a challenge, striven to arouse. The
Cavaliere is sincerely confused and uses the occasion to examine his feelings (see Example 5-11):

Vo pensando e ripensando,	I am thinking and reflecting,
Son così fra il sì e il nò.	I'm caught between yes and no.
Che far debbo a me domando,	I ask myself what I must do,
E risolvermi non sò.	And do not know how to decide.
Io non sò se m'inganno;	I don't know if I'm deceiving myself,
Ma giurerei, che sono innamorato.	But I could swear I'm in love.
Tal caldo inusitato	Such an unaccustomed fire
Mi sento insinuar entro le vene,	Flows through my veins,
Che riposo non hò.	That I can find no rest.
La pace antica	Where has the former peace
Del mio cor dove andò?	Of my heart gone?
La bella Locandiera	The fair innkeeper
M'incantò, mi sedusse . . .	Has charmed and seduced me . . .
Ma quest'affanno	But can this turmoil
Non potria derivar d'altra cagione?	Come from something else?
Un effetto di bile esser potria;	Perhaps it's the result of bile,
Esser potrebbe anco Ipocondria.	Or maybe hypochondria.
Ma se tu fossi, Amore,	But if it is you, Love,
Cagion del mio penar,	That causes my distress,
Nasconditi nel core,	Hide in my heart,
E non ti palesar.	And don't publicize yourself.

The form, though not a rondò proper, nevertheless refers to that form's
closed slow first part followed by a return to the tonic in a faster tempo, as
well in its intense subjectivity, which is the normal expressive mode for this
form. Despite the Cavaliere's social appropriateness for this sort of aria, and
despite the directness and intensity of his feelings, there is something not
quite straightforwardly sympathetic in it. It is, for example, quite clear from
the conventions of the genre and from the setup of the characters that the
Cavaliere is not going to win Mirandolina (the employee Fabrizio conventionally should—and does—win her hand), and that his newly awakened
sensitivity is going nowhere (there is, after all, no other possible mate for
the Cavaliere in the cast). In addition, his main emotion here is indecision
rather than love—being "fra il sì e il nò" as he puts it—and as James Web-

5-11: Salieri, *La locandiera,* II,1
Cavaliere Ripafratta: "Vo pensando, e ripensando," 10–18; 77–87
Source: Transcription in James Webster, "Understanding Opera
Buffa: Analysis = Interpretation," in Hunter and Webster, *Opera
Buffa in Mozart's Vienna,* pp. 350–61. Reprinted with permission.

5-11: *(Continued)*

Ma se tu fos - si, A - mo - re,   Ca - gion del mio   pe -

- nar,   Na - scon - di - ti nel co - re,   E   non   ti

pa -   le - sar, e non ti pa - le - sar.

ster has demonstrated in a close analysis of this piece,[40] there are various ways in which indecision and "failure to achieve" are structural themes of the piece. Amorous indecision is absolutely characteristic of sentimental heros,[41] and it can be touching, but here its function as a dismantling of the Cavaliere's original position and its clearly hopeless prognosis undercut the sympathy one might feel for someone undergoing the confusions of first love. (And the Cavaliere's own attribution of his tinglings to bile or hypochondria do not help his case.) The sentimental moment, then, is for the Cavaliere, a double comedown. Not only is it an embarrassment to find himself in the position of needing a sentimental aria, but he cannot even produce a conventional (or competent) example of the species.

For many men from various social strata, then, the sentimental moment is not where they most characteristically come to life, or their most advantageous opportunity for self-representation. For women, however, the sentimental realm is precisely the place where their core attributes are exposed; it is their primary opportunity for serious self-representation. It is, then, the greater naturalness and emotional effectiveness of female sentimental statement that indicates the feminization of the sentimental middle, making it a realm, like the female-dominated salon, where "private actions [have] public significance,"[42] or like the emerging bourgeois household, where women exercised the power of moral authority by both demonstrating and appealing to sentimental capacities. Nancy Armstrong describes the rise of the domestic novel in English fiction as an agent in the "gendering of subjectivity," or the process by which women, as possessors of a special capacity both for feeling and for the means of conveying it, became associated with a realm apart from the materiality of politics and temporal power. She writes: "Of the female alone did [literature] presume to say that neither birth nor the accoutrements of title and status accurately represented the individual: only the more subtle nuances of behavior indicated what one was really worth."[43] The aria of sentiment in this repertory of opera buffa is part of the same redefinition of woman's sphere. However, in this repertory at least, the sentimental style in the mouths of women from (or apparently from) below the upper ranks of society does not indicate the erasure of class distinctions or even articulate in any very consistent way a middle-class sensibility. Rather, the sentimental mode in the throats of many of opera buffa's women draws on the "noble" capacities

[40] James Webster, "Understanding Opera Buffa: Analysis = Interpretation," in Hunter and Webster, *Opera Buffa in Mozart's Vienna*, pp. 373–74.

[41] One common device is "tell her I'm dead—no, tell her I'm in [Illyria]." See Chapter 4, p. 96 and n. 8.

[42] Daniel Gordon, "Philosophy, Sociology, and Gender in the Enlightenment Conception of Public Opinion," *French Historical Studies* 17 (1992) p. 905.

[43] Nancy Armstrong, *Desire and Domestic Fiction* (Oxford: Oxford University Press, 1987) p. 4. The phrase "the gendering of subjectivity" occurs on p. 20.

of the audience to respond with sympathy and generosity[44] and redefines the relations between gender and class.

It is impossible to describe with any certainty the social implications of the sentimental mode in Vienna. In particular, it is hard to gauge the extent to which the bourgeois model of the home had begun to supplant the older aristocratic model of the household. On the one hand, Mozart's evocation of an affectionate home life in his letters, and Joseph II's lamentations about his lack of a wife to "come home to," suggest that the home in the bourgeois sense of a domain given meaning by the ministrations of a woman, and dependent on companionate marriage, was by no means a foreign notion.[45] On the other, the persistence of complaints about cicisbeism by foreigners and natives alike,[46] and both Pezzl's and Riesbeck's comments about the lovelessness of marital relations,[47] suggest that this bourgeois ideal was not even aimed at by a significant portion of the population. In this context, then, opera buffa's coordinated naturalization and feminization of the sentimental statement seems unusually prescriptive.

CONCLUSION

These aria types not only differentiate characters by class and gender, but also, to a greater or lesser extent, suggest different responses to those classes and genders as these aria types represent their circumstances: ridicule for the pretentious man, sympathy for the passive and victimized woman, a mixture of awe and disdain for the proud aristocrat, and a combination of delight and distance for the flirtatious serving girls. No monolithic ideology emerges from this play of sympathy, ridicule, and various sort of pleasure. However, one of the striking things about this repertory—especially its later phase—is the extent to which women are the focus of its sympathies. There is no paradigmatic male utterance as uncomplicatedly sympathetic as the sentimental heroine's lament, and no paradigmatic female utterance for which the delight in performance is as mixed with ridicule as the buffa aria. And perhaps it is the way in which opera buffa's gender distinctions begin to take on its markers of class distinction without erasing them which most closely embodies the contradictory tendencies of late-eighteenth-century Viennese society.

[44] The class associations of sentimental generosity are discussed in Robert Markley, "Sentimentality as Performance: Shaftesbury, Sterne, and the Theatrics of Virtue," in Felicity Nussbaum and Laura Brown, eds., *The New Eighteenth Century: Theory, Politics, English Literature* (New York and London: Routledge, 1987) pp. 210–30.

[45] Beales, *Joseph II* (Cambridge: Cambridge University Press, 1987) vol. 1, pp. 335–36.

[46] Riesbeck, *Briefe eines reisenden Franzosen*, p. 204, Pezzl, *Skizze von Wien*, trans. in Landon, *Mozart and Vienna* (London: Thames and Hudson, 1991) pp. 111–12.

[47] Pezzl, *Skizze von Wien*, trans. Landon, pp. 110–13; Riesbeck, *Briefe*, p. 165: "It is striking how indifferent married couples are to each other here."

Chapter Six

ENSEMBLES

SOME ISSUES

Ensembles are often taken to exemplify the spirit of opera buffa. This is partly because they are more numerous in, and more characteristic of, the genre than opera seria,[1] partly because they focus on groups rather than individuals and are thus felt to embody the spirit of comedy more fully than the seriatim statements of personal positions represented by arias, and partly because their flexible forms and various textures allow an apparent "naturalness" of interaction that contrasts with the supposed "stiff artificiality" of opera seria. Ensembles have also traditionally been taken as the element of opera buffa closest to the essence of the "high classical" instrumental style and have been essentially canonized in the context of opera buffa in relation to that. Wolfgang Osthoff, for example, comments that opera buffa's spirit of community is most aptly expressed through resources of polyphony and practices *based in* instrumental music (emphasis mine) and describes the genre as a whole as being suffused with an *Ensemblegeist*.[2] Reinhard Strohm does not assert the priority of instrumental music but notes that opera buffa's pervasive themes of social differentiation and the relation of the individual to the group are in fact questions of "harmony" and are naturally expressed in ensembles, in which participants are both soloists and members of the group.[3] In the following two chapters, I do not address the relation of the opera buffa ensemble to instrumental music of the same period, but I take seriously the notion of the genre's "ensemble spirit" in the sense of its preoccupation with social groups. Unlike arias, which tend to articulate the "fixed" stratification of society by rank and

[1] See, however, Daniel Heartz and Marita McClymonds, s.v. "Opera seria," *NGO,* on the increasing seria use of ensembles in the 1780s and 1790s.

[2] Wolfgang Osthoff, "Die Opera buffa," in Wulf Arlt, Ernst Lichtenhahn, and Hans Oesch, eds., *Gattungen der Musik in Einzeldarstellungen. Gedenkschrift Leo Schrade,* erste Folge (Berlin and Munich: Francke, 1973) pp. 680–84, *et passim.* Charles Rosen, *The Classical Style* (London: Faber & Faber, 1971) *passim,* often comments on the relation between the pacing of instrumental music and that of the buffa ensemble (by which he means Mozart's Da Ponte operas). For a more detailed discussion of one sort of relation between instrumental music and opera buffa, see James Webster, "How 'Operatic' are Mozart's Concertos?" in Neal Zaslaw, ed., *Mozart's Piano Concertos: Text, Context, Interpretation* (Ann Arbor: University of Michigan Press, 1996) pp. 107–37.

[3] Reinhard Strohm, *Die italienische Oper* (Wilhelmshaven: Heinrichshofen, 1979) p. 250. This is, to my knowledge, the most insightful (and also the most compact) discussion of the socially embedded nature of opera buffa in the literature.

gender, ensembles are typically more concerned with the relations between individuals and their ad hoc or contingent groupings, particularly with the ways in which individuality emerges as the result of circumstances. Thus whereas arias paradoxically invoke groups (type, class, gender) in their very definitions of individuality, ensembles by the same token raise questions about the nature of individuality in their presentations of, and inexorable drive toward, undifferentiated group utterance.

Numbers

Opera buffa's pervasive interest in groups does not, in most cases, translate into a preponderance of ensembles. Indeed, among all the operas performed in Vienna between 1770 and 1790, only *Così fan tutte* includes more ensembles than arias, and the norm in the repertory as a whole is that ensembles represent between a quarter and a third of closed musical numbers. The average opera in the repertory has an ensemble introduction, two finales at the end of the first two acts, a choral or vaudeville number at the end of the third act if there is one, plus two or three other ensembles set among fourteen or so arias. *Così*, however, is not the gross exception that these figures might suggest. There was across the genre as a whole during these years a general increase in the number of ensembles, and this trend appears to have been especially marked in Vienna. Among the imported operas in their pre-Viennese condition, the numbers of mid-act ensembles in these operas rise from an average of two in the 1770s to something more like an average of four in the 1780s. (Paisiello typically includes more ensembles than other composers, and *Il barbiere di Siviglia* includes equal numbers of arias and ensembles.[4]) Once in Vienna, imported operas were not uncommonly furnished with extra ensembles; Mozart's two contributions to Bianchi's *La villanella rapita* are only the most famous of these.[5] At least as striking as the addition of ensembles to imported operas, however, is the predilection of Mozart, Salieri, and Martín y Soler—the three

---

[4] *La frascatana,* for example, includes five mid-act ensembles, and *La molinara* has six. Among the eight ensembles in *Il barbiere di Siviglia,* however, there is an extraordinary amount of solo singing. In the first duet between Figaro and the Count, for example, Figaro has a 67-measure solo before the Count enters.

[5] These are the trio "Mandina amabile" intended for insertion in I,13, and the quartet "Dite almeno in che maniera" for II,12. Anfossi's *Le gelosie fortunate* was also provided with a couple of trios by "Paolo Kirzinger" (Paul Kürzinger); and in the score for what seems to be the second Viennese production of Paisiello's *Le due contesse* (1787), a duet replaces an aria in the first act, thus giving both acts an ensemble in addition to the closing number—the second act closes with a duet followed by a short chorus. There are two Viennese scores for this opera in the Austrian National Library: one (Mus. Hs. 17803) appears to represent the 1776 production (it largely matches the 1776 libretto) and the other (KT 92) the 1787 production (it lists performers who were present at this time). Guglielmi's *La quacquera spiritosa* seems to have been furnished with at least three ensembles by Paisiello, two of which were additions to the score rather than replacements.

most significant composers writing regularly *for* Vienna during this latter period—for concerted numbers. Whether this was a response to Viennese taste (Zinzendorf, for example, comments on ensembles at least as often as he comments on arias, and clearly enjoyed them as much as any aspect of the genre), or a particular predilection of Da Ponte is hard to say. *Così* may be the only opera with more ensembles than arias, but *La grotta di Trofonio, La cifra, Don Giovanni, Le nozze di Figaro, L'arbore di Diana,* and *Una cosa rara* include almost as many ensembles as arias.[6] Among the other operas premiered in Vienna, only Da Ponte and Storace's *Gli equivoci* (1786) echoes these proportions, and *Il barbiere di Siviglia* is the only import to come close to these proportions.

Apart from finales, which occur in every opera in this repertory, duets are by far the most common form of ensemble. The vast majority of operas (about 8/9) have at least one duet (often the love duet all but obligatory in the last act of three-act operas), and about two-thirds of these have two or more. There are more than twice as many duets as trios,[7] about twice as many trios as quartets, and these ratios continue with quintets and sextets. Whereas trios and quartets occur in the repertory in both the 1770s and the 1780s, quintets and sextets appear only in the 1780s; Mazzolà and Salieri's *La scuola dei gelosi,* with its second-act quintet, was apparently the first opera performed in Vienna to include a mid-act ensemble with so many participants.[8]

Ensembles and Form

The musical forms of ensembles are extremely various: finales and large ensembles tend to be sectional and through-composed with no highly articulated structural returns of material, though motivic repetition and return (often in the orchestra) often articulates a recurring situation or highlights the common reactions of a variety of characters. Smaller ensembles are also more often than not through-composed, though they also exhibit a variety of binary and ternary forms. Even when through-composed, though, they not infrequently begin with a clearly articulated exposition, often allowing each of the participants a solo statement that corresponds to a particular phase of the expository process. Exposition-like structures are also

---

[6] The numbers are: *La grotta di Trofonio* (Artaria score), 14 arias (including *ariosi*), 1 aria-plus-chorus, 7 ensembles, 2 finales; *Le nozze di Figaro*, 14 arias, 9 ensembles, 3 finales, 2 choruses; *Don Giovanni*, 12 arias (in both Prague and Vienna versions), 8 ensembles (9 in Vienna), 2 finales; *Una cosa rara* (1786 libretto), 17 arias, 8 ensembles, 1 chorus, 2 finales; *L'arbore di Diana* (1787 libretto), 17 arias, 10 ensembles, 1 aria-plus-tutti, 2 finales.

[7] Rabin, "Mozart, Da Ponte, and the Dramaturgy of Opera Buffa" (Ph.D. dissertation, Cornell University, 1996) p. 284, comments that trios are about half as numerous as duets in the 1780s repertory.

[8] Ibid., p. 314; almost all the operas in the 1780s included at least one large ensemble.

not uncommon at the beginnings of bigger or more complex ensembles, but their formal effect is often diminished by the length, complexity, tonal perambulations, and dramatic weight of what follows. Short small ensembles may (like "Soave sia il vento") use the whole text twice, but repetitions of whole texts are relatively rare among even small ensembles. Tonal processes—and not just striking modulations to distant keys—are often used for dramatic effect, but the particular deployment of tonal patterns is at least as dependent on the particular needs of a given text as on abstract musical criteria. In other words, while musical processes are essential to the meaning and effect of any given ensemble, they have little abstract or generalizable meaning or force and never constitute quasi-*topoi* as do, say, the compressed da capo or the rondò among aria forms.

Ronald Rabin has noted what he calls the "ensemble principle" in this wildly various category of number.[9] That is the principle by which a series of solo utterances (more or less long, more or less individualized, and more or less interactive) coalesce into one or more moments of ensemble singing, always at the end of the number and often at the ends of its various sections or phases. Most ensembles in this repertory begin with solos, long or short, melodic or declamatory, and in many the end is the only place with any significant amount of ensemble singing. Such ensemble singing, as Rabin notes, is homophonic more often than not, representing a moment of musical, if not textual, lockstep. John Platoff's description of the "action-expression" cycle in opera buffa finales—the "action" represented by dialogue or solo statements, and the "expression" by tutti or ensemble singing—is a more specific version of this principle.[10] The processes by which this lockstep comes about, whether as a gradual rapprochement or as a sudden snap into unmotivated synchrony, and its effects, which range from profound resolution to the most tenuous truce, vary widely. However, within this variety, introductions, finales, and mid-act ensembles both large and small all have their own characteristic ending types and strategies, and in each instance the process of ending is significant on various levels of the drama, in ways that usually depend on how the ending relates to what precedes and follows it. Is it a consequence of an inexorable process? Does it satisfactorily resolve the tensions preceding it? Does it establish a new status quo from which the drama will now proceed? The answers to these questions vary somewhat predictably among introductions and finales, and among different sorts of mid-act ensembles. Some of the variation has to do with the dramatic function of the number: is it "about" opening things up or closing them down? Does it coil the spring for the next phase of the

[9] Ibid., p. 242.

[10] Platoff, "Music and Drama in the Opera Buffa Finale: Mozart and His Contemporaries in Vienna" (Ph.D. dissertation, University of Pennsylvania, 1984); and "Musical and Dramatic Structure in the Opera Buffa Finale," *JM* 7 (1989) pp. 191–230.

action? Some of the variation in the significance of ensemble-endings, however, has to do with the social configurations of the ensembles; whether the characters represent a stable grouping with respect to the terms of the drama, whether the alliances forged in the course of the ensemble are plausible, and whether the ensemble represents its participants as a collection of individuals or as a more closely knit group.

Social Configurations

The social configurations of ensembles—the choice of participants with respect to gender and class—are almost as dependent on particular circumstances as their musical forms. There is no category of character exempt or excluded from ensemble participation, and no prescribed configuration of characters for any given type of ensemble, with the obvious exception of the third-act love duet, which is normally sung by the central pair of lovers.[11] There is, however, some tendency for ensembles apart from these final love duets to suggest the social middle. There are, for example, no introductory ensembles sung only by aristocrats or secondary servants (i.e., the equivalents of Barbarina or Antonio in *Figaro*): such ensembles either include characters in the middle or delineate the total social space of the opera by including both ends of the social scale. And in finales (which normally involve all the characters) an omitted character is either a *parte seria* (perhaps echoing the older practice of excluding such characters from ensembles with the *parti buffe*) or a secondary servant. Mid-act ensembles seem to choose the participants for dramatic rather than social reasons: the characters who sing in any given ensemble are the ones most immediately involved in the situation that the number either resolves or intensifies. Again, there is some preponderance of "middling" characters in these ensembles, but that reflects their greater engagement in the imbroglio. The overall class picture represented by ensembles, then, is inclusive and "democratic." In this sense ensembles—at least in their most superficial aspects—present a counterbalance to the overdetermined stratification evident in most other aspects of the genre.

Gender representation in ensembles is slightly more complex than class representation: finales obviously represent the gender distribution of their operas; normally this comes out to one or two more men than women,[12]

---

[11] *La fiera di Venezia* includes a comic parody of this type of final duet in "Scordati o Donna ingrata," sung by the nobleman Ostrogoto and the minx Falsirena, who has been teasing him throughout.

[12] The norm is four male characters to three female, but occasionally (as in *Il barbiere di Siviglia*) the opera includes only one woman. Only three operas out of the whole repertory (Cipretti and Salieri's *La moda*, Goldoni and Gassmann's *L'opera seria*, and Da Ponte and Martín's *L'arbore di Diana*) include more women than men, and only twelve include equal numbers. This means of course that the mating game almost always leaves remainders, and that they are almost without exception male.

while in introductory ensembles women are slightly overrepresented—
often appearing in equal numbers to men—perhaps to prefigure the pervasive trajectory toward happy coupling. In large ensembles, however
(quartets and up), men almost without exception outnumber women—
over two-thirds of quartets involve three male and a single female character, who is normally the much-desired center of the plot. (None reverse
this balance, with three women and one man.) Such ensembles thus crystallize and magnify the underlying gendered narrative of many *opere buffe.*
Among the smaller ensembles (duets and trios), however, a surprisingly
large number—about a third—are sung by all-male or all-female groups.
There are many more all-male ensembles than all-female—indeed three
quarters of the single-sex ensembles are male. These ensembles may on the
one hand seem to pull against the pervasive theme of happy coupling, but
on the other, the typically competitive or antagonistic qualities of all-male
ensembles (the opening trio of *Così* is a well-known example) and the pre-
ponderantly co-operative and well-integrated aspects of most female ensembles[13] (the famous canonic trio for the Queen and the shepherdesses
in *Una cosa rara* comes to mind) reinforce the gender stereotypes that permit the normal progress toward marriage. As with musical form, then, gender representation in ensembles is crucial to their meanings, but these
meanings depend on particulars rather than on any abstract principle.

Mid-Act Ensembles

Although almost all the operas in this repertory include at least one mid-
act ensemble, only about a third include ensembles larger than trios, and
most of these originate from the late 1770s and 1780s. Duets, however,
are common throughout the period, as mentioned above; many operas
have two or three, often one in each act. *Figaro,* as Rabin points out, is unusual in including six duets, but (for example) *Così* and *Don Giovanni* both
include five,[14] and *La fiera di Venezia, La grotta di Trofonio,* and *Il barbiere di Siviglia* all include four. In operas with two or more duets, it is almost a rule that one—but only one—of these is sung by the central lovers;
the others are opportunities for a variety of comic or revealing couplings.[15]

---

[13] Susanna and Marcellina's "Via resti servita" in *Figaro* is an obvious exception to this.

[14] *Così* could be said to include six if "Secondate, aure amiche," which ends with a chorus, were counted, and the Viennese version of *Don Giovanni* would also include six if
"Giovinette, che fate all'amore" were counted. The Prague version, without "Per queste due
manine," would include five.

[15] This convention is further evidence, were it needed, that the two opening duettini in
Figaro—both sung by Figaro and Susanna—should be regarded (or would have been perceived) as a single dramatic unit. Even in this duet-filled opera, only these two are sung by
the central lovers; the others are sung by Susanna and Marcellina, Susanna and Cherubino,
Susanna and the Count, and Susanna and the Countess, respectively.

Trios and larger ensembles deploy their participants in no predictable or consistent way.

Typically, mid-act ensembles either work a situation through to resolution or establish a point of conflict and freeze it as a way of coiling the dramatic spring for the next phase of the action. Some local resolutions also function as longer-range points of conflict: for example, Don Giovanni's seduction of Zerlina in "Là ci darem la mano," where the local resolution expressed in "Andiam, andiam mio bene" sets up much of the remaining conflict of the drama. However, if we take the characters' perceptions or representations of the ensemble-ending rather than its larger dramatic effect as its "truth," it is generally the case that small ensembles—duets and trios—tend (with many exceptions) to work through to agreement or resolution, while larger ensembles overwhelmingly end with confusion or disagreement. Not only are these dramatic functions different, but the relation they posit between individuality and collectivity also differs. The smaller ensembles are often about relationships—romantic love chief among them, of course, but also relationships about power (usually unequal) or about the capacity to persuade others. The invocation of these sorts of relationships inevitably defines the singers as much in relation to each other as to the larger situation and thus lends them a provisional individuality, or at least a set of characteristics that distinguish them from the other participant(s). The larger mid-act ensembles, in contrast, are less about relationships in the sense of the interactions of fully constituted or internally motivated individuals than about group reactions to situations—reactions that can, nevertheless, reveal individual proclivities and characteristics.

Smaller Ensembles: A Duet and a Trio

Duets are the only ensembles with any structure more predictable than the general progression of the ensemble principle. As in many aria forms, the formal conventions of the ensemble are strongest at the beginning. Ronald Rabin has described the progression as moving "from independent statements for the two participants, through dialogue, to a closing *tutti* in parallel thirds and sixths."[16] The "independent statements" often repeat the same melody, either in an antecedent-consequent (I-V; I-I) pattern, or in a pattern more like a sonata-form exposition (I-I; I-V). The opening statements usually constitute a clear first paragraph, both textually and musically. As Rabin notes; the dialogue section may be modulatory (it may also change tempo or meter) and the unanimous section (which is also often in a new tempo and/or meter) is almost always in the tonic throughout;[17]

---

[16] Rabin, "Mozart, Da Ponte, and the Dramaturgy of Opera Buffa," p. 285.
[17] Ibid., pp. 291–92.

the tonal effect may be reminiscent of the "sonata aesthetic,"[18] but duets are more often thematically through-composed, or at least continuously varied, than in thematically closed forms. Trios are more formally various, as Rabin also notes: they may begin like duets, with lengthy solo statements, but they are equally likely to launch more quickly into interaction and thus tend to present a less formal opening paragraph.

The love duet "Pianin pianino" from *L'arbore di Diana* II,9 exhibits many of the conventions of the duet in this repertory, though Martín's short-breathed style is quite unusual.[19] Like most such pieces, it sets up in the middle a situation that needs to be resolved or commented on in the end. In this case Endimione, the shepherd with whom Diana has illegitimately fallen in love, is pretending to be asleep. Diana wakes him and covers his eyes while she woos him, challenging him to guess her identity. The removal of her hands is the occasion first for surprised dialogue and then for the happy final unanimity. The opening statements, as befits the situation, are textually and musically distinct, though they do not form a strong contrast (see Example 6-1):

DIANA:

Pianin pianino	Quietly quietly
Lo chiamerò;	I'll call him;
Poi quando è desto,	Then when he's awake
Fuggirò presto,	I'll run away immediately.
Indi ben so	Thus I know
Quel che farò!	What I'll do!
Endimione . . .	Endimione . . .
(Lo scuote e poi fugge)	*(Shakes him and runs away)*

ENDIMIONE:

Che voce, oh Dio!	Ye gods, what a voice!
I sonni miei	Who disturbed
Chi mai turbò!	My sleep?
Alcun non vedo,	I see no-one;
Fu sogno credo.	It must have been a dream.
Sonno ancor ho;	I'm still sleepy,
Dormir io vo'.	I want to go back to sleep.

Diana then throws a stone at him, which "wakes" him enough for him to start running away; this happens in two solo statements in the dominant. Diana restrains him by putting her hands over his eyes, and they sing ho-

---

[18] Rosen, *The Classical Style*, p. 296.

[19] Andrew Steptoe, *The Mozart–Da Ponte Operas* (Oxford: Clarendon Press, 1988) p. 242, adduces this piece as a model for Ferrando and Fiordiligi's "Fra gli amplessi" in *Così*. My own opinion is that if it is a model (and there are certain tonal correspondences), it is (as I will argue about *La grotta di Trofonio*) an "anti-model," or a point of competitive departure rather than an object of homage.

6-1: Martín y Soler, *L'arbore di Diana,* II, 9
Duet: Diana and Endimione, "Pianin, pianino," mm. 8–19; 28–35

mophonically together about the flames of love, as they close the expository paragraph. As Endimione plays at pretending not to know who Diana
is, they exchange decorous four-measure phrases moving back to the tonic.
The climax of the duet comes as Diana can no longer resist revealing her
identity and tells Endimione, in a striking modulation to E♭ (♭III) to un-

cover his eyes. This is also the only point in the duet where anything re-
sembling dialogue happens: it segues immediately into the expected parallel thirds in the tonic, as the lovers, now certain of each other's affection,
celebrate their union (see Example 6-2).

DIANA:
    Tacita il passo   With quiet step
    Voglio avanzar,   I want to approach,
    E questo sasso   And throw this pebble
    Ver lui gittar.   At him.

ENDIMIONE:
    Un sasso, un sasso!   A stone! A stone!
    Che cosa è questa!   What's going on?
    Fuggiam,   Let's flee,

DIANA:
      No, resta,   No, stay,
    No, resta,   No, stay,
    Mio caro ben.   My dear love.

      (Diana trattiene Endimione: *(Diana restrains Endimione,*
      coprendogli gli occhi   *covering his eyes*
      colla mano.)   *with her hand.)*

DIANA:
    Lieta di stringere   Happily clasping
    Luci sì belle,   Such beautiful eyes,
    Sento in me nascere   I feel new flames
    Fiamme novelle;   Coming to life in me.
    Mi par che l'anima   It seems as if my soul
    Languisca in sen.   Were languishing in my breast.

ENDIMIONE:
    Al dolce stringere   With the sweet clasp
    Di man sì bella,   Of such a beautiful hand,
    Sento in me nascere   I feel a new flame
    Fiamma novella.   Coming to life in me.
    Mi par che l'anima   It seems as if my soul
    Languisca in sen.   Were languishing in my breast.

ENDIMIONE:
    Ah di chi siete   Ah, whose are you,
    Dite vezzose;   Charming fingers?

DIANA:
    Il cor te'l dica   Your heart should tell you,
    Bocca di rose.   Rosebud-lips.

      (Sempre colle mani   *(Keeping her hands*
      sopra gli occhi   *over Endimione's*
      di Endimione)   *eyes)*

ENDIMIONE:

   Il cor mi dice

   Che tu sei mia,

   Ma chi tu sia

   Non dice il cor.

DIANA:

   Ah che resistere

   Non posso ancor!

   Apri quei lumi,

   Mio bel tesor.

    (Qui cava le mani)

ENDIMIONE:

   Cintia!

DIANA:

   Si, caro!

ENDIMIONE:

   Sogno, o son desto?

À 2:

   Deh, fate o Numi,[20]

   Se un sogno è questo,

   Che ambi possiamo

   Dormire ognor.

My heart tells me

That you are mine,

But who you are

My heart does not reveal.

Ah, I can no longer

Resist.

Open those eyes,

My beautiful treasure.

(Here removes her hands)

Cynthia!

Yes dear!

Am I dreaming, or awake?

Oh Gods, grant that

If this is a dream,

We will be able to stay asleep like this

Forever.

Somewhat less typical than the trumped-up tension in the middle is Martín's adherence not only to a single tempo and meter, but also to the repeated use of the three-eighth-note pattern with which Diana's part begins. The two characters are not strongly differentiated by their musical material, but Diana's move to faster declamation (prompted by the *sdrucciolo* line "Ah che resistere"), and the rising line as she succumbs to temptation, as well as her surprising move to E♭ as she decides to reveal herself, suggest a level of feeling and self-determination absent from most larger ensembles. It is, after all, not an external stage situation that prompts her "shock solo," to paraphrase John Platoff,[21] but the promptings of her heart—however artificially assisted by Amore. Endimione is essentially a foil in this duet; we already know that he is in love, and it is Diana's change of heart that forms the real emotional topic of the opera. In this respect it

[20] These words, and "che ambi possiamo" two lines later, are the words in the score (Mus. Hs. 17795). The 1787 Viennese libretto reads "Andiam, andiamo/ . . . /Così vogliamo/. The practical score, KT 37, (which seems also to have been used in the German-language productions of this opera) has crossed out the section from "Ah di chi siete" until "Apri quei lumi," thus deleting (among other things) Diana's "Ah che resistere non posso ancor."

[21] Platoff, "Music and Drama in the Opera Buffa . . ." pp. 288ff., describes the "shock tutti" as a frequent feature of finales: it is a place where the assembled cast reacts "in unison" to a surprising turn of events.

6-2: Martín y Soler, *L'arbore di Diana*, II, 9
Duet: Diana and Endimione, "Pianin, pianino," mm. 105–33

6-2: *(Continued)*

que - sto, ch'am - bi pos - sia - mo dor - mi - re o - gnor?

is telling that Diana begins the piece; this contradicts the more usual practice of male beginnings in romantic duets.

The happy end of the duet is also the resolution of a dramatic process
that has been going on since the beginning of the opera. Relatively in-
significant and utterly conventional though it may seem (and in fact be) in
the context of the duet, in the context of the opera as a whole, this resolution is of major importance, because it completes Diana's trajectory from
proud goddess to woman in love. In establishing Diana's basic position for
the rest of the opera, as human, ruled by sentiment, and thus subject to,
rather than ruler of, events, this ensemble ending also permits the narrative denouement of the opera (in which Diana is quite passive) to proceed.[22] Thus, like many small ensembles in this repertory, it combines an
interpersonal process with a dramaturgical function. And like many aspects
of opera buffa, this ensemble has its paradoxes. If the duet exposes Diana's
true feelings for Endimione, and in a sense renders her more fully an individual through her interaction with him, it also renders her more like "all
women" (*tutte*) who cannot resist the power of love. Similarly, if the duet
represents a particular interpersonal process, delineating a unique relationship, the result of that relationship is to open the door to the opera's
ultimately and literally "mechanistic" end, in which Cupid appears in a machine and dispenses happiness all around.

The trio "Deh, caro Padre amato" in Grandi and Sarti's *Le gelosie villane*
II,12 does not suggest its participants' inner lives to the same extent as
Martín's duet does for Diana, but it is no less concerned with the affective
aspect of relationships.[23] Giannina's lover Tognino and her father,
Cecchino, have (by dint of hiding in a cupboard) overheard her flirting
with the local Marchese. They are discovered, the Marchese sings an aria
protesting his respect for them, then leaves in a hurry; and Giannina is left

---

[22] Diana's big moment of subjectivity, her rondò, "Teco porta" (and its substitution, Luigi
Tarchi's "Ah sol bramo o mia speranza" in the later reworking of the opera for Ferrarese)
comes after this duet, in the midst of the imbroglio about her status as priestess. Although
this is the musical climax of Diana's psychological trajectory, it merely confirms the state of
mind and heart revealed in this duet.
[23] Rabin, "Mozart, Da Ponte and the Dramaturgy of Opera Buffa," pp. 310–11, also discusses this trio.

to face her family. She pleads sweetly with her father, who resists her blandishments, both verbally and musically. Trying the same tune with her lover, she is met with another rebuff (see Example 6-3):

GIANNINA:

Deh, caro Padre amato,	Ah beloved father,
Donatemi il perdono,	Give me your pardon,
Non vi mostrate ingrato.	Don't be unpleasant.
Se vostra figlia sono	If I'm your daughter
Ancor vi parli il cor.	Your heart will speak to you.

CECCHINO:

Sì, che mia figlia sei	Of course you are my daughter,
(Per quello che si dice),[24]	As they say,
Ma dica un poco lei	But tell me now
Se ad una figlia lice	Whether a daughter is allowed
Sprezzare il proprio onor.	To forget her honor.

GIANNINA:

Caro Tognino amato . . .	Dear beloved Tognino . . .

TOGNINO:

Nò nò più non ti credo.	No no, I don't believe you.
Da te fui ingannato,	I was deceived by you once,
E tu m'inganni ancor.	And you're at it again.

Giannina then tries the minor mode, which unites the men in tears. The dialogue section comes when she makes them look at her "before she leaves," at which point she presents an ornamented version of her opening melody. The three characters then admit the power of love, change tempo and meter, and sing in familial homophony until the end (see Example 6-4).

GIANNINA:

Per questo pianto mio	For the sake of my tears
Calmate quel furor.	Calm your fury.
(s'inginocchia)	*(kneels)*

MEN:

Or ora piango anch'io	Now I'm crying too
E già mi sento il core	And I feel the heart
In petto a intenerir.	In my breast softening.

GIANNINA:

Guardatemi	Look at me

CECCHINO:

Ti guardo.	I'm looking.

[24] This is the version of the line in KT 182. The Vienna 1777 libretto has "Ma sei una temeraria."

6-3: Sarti, *Le gelosie villane,* II,3
Trio: Giannina, Cecchino, Tognino, "Deh, caro Padre amato,"
mm. 1–31; 39–45

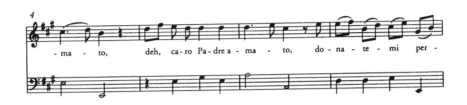

6-3: *(Continued)*

cor vi par - li il cor.   Cecchino: Sì, che mia fi - glia se - i per

p   *cresc.*   *fp*

quel - la che mi di - ce,   ma di - ca un po - co le - i   se ad

cresc.   *fp*   *cresc.*

u - na fi - glia li - ce   sprez - za - re il pro - prio o - nor

Tognino:
No, no più non ti cre - do,   da te fu in - gan - na - to,   e tu m'in-gan-ni an - cor

GIANNINA:
 Tognino   Tognino

TOGNINO:
  Cosa vuoi?   What do you want?

GIANNINA:
 Donami almen un guardo   At least look at me
 In prima di partir.   Before I leave.

  (La guardano,   *(They look at her*
   e la fanno alzare)   *and help her up)*

À 3:
 Amor di natura   Love, you are by nature
 Sei pur portentoso!   Portentous!
 Lo sdegno non dura: Anger does not last,
 E un cuor amoroso   And a loving heart
 Non puote nel seno   Cannot nourish poison
 Nutrire il veleno.[25]   In its breast.
 Si cangia in affetto   Misery and anger
 Lo sdegno il dispetto   Change to affection:
 Trionfa l'amor.   Love triumphs.

The form of this trio is through-composed overall, with barely a change of key. However, the several repetitions of Giannina's melody in the opening section give both a musical and dramatic focus to what might otherwise be a rather meandering piece. The ensemble singing also "accumulates" from the male *à 2* as they respond to Giannina, to the final tutti, which enhances the number's sense of direction. The change of heart on the part of the men is undoubtedly abrupt and is not given even the musical clothing that Martín grants Diana's decision to reveal herself in the duet discussed above. But this change of heart is not the psychologically unmotivated snap into good cheer that we find at the ends of some ensembles, especially introductory ones; it is, rather, an ellipsis that assumes a knowledge of the conventional emotional processes between fathers and daughters, lovers and beloveds. Because the relationships are well understood, because Sarti's music distinguishes the participants in ways that arise directly from their characters, and because he dramatizes Giannina's progression from sweetness through misery to confidence in her powers of persuasion, as well as the larger progression from individual isolation to group cohesion, this piece, for all its conventionality, does suggest the potential for small ensembles to delineate, and then merge, individual consciousnesses. In this case the ending is, like the ending of Diana's and Endimione's duet, a resolution not only to the immediate conflict between

---

[25] The libretto has "Non puote il veleno / Nutrire nel seno" (text in example follows the score).

6-4: Sarti, *Le gelosie villane,* II, 3
Trio: Giannina, Cecchino, Tognino, "Deh, caro Padre amato,"
mm. 100–110

Giannina and her family, but to the potential class conflicts of the plot over-all. With Giannina safely resituated where she belongs (rather than with the Marchese), the chaos of the second-act finale, in which the Marchese's crepuscular philanderings get him soundly beaten by the *villane,* and in which Cecchino's suspicions about Giannina are reawakened, operates as sheer comedy rather than as socially destabilizing commentary.[26] The abruptness and extent of the trio's celebration, then, may seem *de trop* within the number itself, but in terms of the social (and to some extent psychological) themes of the opera as a whole, the abruptness is justified by the conventional frame within which these tensions occur, and the amount of time

---

[26] The contrast with the fourth-act finale of *Figaro* is obvious. There, not only do we find the conventional mechanical comedy of social reversals in the dark, but a deeper psychological comedy, in which the correct alliance, between the Count and the Countess, seems attractive to the Count because he thinks it is illicit and socially destabilizing.

spent asserting familial and class solidarity is altogether appropriate in an opera about the attempt to disrupt the "natural" bonds of same-class love and marriage.[27]

This trio and Diana's and Endimione's duet are both second-act pieces: the long-range functions of their resolutions are obviously related to their late placement in the drama. Duets between characters for whom there is either no need or no hope of resolution—all-male duets are often of this sort—more often occur in first acts than in second, and their endings do not participate in this pattern of double resolution. However, the process of rapprochement and resolution demonstrated in both Martín's duet and Sarti's trio is by no means limited to second-act ensembles: the opening duets in *Figaro* exemplify this process, for example, as does Don Ottavio and Donna Anna's "Fuggi, crudele" in *Don Giovanni*, despite the difference in subject matter.

Both this trio and the duet for Diana and Endimione could also be read as justifying or supporting a conventional social order through a central character's individual desire for, or will to belong to, it. If some rules of the social order (women contained in marriage, no marriages across class boundaries) are taken as primary social messages of these ensembles, then they seem rather uncomplicatedly related to the "conservative" frames of the genre. On the other hand, if the "will to belong" eventuating in the happy ending is taken as the main social characteristic of these ensembles, then their social implications are more complex, more interesting, and possibly more realistic. Both these ensembles (and many similar ones) represent a social order (marriage, family, rank) that presents itself as dependent on certain individuals' will to belong, but to which those individuals are in fact subject without negotiation. In this respect these ensembles seem to agree with Theresian political theorist J.H.G. von Justi[28] that it was the duty of the individual to "promote all the ways and means adopted by the ruler for their happiness."[29] In other words, self-realization was to consist solely in internalizing the aims of the larger order, or, as Peter Gay puts it, the duty of a citizen in response to the efforts of a ruler to make him happy was to "obey . . . and *be* happy."[30] Ernst Bruckmüller describes the "newly formulated interest in critical and independent bourgeois co-operation in

---

[27] There is a third-act trio for Giannina, her father, and the Marchese, which follows rather the same progression, though with different personnel and a different social object: Giannina and her father beg the Marchese for forgiveness for the events of the previous evening (the second-act finale), he refuses, they cry, he gives in and is reintegrated into the community, much as Giannina is reintegrated into her family in the trio just discussed.

[28] Johann Heinrich Gottlob von Justi was the author of *Die Grundfeste zu der Macht und der Glückseligkeit der Staaten* (The Basic Principles of the Power and Happiness of States), 2 vols. (Leipzig, 1760/61).

[29] Quoted in Peter Gay, *The Enlightenment: An Interpretation*, vol. 2, *The Science of Freedom* (New York: Norton, 1977) p. 489.

[30] Ibid.

public affairs" characteristic of the highest and most educated layers of the Austrian bourgeoisie in the late eighteenth century,[31] but he mentions this only to point out how thoroughly bound to the court such "independent co-operation" was, and how difficult it turned out to be to develop truly independent (and thus effectively critical) agencies of public opinion. Giannina's tearful re-entry into the family fold and Diana's embrace of a loving relationship are, of course, not self-conscious allegories for the tentative and contradictory place of public opinion under the Habsburgs, but they do celebrate the same apparently voluntary but fundamentally predestined relation between the individual and the larger polity that underpinned enlightened despotism.

Larger Ensembles: A Quartet

A different picture of the relationship of individuals and groups, and of the meanings of endings, emerges from most larger mid-act ensembles. The beginnings of larger ensembles are more various than the beginnings of duets and trios. Although it is the norm for larger ensembles to begin with solo singing, and some even begin with complete solo statements by all the characters, it is not unusual for this process to be compacted, either by having characters enter in pairs, or by making the entrances brief. The second-act sextet in *Una cosa rara,* "Dammi la cara mano," combines both methods. The peasant girls Lilla and Ghita, mistaking the duplicitous Prince and Corrado for their peasant lovers, sing twelve measures in thirds asking for the men's hands. The men respond in kind. These statements give way to shorter exchanges, after which Lubino and Titta, the peasant lovers, come in on the scene with two-measure declamatory interjections (see Example 6-5). Vocal material in larger ensembles, even as they open, is often rather fragmented and neutral in topic, blurring the distinctions between individuals. However, the orchestra often presents a compensatory continuity and energy; in such instances the orchestral music has the acoustic function of providing continuity, the rhythmic function of suggesting one or more expressive *topoi,* and the textural function of allowing pliable and responsive vocal lines from several characters. It may also indicate the tone or the mood of a segment of action. More importantly, its dramatic function often resembles that of a general lighting effect or a scrim: it flattens out or clouds over individual features in favor of the tableau.[32]

[31] Bruckmüller, *Sozialgeschichte Österreichs* (Vienna and Munich: Herold, 1985) p. 286.
[32] In this connection it is striking how little attention Allanbrook pays to the big ensembles in *Rhythmic Gesture in Mozart,* particularly once the characters start to sing together (the obvious exception is the contrast between Don Giovanni and Elvira's patter and Donna Anna and Don Ottavio's higher-flown material in "Non ti fidar"). This reinforces the idea that even in Mozart, vocal material in the big ensembles is in the truest sense lacking, or weak in character.

6-5: Martín y Soler, *Una cosa rara*, II,12
Sextet: Lilla, Ghita, Prince, Corrado, Lubino, Tita, "Dammi la cara
mano," mm. 1–18; 37–41

Translation:

Lilla and Ghita:	Give me your dear hand, embrace me my heart, you are my sweet love. You don't answer me?
Prince and Corrado:	I am the faithful adorer of your lovely eyes.
Lubino and Tita:	I think I hear people.
Lubino:	Lilla!
Tita:	Ghita!

The "ensemble principle" is often enacted more than once in large ensembles, as each phase of the action ends with some sort of ensemble singing, either by subgroups or by the whole cast of the number.[33] The only norm about the middles of larger ensembles is that interaction among the characters becomes either faster or more complex. Unlike the opening and middle sections, however, the endings of mid-act large ensembles in the repertory are remarkably uniform. With very few exceptions (the clapped-on "goodnight" happy end in the septet in *Una cosa rara* is one), mid-act ensembles of this sort end either with a moment of shared confusion or misery, with multiple texts indicating a frozen moment of conflict, or occasionally with a shared text of celebration meant ironically or stupidly by at least one character. Multiple texts may (like the end of the sextets in both *Figaro* and *Don Giovanni*) be set to two or more distinct musical ideas, or they may be disguised by homophonic and homorhythmic music. Dramatically, then, the endings of these numbers can function somewhat like John Platoff's "shock tutti" in a finale; they crystallize a moment of shared dramatic tension, they ensure that a plot-knot is tied as tightly as possible and held firm for some period of time. Like the endings of many finales, the endings of mid-act large ensembles are typically also repetitive, and harmonically and melodically spectacularly uninteresting—often almost minimalist in content. The musical material is often neutral in tone, content, and topic, emphasizing the collision of trajectories rather than individual emotional reactions. Mid-act large ensembles thus do not typically work a situation through to resolution; rather they expose and exacerbate its tensions and confusions. When the impasse of the ending is combined with the often "unstable" grouping of characters (disproportionate numbers of one gender, conspicuous absences, etc.), it becomes clear that the dramaturgical function of these numbers is to "coil the spring" for the next phase of the drama rather than to resolve either local or long-range tensions; and that their social significance lies in the way they play self-definition off against the power of circumstance.

The quartet from Palomba and Paisiello's *Le gare generose* I,5 exemplifies a number of these traits; it is reproduced essentially whole in Example 6-6 at the end of this chapter. Mr. Dull, the broad-minded Boston businessman, and Miss Meri, his niece, have each made marriage proposals to their servants, who are, as it happens, an eloped, already-married couple. They are, naturally enough, struck dumb by the offers, and the piece begins as Mr. Dull and Miss Meri take their horror for an excess of pleasure. The piece begins with Mr. Dull using a fairly neutral triadic *buffo*-like figure to point out his desire for some reciprocation for his generous offer.

---

[33] Rabin, "Mozart, Da Ponte, and the Dramaturgy of Opera Buffa," p. 329, describes a characteristic ensemble structure in which "strict homorhythmic response [alternates freely with] free dialogue."

Miss Meri chimes in with a similar message—she likes to do good but has no patience for ingrates. Paisello distinguishes these two characters from each other; unlike Mr. Dull, Miss Meri has a scalar, legato cantabile motive, presumably illustrating her peaceable nature. But in fact, she is not particularly peaceable, and she excites little sympathetic or sentimental interest in the course of the opera—the little dotted figure she uses at "ma da furia posso oprar" is much more characteristic of her role. If one were looking for psychological or interpersonal plausibility, one might read the cantabile phrase as an attempt to ingratiate herself with Bastiano (the slave whom she wishes to marry). But when Gelinda (the slave girl and female focus of the plot) uses the same material gingerly to ward off Mr. Dull, it becomes evident that the contrast in musical material (dotted-neutral vs. cantabile-sentimental) refers not so much to the inner lives of the characters as to the way the *situation* necessitates a balance between ingratiation and understanding, or between communication and reserve. Both Gelinda and Miss Meri do have little moments that indicate their individuality— Meri's dotted figure on "ma da furia posso oprar" and Gelinda's smoother line on "è un effetto d'umiltà" indicate the contrast between the more seria-like character[34] and the lower-status but more ingratiating *prima buffa*. Similarly, Bastiano begins with the ♪·♪|♫ figure borrowed from Mr. Dull, moving later into eighth- and then sixteenth-note patter; his distinctness as a character is not asserted until after he has musically established his conformity with the group. The first phase of the ensemble ends with dialogue singing based on the "neutral" or group material established by all the characters except Meri (mm. 52–56), then moves to an ensemble passage using material based on Bastiano's three-eighth-note figure in mm. 41ff. In the second large section of the piece (mm. 69–100), a continuous eighth-note orchestral figure forms the opening background, and all four characters enter with the same material. It is characteristic of this repertory that the utterances of the characters at this point in the number are distinguished not by the "substance" of the material, but by its articulation—Dull and Gelinda are accompanied by eighth notes with no slurs, and Meri and Bastiano's accompaniments have slurs (see mm. 69–84). Thereafter, Bastiano and Gelinda are distinguished from the masters by periods of panicked patter, and the pairs are indicated by staggered entrances and hocket effects. In these instances what we hear is not so much a description of an emotional or psychological condition or reaction as an em-

---

[34] Miss Meri is a good example of a character hovering on the edge of a seria characterization. Dittersdorf's substitution aria for her, "Così destino, e voglio," is an effective mixture of noble pride and flirtatiousness. (This aria is in the Library of Congress copy of the opera, whose Viennese origins are proclaimed on its title page. Paisello's own setting of the same text is transmitted in the Austrian National Library manuscript, Mus. Hs. 17807.)

bodiment of the alliances and mésalliances that the situation has brought about.

This quartet is characteristic of these ensembles (and finales, for that matter) in this repertory in the amount of time it spends ending, and the harmonic and melodic redundancy of the process. From the beginning of the end (ensemble "Vorrei dir" at m. 139) to the end there are 19 perfect authentic cadences for the voices (and more in the succeeding ritornello, not shown), and 21 complete bars of tonic harmony. It is hard to justify this in terms of grounding the tonic, since the piece has scarcely left it. There are also four simultaneous texts at the end, which Paisiello is careful to articulate as distinctly as possible—see, for example, mm. 145ff., where every character has a different rhythm, and is in any case singing words they have sung alone before. The combination of harmonic stasis and predictable cadences, and the careful dovetailing of the different rhythms, directs attention to the rhythmic and textural elements of the music, and perhaps more importantly to the singers' clockwork precision.

The significance of this ending, and others like it, is, I think, that a comically frozen moment of conflict coexists with a larger message of accommodation. That is, on the immediate level it is quite funny to see characters locked in disagreement or misunderstanding but still, in a spirit of obvious cooperation, singing the same music—and the length of the ending emphasizes this comedy. At the same time, the way in which the conventions of tonal music and the syntactical demands of number opera can contain and even partially reconcile different interests suggests that even at a moment of interpersonal conflict and dramatic tension, it is important to remember the common enterprise in which all parties are engaged. And the longer the ending goes on, the more the details of the conflict recede behind the surface message of unanimity. As with so many aspects of these works, conflict and atomization are delicately balanced against resolution and cohesion. It is a foregone conclusion that neither side of the equation will ever disappear; they remain in a state of perpetual and delightful flux. The social issues in this sort of ending, then, do not have to do with individuals "internalizing" the values of the group, as they do in the smaller ensembles discussed above; nor do these endings demand a sympathetic response from the audience, as do the smaller ensemble endings. Rather, the social value of the lockstep conflict at the end of the larger ensemble derives precisely from its comedy; the good humor of the moment encourages tolerance toward oppositional behaviors as long as they are contained in a harmonious frame.

6-6: Paisiello, *Le gare generose,* I,5
Quartet: Dull, Meri, Gelinda, Bastiano, "Ola, dico," [entire except
for final ritornello]

6-6: *(Continued)*

6-6: *(Continued)*

6-6: *(Continued)*

6-6: *(Continued)*

6-6: *(Continued)*

6-6: *(Continued)*

6-6: *(Continued)*

6-6: *(Continued)*

6-6: *(Continued)*

6-6: (Continued)

6-6: *(Continued)*

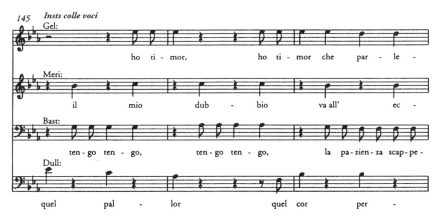

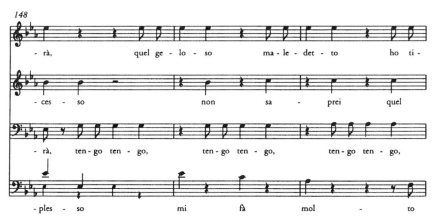

6-6: *(Continued)*

6-6: *(Continued)*

6-6: *(Continued)*

6-6: *(Continued)*

plus 11 mm. of rit.

Dull: Hey, I say, I'm the master, I make a ceremony out of my clemency, but I want something in return for my niceness. **Meri:** I am peaceable and good, it pleases me to do good, but I can get really angry with those who show ingratitude. **Gelinda:** What should I say to them? I'm confounded. For heavens' sake, dear master, if I do not respond properly to your love, it's the result of humility. **Bastiano:** If I answer, and the world comes tumbling down, that I'd like... but wouldn't like, because this... that... she... I know she'll tell me that's enough.

Dull: What's he saying to you? **Meri:** What do you think? **Gel:** There are gaps. **Bast:** There are problems...

All: I want to speak, but what can I say? I want to do something, but what can I do?

Dull: Dianina, I'll give you time to think about your circumstances. **Gel:** Why do you want to add remorse to my misery? **Meri:** Bronton, think about the fact that you could settle your fate. **Bast:** I'll think, thinking, and then, in thinking, a thought will come. I'll hang on, and finally I bet her patience will give out. **Gel:** That cursed jealous [Bastiano], I'm scared he'll say something.

Dull: What pallor, what a perplexed look: I'm really beginning to suspect. **Meri:** My doubts are increasing by leaps and bounds; I don't know what to think. **Bast:** What on earth am I supposed to do? **Gel:** What on earth am I supposed to say?

Chapter Seven

BEGINNING AND ENDING
TOGETHER: *INTRODUZIONI*
AND FINALES

ENSEMBLE *INTRODUZIONI* AND FINALES are among the most universal and durable features of Goldonian and post-Goldonian opera buffa. As ensembles, they frame each work with assertions about the primacy of groups and social processes. They also encapsulate the tension between individual self-determination and group conformity characteristic of the genre as a whole. On a more particular level, *introduzioni* and finales also typically convey something in miniature about the work in which they occur. For example, *introduzioni* often prefigure the overarching feel, or ethos, of the work: the multisectional form of the introduction to *Fra i due litiganti*, with its late entrance of two characters, and the almost manneristic double crescendo of the ending prefigures the imbroglio-ridden quality of the opera as a whole, while the chorus-framed hunting scene at the beginning of *Una cosa rara* anticipates not only the pastoral setting, but also the relative dramatic stasis of the work. Finales may not reiterate the "feel" of the work, but they often replay in miniature the central narrative. Thus operas centering on a persecuted heroine usually have at least one finale in which all the other characters look for her (often in the dark);[1] operas revolving around one or more dupes usually include at least one finale that is the climax or immediate aftermath of the trick played on him or them;[2] and operas in which the happy end is dependent on the exposure and neutralization of villainy usually discover and punish the villain in a finale.[3] And in both *introduzioni* and finales, the general social topic of individuals and groups plays with and against the musical and dramaturgical exigencies of beginning and ending.

---

[1] *Fra i due litiganti* I and II, *L'incognita perseguitata* I and II, *Giannina e Bernardone* I, *Una cosa rara* I, and *La frascatana* II are examples from the repertory. *Figaro* IV obviously connects to this type.

[2] *I filosofi immaginari* I and II, *L'arbore di Diana* II, *Il barbiere* IV, *Il curioso indiscreto* I and II, *L'astratto* I and II, *Il mondo della luna* I and II, and *Così* I and II also fall into this category.

[3] *Una cosa rara* II, *Il convitato di pietra* II, *Le gare generose* II. Also *Don Giovanni* II.

INTRODUZIONI

Almost all operas in this repertory begin with an introductory ensemble, often designated *introduzione*.[4] This term is found in scores more often than in librettos, unlike the term *finale*, which is regularly indicated in the librettos. Whether this has to do with obvious practical matters like the redundancy of the word *introduction* at the beginning of an opera, or the need for the multi-scene structures of many finales to be held together with a title, or whether it has to do with some aesthetic or dramaturgical distinction between these two sorts of numbers, is impossible to determine. However, without using the word *introduzione*, many librettos indicate the "set piece" aspect of the opening number by means of unusually elaborate stage sets and blocking directions. *La villanella rapita,* for example, begins: "Countryside, with Biagio's house, with a practicable porch. Hill in the distance, and a river crossing the landscape. From one side of the river, part of a city not too far away. Biagio, Ninetta, and Giannina with two other peasants under the porch of the house, all occupied in various culinary tasks."[5] This opening is designated *introduzione* in the score, but works without such designations often have equally elaborate stage directions in the libretti, with a comparable sense of introducing a group or set of relationships. Among the Mozart-Da Ponte operas, for example, of which only *Don Giovanni* has a so-designated *introduzione, Figaro* has the most elaborate stage instructions: "Not-yet furnished room, a sofa in the middle. Figaro with a ruler in his hand, and Susanna at the mirror, trying on a hat decorated with flowers." Both *Don Giovanni* and *Così,* on the other hand, open with very spare textual instructions: "Giardino. Notte," and "Bottega di caffè," respectively. This scenic spareness is, of course, more than compensated for in the tumultuous *introduzione* of the former and the unprecedented three-trio opening of the latter.

The term *introduzione* as used in this repertory, then, seems to have no watertight dramatic or structural meaning: the little duet at the beginning of *Figaro* has no designation other than "scene 1," which might be thought to arise from its small scale, but the comparably small-scale master-servant duet that opens Livigni and Paisiello's *La frascatana* is, however, called *introduzione.* By the same token, the pastoral chorus-aria-chorus complex at

---

[4] The very few that don't—among them *La buona figliuola* and Goldoni's *Lo speziale* (set by Haydn in 1768)—open with a self-introductory song for a character below the highest rank. Leporello's "Notte e giorno faticar" is related to this model, though it forms part of a larger ensemble introduction.

[5] Campagna, dov'è situata la Casa di Biagio con Sottoportico pratticabile [*sic*]. Colline in prospetto, e fiume, che attraversa la Campagna. Da un lato di là dal fiume parte della Città in poca distanza. Biagio, Ninetta, e Giannina con due altri Villani sotto il portico della Casa tutti occupati in varie faccende per la Cucina.

the beginning of *Una cosa rara* has no designation, which might be thought to arise from its encompassing more than one scene, but the four-scene introductory complex in Goldoni and Gassmann's *L'amore artigiano* is entitled *introduzione*. Numbers with this designation range from static elegies to full imbroglios, as do opening ensembles with no designation. There seems to be some chronological progression in the Viennese repertory to a less-frequent use of the term, but like all such progressions, it is neither uniform nor inexorable. However, within the variety of form and designation I have just described, there is a central core of introductory ensembles (most designated *introduzione* in the score) with common features. These features include a cast of more than two singers (usually three or four but occasionally up to seven[6]), a structure that permits both solo and ensemble singing, and (normally) a homophonic tutti ending. It is to these ensembles—which I will designate *introduzioni* whether or not they are so called in the score—that we now turn.

The Ternary Structures of Introduzioni

The most pervasive structural principle of *introduzioni* is a ternary design that begins with a more or less static statement about the situation or the occasion, continues with a disruption, complication, or minor imbroglio, followed in turn by an ensemble statement.[7] The beginnings of *introduzioni* can involve ensemble singing but more often include a series of solos; the middle sections, which introduce the conflict of the drama, or a social disruption or disagreement relevant to it, almost uniformly involve dialogue among the characters; and the endings, which are essentially always tuttis, can represent reasonable agreement, clapped-on celebration, or general confusion or dismay. Although the realization of the ternary principle varies widely in the repertory, the tripartiteness of these beginning numbers is so common that one might argue that contemporary audiences would have heard both the duettino-recitative-duettino opening of *Le nozze di Figaro* and the unprecedented three-trio opening of *Così* as variants on the *introduzione,* regardless of their designation (or lack thereof).[8] Indeed, the toast to Venus and Cupid proposed in "Una bella serenata" (the third of *Così*'s three opening trios) is closely related to the celebratory endings of many introduzioni in this repertory, and its fuller orchestration (while it belies the pastoral elements of the text) also makes it a suitable conclusion to the set. "È la fede delle femmine," the middle

---

[6] Most *introduzioni* do not use the whole cast.

[7] Rabin, "Mozart, Da Ponte, and the Dramaturgy of Opera Buffa" (Ph.D. dissertation, Cornell University, 1996) pp. 249–84, describes a number of *introduzioni* using this ternary principle.

[8] See Bruce Alan Brown and John A. Rice, "Salieri's *Così fan tutte,*" *COJ* 8 (1996) p. 29.

trio of the three, is also the most "dialogic" (as well as the least conclusive).

One obvious function of all ensemble introductions is to assert immediately the *Ensemblegeist* of the genre, to assert that these operas are about groups and institutions before they are about self-determining individuals, or at least that moments of subjectivity or self-determination are always contained within a well-understood set of social expectations. The beginnings of *introduzioni* assert the genre's orientation toward groups in various ways. A very small number of operas in this repertory begin with a chorus consisting of an undifferentiated collective: *La fiera di Venezia*, for example, opens with a chorus of Venetian petty merchants, and *Una cosa rara* begins with a chorus of hunters. *I filosofi immaginari* includes a section for the resident students of the old philosopher Petronio, though it does not begin with it. Despite these occasional representations of undifferentiated but locally specific groups, this repertory almost never features the "popolo" in the sense of a mass of citzens. (Da Ponte and Salieri's *Axur re di Ormus* is the most striking exception; its concern with, and demonstration of, a population's sentiments about a ruler, relate to its origins as a French-language *opéra* (*Tarare*), written by Salieri for Paris to a text by Beaumarchais.) The expense of representing a whole citizenry on stage was certainly a relevant consideration in opera buffa's general avoidance of citizen-masses, but it is also the case that, unlike the ruling-class characters of opera seria, opera buffa characters are almost never defined in relation to society in the aggregate. Even in Casti and Paisiello's *Il re Teodoro in Venezia*, whose *argomento* describes King Theodore's rout by the people of Corsica, the action of the opera itself concerns the immediate and local interactions of the people (including King Theodore) in the Venetian inn. The opera invokes the notion of a ruler's larger obligation to his people by having a Venetian official indict and imprison the King for his debt rather than by showing an angry mob.

Opera buffa, then, typically represents "society" by means of a carefully selected sample of identifiable individuals. These individuals, however, do sometimes take over the chorus function of larger groups and utter their first sounds on stage as members of an undifferentiated tutti ensemble. The texts of such opening tuttis may further deindividuate the participants by expressing the most generalized celebratory or pastoral sentiments. The opening of *La finta giardiniera*, quoted in Chapter 3, exemplifies this, as does the beginning of Anfossi's *L'incognita perseguitata*, shown in Example 7-1. The steady rhythm, the uncomplicated harmonies, and the tenor doubling of the soprano are all quite usual in four-part homophonic vocal writing in this repertory, but the slightly oversweet blandness lent by these musical devices seems to express the general tone of the entertainment to come rather than the experience of the individuals who will construct it.

7-1: Anfossi, *L'incognita perseguitata,* introduzione, mm. 24–31

Translation: [What] beautiful pleasure in this day, which makes our hearts rejoice.

Introduzioni more often begin with a series of closed solos introducing the characters than with any sort of ensemble singing. Such solos often comment on or arise from the immediate situation, which may or may not be directly related to the issues of the drama: some, for example, comment on the weather,[9] or engage in desultory tea-party or card-game conversation,[10] while others allow the characters to introduce themselves more directly. The characters are, however, typically presented in juxtaposition rather than in interaction with each other; often the individual utterances are addressed to the audience, and sometimes they are apostrophic. The lack of active engagement among the characters and the often rather disengaged content of the speeches connects these openings with the tutti beginnings just discussed, even though the singing is solo. The opening of Goldoni and Gassmann's *L'amore artigiano* can serve as an example. The stage set is unusually picturesque, and the singers are, to begin with, literally "set in" the stage picture, as they appear in their windows: "Little square with various houses and shops, still closed. It is barely dawn, and little by little [the stage] lights up. Rosina opens the window and becomes

[9] As, for example, in *Il convitato di pietra, L'isola di Alcina, La vera costanza,* Cavalieri and Guglielmi's *L'impresa dell'opera,* and Piccinni's *Gli stravaganti* (librettist unknown).
[10] For example, *L'astratto,* or Petrosellini and Cimarosa's *L'italiana in Londra. Le gare generose* also begins with a tea party, but the introductory statements are shorter and more dialogic.

visible; Angiolina does the same from her house, right opposite Rosina's; then Giannino comes along the street, playing his guitar and singing."[11] The piece opens with a duet for the women, consisting of two full solo statements (the first one moving to V and the second in I) and an ensemble stanza, then segues (with a change of tempo and meter) into Giannino's serenade (see Example 7-2):

ROSINA:

Bella cosa gli è il vedere	It is a beautiful thing to see
Spuntar l'alba in sul mattino:	The dawn break in the morning:
Ma se passa il mio Giannino,	But if my Giannino goes by,
Fugge l'alba e spunta il sol.	Twilight flees and the sun rises.

ANGIOLINA:

Sorge l'alba, e sto a vedere	Dawn rises and I stand watching
Far il sole il suo cammino;	The sun on its path;
Ma dagli occhi di Giannino	But Giannino's eyes
Vinta è l'alba, e vinto è il sol.	Conquer the dawn and the sun.

À 2:

Pria ch'io vada al mio lavoro	Before I go to work
Deh vedessi il mio tesoro,	Ah, let me see my beloved,
Deh venisse il mio bel sol.	Let my lovely sun come by.

GIANNINO:

Non posso riposar, non trovo loco,	I cannot rest, or find a place.
Cerco qualche ristoro alla frescura,	I seek some rest in the cool air,
Ma dove i'vado porto meco il foco,	But wherever I go, I carry a fire with me,
Ed è il mantice mio fra quelle mura.	And the bellows for it are within these walls.

The repetitiousness of the opening duet contributes to the sense that this opening is as much about the stage set as about the feelings of the women, and the fact that these two women love the same man is (perhaps comically) hidden behind each participant's isolated enjoyment of the scene and of the sensation of being in love.[12]

The third characteristic opening to the ensemble introduction, less frequent than the static solos but more so than the choral opening, is a series of solos shorter than a stanza, often placed in more or less dialogic relation to one another: these solos often delineate the principal conflict of the opera and give the impression not of framing the opera but of launching

[11] Piazzetta con varie case e botteghe ancora chiuse. Vedesi appena l'alba, e a poco a poco si va rischiarando. Rosina apre la finestra e si fa vedere; poi Angiolina fa lo stesso nell'abitazione sua dirimpetto a quella della Rosina, poi Giannino viene di strada, suonando il chitarrino e cantando.

[12] See Heartz, *Haydn, Mozart and the Viennese School 1740–1780* (New York: Norton, 1995) pp. 414–15, for admiring commentary on this *introduzione*.

7-2: Gassmann, *L'amore artigiano*, introduzione, mm. 22–49;
86–89; Allegretto, 7–14

7-2: *(Continued)*

precipitately into the nub of the action. The opening of *Fra i due litiganti* is a case in point, as the Conte and Contessa walk in quarreling:

CONTESSA:
  La voglio così,   I want it thus.

CONTE:
  Così non sarà.   It will not be that way.

CONTESSA:
  Prevale il mio sì.   My say-so will prevail.

CONTE:
  Adesso non già.   Not in this situation.

These two exchanges are each presented as repeated little periods, whose melodies show no distinction in character, and which match the *abab* rhyme of the text with comparable musical symmetry (see Example 7-3). This paragraph is followed immediately by a homophonic duet passage in which they both assert their determination to win (see Example 7-4).

7-3: Sarti, *Fra i due litiganti il terzo gode,* introduzione, mm. 12–20

Thus, even though the text suggests conflict and individual differentiation, the musical symmetries of this beginning, the identical qualities of the characters' phrases even before the homophonic passage, and the alacrity with which they fall into simultaneity suggest the static and institutional nature of their disagreement: the beginning of this *introduzione* seems more a comment on the nature of aristocratic marriage than a depiction of these characters' inner lives.[13]

Whether an *introduzione* begins with an ensemble or some sort of solo singing, it almost always moves to a section in which the characters (plus occasionally one or two new ones) interact more directly with each other, often delineating the drama's principal tension or conflict, and disrupting the pastoral celebration or the stability or institutionality of the beginning.

[13] The expression of institutionalized discord is also one function of Leporello's "Notte e giorno faticar" at the beginning of *Don Giovanni.* Servants have always complained about their jobs and maligned their bosses behind their backs; Leporello thus represents the expected order so shockingly disrupted by Don Giovanni's assault on Donna Anna and murder of the Commendatore.

7-4: Sarti, *Fra i due litiganti il terzo gode*, introduzione, mm. 20–28

Translation: I swear and protest that no-one will see me believing this.

This gives a sense of increasing embroilment in the drama and typically provides some insight into the individual situations of the characters. In *L'incognita perseguitata*, after the opening cheerful chorus, the two pairs of characters, the noble Asdrubale and the apparently lowly Giannetta, then the servants Fabrizio and Nannina, speak to each other in full quatrains, indicating the point of tension between them: Giannetta thinks herself unworthy of Asdrubale's attentions, while Fabrizio has turned his attentions from Nannina to Giannetta:

GIANNETTA:

Ah Signore, il Ciel vi renda
Quel gentil virtuoso affetto,
Che per me serbate in petto,
Ch'io non so di meritar.

Ah Sir, let Heaven return to you
That noble and virtuous affection
That you have in your heart for me,
[And] of which I am unworthy.

ASDRUBALE:

Che beltà, che leggiadria,
Quei begl'occhi spiritosi
Hanno i rai del sole ascosi,
Mi fan l'alma in sen brillar.

What beauty, what loveliness,
Those beautiful lively eyes
Have hidden the rays of the sun,
And make my soul shine in my breast.

NANNINA:

Dammi sol mio caro bene,
Amorosa un'occhiatina,
Che saprà la tua Nannina
Fido il cor per te serbar.

Give me, my only sweet love,
A loving glance,
So that your Nannina will be able to
Hold her heart faithful to you.

7-5: Anfossi, *L'incognita perseguitata,* introduzione, mm. 48–60; 72–90

FABRIZIO:

Datti pace, non sdegnarti,   Don't worry, don't be angry,
Il tuo amor più non desio;   I don't want your love anymore.
Sol Giannetta è l'idol mio,   Giannetta is my only idol
E lei solo voglio amar.   And I want to love her alone.

Anfossi's music differentiates the characters less strongly than does the text; all the characters (including Asdrubale, not shown here) engage in cantabile/sentimental slurred pairs of eighth notes, and even Fabrizio's use of the characteristically *buffo* dotted-quarter, eighth figure does not last long. The dramatic pace picks up slightly after this section, as Giannetta and Asdrubale declare their love in musically matched single lines, Fabrizio joins in with a couplet, and Nannina (also in a couplet) dissents from the general satisfaction.

The disruption in this *introduzione* concerns the conflict between individual desires and a stable or rigid social order. Asdrubale's desire for the apparently lowborn Giannetta suggests a potentially destabilizing disregard for social boundaries, while Fabrizio's spurning of Nannina for the actually noble Giannetta suggests the dangers of pretension. This double misinterpretation of Giannetta's status is the mainspring of the plot. This *introduzione* does not explore the psyches of its participants; the music is too conventional and too little differentiated for that. Nevertheless, it clearly and schematically illustrates their positions in relation to each other, particularly when the dialogue gets going. Thus, on the one hand, this number suggests that individuality will emerge from the negotiation and renegotiation of socially determined relationships; on the other, the musical continuities of tempo, meter, and topic suggest that such individual differences as emerge will be subsumed into a predominantly pleasant or easily entertaining aesthetic.

In *Fra i due litiganti,* the change from the opening paragraph comes not as the participants identify their individual positions in the drama, but with the entry of the servants Livietta and Masotto, who rush in to see what the racket is. Their music—beginning as recitative-like vocal lines over a continuous orchestral figure in a new meter ($\frac{4}{4}$ rather than $\frac{3}{8}$)—identifies them as different from the Conte and Contessa, but not from each other: again, institutional rather than individual characteristics are the issue here, and the "disruption" characteristic of the middle section of most *introduzioni* is here represented by the suggestion that the servants will intervene (as in fact they do) to settle the apparently irreconcilable disagreement between the aristocrats, controlling the action in the process. Although the particulars are quite different from those in *L'incognita perseguitata,* the larger message that individuality is revealed through the juxtaposition of differences, and through behaviors in reaction to circumstances, holds in both cases (see Example 7-6).

The end of this *introduzione* unites these two pairs of characters in a largely homophonic holding-pattern of uncertainty:

Con tanto strepito,	With so much disagreement,
Con tal fracasso,	With such a racket,
Senza concludere	We stand here
Si resterà.	Without resolution.

7-6: Sarti, *Fra i due litiganti il terzo gode,* introduzione, mm. 82–94

Translation: **Livietta:** What's up? **Masotto:** What's happened? **Both:** I heard screaming here. **Livietta:** And I ran… **Masotto:** I came… **Both:** weakly to help, for reasons of justice and duty.

There are no musical differences among the characters in this section, and the fourfold (!) repetition of the final quatrain drives home both the comically unifying effect of the situation and the amusing incongruity between the uncertainty of the situation and the joyful finality of the music. Thus, although this *introduzione* presents more conflict—and presents it with less ceremony—than many, it never allows any of the individuals involved to step out from behind their statuses or their situations. Rather, it represents the animating tension of the drama (whom will Dorina marry?) as a matter of institutional rather than personal interest. In fact, as the opera gets going, the individuals (especially Dorina and Masotto) do gain depth and interest, but the *introduzione* erects a sturdy institutional frame to contain their more "human" qualities.

The end of the *introduzione* to *L'incognita perseguitata* simply repeats the jolly opening chorus to the same cheerful words. I suggested in Chapter 2 that the sudden celebratory ending, which is at least as common among *introduzioni* as the collective statement of uncertainty or confusion, enacts in miniature the overall process of comedy, and that on certain occasions, where the good cheer of the opening is literally repeated at the end of the *introduzione,* the ternary structure of the introduction plays out explicitly and on a small scale the implicit broad ternary structure of comedy. On a more immediate level, the little happy end of the *introduzione* encapsulates the situation that must be disrupted in order for the opera to proceed. And in social terms these suddenly cheery endings efficiently co-opt the individual into the group, the idiosyncratic into the norm, and self-expression into agreement, a process reenacted in various ways and on various levels throughout most operas in this repertory.

Functions of Introduzioni

The few scholars who have looked in any detail at opera buffa *introduzioni* have typically thought in dramatic rather than social terms and divided them into "tableaux" and "action pieces." The former involve no action, are quite distinct from the body of the drama, and as Stefan Kunze notes, form the aural dimension of the opening stage set, while the latter serve as "springboards" into the nub of the action—often with a quarrel or difference of opinion.[14] Although "tableau" and "springboard" are useful con-

---

[14] Stefan Kunze, "Per una descrizione tipologica della 'introduzione' nell'opera buffa del settecento e particolarmente nei drammi giocosi di Carlo Goldoni e Baldassare Galuppi," in Maria Teresa Muraro and Franco Rossi, eds., *Galuppiana 1985: Studi e Ricerche: Atti del Convegno Internazionale, Venezia . . . 1985* (Florence: Olschki, 1986) pp. 165–77, was among the first scholars to identify the pastoral *introduzione* in mid-century opera buffa; he locates it not only among sheep but also in gardens and other natural settings. He contrasts this with the *introduzione* in which people are presented not as indistinguishable parts of the scenery but as interacting individuals having something like a conversation. He notes that the *intro-*

ceptual poles around which to organize the dramatic functions of *intro-duzioni,* most such pieces in this repertory include elements of both. Thus, just as *Fra i due litiganti's* "springboard" *introduzione* institutionalizes the differences among the characters into something like a tableau of the opera's social world, so the apparently tableau-like opening of *L'incognita perseguitata,* with its explicitly pastoral content and its literally ternary form, also sows the seeds of the drama to come by exposing the conflicting personal positions that will drive it.

Both dramatically and socially then, *introduzioni* present frames in unstable relations with their contents: tableaux include springboard elements and vice versa, quarreling individuals turn out to be part of a static social structure, and apparently happy social groups turn out to consist of members whose interests are incommensurable. As with so many aspects of opera buffa, it is these abstract structures or relationships that most closely connect with the world in which these operas played. In other words, the social relevance of many *introduzioni* lies in the way they cheerfully normalize the tensions between framing social structures and individual proclivities. The pleasure provided by the framing good cheer or static institutionality of most *introduzioni* is essential to the message that it is not conflict between individuals and society that matters, but ease of accommodation on both sides.

FINALES

Finales are the most-discussed ensemble-type in opera buffa: indeed they are probably the most-discussed aspect of opera buffa altogether. Almost all the operas in this repertory include two ensemble finales, one at the end of the first act, and the other at the end of the second.[15] It is normal in a three-act piece for the second-act finale to end with something still unresolved and a general expression of puzzlement, confusion, or misunderstanding, though this is rarely as strong or as desperate as the end of the first act.[16] In two-act operas, the second-act finale typically includes the de-

---

duzione presented as an "ensemble proper" is a rather late development that leads to the dramatically integral opening numbers of the Mozart–Da Ponte operas. Francesco Blanchetti, "Tipologia musicale dei concertati nell'opera buffa di Giovanni Paisiello," *RIM* 19 (1984) pp. 237–38, also makes a primary distinction between *introduzioni* primarily concerned to exhibit the ambience of the work to come, and those primarily concerned to introduce the action. Hermann Abert makes a similar distinction in "Paisiellos Buffokunst und ihre Beziehungen zu Mozart," *Gesammelte Schriften und Vorträge* (Halle: Niemeyer, 1929) p. 387.

[15] Paisiello's *Barbiere* is an exception, having only one real ensemble finale, at the end of the last act.

[16] Friedrich Lippmann, "Il 'Grande Finale' nell'opera buffa e nell'opera seria: Paisiello e Rossini," *RIM* 27 (1992) p. 225, goes so far as to say that only "internal finales" (the first-act finale in a two-act opera, and the first two finales in a three-act piece) count as "grande."

nouement and resolution of the plot, and ends with general celebration or moralizing. Third acts, where they exist, usually end with a brief chorus, or a chorus alternating with solo or duet statements of resolution or intention. Third act ensemble-endings never involve denouement or plot-work; they merely enact the dramatic as well as the musical cadence to an already-completed process.

Dramatic and Musical Structures in Finales

The finales in this repertory are essentially all of the "chain" type. That is, they are basically through-composed, with a number of musical sections in different tempi, meters, and keys.[17] As John Platoff notes about the operas composed for Vienna in the 1780s, the musical sections correspond to phases in the action, and the musical changes usually come as a result of a change in scene, a new poetic meter, and/or a new topic of discussion. Sections often begin with solo statements or dialogue and move toward ensemble singing of some sort, thus multiply reiterating Rabin's "ensemble principle." The musical sections are usually but not always closed with clear cadences, and the range of modulation can be as narrow as tonic, dominant, subdominant, and/or supertonic (in which case there may be no change of key signature) or broad enough to encompass sections in distantly related keys. Many finales include at least one modulation up or down by a third; this may or may not coincide with the crucial or most surprising event of the finale, or with a radical change in tempo or meter. There is a general chronological progression toward longer finales with more discrete sections and more distant modulations, but as early as 1772 the first-act finale to Gazzaniga's *L'isola di Alcina* includes 12 discrete musical sections and modulations to E♭ and B♭ in an overall context of C major, while as late as 1786 the first-act finale of Paisiello's *Le gare generose* includes only 5 big musical sections (plus a short section in accompanied recitative) and remains in keys closely related to the tonic, F major: the most distant modulation being to E♭ in a section in B♭.

Osthoff mentions the "Gesetz der Steigerung" in finales—that is, the rule of accumulation or increase, both in the numbers of people on stage

---

Where the third-act finale is simply a chorus, I would of course agree, but there are plenty of two-act operas in this repertory whose "final finale" would surely count as "grande."

[17] All the finales in this repertory include substantial segments away from the tonic. In some cases, however, particularly among the earlier operas, the basic key signature never changes and modulations are simply signaled with local accidentals. These finales typically do not move very far away from the tonic. Examples of such finales can be found in the first act of Anfossi's *L'incognita perseguitata*, the second act of Paisiello's *Le gare generose* (which, however, does have one section in ♭III), both acts of the same composer's *La frascatana*, *Il barbiere di Siviglia*, and *I filosofi immaginari*, and both acts of Piccinni's *L'astratto* and *La buona figliuola*. Paisiello's propensity not to mark overall key changes is particularly strong.

and in the prevailing tempo;[18] this "rule" is in a sense the large-scale and dramatic analogue to the smaller-scale musical "ensemble principle" that pertains in essentially all ensembles in this repertory. The rule of accumulation is the chief feature both described and enacted by Da Ponte in his famous comic account of the finale:

> This finale, which, in addition, must be intimately connected with the rest of the opera, is a sort of comedy-let or little drama in itself, and needs a new intrigue and an extraordinary point of interest. In this [sort of number] it is chiefly the genius of the composer, the power of the singers, and the greatest dramatic effect that needs to shine. Recitative is excluded: everything is sung, and all sorts of singing are found here. The adagio, the allegro, the andante, the amorous, the harmonious, the noisy, the uproarious, [and] the positively frenetic, with which the above-mentioned finale always closes. The proper musical term for this last is the "close" or the "stretta"; I don't know whether this is because the drama tightens and intensifies there, or because it stresses, not once but a hundredfold the poor brain of the poet who has to write the words. In this finale theatrical convention dictates that all the singers—even if there are three hundred—appear alone, in pairs, in threes, in sixes, in tens, in sixties, to sing solos, duets, trios, sextets, and sixty-ets; and if the plot doesn't permit this, then the poet has to find a way to make it happen, regardless of the criterion of reason, and of all the Aristotelian [rules] in the world. And if he finds that it doesn't work, so much the worse for him.[19]

Certain libretti also indicate the widespread understanding of this process when, rather than marking a new scene for each entrance, they simply indicate that the characters enter "tutti a suo tempo," or as in Porta and Righini's *L'incontro inaspettato* I, "indi tutte [*sic*] come siegue nel finale." Other libretti divide the finale into two or more (sometimes as many as five or six) scenes, with each scene change marking an entrance and sometimes an exit. Most finales adhere to the rule of accumulation, and almost all end with more characters on stage than at the beginning. Never-

---

[18] Osthoff, "Die Opera buffa," in *Gattungen der Musik in Einzeldarstellungen,* ed. Wulf Arlt et al. (Berlin and Munich: Francke, 1973) p. 724.

[19] Lorenzo Da Ponte, *Memorie,* ed. Giuseppe Armani, 2d ed. (Milan: Garzanti, 1980) pp. 92–93: Questo finale, che deve essere per altro intimamente connesso col rimanente dell'-opera, è una spezie di commediola o di picciol dramma da sé, e richiede un novello intreccio ed un interesse straordinario. In questo principalmente deve brillare il genio del maestro di cappella, la forza de' cantanti, il più grande effetto del dramma. Il recitativo n'è escluso, si canta tutto; e trovar vi si deve ogni genere di canto. L'adagio, l'allegro, l'andante, l'amabile, l'armonioso, lo strepitoso, l'arcistrepitoso, lo strepitosissimo, con cui quasi sempre il suddetto finale si chiude; il che in voce musico-tecnica si chiama la "chiusa" oppure la "stretta," non so se perché in quella la forza del dramma si stringe, o perché dà generalmente non una stretta ma cento al povero cerebro del poeta che deve scrivere le parole. In questo finale devono per teatrale domma comparir in scena tutti i cantanti, se fosser trecento, a uno, a due, a tre, a sei, a dieci, a sessanta, per cantarvi de' soli, de' duetti, de' terzetti, de' sestetti, de' sessantetti; e se l'intreccio del dramma nol permette, bisogna che il poeta trovi la strada di farselo permettere, a dispetto del criterio, della ragione e di tutti gli Aristotili della terra; e, se trovasi poi che va male, tanto peggio per lui.

theless, the rule plays out in a variety of different ways. Some finales, like *L'arbore di Diana* I, accumulate the characters gradually and inexorably: the piece starts with Doristo (the guardian of the garden) and a chorus of spirits; Diana and three nymphs enter in the next scene; Amore comes in next, followed by Silvio and finally by Endimione. No-one leaves in the course of the finale and the stage simply gets fuller as the finale proceeds. The second-act finale to *I filosofi immaginari,* whose text is given at the end of this chapter, also follows this pattern of unbroken accumulation. Most finales follow this pattern, but in some, *Fra i due litiganti* II, for example, whose text also appears at the end of the chapter, individual characters come and go once or twice in the course of the finale, slightly complicating the overall pattern of increase, while in a few others there is a "double wave" of accumulation—an increase in numbers until a break, followed by a soliloquy or a duet and a second increase. On rare occasions, as in *L'arbore di Diana* II, there is a change of stage set in the middle of the finale—in this case from Diana's garden to the realm of love.[20]

Just as finales typically end with more characters on stage than they had at the beginning, the vast majority of finales end in a faster tempo than that in which they began. But unlike the number of characters on stage, which can be comfortably explained by an overall rule of increase, the changes in tempo and meter in these finales (sometimes as many as 13, and in the exceptional case of *Figaro* II, 17) cannot be fully explained by this rule but rather follow the demands of text and action. Opening tempi range from *Largo* to *Allegro assai,* and the number, range, and order of tempi in the bodies of finales is infinitely various. Almost all finales include at least one *Andante* or *Larghetto* section; this often corresponds to a private or sentimental moment in the action. However, whatever the particulars of any given finale, it is often the case that a section in slow or moderate tempo precedes the final or penultimate fast section, and in many, the final *stretta,* in which the final argument is played out and the moral or concluding sentiment of the number is declaimed, is faster than what has immediately preceded it. Thus the last two or three sections of most finales typically project a sense of acceleration, intensified in many instances by the rush to impasse or denouement. In addition, the end of the finale may be the only place where all the characters sing together for any length of time; it is almost always the only place where all characters sing more or less homophonically for more than a measure or two, and thus in addition to an increase in tempo and stage-fullness, so to speak, there is also an overall increase in vocal power.

Until recently the standard comment about finales in general, transmit-

---

[20] Platoff, "Music and Drama in the Opera Buffa Finale" (Ph.D. dissertation, University of Pennsylvania, 1984) p. 34, suggests that such changes are relatively common in the operas written for Vienna in the 1780s; they are less so in my somewhat broader repertory.

ted more or less verbatim from one writer to another, was that they represented the match of abstract formal procedures, often assumed to be based on sonata form or principles, with dramatic flow; the "purely musical" means of organization often being considered the primary structural model or layer.[21] Such an idea seems to underlie Osthoff's claim that opera buffa in general (and ensembles and finales in particular) can be understood as a theatrical application of practices first developed in instrumental music.[22] This attitude is intensified by most historians' concentration on Mozart; the second-act finale of *Le nozze di Figaro* has been particularly subject to this sort of treatment, largely because of its long series of modulations by fifth back to the tonic.[23] This finale is commonly seen as the apex of the genre, the culmination of years of attempts by other librettists and composers.[24] John Platoff has gone to great pains to point out the determining function of the text (both in terms of form and content) in the musical structures of finales by Mozart and his contemporaries:[25] he has also identified the basic structural principle of the "action-expression cycle" in which passages of activity, mostly carried on in dialogue, alternate with passages of corporate reflection, carried on in various sorts of ensemble singing. Platoff's purpose is primarily to debunk the notion that instrumental-formal models underlie such a fundamentally theatrical genre as the finale, and to assert that dramatic action in general is a major determinant of musical procedures.[26]

[21] Edward Dent succinctly notes that the ideal of modern opera (which implicitly starts with Mozart's buffa finales) is that the "music should be continuously dramatic, and the drama continuously musical" ("Ensembles and Finales in 18th Century Italian Opera," I, *SIMG* 11 [1909–10], 543-69). Donald Jay Grout, *A Short History of Opera*, 3d ed., with Hermine Wiegel Williams (New York: Columbia University Press, 1988) pp. 330–31 notes: "Mozart never loses sight of the individuality of his persons. . . . Then too, Mozart's music in these finales is . . . truly symphonic."

[22] See Chapter 6, n. 2.

[23] Rosen, *The Classical Style* (London: Faber & Faber, 1971) pp. 302–5. Among the more recent examples of treating this number as profoundly based on sonata principles is Steptoe, *The Mozart–Da Ponte Operas* (Oxford: Clarendon Press, 1988) pp. 173–79. See John Platoff, "Tonal Organization in 'Buffa' Finales and the Act II Finale of *Le nozze di Figaro*," *M&L* 72 (1991) pp. 387–403, for a reconsideration of the formal principles of this finale.

[24] Hermann Abert, *W. A. Mozart: Neubearbeitete und erweiterte Ausgabe von Otto Jahns Mozart*, 6th ed. (Leipzig: Breitkopf & Härtel, 1923–24) pp. 347–48, expresses the general teleological narrative of the development of the finale particularly clearly: "Already before Mozart, composers were not simply striving towards an abruptly changing series of pictures, rather they were trying to develop and exploit the process psychologically, to conceive the outer situation as a result of emotional tensions, and, with increasing artfulness, to prepare and eventually discharge these. It is remarkable that this more sophisticated (*feinere*) sort of comedy reached the highest peak of its development just in Germany."

[25] "Music and Drama in the Opera Buffa Finale: Mozart and His Contemporaries in Vienna"; "Musical and Dramatic Structure in the Opera Buffa Finale" *JM* 7 (1989) pp. 191–230; and "Tonal Organization in 'Buffa' Finales and the Act II Finale of *Le nozze di Figaro*."

[26] Edmund J. Goehring, "The Comic Vision of *Così fan Tutte*: Literary and Operatic Traditions" (Ph.D. dissertation, Columbia University, 1993) pp. 189–90, has suggested in re-

At the same time as Platoff separates the opera buffa finale from the conventions of instrumental music, he also points out that it is in other ways a "thoroughly conventional" sort of number.[27] Here he is close to eighteenth-century opinion, though he does not elaborate on the eighteenth-century idea that the conventionality of the finale was inextricably bound up with its lack of verisimilitude. Lorenzo Da Ponte's description of the finale, quoted above, suggests that the convention of the stretta outweighed every other consideration, and at least one comment in an early-nineteenth-century issue of the *Allgemeine Musikalische Zeitung* also identifies the finale as part of a relentlessly mechanical theatrical process: "Everyone must sing an aria in turn and these arias give place, without the slightest touch of probability, to the finale which ends in the hurly burly of a battle, an earthquake, or a thunderstorm."[28]

Almost all the claimed characteristics of finales, from their capacity to mimic the motions of complex social and emotional activity to their unalloyed mechanism, from their musical coherence to their dependence on the text, have something to them. Whatever their length and complexity, finales in this repertory do begin and end in the same key and use the tensions and relaxations inherent in close and distant, short- and long-range key relations to structure and pace the action. Some units within finales do take on "key-area-form" characteristics. Moreover, the prominence and authority of the orchestra in shaping the flow of the action and in lending it emotional specificity, make the claims of fundamentally instrumental forms understandable if not totally convincing.[29] Many finales do also have a mechanistic aspect that works against literal realism; certain plot "riffs" occur again and again, and particularly where a trick is at issue, there is often the sense that it is played for more than it is worth. At the same time, with its capacity to propel or envelop more or less mundane and characterless dialogue in a blanket of sound,[30] and its potential to allow both smooth transitions between solo and group utterances and surprising juxtapositions of styles and *topoi*, the music of finales both approximates the surface rhythm of social intercourse and invests that intercourse with extraordinary emotional specificity. Relentless mechanism, then, coexists

---

sponse to Platoff that the use of sonata-like principles such as general tonal balance and long-range resolution is not necessarily incommensurate with responsiveness to the text.

[27] Platoff, "Music and Drama in the Opera Buffa Finale," p. 9.

[28] Quoted in Leonard Ratner, *Classic Music* (New York: Schirmer, 1980) p. 393.

[29] See Strohm's comments on Gassmann's *La contessina* in *Die italienische Oper* (Wilhelmshaven: Heinrichshofen, 1979) p. 285 (which applies to arias and other ensembles as well as finales). See also Friedrich Lippmann, "Il 'Grande Finale' nell'opera buffa e nell'opera seria" pp. 225–55, especially his description of the continuous and varied orchestral motives in the first-act finale of *La frascatana* (231–35).

[30] Sabine Henze-Döhring, "La tecnica del concertato in Paisiello e Rossini," *NRMI* 22 (1988) p. 5, describes the orchestral part as "a sort of frame into which the vocal parts are irregularly inserted."

with the illusion of naturalness, and music responsive to particular textual and dramatic moments is layered with more abstract musical processes. Obviously certain finales seem more "natural" than others; some have musical structures comprehensible only in terms of the libretto, while others set the action to musical processes more fully explicable in abstract terms. But all these elements coexist in all buffa finales to some degree, and the question here is how this mishmash of apparently contradictory processes and elements might combine to project dramatic and social meanings.

Social Structures in Finales

In terms of the social values of finales, their most relevant tensions arise in the ways they represent individuals in relation to the groups of which they are part. Like other ensembles, but to a greater degree because of their greater length, internal variety, and complexity, finales suggest that identity is developed in reaction to circumstance as much as in isolated cogitation; the central or animating issue in most finales is not how the characters feel about one another, as it is in small ensembles and some *introduzioni,* but rather what class of actions and reactions they pursue with respect to the situations that come about, and the associations they find desirable, necessary, or convenient in the course of the imbroglio.

Although, as John Platoff points out, many finales are structured around the simple principle of colliding subplots,[31] many also echo the character-centered structures of some plot-archetypes. Such finales revolve around a single individual, whose status as victim, manipulator, or scapegoat allows the others to position themselves in relation to him or her and thus to emerge as individuals. In the second-act finale from *Fra i due litiganti,* for example (see appendix to this chapter), Dorina is the central victim whose disappearance from the household occasions the other characters' variously motivated searches for her, and whose reappearance stimulates reactions ranging from vituperation to swooning.

This focal character often does not appear immediately at the beginning of the finale, and there is often a "set-up" phase, in which characters gather, assert their positions, define a situation, or engage in local humor, before the entrance of the focal character or the enactment of the central action galvanizes the plot and starts the rush to the final impasse or denouement. The "set-up" phase of the action can be apparently simple, as in *I filosofi immaginari* II, where the learned spinster Cassandra (Clarice's sister) enjoys the night air with the *scolari* and is interrupted by Petronio announcing the arrival of "Argatifontidas" (Giuliano in disguise). It can also be quite

---

[31] Platoff, "Music and Drama in the Opera Buffa Finale," p. 25.

elaborate, involving different characters or subgroups of characters in different sorts of preparation, as in *Fra i due litiganti* II, where the *litiganti* hope to find their beloved; the ladies (the Contessa and Livietta) hope to punish the woman everyone loves more than them; and the languishing lovers (Masotto, Dorina herself, and Titta) all bewail their lot. Each of these set-up phases (designated Ia, Ib, and Ic in the translation at the end of the chapter) has its own tempo and key (the Contessa's and Livietta's phase has two meters), thus vividly suggesting the different worlds that have to merge in the rest of the finale. Although the three-part setup in *Fra i due litiganti* is structurally more complex than Cassandra's nocturnal musings (beautifully accompanied by a mixture of "heartbeat" motives and murmuring thirty-second-note runs), this "simple" moment in the Paisiello demonstrates the interaction of individual will and general circumstance in the elaboration of character. The music establishes the magic of the night air and thus introduces love as the overarching reason for the finale. The atmosphere also "domesticates" Cassandra, who has unwaveringly proclaimed her devotion to learning and her revulsion at the thought of sex and babies. In the first act, for example, she has sung:

Di marito il nome solo	Just the word "husband"
È una cosa che m'è odiosa,	Is odious to me,
Fastidiosa, tormentosa,	Annoying, [and] a torment,
Che mi fa raccapricciar.	It horrifies me.
Peggio ancora quando io sento	Worse yet, when I hear
Che dei figli s'han da fare,	One has to make babies,
Questa cosa non mi pare	I don't think
Di doverla sopportar.	I could stand such a thing.

In this finale, however, the nocturnal setting induces unfamiliar sensations (see translation): she does not marry in the end because there is no suitable mate in the plot, but this finale-opening may reassure us that she is "properly" feminine. This moment, then, appears to lend insight into Cassandra's inner life; at the same time it also fits her to the type of the susceptible woman. This anticipates and allows her conformity to the group celebration of marriage at the end of the finale, which, after all, is the point of the opera.

Once the set-up phase has finished, the central event that precipitates the final state of affairs—be that resolution or impasse—usually occurs, and this involves the central character or characters, who may not have even appeared until this point. In *I filosofi immaginari* II, for example, the central event is the enactment of "Argatifontidas's" magical self-rejuvenation (which, in a G minor $\frac{3}{8}$ meter, with some *sdrucciolo* lines, and the word "Erebo," unmistakably echoes—if in a rather deformed version—Gluck's famous chorus of the furies in *Orfeo*):

7-7: Paisiello, *I filosofi immaginari*, II, finale, mm. 184–201

Translation: Prepare everything, my students. You help me (to Clarice). You pay attention, and with the chant that I will present to you, you will invoke [the demons of] hell.

It is not the trick per se that precipitates the end, but the effect of the trick—namely, Petronio's recognition that Argatifontidas is actually Giuliano, that he (Petronio) is the dupe, and that he had better make the best of it. This realization, brought about by the pressure of circumstances rather than by introspection, reveals Petronio as an essentially good-hearted man, as he more or less willingly blesses the marriage and asks only for learned grandchildren:

7-8: Paisiello, *I filosofi immaginari*, II, finale, mm. 445–58

Translation: Either perforce or for love, I must say yes, Sir; go ahead, then, I agree. All I ask from you is learned children, and then [for you to be] happy and healthy.

Just as Petronio's good-heartedness is revealed in his capitulation to events rather than in cogitation, so Giuliano's love for Clarice is revealed in his willingness to perform the elaborate trick rather than in an outpouring of sentiment. For Cassandra, on the other hand (given that she has no power to further or prevent the marriage), a demonstrated change in sentiment is needed to resolve the plot all round; it makes both dramatic and social sense that her little conversion is completed at the beginning of the finale, clearing the way for unalloyed attention to action rather than sheer feeling.

The relation between feeling and action in revealing individuality is also pertinent to the central and end phases of the second-act finale of *Fra i due litiganti,* but it plays out rather differently, partly because this is not in fact the end of the opera, partly because of the larger number of characters involved (seven as opposed to four), and partly because the plot-mechanism differs, revolving around an essentially passive victim rather than an active manipulator. The two central actions, both focusing on Dorina, are her reappearance and her threat to disappear again if she can't pick her own mate. She herself remains essentially unchanged at the center of it all, much as does Giuliano, although in other ways the role of central victim is the inverse of principal trickster. This configuration of the solitary victim versus the persecutors (willing or unwilling) is articulated by the music as well as by the narrative: Dorina's isolation is expressed in her longer-breathed cantabile lines juxtaposed with the more *parlante* music of the others. Her first utterance after being found, for example, sets her apart from the spiteful chatter of Livietta and the Contessa (see Example 7-9). However, the real interest of this configuration of characters and events lies in the ways the characters other than Dorina are galvanized and made to forge sometimes unexpected alliances, which reveal aspects of their personalities not evident in their solo utterances. Thus, the first reaction of the men to the news of her continues the tone of Livietta and the Contessa's music, in its homorhythmic texture, in the dotted-quarter-three-eighths rhythm, and in the bustling quality of the accompaniment (see Example 7-10). This similarity to the musical expression of the ladies' spite (based, as always, in the rhythm of the text) allies the men with them, even though their sentiments are rather different. The effect is that as a group, they seem strikingly ineffectual—a quality not so clear from their individual utterances. However, once Dorina has actually appeared and made her plea, the men continue the rhythm and character of her tune (and the orchestra continues its less frenetic role) (see example 7-11). The men thus appear to change sides, improving their moral standing if not their impression of independence. Not all such sentimental statements in the middle of finales have such an effect: where the victim is truly isolated, and the plot requires that he or she remain so, the lyrical solo line usually remains without obvious motivic or textural consequence.

7-9: Sarti, *Fra i due litiganti il terzo gode,* II, finale, mm. 483–95

Translation:

Livietta: Yes, yes; I want to avenge myself on the gossip.

Countess: In a while, I will mistreat her as she deserves.

Dorina: I myself beg your pardon for my audacity.

7-10: Sarti, *Fra i due litiganti il terzo gode,* II, finale, mm. 454–63

Translation:
Countess: Here's that rascal.
Livietta: Dorina! Alas, what do I see? I'm starting to tremble again.
Men: Dorina, here's Dorina; she's really been found.

7-11: Sarti, *Fra i due litiganti il terzo gode,* II, finale, mm. 503–9

Translation: Leave her alone, my lady, leave her alone now; have mercy.

Where the outcast is not of primarily sentimental interest, the music may not distinguish stylistically between him or her and the rest of the cast but may manifest the social configuration in a rhythmic staggering of similar music. The following example, from the end of the first-act finale of *Le gare generose,* shows the accused Bastiano defending himself unsuccessfully against the accusations of his master who thinks he was trying to escape, his enemy Berlicco who is trying to expose him, the women in the household who are attracted to him, and his wife, who has set him up in order to maintain the secret of their identity:

7-12: Paisiello, *Le gare generose*, I, finale, mm. 722–30

Translation:
  Giannina, Meri, Nab, Berlicco, Dull:
    What gossip, noise, and chatter, what babbling to yourself. You should be put immediately in chains,
    so that then one can think about things. [Your crime] is clear.
  Bastiano: You should know; listen, know, that I cannot say publicly what has been done and said.

The play of groups, defined both musically and dramatically, is among the most important aspects of all finales. Any given grouping can reinforce an already-clear distinction between high-born and low-born, comic and serious, or good and bad characters, or it can subvert these distinctions in both humorous and psychologically or socially insightful ways. Sometimes an unexpected grouping or coupling of characters can suggest individuality rather than commonality. One such example is to be found in the first-act finale of *Una cosa rara*. Here the Prince, who has tried to seduce Lilla, and Lilla, who has firmly refused him, realize that Lubino (Lilla's betrothed) is outside with the Podestà. They are both "caught," but in rather different ways: the Prince is guilty but could, if necessary, bluff his way out of this fix; Lilla is innocent but is unlikely to be able to deflect the blame. As the Podestà and Lubino continue a quarrel they started before the finale, Lilla and the Prince sing parallel lines quite distinct from the bombast and patter of the two men. These parallel lines communicate the Prince and Lilla's common concern, but the incongruous ensemble between the philandering Prince and the righteous Lilla, combined with the fact that lyrical lines in finales tend to indicate moments of subjectivity, ironically throws their differences into relief and emphasizes each one's individuality (see Example 7-13).

As many commentators have noted, disguise and deceit, false identity and illusion, are all standard devices in finales; deception, whether intentional or not, is more often than not their primary content, and the enactment of the deception forms the central narrative phase of many. This is particularly clear in *I filosofi immaginari* II; its relations include *Figaro* IV, where Susanna and the Countess invite misidentification by dressing up in each others' clothes, and *Così* I and II, which use disguise as the primary mechanism. However, even in finales where the central mechanism is the persecution of an innocent, disguise and deceit are not absent. In *Don Giovanni* I, for example, not only are the avengers masked, but Don Giovanni himself is "disguised" as a genial host while Leporello is deputed to distract and deceive Masetto. Darkness, balconies, multiple entrances and exits, closets and floor-length tablecloths all assist in the multiplication of misunderstanding and misidentification that is part and parcel of the comedy of finales. This often contributes to their mechanistic aspect, but it also reveals individual capacities for both nobility and spineless complicity that would be unlikely to emerge in solo utterances.

Finale Endings

Like the groupings of characters in the central portions of finales, the endings of these pieces also send a complex of messages about the relation of the individual to the group. First-act finales and second-act finales in three-

7-13: Martín y Soler, *Una cosa rara,* I, finale, mm. 74–79

Translation:
Lilla: My heart vacillates between grief and fear.
Prince: My heart vacillates between suspicion and love.
Lubino: Traitors, you hope in vain to remove me from here.
Mayor: Drag the culprit away from here, dead or alive.

act operas end either with a commonly declaimed text of general confusion or misery, or with several texts indicating a variety of reactions to the situation at hand. Second-act finales in two-act operas (and other final finales) typically end with a joint declamation of an intention to celebrate, or with a moral. Occasionally, when a villain is defeated, he or she has a dissenting text against the generally celebratory text of the others.[32] The music of all these endings, whether celebratory or miserable, unanimous or inclusive of dissent, typically moves from a fugato texture, or one involving opposing groups (or one against many), to simple homophony. This progression may be repeated several times, but at least twelve measures (and often much more) of complete musical unanimity is standard at the end of finales. Second-act or ending finales may be shorter than first-act ones, as John Platoff points out, but the musical process of ending is not significantly or consistently different between internal and final finales.[33]

However, the significance of this cadential unanimity differs between the middle finale and the final tutti (whether that comes at the end of a second-act finale, or a third-act ensemble). With remarkable consistency, the impasse-ends of internal finales are expressed either in the first person singular or in the impersonal third person referring to essentially individual qualities, while the resolving ends of final finales or third-act tuttis are expressed in either the first person plural or in more general moralizing language, referring to collective qualities or feelings. The first-person responses to the thunderstorm at the end of *Fra i due litiganti* II, for example, contrast with the collective delight of the final chorus (see Chapter 1, p. 28). And in the first-act finale of *I filosofi immaginari,* the characters all admonish themselves to be prudent and patient—virtues they will all have to demonstrate individually in order for them to have any effect:

Silenzio quà si faccia,	Let there be silence here,
Si adopri la prudenza,	Let's learn to be prudent,
Bisogna aver pazienza,	It's necessary to have patience
Per non precipitar.	To avoid a fall.

In the second-act finale, by contrast, they make generalized comment on the solemnity of the moment that envelops them all; in addition, Cassandra and Petronio's use of the collective *ci* at the end emphasize their absorption into the group. One could describe this difference as one of congruence between music and drama; at the end of the first act, there is an unresolvable tension between the two domains, the music indicating closure and the text indicating the need to continue, whereas at the end of the opera both domains are "about" closure. Carolyn Abbate and Roger

---

[32] Bertati and Gazzaniga's *L'isola di Alcina,* which ends with the men leaving Alcina behind on her enchanted island, exemplifies this.

[33] John Platoff, "Music and Drama in the Opera Buffa Finale," p. 27.

Parker have taken this stance about *Le nozze di Figaro*,[34] arguing that the opposing messages of text and music at the end of the second-act finale indicate the radical noncoherence of much opera, and the need for "multivalent" and nontotalizing methods of analysis. This is indisputable from a broadly speaking formalist point of view, but from a more sociological perspective there is an overarching point to be made about a group of characters speaking in unison about their individual experiences, particularly when the next comparable occasion involves the same group of individuals singing about their identity as a group. What happens in the broadest terms between the middle and the end is that a collection of individuals united by the merest circumstance—locked in comic conflict, overcome (for different reasons) by terror or confusion, caught in a thunderstorm or darkest night—turn into a group of people united (if only temporarily) in common purpose, whether that be the denunciation of villainy, the praise of virtue, or simple celebration. The very similarity of the musical means between middle and end reinforces the significance of the move from a collection of individual interests juxtaposed by chance to a community of interest in a larger social order, and emphasizes the value of adjusting individual desires and tendencies to suit that larger order. The social implications of such a message—albeit couched as the delivery of pleasure—could hardly be clearer.

[34] Carolyn Abbate and Roger Parker, "Dismembering Mozart," *COJ* 2 (1990) pp. 187–95.

APPENDIX A

ANNOTATED TEXT OF *I FILOSOFI IMMAGINARI:*
SECOND-ACT FINALE[1]

PHASE I—THE SETUP

The learned Cassandra wanders, philosophizing in the moonlight. Her father Petro-
nio joins her and they discuss the arrival of "Argatifontidas" (actually Giuliano, the
lover of Clarice, Petronio's other daughter).

Giardino con sedili di erbe	*Garden with grass-covered seats*
Notte, luna che risplende	*Moonlit night*

Scene VIII

Cassandra and philosophers, followers of Petronio

Largo $\frac{2}{4}$*:* E♭ major (NB: Key signature remains the same throughout)

CASSANDRA:	
L'ora cheta, ed opportuna,	The quiet and opportune hour,
Il bel raggio della Luna	The lovely rays of the moon
Qui m'invita a passeggiar.	Invite me to stroll here.
CORO:	CHORUS:
Fra il silenzio, all'aer nero	In silence and darkness
Più raccolto stà il pensiero;	One can better collect one's thoughts
Si può meglio meditar.	And meditate.
CASSANDRA:	
Provo in sen certo desio	I feel in my heart a certain desire
Che capire non poss'io,	That I can't understand,
E ci vò filosofar.	And I want to philosophize about it.
CORO:	CHORUS:
Fra il silenzio . . .	In silence and darkness . . .
Siedono separamente	*They all sit down separately*

---

[1] Text taken from autograph score (Mus. Hs. 17048) in the Austrian National Library, and from the Venice 1782 libretto.

Scene IX

Enter Petronio

Andante $\frac{2}{4}$: B♭ major

PETRONIO:
  Vi cerco in ogni lato,
  Alfine qui vi trovo.
  Hai detto, che è arrivato
  Quel gran portento nuovo!
  Io dico Argatifontida:
  Potete ben capir.

CASSANDRA:
  Sicuro che l'ho detto.
  A ritrovarlo andiamo.

PETRONIO:
  Se qui attendete un poco
  Ei quà dovrà venir.
  È vecchio di cent'anni,
  È pieno di malanni;
  Ma udite, e poi stupite;
  Ei dee ringiovenir.

TUTTI:
  È questo un gran portento!
  Che uomo! Oh che talento!
  È cosa da stupir.

I've been looking everywhere for you,
And at last I've found you.
You said that the great new
Wonder has arrived!
I say Argatifontida:
You can well understand.

Certainly I said so.
Let's go and find him.

If we wait here a while
He should come.
He's a hundred years old,
And full of aches and pains;
But listen, and be amazed—
He can rejuvenate himself.

ALL:
  This is a great portent!
  What a man! What a talent!
  It's amazing.

PHASE II—THE TRICK

Argatifontidas arrives and claims that he will rejuvenate himself using a special chant. He makes everyone sign a piece of paper, and while the chorus sings, he takes off his ancient philosopher costume and emerges as a young man. Everyone is amazed.

Scene X

Enter Clarice and Giuliano (dressed as Argatifontidas)

Andante $\frac{3}{8}$: G minor

GIULIANO:
  Per prima prova della mia Scienza
  Voglio di tutti qui alla presenza
  L'antiche spoglie tosto mutar.
  Tutto apprestate, voi miei Studenti:
  (*a Clarice*) Voi m'aiutate

As a first proof of my knowledge
I want to change my ancient trappings
In the presence of everyone here.
Prepare everything, my students:
(*to Clarice*) You help me

Voi state attenti,	You pay attention,
E con il cantico, che io presentovi	And with the chant that I'll present to you
Vogliate l'Erebo tutti invocar.	You will invoke [the demons of] hell.

dà a ciascuno una carta   *gives everyone a piece of paper*

CLARICE AND CASSANDRA:
Che meraviglia sarà mai questa?   What miracle will this be?

PETRONIO:
Che scienza incognita c'è in quella   What arcane science there is in this
testa.   head.

CORO: CHORUS
Tutti restiamo qui ad osservar.   We'll all stay here and watch.

Clarice si appressa a Giuliano   *Clarice moves closer to Giuliano*

GIULIANO:
Dunque principio	Now we'll make a beginning
Noi diamo all'opera.	To this affair.
Prima di tutto,	First of all
Or qui bisogna	It is necessary
Che ognun di voi	That all of you
Qui sottoscriva,	Sign here,
Come è costume,	As is customary,
Il propio nome;	Your own name.
E il fin dell'opera,	And by the end of the operation
Io son sicuro	I am sure
Che tutto bene	That everything
Riuscirà.	Will succeed.

PETRONIO:
Bene benissimo   Good. Very good.
Eccomi quà.   I'm here.

CLARICE:
(Io tutta tremo,   (I'm all a-tremble,
Cosa sarà?)   What's going to happen?)

GIULIANO:
(Non dubitate   (Don't worry;
Lasciate far.)   Let it happen.)

Larghetto $\frac{2}{4}$: E♭ major

GIULIANO:
Vi prego in tal momento,	I beseech you at such a moment,
Per il felice evento,	For this happy event,
Volete con il Cantico	Please accompany this act
Quest'atto accompagnar.	with a chant.

Dopo che hanno sottoscritto, Giuliano riprende la sottoscritta di Petronio mentre cantano il seguente coro, ajutato da Clarice, e dagli studenti, si leva gli abiti da filosofo, e rimane vestito del giovane.

After they have signed, Giuliano re-takes the signature of Petronio, while the following chorus is sung. Helped by Clarice and the students, he takes off his philosopher-suit and appears dressed as a young man.

Largo $\frac{6}{8}$: E♭ major

CORO:	CHORUS:
Sia propizio per Pluton	Let Pluto bless this
Col flin, flin, e col flon, flon,	With a flin flin and a flon flon,
E rinnovi in lui l'età,	And restore his youth
Per virtù del Tapatà.	With the strength of Tapatà.

Allegro $\frac{4}{4}$: E♭ major

GIULIANO:
   Tutto quanto è fatto già.   All this is achieved now.

PETRONIO:
   Che prodigio che fatto è mai questo?   What astonishing feat is this?

PETRONIO AND CASSANDRA:
   Stupefatto davvero ch'io resto.   I'm truly stupefied.

CLARICE:
   Oh che giovane bello e garbato!   Oh what a beautiful young man!
   Quasi agli occhi dar fede non sò.   I'm not sure I can believe my eyes.

PETRONIO:
   Deh! lasciate, che almen io vi tocchi.   Oh please, at least let me touch you.

GIULIANO:
   Si guardate, sentite, toccate . . .   Go ahead, feel, touch . . .

PHASE III—THE AFTERMATH

Petronio recognizes Giuliano, then discovers that the document he signed in the rejuvenation operation was really a marriage contract for Clarice and Giuliano. The lovers plead for mercy and are joined by Cassandra. Petronio gives in, and the opera ends.

Recitative: → B♭ major

PETRONIO:
   Ah! Me meschino! . . .   Oh no! what do I see . . .
   Cosa mai vedo? . . .

   Resta attonito conoscendolo   *Recognizing him, stands astonished*

CASSANDRA:

Non so capire . . . che cosa è stato?	I don't understand . . . what's happened?

Allegro ⁴⁄₄: B♭ major → E♭ major → C minor

PETRONIO:

Ah cara figlia, son disperato . . .	Ah my dear daughter, I'm desperate,
Sono tradito, sono ingannato . . .	I've been betrayed and deceived;
Codesto è un perfido, un impostor.	That man is a traitor and an impostor.

CLARICE:

(da parte) *(aside)*

(Io tremo tutta dalla paura:	(I'm trembling with fear;
Non so che dire; non so che fare,	I don't know what to say or do;
Che gran sconquasso succederà?)	There's going to be a tremendous fuss.)

GIULIANO:

(da parte) *(aside)*

Ah che la cosa è troppa dura	It looks as though it will be too complicated
Potere uscire da questo imbroglio . . .	To get out of this mess . . .

PETRONIO:

con gran trasporto d'ira *in a rage*

Lascia ch'io veda codesto foglio:	Let me see that document
Ciò che vi è scritto, voglio osservar.	I want to see what's written on it.

CLARICE:

Ah che già sento il mio spirito	I really feel that I can't hold up
No, non più reggere, no, no non sà.	Any longer.

GIULIANO:

Ah son contento, che la scrittura	I'm happy that I have here safely
Da lui firmata l'ho qui sicura,	The contract he signed;
Perciò non temo, ciò che farà.	That way I'm not afraid of what he might do.

legge il contratto del matrimonio *reads the marriage contract*

PETRONIO:

Io Petronio Sciatica . . .	I Petronius Backache . . .
Mi obbligo e prometto . . .	Am obliged and promise . . .
Di maritar mia figlia . . .	To marry my daughter . . .
Cioè Clarice Sciatica . . .	That is, Clarissa Backache . . .
Col Sior Giulian Tiburla . . .	To Mr. Julian Trickyou . . .
Presente a testimonj . . .	Present to witness . . .

ironicamente e con rabbia *furiously ironic*

Il Sior Giulian Tiburla	Mr. Julian Trickyou
Mi ha burlato già.	Has really tricked me.

Andante: → *E♭ major*

CASSANDRA:
  E quel che è scritto è scritto,   And what's written is written

Allegro: C minor

  Nè si può cancellar.   And can't be erased.

PETRONIO:
  Ah infedeli, crudeli tiranni,   Ah traitors, cruel tyrants,
  Menzogneri ripieni d'inganni,   Deceitful liars,
  Come un Padre ingannare così?   How could you deceive a father like this?

CORO: CHORUS:
  Che disgrazia! . . . che caso . . .   What a disgrace! What a situation! What
      che orrore! . . .   a horror!

CLARICE:
  (Più non parlo; son pien   (I can't speak anymore; I'm blushing
      di rossore . . .)   all over.)

GIULIANO:
  (Oh che nozze! che pene!   (What a wedding! What pain! What a
      che giorno!)   day!)

CASSANDRA:
  Son rimasti con rabbia con scorno;   They're standing there in fury and shame;
  Così fanno gli amanti oggidì?   Is that how today's young lovers behave?

Maestoso: E♭ major

CLARICE AND GIULIANO:
  Caro Padre voi dovete   Dear father, you must
  Perdonare i nostri errori   Forgive our mistakes
  Se nel seno racchiudete   If you have even a shred of
  Un tantino di pietà.   Mercy in your heart.

PETRONIO:
  Oh che arte! oh che eloquenza!   Oh what acting! what eloquence!
  Avvilito io sono già.   I'm really humiliated.

CASSANDRA:
  Ma ci vuol ormai pazienza,   This calls for forbearance,
  E lasciarli al fin sposar.   And eventual permission for them
                                               to marry.

PETRONIO:
  O per forza, o per amore   Either perforce or for love
  Devo dire, sì Signore: I must say yes, Sir;
  Via su dunque io lo concedo,   Go ahead then, I agree.
  Figli dotti io sol vi chiedo,   All I ask from you is learned children;
  E godete in sanità.   Then [for you to be] be happy
                                               and healthy.

Allegro: F minor → E♭ major

TUTTI:

    Oh che funesta scene,
    Mista di gioia, e pene!
    Oh che fatal momento
    Di smania e di contento.

CLARICE AND GIULIANO:

    Amor provar mi fa.

CASSANDRA AND PETRONIO:

    Amor provar ci fa.

ALL:

    Oh what a solemn scene—
    A mixure of joy and pain!
    Oh what a momentous time
    Of delirium and happiness.

    Love will make me feel.

    Love will make us feel.

Più Presto
(repetition of previous 6 lines)

APPENDIX B

ANNOTATED TEXT OF *FRA I DUE LITIGANTI IL TERZO GODE:* SECOND-ACT FINALE[1]

Phase I—The Setup

In three subphases: the litiganti, the ladies, and the languishing lovers. Masotto accuses Titta and Mingone (the "due litiganti", and respectively, the Count's and the Countess's choices as husbands for the chambermaid Dorina) of making Dorina run away. They quarrel boorishly with each other but are all sympathetic to Dorina. They move aside; the Countess and Livietta enter, both jealous of Dorina (the former on the Count's account, the latter on Titta's) and swear that they will find her come what may.

Dorina enters and laments her fate. Masotto laments his lost love, and Titta bewails his own misery. None of these characters sees each other. Livietta, the Countess, Mingone, and the Count all eventually find each other; each explains his or her reason for wanting to find Dorina. At the other side of the stage, Titta, Dorina, and Masotto all lament the states of their hearts.

Phase Ia: The Litiganti

Folto bosco, con diverse strade formate da varj massi, e da orride spelonche	*Dark wood, with several paths formed by various rocks, and by horrid caverns*

Scene XVII

Allegro $\frac{4}{4}$: D major[2]

MASOTTO:

Coccodrilli, ah che piangete?	Ah crocodiles,
Vano è il punto or che l'avete	There is no point in weeping
Già ridotta a disperar.	Now you have already reduced her to despair.
Sì: Dorina maltrattate;	Yes, you maltreat Dorina;
Per voi altri se n'è andata,	She's left because of you,
Ma l'avete da pagar.	And you'll have to pay for it.

---

[1] Text taken from the scene in the Austrian National Library (Mus. Hs. 17888) and from the Venice 1782 libretto, which supplies the stage directions.
[2] Sarti indicates the keys with new key signatures throughout.

MINGONE:

    Non sò . . . niente, . . . la cagione   I know nothing;

    Fu colui, . . . fu . . . quel . . . birbone   It was because of him, that rascal,

    Che . . . volea . . . rapirla . . . a me.   Who wanted to take her from me.

TITTA:

    A me . . . birbone . . . non è vero . . .   What? Me a rascal? It's not true.

    Per te . . . solo . . . menzognero   It's your fault, you liar,

    Non si trova . . . più non . . . c'è.   That she isn't around any more.

MASOTTO:

    Cosa fate là impazzati,   What are you doing standing there,

    Marmottoni disgraziati?   You great lazy lumps?

    Sù n'andiamo a ricercar.   Let's go and look for her.

MINGONE:

    Vengo vengo.   I'm coming, I'm coming.

TITTA:

    Sono lesto.   I'm running.

À 2:

    Maledetto, per tuo conto   You bastard, it's your fault

    Io mi sento strapazzar.   That I'm in trouble.

MASOTTO:

    Maledetti, al fin del conto   You bastards, at the end of the day

    Voi con me l'avrete a far.   You'll have me to reckon with.

À 2:

    Osserviamo, procuriamo,   Let's watch, let's make an attempt

    L'infelice di trovar.   To find the poor thing.

PHASE IB: THE LADIES

Scene XVIII

La contessa, e Livietta, con alcuni   *The Countess and Livietta, with a few*
paesani   *peasants*

Allegro spiritoso $\frac{3}{4}$: G major

CONTESSA:

    Insolentissima,   Where has that rude

    Pettegolissima,   And insolent girl

    Dov'è fuggita,   Run away to?

    Dov'è sarà?   Where is she?

LIVIETTA:

    In compagnia   In the company

    Di qualche amante.   Of some lover.

CONTESSA:

  Livietta mia,   We already know that,
  Questo si sa.   Livietta.
  Lo sposo ingrato   My ingrate husband
  Colla fraschetta.   [Is] with the minx.

LIVIETTA:

  Come? il padrone   What? the master
  Colla civetta?   With the vixen?

CONTESSA:

  Sì, e quel moscone   Yes, and that bluebottle
  Or me la fà.   Is doing it to me now.

LIVIETTA:

  Parmi impossibile   That seems to me
  Per verità.   Impossible, really.

À 2:

  L'indegna perfida   The unworthy, wicked,
  Scaltrita femmina   Wily woman
  D'offesa simile   Shall feel the pain
  La pena avrà.   Of such a wrong.

Allegro $\frac{2}{4}$: G major

CONTESSA:

  (ai paesani)   *(to the peasants)*

  Nel bosco presto entrate;   Go into the wood quickly
  Cercate l'insolente.   And find the impudent woman.

LIVIETTA:

  Al cenno immantinente   You there! Obey the order
  Pronti ubbidite olà.   Immediately and right away!

  I paesani entrano nel bosco   *The peasants enter the wood*

À 2:

  Unite noi qui entriamo,   Let's enter here together
  L'indegna ricerchiamo,   To seek the wretch.
  Forse si troverà.   Maybe we'll find her.
  Da noi ben schiaffeggiata, Then, thoroughly beaten up,
  A viver ritirata   She'll learn to live
  Allor imparerà.   In retreat.

  Entrando unitamente dalla *They enter [the wood] from the side*
  parte opposta   *opposite to the peasants*

Phase Ic: The Languishing Lovers

Scene XIX

Dorina, Masotto, and Titta

Andante maestoso $\frac{2}{2}$: B♭ major

DORINA:

Oh che orrore! che spavento!
Meschinella, che hò da far?
Vado . . . resto . . . O Dio!
   ch'io sento
Mille affetti a contrastar.

Oh what horror, what fear,
Miserable me; what am I to do?
I go . . . I stay . . . Oh Lord,
   I feel
A thousand conflicting emotions.

Entra dove sono entrate i paesani

Uses the same entrance as the peasants

MASOTTO:

Ah Masotto sventurato,
Quanti affanni hai da provar.
Tu sospiri il bene amato,
E il tuo ben non puoi trovar.

Ah poor Masotto,
How many miseries you have to endure.
You sigh for your beloved
And cannot find her.

Entra dalla parte opposta

*Goes into [the wood] from the side
opposite to the peasants*

TITTA:

Oh che incendio che ho nel petto.
Io mi sento consumar;
Questa volta, poveretto,
Per amor ho da crepar.

Oh what a fire burns in my breast,
I feel as if I'm being consumed.
This time, poor thing,
I think I'm going to die of love.

(Phases Ib, Ic, and Ia—Competition, Vengeance, and Love—Combine)

Scene XX

*Il Conte, e Mingone da parti diverse,
Livietta, e la Contessa unitamente
dalla parte opposta.*

*The Count and Mingone enter from
different sides. Livietta and the Countess enter together from the opposite side.*

Presto $\frac{4}{4}$: G major

CONTESSA:

Il sospetto ch' ognora m'accende,

The suspicions that continually assail me,

MINGONE:

Il dolore che il core m'opprime,

The grief that oppresses my heart,

CONTE:

Il puntiglio che onore mi desta,

The punctilio that honor arouses in me,

À 3:

Di Dorina qui in traccia mi sprona.
Nè la speme per or m'abbandona
Di doverla fra poco trovar.

Spurs me here in search of Dorina.
For now, the hope of finding her soon
Has not abandoned me.

LIVIETTA:

Il desio di punir la rivale
Di Dorina qui in traccia mi sprona.
Ma in amor, se colei non si trova,
Miglior sorte mi resta a sperar.

The desire to punish my rival,
Spurs me here in search of Dorina.
But if she is not to be found here
I can still hope for better luck in love.

Allegro $\frac{6}{8}$: *G major*

CONTE:

alla Contessa

Gelosa imprudente,
Per vostra cagione
Dorina innocente
Da casa fuggì.

to the Countess

You careless, jealous woman,
It is your fault
That innocent Dorina
Ran away from home.

CONTESSA:

al Conte

Amante meschino,
Disgrazia crudele,
Partì il bel visino
Che il cor vi ferì.

to the Count

You poor lover,
What a cruel disgrace
That the lovely face
That wounded your heart has left.

CONTE:

Se stolida siete
Io pazzo non sono.

You may be stupid,
But I am not crazy.

À 2:

Or ora vedrete
Che cosa farò.

In a moment you will see
How things turn out.

MINGONE:

Deluso, schernito,
Perduto ho la sposa,
Chi m'abbia tradito
Comprender non sò.

Spurned and deceived,
I've lost my wife.
I can't understand
Who has betrayed me.

CONTE:

a Mingone
Per te babbuino,
Per te sguaiataccio . . .

to Mingone
For you, blockhead,
For you, boor . . .

CONTESSA E MINGONE À 2:

Pian pian signorino
Non stia a gridar, gridar,
Si calmi un tantino,
Mi lasci parlar.

Calm down, young sir, and
Stop screaming.
Calm down a bit
And let me speak.

LIVIETTA:

> Livietta felice,
> Non ho più rivale.
> Or Titta mi lice
> Consorte sperar.

> Happy Livietta,
> I have no rival anymore.
> Now I can hope
> For Titta as a husband.

CONTESSA:

> Se ancora mi stuzzica . . .

> If you keep teasing me . . .

CONTE:

> Se cresce la colera . . .

> If I get any angrier . . .

À 4:

> Un chiasso, uno strepito
> Or or nascerà.
> Prevedo un disordine
> Che cosa sarà.

> A great racket and fuss
> Will soon break out.
> I foresee confusion.
> What will happen?

> *Si ritirano entro la scena*
> *per diverse parti*

> *They move to various*
> *places upstage*

Scene XXI

*Dorina dal mezzo, Titta, e Masotto da parte opposta, senza avvedendosi l'uno
dall'altro, indi tutti a suo tempo.*

*Dorina enters from the middle; Titta and Masotta from opposite sides, without
noticing each other, then everyone else in turn.*

Andante $\frac{2}{2}$: Bb major

TITTA, DORINA, MASOTTO:

> Il riposo e la sua pace
> Ha perduto questo cor,
> Ah d'uccidermi capace
> Fosse almeno il mio dolor.

> This heart has lost
> Its rest and peace.
> Ah, if only my grief
> Could kill me.

PHASE II—THE CENTRAL EVENT

*Dorina is now the center of attention. She has been bound because the Countess ordered
it so. The litiganti each try to court her but are overcome and ask Masotto to speak for
them. Masotto (her eventual husband) speaks for himself.*

> *Il tempo comincia ad annuvolarsi*

> *The sky begins to cloud over*

Allegro $\frac{3}{4}$: F major

CONTESSA:

> Ecco: quella sfacciata.

> Here's that rascal!

Uscendo co' paesani, a quali
ordina di circondar Dorina,
e di legarla

Appearing with the peasants, whom she
orders to surround Dorina
and tie her up

LIVIETTA:
Dorina! Ahimè! che vedo?
Ritorno già a tremar.

Dorina! Alas, what do I see?
I'm starting to tremble again.

MEN:

Con allegria avvedendosi
tutti di Dorina

Happily, all noticing Dorina

Dorina, ecco Dorina.
Affè che s'è trovata;
Che gioja! che piacer!

Dorina—here's Dorina;
She's really been found;
What happiness, what joy!

CONTE:
Perchè così legata?

Why is she bound like this?

CONTESSA:
Son io che l'ho ordinato,
Deve in castigo andar.

I ordered it.
She is to be punished.

CONTE:
Oibò: la sventurata
Deve frà noi restar.

Oh no, the poor thing
Should stay with us.

LIVIETTA:
Si si, della pettegola
Mi voglio vendicar.

Yes, yes; I want to avenge myself
On the gossip.

CONTESSA:
Fra poco come merita,
La voglio maltrattar.

In a while, I will
Mistreat her, as she deserves.

DORINA:
Perdon vi chiedo i'stessa
Di mia temerità.

I myself beg your pardon
For my audacity.

alla Contessa, e al Conte

to the Count and Countess

D'una fanciulla oppressa
Abbiate carità.

Have pity on
A poor oppressed girl.

MASOTTO, TITTA, MINGONE:
Lasciatela Signora,
Lasciatela in buon ora,
Movetevi a pietà.

Leave her alone, my lady,
Leave her alone now,
Have mercy.

CONTE:
Lasciatela.

Leave her alone.

CONTESSA:
Non voglio.

I don't want to.

CONTE:
  ai paesani, che la slegano   *to the peasants, who untie her*
    Scioglietela.   Untie her.

CONTESSA:
  Non voglio.   I don't want to.

CONTE:
  Lasciatela per Bacco,   Leave her alone, for God's sake,
  Io vi farò pentir.   Or I'll make you regret it.

MASOTTO, TITTA, LIVIETTA, CONTE, DORINA:
  La speme già consolami,   Hope already consoles me,
  Vicino è il mio gioir.   My happiness is near.

CONTESSA:
  La rabbia già divorami,   Rage devours me already,
  Non posso più soffrir.   I can stand it no longer.

Andante $\frac{6}{8}$: D major

DORINA:
  Per dar fine ad ogni contesa,   To put an end to all the quarrels,
  Io da casa son fuggita.   I fled the house.
  Vuò piuttosto dar la vita   I would rather give my life
  Che vedervi ad altercar.   Than see you fight so.
  Vengo a voi; ma del mio core   I'll come with you, but
  Vuò dispor come a me piace.   I want to dispose of my heart as I wish.
  Se il negate io torno in pace   If you deny me, I'll return peacefully
  Fra le selve ad abitar.   To live in the woods.

MASOTTO:
  Ha ragione, poverina,   She's right, poor thing;
  Non si deve violentar.   We shouldn't abuse her.

MINGONE AND TITTA:
  È pur cara, è pur buonina,   She's so dear, she's so good,
  Mi fa tutto liquefar.   She makes me all wobbly inside.

CONTE:
  Obbediente a me Dorina   Obedient to me, Dorina
  A mio modo avrà da far.   Will have to do what I tell her.

CONTESSA AND LIVIETTA:
  Ora fa la modestina   Now she's playing Miss Humility
  Per poterci corbellar.   to deceive us.

PHASE III—THE IMPASSE

Meanwhile, a thunderstorm has been brewing, and while the suitors attempt to woo Dorina, it has worsened. It finally erupts, and everyone unites in fleeing the weather.

Allegro $\frac{12}{8}$: *D major*

MINGONE:
  Io vò dirle all'orrecchio che l'amo.

  Ah mia bella s'io t'a . . .

TUTTI:
  Ahimè!

  Primo lampo

TITTA:
  Vita mia, vo dirle pian piano,
  Ah Dorina mia vi. . . .

TUTTI:
  Che lampo!

  Lampo come sopra

TITTA E MINGONE:
  Voi parlate a Dorina per me.

MASOTTO:
  Parlerò (ma però a mio favore,)
  Caro ben, tu sei l'i . . .

  Altro lampo, indi scoppio di saetta

TUTTI:
  Ajuto!
  Ah soccorso, più scampo non v'è.

I want to whisper in her ear that I love
  her.
Ah, my beauty, if I lov . . .

ALL:
  Oh no!

  First lightning

My life, I'll tell you so gently,
Ah Dorina, my li . . .

ALL:
  What lightning!

  Lightning, as above

You speak to Dorina for me.

I'll speak, but on my own behalf.
My dear love, you are the id . . .

  More lightning, then a burst of
  thunder

ALL:
  Help!
  Ah help, there's no escape!

[Allegro] $\frac{12}{8}$: *E♭ major*

TUTTI:
  Ah che il tempo più cresce e
    s'intorbida,
  La paura mi toglie il respiro.
  Più la luce del giorno non miro;
  Ah si parta, si fugga di quà.

ALL:
  Ah the weather is increasingly
    threatening,
  Fear robs me of breath.
  I no longer see the light of day,
  Ah, let's go; let's leave this place.

Allegro assai $\frac{4}{4}$: *D major*

DORINA:
  Ah meschina, dove andrò?

MASOTTO:
  Il braccio vi darò.

CONTESSA:
  Mingone, tocca a te.

MINGONE:
  Diletta mia sposina . . .

Ah, miserable me, where shall I go?

Let me give you my arm.

Mingone, that's your job.

Sweet little wifey . . .

CONTE:

   (a Titta)   *(to Titta)*

  Và tu, che sei lo sposo.   Go ahead, you're the bridegroom.

TITTA:

  Venite, tocca a me.   Come along. It's my turn.

DORINA:

   (a Titta, e Mingone, che a forza   *(to Titta and Mingone, who have*
   la prendono per un braccio)   *forcibly grabbed her by the arm)*

  Andate tutti al diavolo,   Go to hell, the lot of you,
  Di voi non so che far.   I don't know what to do with you.

TUTTI: ALL:

  Ah che il terror, lo spasimo   Ah, the terror and fear
  Mi fanno vacillar.   Make me reel.

   *Si vede un lampo, ed in seguito odesi un rimbombo di tuono: il temporale cresce
   sino alla fine del Atto.*

   *A bolt of lightning is seen, and then a thunderclap heard: the storm gets
   continuously worse until the end of the act.*

  Ahimè che di spavento   Alas, I'm freezing, sweating, and
                          trembling
  Io gelo, sudo, e fremo.   With fear.
  Dove ci asconderemo?   Where will we hide?
  Di noi che mai sarà?   What will become of us?
  Più torna il tuono a stridere,   Now the thunder is starting to rumble
                          again,
  Il nembo già precipita,   The clouds are beginning to make rain,
  In aria vedo il fulmine,   I see lightning in the sky,
  Fuggiamo via di quà,   Let's flee from here,
  Fuggiamo per pietà.   For heaven's sake, let's flee.

   Partono tutti confusamente   *All leave in confusion*
   per diverse parti   *by various exits*

PART III

Così fan tutte le Opere?
A Masterwork in Context

Chapter Eight

COSÌ FAN TUTTE
IN CONVERSATION

I BEGAN THIS BOOK with a partial re-creation of the operatic "conversation" in which *Le nozze di Figaro* participated: a conversation involving other works, both operatic and literary, other local composers and librettists, the continuing relationship between the performers and the audience, and the broader cultural context. *Così fan tutte*, not surprisingly, also participated in this kind of conversation—using *Figaro* itself (and its web of references) among its interlocutors, as Bruce Alan Brown has recently shown.[1] Like *Figaro, Così* plays on continuities in the Burgtheater's performance personnel, it connects in a variety of ways to other works in the repertory, and it treats themes in common currency in the repertory. However, the balance of elements in *Così*'s conversation with its contexts is rather different from *Figaro*'s. Unlike that opera, for example, *Così* is not based on a single model and is not an explicit narrative sequel to another, as *Figaro* is to *Il barbiere di Siviglia;* thus one of the ready-made, or most obvious elements in an operatic conversation is absent. Despite (or perhaps because of) its lack of a single source or model—a lack unusual among Da Ponte's libretti—*Così* is more pervasively and virtuosically intertextual than *Figaro*.[2] Indeed, Bruce Alan Brown describes it as the result of a "promiscuous miscegenation" of sources, from contemporary operas to ancient myths: a mixture which, given the "conversational" context of this repertory, was surely part of the pleasure of the work for the audience.[3] Another way in which *Così*'s relation to its interlocutors differs from *Figaro*'s is that while the generic and repertorial conversation invoked by the earlier work is in some ways incidental to its transhistorical meanings, *Così*'s "conversations" with its contexts, and especially with the immediate context of the

---

[1] Bruce Alan Brown, "Beaumarchais, Paisiello and the Genesis of *Così*," in Sadie, *Wolfgang Amadè Mozart* (Oxford: Clarendon Press, 1996) pp. 312–38.

[2] Daniel Heartz has argued, in "Citation, Reference and Recall in *Così fan tutte*" (*Mozart's Operas* [Berkeley: University of California Press, 1990] pp. 229–53), that not only does this opera invoke works by other librettists and composers (and Heartz specifically mentions Goldoni's *Le pescatrici* in this connection) but it is also replete with cross-references within itself, and to Mozart's earlier works, including and especially *Idomeneo*. Bruce Alan Brown has also commented on Mozart's self-borrowings in Brown, *Così*, pp. 3–6, and in "Beaumarchais, Paisiello and the Genesis of *Così*," in Sadie, *Wolfgang Amadè Mozart*, pp. 312–38.

[3] Brown, *Così*, p. 14.

Burgtheater repertory, are intimately linked with the meanings that most readily speak to us today. I am not arguing here that only the lucky few who have pored over the *opere buffe* in the Burgtheater repertory can "really" understand *Così* (were that even possible). Rather, I would argue that if one takes convention to be a pertinent issue in this opera—which is a position available to any audience member, since the moral value of conventional social arrangements is an explicit topic of the plot, and since comic conventions like the doctor and notary disguises, and operatic conventions like the exit aria and the rage aria, are all prominently displayed—an examination of *Così*'s historically more local referentiality both confirms and deepens the import of convention on every level of this work.

The astonishing number and variety of references in Da Ponte's libretto constitute a testament to his wide reading, his classical education, his evident need to display both of these, and his ability to integrate the most disparate sources into a coherent whole.[4] Among historical sources are the myth of Cephalus and Procris from Ovid's *Metamorphoses*,[5] tales of infidelity from Boccaccio's *Decameron*,[6] and most importantly and demonstrably, Ariosto's epic *Orlando furioso*, which pervades Da Ponte's work on various levels, from the women's names (two of Ariosto's heroines are called Fiordiligi and Doralice) to various plot-devices, to reiterations of words and phrases from the older text.[7] This layer of Italianist reference (each historical layer embedded in the others, since Ariosto relied on Boccaccio and Boccaccio on the *Metamorphoses*) demonstrated Da Ponte's learning; it probably also constituted one of the pleasures of the text for the better-educated and Italian-oriented members of the audience.[8] There is also a series of more contemporary literary works that have been proposed as models for the libretto, but that all more plausibly count as relevant context than as literal models or references. These include various plays of Marivaux,[9] and Laclos's scandalous novel *Les liaisons dan-*

---

[4] Isabelle Moindrot, "*Così fan tutte* ou les artifices de l'idéal," in *L'Avant-scène opéra* 131–132: *Così fan tutte*, ed. Michel Noiray, pp. 23–24 links this skill to Da Ponte's demand of a finale-librettist that he supply sense and reason even when the materials do not seem to admit of it. See Chapter 7, p. 212 for a quotation of the relevant passage.

[5] E. H. Gombrich, "*Così fan tutte* (Procris included)," *Journal of the Warburg and Courtauld Institutes* 17 (1954) pp. 372–74.

[6] Steptoe, *The Mozart–Da Ponte Operas* (Oxford: Clarendon Press, 1988) pp. 124–25, and Brown, *Così*, p. 59.

[7] Brown, *Così*, pp. 60–70, gives the best available summary of Da Ponte's reliance on Ariosto, describing *Così* as one result of "a life spent in constant communication with Ariosto, and the rest of the Italian literary Parnassus" (p. 62).

[8] Brown, *Così*, p. 14, notes that Count Janos Fekete de Galántha attempted a translation of *Orlando furioso* into Hungarian; and there had been for many years a not inconsiderable community of Italian speakers and Italophiles in the Habsburg capital.

[9] Charles Rosen, *The Classical Style* (London: Faber & Faber, 1971) p. 314, notes the parallels between *Così* and *Le Jeu de l'amour et du Hasard;* Nicholas Till, *Mozart and the Enlightenment: Truth, Virtue, and Beauty in Mozart's Operas* (New York: Norton, 1993) pp.

gereuses;[10] to the extent that these plays and novels were current in Vienna, they may well have constituted a frame of reference for the audience and added to the intertextual pleasures of the work, but none of them is indisputably a source. More demonstrably intentional as the targets of references, both by Da Ponte and by Mozart, are contemporary or slightly older librettos and their musical settings, and it is with particular examples of such references that the rest of this chapter concerns itself.

Many scholars have noticed Don Alfonso's almost-quotation from Metastasio's *Demetrio* in the second terzetto. In that Metastasian opera, set more than fifty times in the eighteenth century and surely known, either as a text or in at least one musical version, to large numbers of the Burgtheater audience, Olinto sings "È la fede degli amanti/ come l'araba fenice." Da Ponte has Don Alfonso change this to "È la fede delle femmine . . ." As Bruce Alan Brown and Daniel Heartz have noted, Goldoni had also quoted this line in *La scuola moderna* (note the *scuola* connection between Goldoni and Da Ponte), and the phoenix metaphor appeared in several other libretti by Da Ponte, before and after *Così*.[11] The resonances of this quotation are further enriched if one knows (as some in the Burgtheater audience of 1790 would have) that Olinto was one of the characters invoked by Clorinda in her comic "madness" in Bertati and Anfossi's *Il curioso indiscreto*, described in Chapter 5.[12] *Il curioso indiscreto* is an opera often suggested as an influence on *Così* on account of its experimental theme and the device of switching lovers;[13] the Viennese production also included two arias by Mozart, in one of which the heroine agonizes, as Fiordiligi does in "Per pietà," about falling in love with the

---

235–36, proposes *La Dispute* as a source; Brown, *Così*, pp. 71–72, regards it as an example of a widespread type rather than a demonstrable model.

[10] Steptoe, *The Mozart–Da Ponte Operas*, pp. 131–32, notes parallels between *Les liaisons dangereuses* and *Così*, as does Hans Mayer in "*Così fan tutte* und die Endzeit des Ancien Régime," in his *Versuche über die Oper* (Frankfurt am Main: Suhrkamp, 1981) pp. 9–52.

[11] Brown, *Così*, p. 75. Heartz, *Mozart's Operas*, p. 229.

[12] See Examples 5-6 and 5-7.

[13] See Brown, *Così*, pp. 79–80; Steptoe, *The Mozart–Da Ponte Operas*, p. 135; Stefan Kunze, *Mozarts Opern* (Stuttgart: Reclam, 1984) p. 441. There are certainly plot-parallels between these two operas, and this small moment of resemblance may have made a connection for members of the Burgtheater audience. But despite its experimental theme, *Il curioso indiscreto* is both musically and dramatically more a comedy of intrigue than a "psychological demonstration." Clorinda and the Contino each try to resist the inevitable in a single aria—Clorinda's "Vorrei spiegarvi oh Dio" is one of the arias that Mozart substituted for Aloysia Lange—but thereafter the problems arise from complications in circumstance and from incidental misunderstandings rather than from inner resistance. *Il curioso indiscreto* also lacks the focus of *Così*, being without the symmetry of reversed pairs of lovers, and switches attention among three couples (Clorinda and the Contino, Emilia and Aurelio, and the servants Serpina and Prospero) rather than two. Unlike Da Ponte and Mozart's work, it moves relatively quickly away from both the strategic and the psychological processes of the test and becomes a more traditional plot centered on the gulling of a manifestly stupid man.

"wrong" man.[14] (However, whereas Fiordiligi bids an apostrophic farewell to Guglielmo, Clorinda tries to tell the onstage Contino to return to his proper betrothed, so she can keep her promise to the Marchese.) Don Alfonso's use of the Metastasian quotation, then, comes across as pedantic and mildly comic on the level of a reference to Metastasio,[15] but as a reference to *Il curioso indiscreto* it has resonances of deception, manipulation, and broader comedy—all of which Don Alfonso initiates in *Così*. The complexity and ambiguity of this apparently simple Metastasian citation is characteristic of the operatic references throughout the work.

Two works—both written for Vienna—stand out as particularly important local points of intertextual reference for *Così*, though they are by no means the only such examples:[16] Da Ponte and Martín y Soler's *L'arbore di Diana* (1787) and Casti and Salieri's *La grotta di Trofonio* (1785). These works function as quite different sorts of interlocutors in *Così*'s operatic dialogues, however. Whereas *L'arbore di Diana* can reasonably be understood as a fairly straightforward "sibling" to *Così*,[17] that relationship emphasized by the continuities in performing personnel between the two works, the relation between *Così* and *La grotta di Trofonio* is both more argumentative and more profound. Indeed, *Così*'s intertextual argument with *Trofonio* raises the question of the conventional nature of the genre as a whole.

L'ARBORE DI DIANA AND COSÌ FAN TUTTE

L'arbore di Diana, premiered in 1787 and reworked in the 1788–89 season when Adriana Ferrarese took over the title role from poor Anna Morichelli Boselli, who evidently had trouble with it and who in any case had left the company,[18] shares various narrative and structural themes with

[14] Clorinda's "Vorrei spiegarvi" K.418 (I,6). The other one is "No che non sei capace," K.419 (II,7). Both were written for Aloysia Lange. Mozart also wrote an insertion aria, "Per pietà non ricercate," K.420, for Valentin Adamberger, but it was not performed, evidently due to intrigues.

[15] Brown, "Beaumarchais, Paisiello and the Genesis of *Così*," p. 329, points out the clearly (if learnedly) comic intent of Don Alfonso's quote as demonstrated in Ferrando's response: "Scioccherie di Poeti!"

[16] Brown, "Beaumarchais, Paisiello and the Genesis of *Così*," pp. 331–37, mentions Paisiello and Casti's *Il re Teodoro* (also written for Vienna, in 1784) as another point of reference.

[17] The possible exception to this is the relation between the duets "Pianin pianino," for Diana and Endimione, and "Fra gli amplessi," for Fiordiligi and Ferrando (see Chapter 6, n. 19).

[18] See the complete quotation of a "Lettre d'un habitant de Vienne à son ami à Prague, qui lui avait demandé ses réflexions sur l'opéra intitulé L'Arbore di Diana," (letter from a resident of Vienna to his friend in Prague who had asked for his comments on the opera, *L'arbore di Diana*) in Michtner, *DAB*, pp. 435–39, in which said inhabitant pours forth his (or her) disgust at the immorality and license of the work. The opera held the stage with great tenacity, however, and in a memo to the direction of the court theatre in 1790, Da Ponte

Così and emphasizes the importance of the singers to the meanings of the works.[19] Along with *Così*, it is one of the small number of Da Ponte's libretti not based on a single model: he considered it "The best of all the dramas I have written, as much for the invention as for the poetry."[20] The "arbore" of Martín's title is a magic tree in Diana's chaste kingdom, which tests the virtue of Diana's presumably virginal nymphs: they walk past it every day, and for the chaste nymphs its enormous apples light up and play music, while for the "bad" ones, the fruit blackens, leaps off the boughs, and pelts and maims the offenders.[21] The main conceit of the plot is the penetration by Amore of Diana's closely guarded realm, and a subsequent series of tricks to corrupt the nymphs (not difficult) and to soften Diana's heart to love (difficult but eventually successful by virtue of Endimione's "receipt" of Cupid's arrow.) The tree disappears at the end of the opera and is replaced by the "realm of love." On the face of it, this story seems to have little to do with *Così*, but there are at least two significant narrative parallels. The first of these is the device of a self-enclosed and self-satisfied little world disrupted by a figure *hors de combat,* or at least *hors de mariage,* (Amore in one case; Don Alfonso in the other) whose principal aim is to manipulate the inhabitants to prove a point.[22] The second and more immediately striking of the two parallels is the trajectory of the central female characters, Diana and Fiordiligi. Both women move from a position of prideful denial to one of submission to love,[23] and the "domesticating"

---

noted that if *L'arbore di Diana* was done in a relatively economical manner, it was always a box office success. ("Memoria da me presentata alla Direzione il mese di Xbre dell'anno 1790" [Memo presented by me, to the Administration in December 1790], quoted in Michtner, *DAB*, p. 442.)

[19] Dorothea Link, "*L'arbore di Diana*: A Model for *Così fan tutte*," in Sadie, *Wolfgang Amadè Mozart,* pp. 362–73, argues that both operas exhibit the essential features of the pastoral drama, *L'arbore* more explicitly than *Così*, but the latter nonetheless strongly.

[20] "il migliore di tutti i drammi da me composte, tanto per l'invenzione che per la poesia." *Memorie,* 2d ed., ed. G. Armani (Milan: Garzanti, 1980) p. 128.

[21] Da Ponte claims in his memoirs (*Memorie,* pp. 126–27) that when he announced the title of the opera to his and Martín's friend Lerchenheim, he had no idea what he meant by it; he produced an outline of the opera in half an hour in the middle of dinner a couple of days later, having promised to show it to some friends.

[22] Dorothea Link, "*L'arbore di Diana*: A Model for *Così*," p. 365, notes that the isolated setting in *Così* is part of the way in which Mozart's opera repeats and comments upon the explicitly pastoral setting of *L'arbore di Diana*.

[23] This may be a classic eighteenth-century dramatic trajectory for women. Cleopatra, in Handel's *Giulio Cesare,* for example, undergoes a similar transformation, as do others of his powerful (often supernatural) women. One might argue that Mozart's Vitellia's move from power-hungry scheming to two pleas for mercy (one implicitly to the audience at the end of "Non più di fiori" and one to Tito) also belongs in the same category. The moment of facing the audience and admitting a sort of defeat (an appropriately womanly move?) seems to be crucial to this trajectory. Alcina's trajectory in *L'isola di Alcina* is comparable—see Example 5-5.

process by which this change of heart takes place is at the center of the opera. The minute examination of this dramatically central conversion process distinguishes Diana and Fiordiligi from other opera buffa characters who first deny and then admit passion. (See below, Chapter 9, on the conventions of the amorous conversion in this repertory.)

As well as the narrative parallels between these two operas, there are also performative connections. The tenor Vincenzo Calvesi played both Endimione and Ferrando, and by January 1790, when *Così* premiered with Adriana Ferrarese as Fiordiligi, she was also the singer associated with the role of Diana. The music for Ferrarese in particular exhibits some striking similarities. Both operas, for example, include a virtuosic aria in B♭ toward the beginning of the piece in which the character proudly asserts her impregnable status (as goddess, as immutably faithful); and both include a pensive Rondò in the second act admitting love. These connections existed even with the original version of *L'arbore di Diana;* "Sento che Dea son io" (see Example 5-3) being the seria-style aria in B♭ and the second-act rondò "Teco porta, o mia speranza," (Example 8-1) a lovely example of Martín's melodic gift. These connections are retained in the reworked version for Ferrarese, despite the replacement of both of these Martín arias with arias by Angelo Tarchi.[24] The first one, "Se il nome mio non basta," contains in its opening phrases the melodic outlines and rhythms of the beginning of "Come scoglio" (see circled notes in Example 8-2) as well as anticipating the general tone of Mozart's aria. The enormous leaps later in Tarchi's aria and the triplet coloratura are also familiar from "Come scoglio (see Example 8-3)." Tarchi's second-act rondo, "Ah sol bramo, o mia speranza," a two-tempo farewell aria, betrays more fugitive melodic similarities to the equivalent moment in *Così* (see Example 8-4).[25] The openings are both triadic and without the usual bass line, and the descending chromatic eighth-note figure at the end of the second full measure of the Tarchi may connect (given the shared singer and situation) with the melodic figure at the beginning of the faster section of "Per pietà." These musical features can, however, also be found in other examples of these aria types; and the significant similarities between Diana's and Fiordiligi's arias seem to me to lie more in the way they chart the psycho-

---

[24] Both these examples are taken from the manuscript piano-vocal scores in the Austrian National Library (Sm. 10777); it is unfortunately impossible to tell the instrumentation from these sources. Despite the indication on this manuscript copy that for the purposes of Viennese consumption the arias belonged in *L'arbore di Diana,* it is not clear whether Tarchi originally composed these arias for this particular occasion, for La Ferrarese to use in general, or whether they come from another (or two other) of Tarchi's operas. Many thanks to Dorothea Link for pointing out this source.

[25] That "Per pietà" is demonstrably connected to Eurilla's rondò "Sola e mesta," in Da Ponte and Salieri's *La cifra* (see Rice, "Rondò vocali di Salieri e Mozart," in Muraro and Bryant, eds., *I vicini di Mozart* [Florence: Olschki, 1989] vol. 1, 185–209) does not preclude the possibility of a relationship between it and "Ah sol bramo."

8-1: Martín y Soler, *L'arbore di Diana*, II,14
Diana, "Teco porta, o mia speranza," mm. 1–8; 54–62

Translation: Oh my hope, carry with you my soul that [departs] with you.
[If only] the lovely moment would return to restore my pleasure.

8-2: Tarchi, insertion in Martín y Soler, *L'arbore di Diana*, I,9
Diana: "Se il nome mio non basta," mm. 1–11

Translation: If my name does not suffice to terrify you, wretches...

logical and dramatic progress of the two women than in particular musical features.

The crucial difference between Fiordiligi and Diana, of course, is that while Diana's discovery of passion "takes" in the course of the drama (and Amore celebrates his victory over the goddess of chastity), Fiordiligi's two-timing passion for her Albanian suitor is relinquished in favor of her original, apparently less passionate pairing with Guglielmo. One might, then, regard *Così* as a sort of "sequel" to *L'arbore di Diana*, at least with respect to their central female characters. If the moral message of *L'arbore di Diana* is that a life involving love is better than a life of forced and in some sense false chastity, one message of *Così* is that love is neither socially nor emotionally simple. If Diana does "turn into" Fiordiligi, her "more mature" self learns both the convenience and the dangers of a first and more or less unexamined love.

There is another singerly parallel between these operas, as both Dorothea Link and Dexter Edge have noted.[26] Luisa Villeneuve, who played Amore (a partially *travesti* role) beginning in June 1789, also created the role of Dorabella. The latter's aria "È amore un ladroncello"—a late addition to the score—could thus function for the audience as an ap-

[26] Dorothea Link, "*Così fan tutte:* Dorabella and Amore," *M-Jb* (1991) pp. 888–94. Dexter Edge, "Mozart's Reception in Vienna," in Sadie, *Wolfgang Amadè Mozart,* p. 95.

8-3: Tarchi, insertion in Martín y Soler, *L'arbore di Diana*, I,9
Diana, "Se il nome mio non basta," mm. 113–27

Translation: that I don't know how to restrain myself.
* The manuscript of this aria is a piano reduction.

8-4: Tarchi, insertion in Martín y Soler, *L'arbore di Diana,* II,14
Diana, "Ah sol bramo o mia speranza," mm. 4–8

Translation: All I desire, o my hope, is to assuage my grief.

parent self-reference, and her notions of love, which combine a sense of necessary disruption with a certain nonchalance, render her philosophically analogous to *L'arbore*'s Amore. (The other Cupid-figure in *Così* is Despina, as Edmund J. Goehring has recently argued.[27]) The Amore-Dorabella connection works less convincingly as a narrative sequence than the connection between Diana and Fiordiligi, however, and the musical connections between the two lighter figures are less striking. In addition Amore's *structural* role as presiding manipulator (or magician) is taken over by Don Alfonso rather than by Dorabella, whereas the structural roles of Diana and Fiordiligi are entirely comparable.

I would suggest that the nature of the conversation between *L'arbore di Diana* and *Così* was both amicable and quite specifically inclusive of the audience; although the pastoral-mode similarities noted by Dorothea Link are perhaps primarily an "author to author" conversation,[28] the continuities between the performers, and the musical and textual elements deriving from those performative continuities were surely addressed to the audience in ways that relied on and flattered their knowledge of the various habits of the repertory. The dialogue between *Così* and *La grotta di Trofonio,* however, is quite different. While no doubt at least potentially perceptible *by* audience members, it seems to me not addressed *to* them; rather, it is a dialogue among the authors, and as I will argue, it raises issues about the genre in the abstract more than about the repertory in its performed specificity.

---

[27] Edmund J. Goehring, "Despina, Cupid and the Pastoral Mode of *Così fan tutte*," *COJ* 7 (1995) pp.107–33.
[28] Link, "*L'arbore di Diana:* A Model for *Così fan tutte.*"

LA GROTTA DI TROFONIO AND COSÌ FAN TUTTE

If the conversation between *Così* and *La grotta di Trofonio* is more argumentative than that between *Così* and *L'arbore di Diana*, that mirrors the relations between their authors. At the time of the premiere of *Così*, Da Ponte was an acknowledged rival of Giambattista Casti, though by the time Da Ponte was to leave Vienna in 1791 they were united in disdain for Giovanni Bertati, and Casti pled Da Ponte's case in front of Leopold II.[29] Da Ponte also became Salieri's enemy after February 1789, when Da Ponte's opera-revue, *L'ape musicale*, excluded Salieri's mistress, Caterina Cavalieri, in favor of Da Ponte's, Adriana Ferrarese.[30] The rivalry between Salieri and Mozart is less reliably documented if more extravagantly fictionalized, but there nevertheless appears to be some truth to it, not only in Mozart's early days in Vienna[31] but also around the time of, and even in connection with, Mozart's composition of *Così*. John A. Rice and Bruce Alan Brown have, for instance, recently discovered that Da Ponte first offered the libretto to Salieri, who started two numbers and gave up;[32] they quote Mary Novello reporting Constanze Mozart's comment that her husband's successful completion of the setting was the cause of Salieri's "enmity."[33] The reason for Salieri's uncharacteristic abandonment of this libretto is not clear; Brown and Rice surmise that it may be connected with a general downturn in his creative energies in the latter part of 1788 and 1789. It does not tell us much about the relationship between the two composers. The relations between *Trofonio* and *Così*, however, do seem to tell a story of unrelieved competitiveness on Mozart's and Da Ponte's parts; whether this was meant

---

[29] Da Ponte, *Memorie,* pp. 159–65. Da Ponte's mixed feelings about Casti are particularly evident in the following passage from the *Memorie* (p. 163): "Fu mio persecutore: per sentimento d'uomo, ma più pel dovere del storico [!] ho dovuto nelle mie *Memorie* tal dipingerlo. Fu mio benefattore, e, come tale, è mio dovere di confessarlo e di professargli l'obbligazione ch'ha meritata." [He was my persecutor; from human sentiment, but more from my duties as a historian, I have felt obliged to depict him as such in my memoirs. He was my benefactor, and as such, it is my duty to confess this, and to profess to him the obligation he has earned.]

[30] Bruce Alan Brown and John A. Rice give a clear account of this in "Salieri's *Così fan tutte,*" *COJ* 8 (1996) pp. 35–36.

[31] See, for example, Mozart's description (*Letters,* July 2, 1783) of the intrigue surrounding his insertion arias in *Il curioso indiscreto*, at least part of which involved Salieri. Despite the braggadocio of this letter ("It failed completely with the exception of my two arias, the second of which, a bravura, had to be repeated"), Mozart's printed disclaimer about his arias being written *for* Aloysia Lange and not *against* Anfossi, is, to my knowledge, unique among Viennese librettos of this period and does suggest that Mozart felt his position as a (non-Italian) outsider very keenly.

[32] Brown and Rice, "Salieri's *Così fan tutte.*" These authors are careful to indicate that we do not know whether Mozart knew that he was second in line for the work, then entitled *La scola degli amanti*.

[33] Brown and Rice, "Salieri's *Così fan tutte,*" p. 20.

more or less amicably or in bitterness, and how it was received, will probably never be known.

The connections between *La grotta di Trofonio* and *Così* do not to any significant extent involve the performing casts. There were correspondences in the casts—at least the casts of the premieres[34] (Vincenzo Calvesi played Artemidoro and Ferrando; Benucci played Trofonio and Guglielmo; and Francesco Bussani played Plistene and Don Alfonso), but the roles are either quite different (Trofonio and Guglielmo, for example), or similar only in broadly typological ways (Artemidoro and Ferrando, for example, are both tenor lovers). The plot of *La grotta di Trofonio,* however, is closer to *Così* than is that of *L'arbore di Diana.* It involves two pairs of lovers: Ofelia and Artemidoro, the high-minded couple who discuss "the sublime Plato" in their strolls through the woods; and Ofelia's twin sister Dori (cf. Dorabella), and Plistene, whose temperaments are more cheerful, down-to-earth, and laughter-loving. The women and their father Aristone rejoice that the contrasting temperaments of the sisters have been so well-matched by the young men. The "philosopher" Trofonio, however, persuades each of the lovers in turn (first the men, then the women) to enter his grotto, which has the magic capacity to change people's temperaments from grave to cheerful and vice versa. The predictable misunderstandings occur when the women meet their altered mates. The girls also enter the grotto, but the men have returned to normal in order to be able to suit the original temperaments of their lovers. There follow the predictably unsatisfactory meetings between the changed women and the temperamentally unchanged men. Finally, Aristone, who has philosophical pretensions himself, decides to consult Trofonio, who makes the women reenter the grotto, and the original order is restored.

Andrea Della Corte bluntly describes Casti's work as "stupido,"[35] a judgment both anticipated and echoed by many, though usually with more circumlocution. Da Ponte's opinion was that "the second act, as far as the libretto is concerned, entirely destroys the effect of the first, of which it is nothing but an exact repetition[.]"[36] Casti's libretto may be "stupid" in its mechanical repetition of events (and even for an admirer of some fairly

---

[34] It is true that the change from Morichelli to Ferrarese in the history of *L'arbore di Diana* was widely trumpeted, but partly because it was Ferrarese's debut performance in Vienna. Most cast changes were not so widely or loudly advertised or, indeed, advertised at all, though the evidence of many scores (especially those designated KT) suggests endless tinkering, no doubt including adaptations for different singers. There is, thus, no certainty either that the correspondences between roles that I have mentioned would have been the most current ones, or that there might not have been more.

[35] Della Corte, *L'opera comica italiana* (Bari: Laterza, 1923) p. 67.

[36] Da Ponte, *Memorie,* p. 116. He continues, with virtuosic vituperation, "but [Trofonio is] in my opinion, a much more beautiful work than *Teodoro*" (. . . il cui secondo atto, quanto alla poesia, distruggeva interamente l'effetto del primo, del quale non era che una perfetta ripetizione; ma che, a mio credere, è un'opera assai più bella del *Teodoro*).

silly *opere buffe* the tedium does set in rather early), but the opera as a whole is very interesting in its relation to *Così*, and certain correspondences suggest not just accidental parallels, but conscious connections. Bruce Alan Brown has dismissed *Trofonio* as a possible "source" for *Così* on the grounds that the resemblances—the switching of the lovers, the symmetry and concentration of the plot, for example—are either too superficial or mismatched, unlike Da Ponte's thoroughgoing use of Ariosto.[37] However, I would argue that the problem is not that the resemblances are merely superficial (which many of them are) but that the deeper points of contact— and they do exist—are negative. Having noted that Trofonio is not a "real" philosopher, and that the opera ends with "no moral whatsoever," Brown also remarks, "One can easily imagine Da Ponte thinking how much more might be done with such a premise."[38] Indeed, *Così* seems to me precisely the proof that Da Ponte (and Mozart) did in fact "do more."

The larger attempt to do more is signaled by a series of large and small superficial resemblances, which the Burgtheater audience might reasonably have been expected to catch and sift out from the merely generic resemblances with which they were constantly presented. Some of these little resemblances are simply that: their largest intertextual function is to indicate the existence of a connection and to provide the relatively trivial pleasure of its identification. Others lead out into the aesthetic and moral dimensions of the works and can engage the listener in the substance of the argument. The most obvious superficial similarity between the two operas is the device of a consciously manipulated, perfectly symmetrical crossing of lovers; multiple pairs of lovers get switched or reconfigured quite regularly in this repertory, but the carefully manipulated symmetry of both *Trofonio* and *Così* and their concentrated narrative focus on the mechanisms of the switch distinguishes them from all other operas in the repertory. The presence of a philosopher-manipulator is another generically unusual point of contact: I discuss this in more detail below. The name resemblance between Dori and Dorabella is also striking, since neither is a usual opera buffa name,[39] and both are the lighter-hearted member of a pair of sisters. Indeed, one might regard Dori as a link between Ariosto's Doralice and Da Ponte's Dorabella, since Ariosto's heroine bears no relation to his Fiordiligi, and Casti's heroine supplies the familial relation. (Casti's serious sister's name, Ofelia, is also unique in the repertory: quite apart from its Shakespearian resonances, one might note the "fe" sound, unusual in female *parte seria* names, and which "Fiordiligi" might be thought to evoke.)

[37] Brown, *Così*, pp. 78–79.
[38] Ibid.
[39] To say that "Dorabella" refers to "Dori" is not to deny that it also refers to Ariosto's "Doralice." Indeed, as Don Alfonso's Metastasian quotation suggests, *Così* is not only full of allusions, but any given allusion can resonate in several different ways simultaneously.

An internal connection between the librettos occurs in the first-act finales of both operas: right at the beginning of that portion of *Così*, the women sing:

Ah tutta in un momento	Ah, all in a moment
Si cangiò la sorte mia.	My fate has changed.

In the first act finale of *Trofonio* the stretta begins (in choral homorhythm):

In un momento	In a moment
Tal cangiamento	Such a change
Di verisimile	Has no shadow
Ombra non ha.	Of likelihood.

At both moments the words are clearly audible; both come at crucial formal junctures, both are sung homophonically by the relevant characters, and both involve disbelief at a change of state.[40] And in both librettos the lovers borrow rock similes from Ariosto to indicate constancy—Fiordiligi's "Come scoglio" and Plistene's comment (I/9) "Ma io per la mia Dori/ Duro, e costante come uno scoglio."[41] Mozart also engages in this play of small references. For example, the dialogue between the young men and Alfonso in the opening scene of *Così*, where the older man persuades the younger ones into the bet, is reminiscent of Act I scene 6 of *La grotta di Trofonio* where Aristone (the girls' father) assures himself that each young man wants the proper (i.e., temperamentally matched) bride. Both scenes involve the young men assuring an older one that they will keep their promise, both involve the young men singing responses in chorus, and both involve the question "Parola?" ("Your word on it?") from the old man and an enthusiastic response from the juniors (see Examples 8-5a and 8-5b). Another small musical connection between the two operas is the relation between Despina's intonations as the notary in the second-act finale of *Così*, and Trofonio's descriptions of the biological effects of his grotto; the musical connection being the repeated-note, end-accented vocal line with its spiky fourth, and the syncopated accompaniment (see especially mm. 4–8 of the *Così* example), and the dramatic connection being the exercise of authority. The monotone text with spiked fourth leap, often in triple meter with sdrucciolo line-endings, is something of a topic in opera buffa, as Giuliano's ridiculous self-rejuvenating spell in the second-act finale of *I filosofi immaginari* demonstrates (see Example 7-9, especially the first 4 measures). Thus, even if one wanted to argue that Despina was merely spoofing quackery in general, Trofonio would have been a memorable example in the repertory. A

---

[40] Link, "*L'arbore di Diana:* A Model for *Così fan tutte*," p. 371, might point out that the attention to mutability of character, brought about by magic (or its equivalent), links all three operas as pastorals.

[41] This is pointed out both by Brown, *Così*, pp. 65–66, and Isabelle Moindrot, "*Così fan tutte* et les artifices de l'idéal," p. 27 and n. 4.

8-5a: Salieri, *La grotta di Trofonio,* I,7
Recitative, "Amici, a quel che veggio," Artemidoro,
Plistene, Aristone, mm. 37–42

Translation:
Artemidoro:	Well, if it pleases you you, I'll marry Ofelia.
Plistene:	I'll take Dori.
Aristone:	Your word?
Plist. and Art.:	Yes, our word.
Aristone:	Done?
Plist. and Art.:	Done.

further textual connection between them is Trofonio's mumbo jumbo about electrical emanations and Despina's first-act disguise as a doctor versed in the magnetic mysteries of mesmerism (see Examples 8-6a and 8-6b).

Even these small resemblances are not simple imitation, however. In every example of significant resemblance between the two operas, *Così* either improves upon or mocks *Trofonio.* Despina's ridiculous intoning of the marriage contract is obviously a parody, if not only of Trofonio. But with respect to the opening scene of *Così,* and the betrothal agreement scene between Aristone and the young men, the dramatic point of that interaction in *Così* is the tension between the lovers and Don Alfonso, between blind faith and open-eyed skepticism, which sets up both the mechanism and the moral *agon* of the plot. In *Trofonio,* on the other hand, there is no such tension, merely a fixing of already-known positions. As far as the mechanism of the switch and the "cangiamento" is concerned, the lovers in *Così* change only their superficial features, but this trivial change has profound consequences. The lovers in *Trofonio,* on the other hand, change

8-5b: Mozart, *Così fan tutte*, I,1
Recitative, "Scioccherie di poeti," Don Alfonso, Ferrando,
Guglielmo, mm. 25–26; 34–37

Translation:
Don Alfonso:	Your word.
Ferrando:	Absolutely my word.
Guglielmo:	With all my heart.
Don Alfonso:	Bravo!
Ferr. and Gugl.:	Bravo, Mr. Don Alfonso!

temperaments, but this profound change leads to no new understandings and no new relationships. (The distinction between the possibility of profundity in superficial changes and the potential triviality of apparent revolution has implications for the larger generic messages of these works, as I argue below.) In addition, the notion of relationship as the active engagement of one person with another is largely lacking in *Trofonio,* being replaced by the notion of abstractly matched temperaments and a fixed order between the father and Trofonio and the young people. Relationships in *Così,* however—between the women and their lovers (and particularly the "wrong" ones), between the two same-sex pairs (especially the men) and

8-6a: Salieri, *La grotta di Trofonio,* I,10
Trofonio, "Spirti invisibili," mm. 58–69

Translation: Then come the electric effluvia that knock and shake the nerves and muscles.

between Despina and her mistresses—are the essence of the matter. Like the switched lovers, whose structure Mozart and Da Ponte appropriate but also alter, the principle of concentrated symmetry—which Casti adhered to with such monotonous results, and which Salieri could not do much to enliven—becomes in *Così,* because of its concern with relationships, a frame in tension with its contents. As Joseph Kerman writes: "It is the asymmetries in this highly symmetrical plot that provide the dramatic drive. Dorabella falls at once, but Fiordiligi puts up an unexpected struggle, around which the second act comes to revolve."[42] Once again, the appropriated element of *La grotta di Trofonio* is "corrected" in *Così.*

[42] Joseph Kerman, *Opera as Drama,* new and revised ed. (Berkeley: University of California Press, 1988) p. 94.

8-6b: Mozart, *Così fan tutte*, II, finale, mm. 255–62

Translation: join you in matrimony: Fiordiligi with Sempronio

Don Alfonso, Trofonio and "Filosofia"

The superficial connection between Don Alfonso and Trofonio is in their titles—"vecchio filosofo" and "filosofo." The most obvious result of this connection is an awareness of the differences between the two figures— differences that mirror the two primary associations of "filosofo" and "filosofia" in late-eighteenth-century opera buffa. These associations are on the one hand with astronomy, astrology, and magic and on the other (less commonly) with the exercise of reason and moderation, justified or bolstered by the ancients. This operatic mixing of what we may perceive as quite different categories under a single heading appears to mirror more general and deeply rooted cultural practices. As John Passmore writes: "In general [medieval and renaissance philosophers] used "philosophy" as often to refer to what we now call "science" as to refer to what we now call "philosophy." . . . If we can now distinguish with sufficient clarity between cosmological speculation and descriptive metaphysics, the fact remains that, as we can see from Aristotle's *Physics,* the distinction was not an easy one for men to make."[43] Trofonio is a clear example of a cosmological manipulator. He calls forth spirits, his grotto has obviously magic properties, and he relies on arcane theories and prescriptions. His activities and interests associate him with other opera buffa "filosofi" like Petronio in *I filosofi immaginari,* or Ecclitico the "finto astrologo" of Goldoni's libretto *Il mondo della luna,* or (to a lesser extent) to figures like Don Polidoro in Petrosellini and Cimarosa's *L'italiana in Londra,* who spends the opera in search of the heliotrope said to guarantee invisibility.[44] Trofonio differs from these figures, however, in being neither the butt of the plot nor a trickster working for material (financial, social, or sexual) interests. Trofonio also differs from these other figures in having palpable (if implausible) powers rather than deluded pretensions: neither Buonafede (*Il mondo della luna*) nor Petronio (*I filosofi immaginari*) can actually do anything.

Don Alfonso resembles Trofonio in not being the gullible object of the other characters' tricks and in having demonstrable power over the other characters. However, unlike Trofonio (and for that matter, unlike Amore in *L'arbore di Diana*), Don Alfonso's power is the force of reason, and his stance is one of psychological distance or suspension of belief; he demonstrates a faith in the reconciliation of reason and desire that, as Bruce Alan Brown notes, was coming to the end of its cultural currency.[45] Like Trofonio, Don Alfonso is learned, as his occasional excursion into Latin and his ability with classical references show, but he wears that learning lightly and uses it in the service of his larger purposes, rather than for its own sake, as Trofonio does.[46] Indeed, Stefan Kunze goes so far as to suggest that he is Mozart's attempt to make good again with Voltaire, whom the musician had maligned to his father in his youth.[47] The manifest demonstration of Don Alfonso's power is rhetoric rather than magic; his effect is made through the medium of persuasion rather than trickery, and his pragmatic

[43] See s.v. "Philosophy" in *The Encyclopedia of Philosophy.*

[44] William Gerber, s.v. "Philosophical Dictionaries and Encyclopedias" in *The Encyclopedia of Philosophy,* notes the publication in 1738 of Frederick Christian Baumeister's *Philosophia Definitiva, Hoc Est Definitiones Philosophicae,* which contained about 1300 definitions, nearly one hundred of which were (still) on cosmology. This dictionary was enlarged and reprinted in 1767. There was no significant Italian dictionary or encyclopedia of philosophy published in the eighteenth century.

[45] Brown, *Così,* pp. 2–3; 89–94.

[46] Brown, "Beaumarchais, Paisiello and the Genesis of *Così,*" p. 332, also notes the "lighter hand" with which Da Ponte incorporated topical references in *Così,* compared to those in Casti's *Il re Teodoro in Venezia.*

[47] Stefan Kunze, *Mozarts Opern,* p. 450. The maligning of Voltaire comes in a letter to his father from Paris (July 3, 1778), "that godless arch-rascal Voltaire has pegged out like a dog, like a beast! That is his reward!" Four days earlier (June 29, 1778), but evidently not seen by Wolfgang when he wrote his letter, Leopold had written, "So Voltaire is dead too! and died just as he lived; he ought to have done something better for the sake of his reputation with posterity."

notion that wisdom lies in accepting things as they are and not searching after an ultimate truth[48] contrasts pointedly with Trofonio's renunciation of society in pursuit of arcane verities.[49] At the same time, however, as both Dorothea Link and Maria Antonella Balsano have pointed out, Don Alfonso is easy to associate with the world of pastoral magic: this substrate in his character may project a sense that he has consciously renounced the supernatural for the reasonable, and thus strengthen both his connection and his contrast with Trofonio.[50]

Another point of similarity between these two figures which immediately reveals their differences lies in the music they sing. Both are associated with the only minor-mode numbers in their respective operas; Don Alfonso's "Vorrei dir" is a "textbook" example of the *aria agitata* or panic aria (see below, Chapter 9), and his homiletic eruption "Nel mare solca"—a quotation from Jacopo Sannazaro's *L'Arcadia*[51]—also begins in the minor, though it moves after four measures to its major-mode goal. Trofonio's opening aria, in which he calls forth his spirits and describes the powers of his grotto, is a splendid D minor fantasy.[52] D minor returns at the opening of the second-act finale in which Aristone calls Trofonio from his grotto. Although both characters have highly distinctive key associations, their manners of utterance are quite different. Don Alfonso is famous for the brevity of his arias; his rhetorical power over the other characters seems in inverse proportion to his somewhat meager "performative" presence.[53] Trofonio, on the other hand, has two substantial arias, the first, at least, highly unconventional for opera buffa, with its frequent brief tempo and meter changes, its inclusion of the chorus, and its complex harmonies. His power (embodied, according to Salieri's wishes, in a voice "di gran forza e tenebrosa"[54]) is largely "performative" and is directed at the audience at least as much as at the other characters.

[48] I,1: "O pazzo desire! / Cercar di scoprire / Quel mal che, trovato, / Meschini ci fa" [O mad desire to try to discover that harm that, once found, makes us miserable]. Brown, "Beaumarchais, Paisiello" p. 314, links this "proverbial" statement to a comment of Bartholo's in *Le barbier de Séville,* and Heartz, *Mozart's Operas,* pp. 230–32, connects it to Goldoni's *Le pescatrici.* Proverbial or not, it is advice the overcurious Marchese in *Il curioso indiscreto* could well have heeded.

[49] I,11: "Trofonio sono, abitator di questa grotta ov'io fra studi ignoti arcani lungi dal folle mondo solitario m'ascondo" [I am Trofonio, inhabitant of this grotto, where I solitarily hide myself to pursue secret arcane studies far from the mad world].

[50] Link, *L'arbore di Diana:* A Model for *Così fan tutte,* p. 372. Maria Antonella Balsano, "L'ottava di *Così fan tutte,*" in *Liedstudien: Wolfgang Osthoff zum 60. Geburtstag,* ed. Martin Just and Reinhard Wiesend (Tutzing: Schneider, 1989) p. 280.

[51] Brown, *Così,* pp. 69–70.

[52] The opening of this aria echoes the C minor opening of the overture.

[53] The small number and brevity of Don Alfonso's arias has also been attributed to the musical limitations of the first performer of the role, Francesco Bussani. See Brown, *Così,* pp. 135–36.

[54] Salieri's autograph notes to the opera, quoted in Rudolph Angermüller, *Antonio Salieri: Sein Leben und seine weltliche Werke unter besonderer Berücksichtigung seiner "grossen" Opern* (Munich: Katzbichler, 1971) vol. 3, p. 32.

These rather obvious differences-in-similarities between Don Alfonso and Trofonio, however, point to deeper connections between them. Although these figures evoke different aspects of the designation "filosofo," they share an overriding interest in demonstrating a theory or principle apparently for its own sake, but in fact through, and in some sense for, their own demonstration and exercise of power. Writers on *Così* have described Don Alfonso's power in a number of ways, and with varying degrees of detachment and approval. The metaphor of the puppetmaster pulling the strings of the lover-marionettes is now a cliché; it appeared first in Edward J. Dent's *Mozart's Operas* and was revived in Joseph Kerman's *Opera as Drama*.[55] Others have seen him as the embodiment of the principles of the French philosophes.[56] Stefan Kunze, as I noted above, describes Don Alfonso as a "demythologized deity," presiding over the predetermined and inevitable unfolding of events. More political readings include Hans Mayer's:[57] he uses Adorno and Horkheimer's reading of the Enlightenment ethos as proto-totalitarian to connect Don Alfonso's insistence on the rule of reason with his unapologetic control over the lovers, while Isabelle Moindrot sees him, like Trofonio, as the power-hungry purveyor of a self-satisfied and sterile set of values.[58]

Whatever the critics' views of the nature of Don Alfonso's power, most of them agree that Da Ponte's libretto does not in any obvious way undercut or parody Don Alfonso's rationalistic values. Casti's satiric intentions vis à vis Trofonio, however, are evident both in the libretto and in his own comments about it. According to a verse written later, Casti's avowed purpose in writing this libretto was to "deride the devil and magic exorcisms of sorcerers and swindlers, and the fake paroxysms of demoniac impostors."[59] Within the libretto Trofonio's own chorus of spirits call him a swindler (*ciurmatore*),[60] and his breast-beating comments on his own

[55] *Opera as Drama*, p. 93.

[56] Brown, *Così*, pp. 82–86, makes this connection in some detail, as does Gerhard Splitt, "Gespielte Aufklärung: *Così fan tutte* oder die Umkehrung der Moral," in *Freiburger Universitätsblätter* 27 (Sept. 1988) pp. 62–69. See also Cornelia Kritsch and Herbert Zeman, "Das Rätsel eines genialen Opernentwurf—Da Ponte's Libretto zu 'Così fan tutte' und das literarische Umfeld," in Herbert Zeman, ed., *Die österreichische Literatur: Ihr Profil an der Wende vom 18. zum 19. Jahrhundert (1750–1830)*, Part I (Graz: Akademische Druck- und Verlagsanstalt, 1979) pp. 359–64.

[57] "*Così* und die Endzeit des Ancien Régime," in his *Versuche über die Oper* (Frankfurt am Main: Suhrkamp, 1981) pp. 9–52.

[58] Moindrot, "*Così fan tutte* ou les artifices de l'idéal," pp. 31–32.

[59] "[Poscia l'opera ho composta / della GROTTA DI TROFONIO / Che composi a bella posta] / Per deridere il Demonio; / Ed i magici esorcismi / Di stregoni e ciurmatori / Ed i finti parossismi / D'energumeni impostori." Casti published this verse in his *Memorial given as a joke on the occasion of the recess of the diocese of V . . . ; it appeared in his complete works. Quoted in Laura Callegari Hill's introduction to *La grotta di Trofonio* (Artaria, 1785; rpt. Bologna: Forni, 1984).

[60] I, 10; "Perchè l'infochi / con gridi rochi? / Perchè ci evochi / dai stigi lochi / gran ciurmator." [Why dost thou kindle [us] with hoarse cries? Why dost thou call us from Sty-

power (e.g., II,8: "This enchanted hovel will stand as testimony to the power of Trofonio for centuries to come")[61] are quite out of proportion with its effect. As far as the plot is concerned, Trofonio gets what he deserves at the end, when the lovers and Aristone politely but desperately refuse his further aid in their marriage plans, despite his threats. Don Alfonso, on the other hand, is proved right (at least on the level of the plot); far from being rejected by the other characters, he is absorbed by them, as they all preach his message in chorus at the end. On the level of the libretto, then, Don Alfonso serves as a largely positive example of Enlightenment principles, while Trofonio serves a negative function in support of those same principles.[62] The music of both operas complicates this reading, however; this complication is treated below.

The libretto of *La grotta di Trofonio* is unique in the repertory in having scholarly footnotes explaining the various classical references in the text. Its setting, amid the rocks and forests of exotic Boeotia, and explicit references to the "bizzarre stravaganze" of the plot and its roots in Ovid,[63] are also unusual. Casti's characters discuss Theophrastus and read Plato, and the text as a whole exudes a learned authority quite exceptional amid the *galanterie,* low humor, and tossed-off wit of most of this repertory. Salieri's music is not as obviously "learned" as the text, but his use of the supernatural chorus to interrupt Trofonio's aria, the rich mixture of long and short arias, the fluid way in which solo and ensemble utterances connect, the occasional use of distant modulations or chromatic harmonies (Aristone's first comic aria is a surprising case in point), and the unusually elaborate writing for winds all suggest a musical ambition generally speaking foreign to the genre. (Salieri's recent composition of *Les Danaïdes* for Paris surely played into his compositional choices for *Trofonio.*) Rudolf Angermüller also quotes Salieri as saying that the music was "not in the usual style, as the text demanded."[64] Da Ponte's libretto for *Così* is, as we have seen, at least as richly learned as Casti's, but the learning is subtly woven into the texture of the piece (and there are neither footnotes nor an introduction). In this context Da Ponte's determinedly ordinary household setting for *Così,* and his use of the utterly unremarkable buffa device

---

gian places, great swindler?]. The doggerel verse, related in meter to Gluck's chorus of the furies in *Orfeo,* must also have added to the satiric effect.

[61] Questo magico abituro / ogni secolo futuro / del potere di Trofonio / testimonio ognor sarà.

[62] Michael Robinson, "Paisiello, Mozart and Casti," in *Internationaler Musikwissenschaftlicher Kongress zum Mozartjahr 1991, Baden-Wien* (Tutzing: Schneider, 1993) pp. 71–79, suggests that Da Ponte's libretto *Demogorgone, o sia il filosofo confuso,* written for Vincenzo Righini and also performed in Laxenburg (an imperial country-house just outside Vienna) a year after Salieri's opera, was also a public debunking of *Trofonio.*

[63] Casti, preface to the Vienna 1785 libretto, and also to the printed Artaria score.

[64] Angermüller, *Antonio Salieri,* vol. 2, p. 119.

of the disguise to propel the plot, seem like acerbic comments on the place of self-advertising originality in this most conventional of genres. And Mozart's music, which quotes a cadential motto from the overture rather than a whole symphonic paragraph, and which, rather than creating avant-garde *scena*s, deploys entirely recognizable ensemble-types in quite new ways, makes a similar point about aesthetic values.

Text and Music in Trofonio and Così

Eighteenth-century comments on Casti's libretto uniformly point to the dramatic redundancy of the second act. Da Ponte's comment has been noted above; an anonymous reviewer for the Paris *Moniteur* in 1790 commented in comparable terms, though with less personal bile: "One sees that this uniform succession of metamorphoses, so easily foreseen, offers nothing but a repeat (*rédite*) of symmetrical scenes; their monotony arises also from the fact that any other point of interest in the piece was unable to introduce any nuance of variety. I think this is a defect inherent in the conception of this poem."[65] At the same time as contemporary observers heaped opprobrium on the libretto, however, they praised the competence and beauty of the music. Da Ponte described the music as "very lovely" (*bellissima*);[66] the French reviewer for the *Moniteur* did the same, and Count Zinzendorf wrote, "The music charming . . . but the subject [has] no spirit [génie], no art, no decoration [subplots or subsidiary interests]; [it is] always the garden, always the grotto, and nothing but transformations."[67] *La grotta di Trofonio* was, nevertheless, not by any means a failure; it was well-written for its singers, and its musical beauties, which are considerable, especially the inventive and colorful use of wind instruments, evidently outweighed its dramatic difficulties in the public mind.

What was in the eighteenth century perceived as a straightforward imbalance of quality between text and music may also be understood as a difference in tone. Although Casti's satiric intent is quite clear from his later verse about the libretto, and from certain moments in the libretto itself (see above), Salieri's setting does not evidently honor that intent.[68] In his au-

---

[65] Paris, *Moniteur*, 15 March 1790. Quoted in Angermüller, *Antonio Salieri*, vol. 3, p. 35.
[66] *Memorie*, p. 116.
[67] "La musique charmante . . . Mais le sujet sans génie, sans art, point de decorations, toujours le jardin, toujours la grotte, toujours les transmutations." Quoted in Michtner, *DAB*, p. 398 n. 36.
[68] My view that the *tone* of Salieri's music sits so uncomfortably with the libretto contrasts with that of Angermüller (*Antonio Salieri*, vol. 2, pp. 118–19) and Sergio Martinotti ("Per un altro ritratto di Salieri," in Muraro, *I vicini*, pp. 282–83), both of whom suggest that the satirical tone pervades all domains of the opera. I also differ somewhat from Andrew Steptoe's view (*The Mozart–Da Ponte Operas*, pp. 135–36) that Casti's "brilliantly ironic" libretto is "compromised by Salieri's somewhat pedestrian setting."

tograph notes on the score,[69] he makes several mentions of the "system" of the opera, by which he means the sets of contrasting temperaments, and gives no indication that this is meant as anything but a straightforward distinction. Thus, although Salieri describes Trofonio's music as "magica," and despite the fact (not to be underestimated) that the role of Trofonio was sung (*à merveille*, according to Zinzendorf) by the celebrated comic bass Francesco Benucci, the music itself—particularly Trofonio's first-act invocation of his spirits, with its orchestral opening unison, its unmediated dynamic alternations, and its pervasive chromatic lines—shows no hint of the grotesque exaggeration that might indicate parody (see Example 8-7).[70]

The notion that the music of an opera was in some sense better than the text is relatively commonplace in commentaries on opera buffa as a genre, but awareness of the discontinuity or noncongruence of the two domains seems particularly strong in comments on both *Trofonio* and *Così*. The well-known opinion of *Così* which appeared in the Berlin *Journal des modes* (1792) expresses the dichotomy at its most extreme: "It is really regrettable that our best composers generally waste their time and talents on miserable and deplorable subjects. . . . The present composition is the silliest thing in the world and should only be attended on account of its splendid music."[71] Even Zinzendorf, who was more forgiving toward the text than the Berlin commentator, called the music "charming" but the "subject" only "assez amusant."[72] The perceived incommensurability between the frivolity or triviality of the libretto and the extraordinary beauty of the music of *Così* has been at the heart of criticism of the opera throughout the nineteenth century and well into our own. That perception is undoubtedly due at least in part to the entrenched notion of Mozart as a transcendent genius saddled with hack librettists (an attitude not generally associated with Salieri studies). It is, however, also due to something more objectively present in *Così*, which is a seriousness in the music apparently incommensurable with the playfulness of the plot. Joseph Kerman, for example, speaks for many when he says, "I have never seen an explanation of any convention that makes sense both of the action . . . and also of the remarkable expressivity of some of the music."[73] In the context of claiming *Così* as a "refutation" of *La grotta di Trofonio*, it may not be out of line to suggest that Mozart took the notion of music "too serious" or "too beau-

---

[69] These were evidently written after the piece had been performed. About the second-act trio "Venite o Donne meco," he writes that "it has always been regarded as one of the best pieces in the opera" [fu sempre riguardato come una dei pezzi particolari dell'opera]. Quoted in Angermüller, *Antonio Salieri,* vol. 3, pp. 32–33.

[70] Operas on the comparably supernatural Don Giovanni theme—Mozart's not excepted—seem also to have stimulated this sort of minor-mode, coloristically orchestrated, music.

[71] Quoted in Michtner, *DAB*, p. 293.

[72] Quoted in ibid., p. 421 n. 25.

[73] Kerman, *Opera as Drama*, p. 92.

8-7: Salieri, *La grotta di Trofonio*, I,10
Trofonio, "Spirti invisibili," mm. 1–17

Translation: Invisible spirits of the air, of thunder and lightning.

tiful" for a cynical or ironic libretto at least partly from Salieri, and in ap-
plying that beauty to the portrayal of human relations rather than to the
evocation of the supernatural world, made it serve dramatic rather than il-
lustrative ends.

The point-by-point commentary of the previous paragraphs easily ram-
ifies into a more general reading of the relation between the two works, in
which *Così* can be understood as an exemplar of the genre, as a "scuola"
not only for lovers, but also for librettists and composers.[74] In deploying
generic cliches in an entirely "ordinary" setting, rather than striving might-
ily after originality, *Così* draws attention to the dramatic potential of the
manipulation of convention; a potential of crucial importance to opera
buffa. Also, in its concentration on the vagaries of the relationships that
arise in an artificial situation, rather than on an irreducible and immutable
system of kindred temperaments, *Così* raises the question of the fit between
individual desires and the stability of some larger group (family, fief, or
polity), which is perhaps *the* fundamental social issue in opera buffa. *Così*'s
generic virtuosity has long been noted in a general way, but to see its relation to *La grotta di Trofonio* is to sharpen our perception of the nature of
that virtuosity.

[74] *Così*'s commentary on its own genre has been noticed in various ways by a number of
critics. Brown, *Così*, pp. 73–81, describes various verifiable connections to the Viennese repertory; Heartz, *Mozart's Operas*, p. 233, writes, "Mozart [makes] his music a commentary on
what had been achieved in opera up to 1790, and most especially in his own operas." John
Rosselli, "Balanced on a Turning Point: *Così fan tutte's* Difficult History" (*The Times Literary Supplement*, June 7, 1991, 15–16), posits the ladies as opera singers in an argument that
the work is in some sense "about" opera. Silke Leopold also comments in *Die Musik der 18.
Jahrhunderts*, ed. Ludwig Finscher (Laaber: Laaber-Verlag, 1985) p. 266, that opera buffa is
"at issue" in *Così*.

Chapter Nine

COSÌ FAN TUTTE
AND CONVENTION

COSÌ FAN TUTTE's pointed dialogue with *La grotta di Trofonio* suggests how its specific intertextual references shade into less palpable, if more deeply meaningful, references to and discussions of convention. Moreover, just as the opera's intertextual references are astonishingly various and convey multiple meanings on many levels, so the conventions it puts up for discussion also range widely and signify on various levels. These conventions range from those as specific as Despina's *commedia dell'arte* disguises and tricks or Fiordiligi's simile aria, to those as pervasive as the "pastoral mode" or "sentimentality"; and from those as formal as the strettas of both finales, to those as genre-oriented and ideological as the *lieto fine*. If *Così*'s specific references provide the self-contained pleasures of a game, playable by connoisseurs and amateurs (*Kenner* and *Liebhaber*) alike, its equally virtuosic deployment of broader conventions may have offered the pleasures of familiarity to those paying slight attention, along with a more sophisticated delight to those who could appreciate the subtlety and self-consciousness with which those conventions were both inspected and reconfigured.[1]

Although the conventions used and manipulated in this opera can be traced to a wide variety of origins, it is *Così*'s treatment of the habits of opera buffa that most compellingly signals its deepest meanings. Some generic habits seem to have been chosen to illustrate a social theme of the work—Despina's relation to her superiors is such an example. Some moments announce their conventionality and make a point about the characters by highlighting their choice of prepackaged utterance: Don Alfonso's "Vorrei dir" and the sisters' first arias are three cases in point. Other conventions, like the household setting and the *lieto fine,* are quietly skewed relative to the majority of the repertory; this locates *Così* rather precisely in its immediate context and raises questions about the nature and value of originality. And finally, one aspect of this opera not normally thought of as "conventional"—namely, its extraordinary moments of sensuous beauty—can, in the context of this repertory, be seen to rest on a convention—a convention, moreover, that illuminates the knife-edge sensibility of the work.

[1] See Brown, "Beaumarchais, Paisiello and the Genesis of *Così fan tutte*," in Sadie, *Wolfgang Amadè Mozart* (Oxford: Clarendon Press, 1996) p. 329, on connoisseurship in *Così*.

A DOUBLE-EDGED CONVENTION EMBRACED: DESPINA

The vast majority of the generic conventions in *Così* are "silent"—that is, deployed both without self-reflexive comment and without obvious irony; these range from Da Ponte's division of the work into two acts with a finale at the end of each to both authors' apportioning of serious and light-hearted qualities between the sisters, and from Mozart's use of the march topos to indicate the military life to the more generalized juxtapositions of high, low, and "middling" styles and manners to delineate a whole social and emotional world. It is, however, characteristic of this most ambiguous of operas that one of the conventions it uses without evident comment and with no ironic intent is itself double-edged. It is the comic convention of the controlling-yet-circumscribed servant, represented by Despina. Despina's attitudes associate her unambiguously with other pert and worldly-wise female servants; her sense that money is what makes the world go round (I,10 "È l'oro per me giulebbe"), that women are in charge of relationships ("Una donna à quindici anni . . ."), and that men are a dime a dozen ("Di pasta simile . . ."), are echoes of generations of comic servants, as critics rarely fail to point out.[2] Her two primary functions in the drama—plot-engine and perpetual servant—are both dialectically related and entirely conventional, as is their capacity both to test the limits of the social order and to reinforce its boundaries.

Despina's engagement with action is obvious: she engineers most of the mischief in the first act finale and persuades the women to flirt a little with the strangers at the beginning of the second act. Once the women have decided to play along with the strangers, however, Despina drops back as an active mover of events, and, as she suggests at the end of the second-act finale, her playful activities lead to actions and emotional movement beyond her control and understanding:

Io non so se questo è sogno:	I don't know if this is a dream:
Mi confondo, mi vergogno.	I'm confused and ashamed.
Manco mal, se a me l'han fatta,	So much the better, if others have done
Che a molt'altri anch'io la fo.	To me, what I've done to them.

Despina's power of action, particularly in the first half of the opera, is, however, by no means confined to the plot. Mozart's music suggests an unusual level of independence and self-determination, especially at the beginning of "In uomini," which, as a first musical impression, carries considerable weight. Many critics have noted that Mozart appropriated the last three lines of the previous recitative, in *versi sciolti*—freely alternating seven- and eleven-syllable lines—for the beginning of this aria; Despina takes this process one step further by interrupting the orchestra's opening

---

[2] See Chapter 3 for a discussion of the characteristic aria types of serving women.

flourish, derailing what could have been a perfectly decorous opening, even given its declamatory character and textual irregularities.[3] When the violins start again in m. 5 with a smooth *galant* figure, Despina again "interrupts," not phraseologically this time but by refusing to take them up on their offer of material, and changing topic to a rawer, spiky comic figure with syllabic declamation (see Example 9-1). The voice and the orchestra only properly adjust to one another after the violins have, as it were, taken her up on her offer in mm. 10ff., in repeating and ornamenting her spiky tune on "Sperare fedeltà." Her bossiness with respect to the orchestra in this opening musically anticipates the dramatic device of pushing the lovers around in "La mano a me date," though by that point in the opera the limits of her power are more evident—indeed, she follows Don Alfonso's lead in that particular piece of puppetry.

The level of dialogic engagement between Despina and the orchestra, which functions almost as another character at the beginning of "In uomini," is unique in the opera and contrasts with the voice-orchestra relations in the ladies' arias, which are both more decorous (the alternations between voice and orchestra at the beginning of "Come scoglio," for example, follow the normal punctuation patterns of accompanied recitative) and less interlocutory (the orchestra in "Smanie implacabili" acting more as the substrate of Dorabella's passion than as another "voice" to be argued with or subdued). Despina's enactment of the modulation to the dominant simultaneously with the orchestra in mm. 33–36 of "In uomini" also contrasts with the equivalent structural moments in "Smanie implacabili" (mm. 16–19) and "Come scoglio" (mm. 22–27), both of which are initiated by the orchestra and completed by the voice (see Examples 9-2a,b,c).

The relations between Despina and the ladies change in the second act, as the focus of the drama moves from mechanistic intrigue to emotional progress. The new state of affairs is embodied immediately in the two opening numbers of the act; Despina's aria "Una donna a quindici anni" and the ladies' duet "Prenderò quel brunettino." In contrast to her first aria, the vocal line in Despina's second number is less conversationally engaged with the orchestra; there is no opening orchestral ritornello to converse with, and in the *Allegretto* section, Despina mostly repeats material introduced in the orchestra. The orchestra performs the modulation to the dominant in mm. 27–29, which Despina repeats. All in all, this aria is more a statement of a predetermined, conventional, and immovable position

---

[3] Goehring, "Despina, Cupid and the Pastoral Mode of *Così fan tutte*," *COJ* (1995) p. 113, sees this opening as a buffa analogue to accompanied recitative, which lends Despina an "authority" unusual for buffa servants. My reading is related to his, but I see this opening as more integrated with the dramatic and social norms for servants in this repertory than he does. See also Webster, "The Analysis of Mozart's Arias," in *Mozart Studies,* ed. Cliff Eisen (Oxford: Clarendon Press, 1991) p. 140, and n. 82.

9-1: Mozart, *Così fan tutte,* no. 12
Despina, "In uomini," mm. 1–11

Translation: To hope for fidelity in men? in soldiers?

9-2a: Mozart, *Così fan tutte*, no. 12
Despina, "In uomini," mm. 31–37

Translation: [The fickle breeze] has more constancy than men. Lying tears, false looks...

than evidence of an inventive and engaged response to a new situation. There is much more literal repetition of material than in "In uomini"; this, combined with her less engaged relation to the orchestra and her diminished harmonic initiative, suggests that at least in terms of exercising psychological power over the ladies, Despina has reached her limit.

As Despina betrays her limits at the beginning of the second act, the ladies begin to show signs of initiative and movement. In their duet deciding to flirt a little, "Prenderò quel brunettino," they repeat no orchestral material; indeed, they seem so eager to flirt that there is no independent room for the orchestra at all until the very end. The modulation to the dominant is enacted in mm. 17–19 by Dorabella and the bass, and confirmed in mm. 19–21 by Fiordiligi, with orchestral support, to be sure, but no prompting (see Example 9-3).

Her two disguised appearances also chart a progression from efficacy to futility: whereas the "doctor" persuades the ladies to take a sympathetic interest in the languishing Albanians, thus furthering both the plot and Despina's own philosophy of love, the "notary" merely enacts a farce whose main purpose is to exaggerate the effect of the inevitable "return" of the original lovers. Thus Despina's eventual immobility, made all the more striking by the apparent authority and self-determination with which she begins her musical role in the opera, strengthens the opera's comparatively underarticulated social distinctions and emphasizes by contrast both the

9-2b: Mozart, *Così fan tutte,* no. 11
Dorabella, "Smanie implacabili," mm. 15–19

Translation: miserable example

emotional significance and the social particularity of the sisters' progress. In this instance, then, the generic convention, used with unusual subtlety and perspicacity, has far-reaching consequences.

SELF-CONSCIOUS CONVENTIONS: ARIA TYPES

If Mozart's (and it is mostly Mozart's) deployment of the "controlling servant" convention makes a point about the social structure of *Così,* it is a point made, as it were, from outside the narrative world of the opera: Despina may in some sense know her place but there is no indication that she manipulates it in complicity with the audience. However, other more or less literal uses of generic conventions do exhibit clear, and telling, self-consciousness. Don Alfonso's "Vorrei dir," the aria Stefan Kunze calls his

9-2c: Mozart, *Così fan tutte,* no. 14
Fiordiligi, "Come scoglio," mm. 21–27

Translation: . . . in love. With us that flame is kindled.

9-3: Mozart, *Così fan tutte,* no. 20
Duet: Fiordiligi and Dorabella, "Prenderò quel brunettino,"
mm. 17–21

Translation:
   Dorabella: He'll say, "my love, I'm dying!"
   Fiordiligi: He'll say, "my beautiful treasure!"

"textbook" aria agitata, is probably the best example of this.[4] As a number of critics have noted, Don Alfonso uses this ready-made aria type to indicate to the audience that he is producing a stock reaction to the fictitious calling-up of the young men. The fact that this little aria also refers specifically to at least one and possibly two other utterances in the repertory—Lilla's desperate entrance aria "Ah pietade, mercede," in *Una cosa rara* and Figaro's "L'invidia, o ciel," in his recitative description of his adventures in *Il barbiere di Siviglia*—also signals to the audience that Don Alfonso is putting it on.[5] The two references have rather different effects, both of which inform the drama of *Così fan tutte*. For Don Alfonso to act like a desperate shepherdess is, of course, very funny, but it also suggests that this overwrought language is the one he thinks the sentimental young ladies will understand. His quotation of Figaro's apparent quotation of his own overdone song connects the two men in wit and wile; the content of Figaro's song—"envy is the cause of all my miseries"—is also another way of stating Don Alfonso's philosophy of the virtues of "bella calma." Thus, while the sisters may only hear the panic and misery, the audience hears a range of witty and significant associations. The referentiality of "Vorrei dir" is anticipated by Don Alfonso's earlier essay in adaptation, namely his reworking of the Metastasian phoenix metaphor in the second terzetto. In other words he is already known to the audience as a man who can turn preexistent material or commonplaces to his own ends, who uses his borrowed material to good effect, and thus whose understanding of convention is explicit and assured.

Don Alfonso's clever use of an aria perfect of its type, but still "the wrong song" for its true circumstances, sets up the two ladies' first-act arias: Dorabella's rage aria "Smanie implacabili" and Fiordiligi's proud simile-aria "Come scoglio." These are also perfect examples of their types,[6] but they call attention to their conventionality by their comic lack of proportion in relation to their circumstances. This lack of proportion has often led students of *Così* to describe them as parodies,[7] or to find incongruous or

---

[4] Kunze, *Mozarts Opern* (Stuttgart: Reclam, 1984) p. 492.

[5] Brown, "Beaumarchais, Paisiello," pp. 315–19, notes both these quotations. Platoff, "How Original Was Mozart? Evidence from Opera Buffa" (*EM* 20 [1992]) pp. 107–8, notes the connection with Lilla's "Ah pietade, mercede," as does Goehring, "The Sentimental Muse of Opera Buffa," in Hunter and Webster, *Opera Buffa in Mozart's Vienna* (Cambridge: Cambridge University Press, 1997) pp. 138–42. There is a further connection between Don Alfonso's "Nel mare solca" and Figaro's "L'invidia, o ciel," which latter is also an eruption in a recitative, also a quotation, and also in the minor (at least to begin with).

[6] Brown, *Così*, p.127, and Heartz, "Citation, Reference and Recall in *Così fan tutte*," in *Mozart's Operas*, ed. Thomas Bauman (Berkeley: University of California Press, 1990) pp. 247–48, both note the echoes of Elettra's "D'Oreste, D'Ajace," from *Idomeneo* in Dorabella's "Smanie implacabili."

[7] Abert, *W. A. Mozart*, 6th ed. (Leipzig: Breitkopf & Härtel, 1923–24) pp. 544, 547. Like many others, he understands Dorabella's aria as a clearer case of parody than Fiordiligi's, since Dorabella is a shallower character than Fiordiligi. Stefan Kunze, on the other hand, sees the

comic elements in the music,[8] but as I have argued elsewhere, the matter cannot really be decided from the text alone.[9] Whether or not "parody" is the correct term for either aria (and that depends in part on who is said to be parodying whom or what), both are certainly ironic, in the sense that the women's perceptions of their situations are diametrically opposed to everyone else's—on and off stage.[10] More relevant to an argument about Mozart's and Da Ponte's use of conventions than trying to "fix" their status as parodies or not is to note that their overwrought characteristics draw attention to their status as conventional exemplars. Indeed, the concentrated and unselfconscious fury of Dorabella's emotion is unparalleled in this repertory of opera buffa—female rage being, as I argue above,[11] typically defused, domesticated, or unambiguously parodied by the character singing. Contextually speaking, it is in its uniqueness a much more "perfect" visitor from the seria realm than "Come scoglio." The latter nevertheless refers so fully to textual and musical predecessors, both specific and general,[12] that even though its seria pedigree may not be perfect,[13] its status as conventional exemplar is not in doubt. Thus if the dramatic contents of "Smanie implacabili" and "Come scoglio" project a (mistaken) certainty about the immutability of the emotional status quo, their striking typological conventionality also suggests with equally mistaken certainty that a rage aria complete with references to the Eumenides, and a simile aria in

---

music of "Smanie implacabili" as entirely serious, even if the text has an ironic element (*Mozarts Opern*, pp. 521–22). And Goehring, "Despina, Cupid," p. 129, stresses the importance of taking "Smanie implacabili" seriously. Heartz, "Citation, Reference and Recall," p. 249, noting references to *Idomeneo* in the accompanied recitatives preceding both "Smanie implacabili" and "Come scoglio," comments that these moments indicate that the ladies sound as if they are taking themselves seriously, a remark that leaves room for a variety of interpretations of these arias. See also Rodney Farnsworth, "*Così fan tutte* as Parody and Burlesque," *OQ* 6 (1988/89) pp. 50–68.

[8] Michel Noiray, "Commentaire musical et littéraire," in *L'Avant-scène opéra 131–132: Così fan tutte*, (Paris: L'avant-scène opéra, 1990) p. 76–77, notes the emphasis of the unimportant words "e la" [tempesta] and the routineness (and repetition) of the ornamented-scale figure in measures 53–55; Brown, *Così*, pp. 128–30, notes various musical "inconstancies" undermining Fiordiligi's assertion of eternal immutability.

[9] Hunter, "*Così fan tutte* et les Conventions musicales de son Temps," in *L'Avant-scène opéra 131–132*, pp. 158–64. See also Hunter, "Some Representations of Opera Seria in Opera Buffa," *COJ* 3 (1991) p. 107: the most likely occasion for an unambiguous parody of opera seria is a reference to a particular opera, character, or aria from the serious genre.

[10] Frits Noske, *The Signifier and the Signified: Studies in the Operas of Mozart and Verdi* (The Hague: Nijhoff, 1977) pp. 99–100, distinguishes between parody and irony in *Così*, finding both in "Come scoglio." He then goes on to read some of the opera's many motivic recurrences as instances of the opera's pervasive dramatic irony.

[11] Chapter 5, pp. 144–45.

[12] See the previous chapter for descriptions of its references both to the Ariostan rock simile in *Trofonio* and "Come scoglio"'s close relation to the Tarchi substitution aria sung by Ferrarese in *L'arbore di Diana*.

[13] Brown, *Così*, p. 128, points out that the "Come/Così" construction of this aria is in fact not Metastasian but properly speaking originates with Apostolo Zeno and was used by both comic and serious librettists throughout the century.

which vocal virtuosity stands for pride and steadfastness, are the appropriate responses to the departure of the lovers, and to the strangers' importunities. The double edge of these arias, as of "Vorrei dir," is that at the same time as they induce a sort of complacency by their easy apprehensibility and clear typological reference, the dramatic situation in which they are deployed undercuts the straightforward and apparently immutable system of signification on which they rely. The conventions they so perfectly embody constitute both their meaning and their undoing.

CONVENTIONS RECONFIGURED: THE HOUSEHOLD AND THE HAPPY END

Other aspects of *Così* appear conventional but actually skew or alter a crucial element of the convention they seem to embody. The setup of the characters is one example where an apparently ordinary arrangement turns out to be actually rather different from the norm. Although contrasting pairs of sisters (or cousins) are perfectly ordinary for the repertory, although the "filosofo" is a conventional character type, although the household is the most normal setting for opera buffa, and although *Così* has all of these attributes, it is different from repertorial norms in the ways these attributes are combined. The chief difference is in the relation of Don Alfonso to the young women. Unlike, say, the *filosofo* Petronio in *I filosofi immaginari,* or Buonafede in *Il mondo della luna,* who are the fathers of the pairs of sisters, Don Alfonso has no natural or legal authority over Fiordiligi and Dorabella, and unlike most pairs of sisters in the Viennese repertory of opera buffa, the ladies have no father. Fiordiligi and Dorabella have no male relations and are defined in relation to no authority. They are, in the context of the repertory, extraordinarily dislocated from the normal social web of hierarchy and obligation.[14] The characters in the repertory that they most resemble are the cousins Cintia and Eurilla in Petrosellini and Cimarosa's *Il pittore parigino,*[15] and even there—in the absence of a father figure—patriarchal authority resonates from the grave; Eurilla's receipt of her inheritance depends on her fulfilling her dead father's wish that she should marry the Baron, and her lack of interest in him despite her father's wishes is the trigger for the plot. The separation of Fiordiligi and Dorabella from the normal structures of authority has led at least one writer to suggest that they were to be understood as opera singers.[16] This idea is at-

[14] Hanns Wienold and Eberhard Hüppe also make this point in "*Così fan tutte* oder die hohe Kunst der Konvention," in *Mozart: die Da Ponte-Opern* (Munich: text & kritik Gmbtl, 1991), Special issue (Dec. 1991) of *Musik-Konzepte,* pp. 318–19. See also Till, *Mozart and the Enlightenment* (New York: Norton, 1993) p. 237.

[15] Cast list given in Chapter 1, p. 56.

[16] John Rosselli, "Balanced on a Turning Point," *The Times Literary Supplement,* June 7, 1991, p. 16.

tractive but unsupported by any other evidence. Fiordiligi and Dorabella do not evidently think of themselves as singers, despite their abilities to "perform" rage and pride; and unlike operas explicitly about theatrical performers, which are typically set either in the theatre or in rented lodgings of one sort or another, *Così* apparently takes place in the ladies' home.[17] Don Alfonso seems not to live in the house with them, though that is never established definitively; and although he discharges the fatherly function of joining the lovers' hands at the end of the opera, he has not performed the normal patriarchal role of objecting to the ladies' marriage plans—though he does in some deeper sense serve the structural function of "obstructing character."[18] *Così*'s simulation of the household structure common to so many *opere buffe,* then, actually serves to emphasize its separation from the clearly structured social world represented by most operas in the repertory; and by negative relation to that convention, defines its world almost exclusively in the terms of the experiment.

The end of *Così* is problematic in rather the same way as its setup. It uses the ending-conventions of the genre—the wedding, the return to a presumed social norm, and the final joining of couples by an authority-figure—but it also calls them into question. This questioning takes place not only on the often-noted global level of the incongruity between the musical depths of the wrong couplings and the apparent facility of the return to the original pairings, but also on the more particular and local level of *Così*'s relation to the repertory that surrounded it. Despite the entirely conventional multiple-wedding ending, the relation of those weddings to what precedes them is in fact rather different from that in operas on comparable subjects or with comparable characters. For example, in *Il curioso indiscreto* Clorinda takes the Contino as her second lover, as Fiordiligi takes Ferrando (albeit with much more agonizing), but unlike Fiordiligi, Clorinda marries the object of her conversion experience. The outcome of this plot is made right by having the Marchese (Clorinda's first fiancé) be a buffoon, subject to inevitable defeat. The opera makes clear that the initial coupling was untenable, whereas this is obviously not the case in *Così*. In *L'arbore di Diana,* whose central love affair is also the result of a conversion experience, Diana loses the initial battle over the reign of chastity but remains attached to the object of her conversion. Other operas where the central female character changes the object of her affections also either allow the conversion to "stick," or return the woman to her original lover for reasons of class. Thus, in *I finti eredi,* Giannina returns to

---

[17] Other operas featuring singers as characters are set either in a theatrical milieu, e.g., Salieri and Casti's *Prima la musica e poi le parole,* or in rented lodgings, as in Cavalieri and Guglielmi's *L'impresa dell'opera.*

[18] Northrop Frye, "Comedy: The Mythos of Spring," in his *Anatomy of Criticism* (Princeton: Princeton University Press, 1957) p. 163.

her peasant lover Pierotto, in *La villanella rapita* Mandina's brief attraction to the Count is rapidly terminated in favor of her Pippo, and in *La fiera di Venezia,* the middle-class Falsirena's continuous flirtation with the Duke Ostrogoto is shown to have no future. These returns are uniformly shown to be both socially desirable and, in the event, the felt wish of the protagonists. The only opera buffa in this repertory with an amorous trajectory comparable to *Così fan tutte* is Bertati and Anfossi's *Lo sposo disperato,* in which Donna Aurora unwillingly marries the boor Canziano at the end. But both the topic and the tone of this piece are utterly different from *Così;* it is quite explicitly about class (Canziano is the classic rich but socially hopeless parvenu chosen by the heroine's father for the obvious material reasons), and there is no significant exploration of emotion. What is more, Donna Aurora is quite unambiguous about her dislike for Canziano and her intentions to engage a *cicisbeo,* whereas Fiordiligi and Dorabella exhibit only fondness for their original partners.

Thus, although the amorous conversion is a convention in this repertory of opera buffa, its function in *Così* as a socially plausible but dramatically unworkable diversion from the proper order is quite distinct. However, a "blank"[19] turn (or return) to the socially or dramatically obvious partner at the end of the opera is also a buffa convention. At the end of *I finti eredi,* for example, when it becomes all too clear to the Marchese that the peasant Giannina will not be his wife, he turns without ceremony to the upperclass Donna Isabella, who accepts his offer immediately. Similarly, at the end of *La buona figliuola,* the bumpkin Mengotto, who has nursed a hopeless affection for the heroine Cecchina, betrothes himself to the farm girl Sandrina, who has spent the opera in spasms of jealous interest in the Marchese. These sudden alliances are like the sudden return to the original partners in *Così,* insofar as they are both socially proper and not altogether unanticipated. On the other hand, these couplings and the many others like them all involve secondary characters, they always explicitly reinforce the proper class structure of the opera, which the body of the plot has disturbed, and they usually create couples who have never before been united, none of which is the case in *Così.* In the context of other *opere buffe,* then, the end of *Così* can be understood both to be thoroughly "conventional" in its references to the habits of the repertory, and thoroughly "original" in its particular combination of conventional elements. It is crucial to the aesthetic of this opera that neither the "pseudo-household" arrangement of characters nor the ending shout out their originality; the point appears to be precisely *not* startling novelty or the forging of obviously new musico-dramatic paths. Rather, in quietly reconfiguring some of

---

[19] Kerman, *Opera as Drama* (Berkeley: University of California Press, 1988) p. 116.

the basic stereotypes of opera buffa, *Così* makes norms and conventions its aesthetic subject.

Così, Convention, and Comedy: Musical Beauty and the Relations between Text and Music

One of the most problematic and ambiguous aspects of *Così* is the fit between music and text, whose incongruity and mutual irritation have been noted continuously since the work's first appearance, and have been touched on at various points in this chapter. *Così*'s exquisite equipoise between laughter and tears, ridicule and sympathy, seeming and being, and play and reality is in large part created by the "mismatch" between the apparently deeply felt beauty of Mozart's music and the polished symmetries, literary games, and playful atmosphere of Da Ponte's text. As I noted above in connection with *Così*'s relation to *La grotta di Trofonio*, one still-healthy strand of criticism which reaches back to the time of *Così*'s origin implies that this mismatch arises essentially from the conjunction of Mozart's genius with the mere talent of Da Ponte, and that, whether wilfully or because he could not help himself, Mozart made something of the opera that Da Ponte could not have intended. Among some of the more recent writers on the opera, for example, Silke Leopold describes the way Mozart "elevates" the characters above an "all-too-trite" story;[20] Nicholas Till notes that "the true moral experiment of *Così fan tutte* is conducted beyond the blinkered gaze of Don Alfonso (and perhaps by implication of Da Ponte),"[21] and Francesco Degrada describes Mozart looking "from an enormous height" at the human comedy contained in *Così,* and imbuing it with the "inexpressible longing" Mozart described in his last letters to Constanze.[22] Another strand of criticism about the opera, more modern in origin, implies that the mismatch has a dramatic or aesthetic purpose, which is to suggest the complex relations between inner and outer worlds—of experience and behavior, truth and convention, tragedy and comedy, life and art. Stefan Kunze, for example, notes that when the narrative has completely undone the lovers' sense of the meaning of relationships, and the abyss has opened, the music is "powerful" enough to span the chasm without "entering into utopias of redemption"; and that it "ad-

---

[20] *Die Musik des 18. Jahrhunderts,* ed. Ludwig Finscher, *Neues Handbuch der Musikwissenschaft,* vol. 5, ed. L. Finscher (Laaber: Laaber-Verlag, 1985) p. 266.

[21] Till, *Mozart and the Enlightenment,* p. 242.

[22] Francesco Degrada, "Splendore e miseria della ragione; a proposito di *Così fan tutte,*" in his *Il palazzo incantato: Studi sulla tradizione del melodramma dal barocco al romanticismo* (Fiesole: Discanto, 1979) vol. 2, p. 15.

heres to the notion (*Bild*) of responsibility, which is what the work is principally about."[23] Yet another emerging strand is the postmodern argument that the various domains of *Così* are simply incommensurable, and that as critics we should celebrate the interpretative windows opened by these instances of *différance*.[24] Bruce Alan Brown's learned and sensitive treatment of Da Ponte's text elevates it to a position equal to Mozart's music, and Da Ponte's understanding of the dynamics of the experiment to a subtlety comparable to Mozart's, but he also acknowledges the "unsettling" effect of the "conjunction . . . of comic texts and sublime music." He argues that this conjunction is "a [presumably intended] acknowledgement of the opera's theatricality—of the fact that very real emotions are being stimulated through artificial means."

The rub between music and text in *Così* is the aspect that most clearly links it to some of the fundamental ambiguities or paradoxes of comedy—striving toward harmony vs. ridicule, orderly norms vs. topsy-turvy social relations, and instruction vs. diversion. It raises the aesthetic question of the relation of music to drama; and on the moral level it questions the relations of essence to appearance and the identity of beauty and truth. *Così* does not raise these transhistorical issues and achieve its place in the pantheon by ignoring its genre, however; rather it engages in the generic practice of manipulating well-recognized conventions, in order to bring them to consciousness and to make them topics for aesthetic and moral consideration. One such convention is the "device" of extravagantly beautiful music, which, while certainly permitted, and even encouraged by the libretto, nevertheless sits uncomfortably with the situations in which it is deployed.[25] Three numbers most often remarked on for their striking beauty are the quintet "Di scrivermi" and the trio "Soave sia il vento" in the first-act farewell sequence, and the so-called Wedding Quartet in the second-act finale, "E nel tuo, nel mio bicchiero," where three of the now-switched-over lovers toast each other and celebrate their love, while the fourth (Guglielmo) mutters in grumpy dissent. Hellmuth Christian Wolff cites the Wedding Quartet as one of the most beautiful pieces in Mozart's entire oeuvre.[26] Anna Amalie Abert suggests that in this number the char-

---

[23] Kunze, *Mozarts Opern*, p. 453.

[24] Wienold and Hüppe, "*Così fan tutte* oder die hohe Kunst der Konvention," use this Derridean term (p. 300) to indicate that the noncongruence between "textual levels" in *Così* is analogous to the opera's shattering of the association between Affekt and morality. They also (p. 301) take Stefan Kunze to task for attempting to "conquer" the opera's incommensurabilities by assuming them into larger hermeneutic explanations.

[25] Thanks to Bruce Alan Brown for pointing out to me that Da Ponte (who was self-confessedly alert to the differing demands of different composers), having already collaborated twice with Mozart, could well have anticipated that Mozart would lavish his "purely" musical attentions on certain places in the text, and write his poetry accordingly.

[26] H. C. Wolff, *Geschichte der Komischen Oper* (Wilhelmshaven: Heinrichshofen, 1981) p. 132.

acters are elevated above themselves, evidently by the beauty of the mo-ment.[27] Alfred Einstein writes of "Di scrivermi": "To [both genuine and simulated emotion] is added the color of pure beauty. We have already mentioned, as a moment of such pure beauty, the Quartet in A♭ in the sec-ond Act Finale. . . . Another piece of this sort is the farewell quintet in the first act. What was Mozart to do at this point? The two young ladies were weeping real tears, while the officers knew there was no reason to do so. Mozart raises the banner of pure beauty, without forgetting the old cynic in the background, 'laughing himself to death.'"[28] Gerald Abraham writes of "Soave sia il vento": "Mozart forgets the action and the characters—or gives them up as hopeless. . . . The girls forget to be sad; Don Alfonso for-gets to be cynical; they unite their voices in three-part harmony, sometimes doubled by clarinets and bassoons, while the muted violins murmur inces-santly throughout."[29]

In their helplessness in the face of Mozart's unbelievably gorgeous music, these critics abandon any attempt to make dramatic sense of the gor-geousness and seem to want to outdo each other in their race to leave both the characters and Da Ponte behind. It is true, of course, that all three en-sembles bring the imbroglio to a temporary halt, as they project an intense stillness or a sense of frozen motion:[30] the pulsing accompaniments in the farewell numbers mark off the seconds without leading anywhere very def-inite, and the canon in the Wedding Quartet embodies the notion of po-tentially endless circularity. The moderate or slow tempos, the lack of sig-nificant modulations to the dominant, the unchanging affects, the use of smooth cantabile melodies, the striking textures, colorful orchestrations, and the absence of dance-like or other gestural connotations in these num-bers all also add to the ways in which they draw attention to their sensu-ous surfaces and thus to the quality of the moments they enact. However, these numbers do not escape the drama to give the audience a bit of "pure musical" pleasure; they are an essential part of its dramaturgy. For one thing, they crystallize the eternally ambiguous relation between sympathy and ridicule that is one of the opera's principal topics. In all of them the music draws the audience—and at least one male character—into the women's emotional world. At the same time, both the explicit artificiality of the situations and the double-edged significance of the men's various

[27] Anna Amalie Abert, "The Operas of Mozart," in *The New Oxford History of Music,* vol. 7, *The Age of Enlightenment,* ed. Egon Wellesz and Frederick Sternfeld (Oxford: Oxford Uni-versity Press, 1973) p. 161.
[28] Alfred Einstein, *Mozart, His Character, His Work,* trans. Arthur Mendel and Nathan Broder (London and New York: Oxford University Press, 1945) p. 446.
[29] Gerald Abraham, "The Operas," in *The Mozart Companion,* ed. H. C. Robbins Lan-don and Donald Mitchell, corrected ed. (New York: Norton, 1969) p. 315.
[30] Kunze, *Mozarts Opern,* p. 495: "Moments of farewell are the pauses [Haltepunkte] in the flow of events."

sorts of participation in these ensembles serve as reminders of the trick being played.

The significance of their dramatic function depends at least in part on their relation to the repertory's deployment of moments of self-conscious beauty—moments that draw attention to, and ensnare the listener in, the sensuous quality of the sound. Any sentient listener can appreciate the tension between the expressive qualities of these moments in *Così fan tutte* and their dramatic circumstances, or the contradiction between the truth implied by the music and the trick being played in the drama, but to put these tensions and contradictions in the context of the repertory illuminates both how rooted in convention and how novel is Mozart's deployment of exceptional musical beauty.

In the repertory at large, cantabile melodies, rhythmically active (pulsing or rippling) accompaniments, colorful orchestration prominently featuring the winds, a slow harmonic rhythm, and a strongly projected sense of stillness—or at least of no urge to finish—are typically found (though not necessarily all together) fulfilling two sorts of dramatic functions. The first occurs where all the composer's expressive resources are poured into emphasizing the immediacy of a character's plight or the depth of his or her feelings. In the Act II finale of *Fra i due litiganti,* for example, where three *innamorati* describe their oppression in a series of solos, the music features a series of wind solos interacting with the vocal line over layered, pulsing accompaniments. (Dorina's moment of misery is quoted in Example 3-3.) The length and "stillness" of this tripartite segment in the finale is emphasized by its repetitiveness. Rosina's aria "Giusto ciel, non conoscete" at the end of the first act of *Il barbiere di Siviglia* has a rather different texture, but the elaborate intertwining of the wind instruments, the pulsing bass, and the *Andante* cantabile vocal melody all serve to suggest the seriousness of her love for Almaviva, a seriousness not so convincingly evident beforehand.[31] Among ensembles in the repertory, the famous canonic trio for the two shepherdesses and the Queen in *Una cosa rara* lacks the wind-oriented orchestration, but the Andante tempo, and the intertwining of arpeggiated quarter notes and scalar eighths conveys a similar sense of attention to texture and to the feel of the moment, which holds in its tender grip the quarreling sisters horrified by the arrival of the queen, and the queen herself, touched by the girls' innocence:[32]

---

[31] A somewhat comparable case is Ofelia's opening aria, "D'un dolce amor la face," in *La grotta di Trofonio,* where Salieri's sweet and elaborate writing for the wind band makes Ofelia's solemnity and pedantry more appealing. His aria for Aspasia, "Son queste le speranze," in the fourth act of *Axur, re di Ormus,* is comparably orchestrated and quite beautiful, but it emphasizes the already-evident seriousness of this captive heroine rather than startling us into taking her more seriously, as do "Giusto ciel" and "D'un dolce amor."

[32] Dorothea Link, "The Viennese Operatic Canon and Mozart's *Così fan tutte,*" *Mitteilungen der internationales Stiftung Mozarteum* 38 (1990) pp. 111–21.

9-4: Martín y Soler, *Una cosa rara*, no. 12
Trio: Queen, Lilla, Ghita, mm. 83–102
Reproduced from Hunter, "Bourgeois Values and Opera Buffa in
1780s Vienna," in Hunter and Webster, *Opera Buffa in Mozart's
Vienna*, pp. 192–93. Reprinted with permission.

9-4: *(Continued)*

Translation:

Lilla and Ghita: For pity's sake don't be disdainful; please listen. This lament about the torment of my heart will move you.

Queen: Their lament moves me.

The second occasion on which intensely expressive music is used in opera buffa naturally depends on the first; it is the mock-pathetic moment, where a comic character tries to persuade another onstage character of his or her sincerity and depth of feeling by "laying it on thick." In the example from Naumann's *Le nozze disturbate* quoted above as Example 1-4, the minx Ninetta threatens to kill herself if the old man she is addressing does not do what she wants; but she persuades him through pathos rather than through rage. In both of these examples, the cantabile melody is a primary factor in creating the pathos of the moment, and the elaborate accompaniment enhances the atmosphere that the melody already creates. (Haydn creates a similar scene in *La vera costanza* in Villotto's "Già la morte in manto nero.")

It was also not unusual for rich and atmospheric accompaniments to be used in ensembles, especially finales, in situations of group confusion or mystery, and often in nocturnal scenes. In these cases the accompaniment provides an expressive "blanket," in which the (sometimes disparate) reactions of the characters are wrapped; such accompaniments are distinct from the motivically rich, rhythmically active, and highly "gestural" orchestral parts in many finales, partly because they so strongly project physical stillness. Example 9-5, from a "shock tutti" in the first-act finale of Gazzaniga's *La locanda*, represents a moment of revelation in the action; the accompaniment holds the characters temporarily frozen as they react, and emphasizes the intensity of their shock (at the end of this section they faint and have to be held up).[33]

The three numbers from *Così* under discussion here thus all connect in one way or another to other moments in the repertory where musical sensuousness indicates seriousness or truth, the illusion of such seriousness, or a still point in the action. However, as with other conventions of the repertory, Mozart and Da Ponte make new use of the "moment of beauty," Mozart not least with his exceptionally rich harmonic palette (the hair-raising diminished seventh chords over the dominant pedal on "desir" in "Soave sia il vento" being only the most spectacular example). When his contemporaries use the "beauty as trick" convention, they almost without exception deploy their intensified pathetic modes of expression to enliven *onstage* moments of deceit, inviting the auditorium audience to see through the ruse of "beautiful" music, and enjoy the spectacle of an onstage dupe being seduced by it. "Too-beautiful" arias thus typically end

[33] The extraordinarily elaborate instrumental accompaniment in the first part of the second-act quintet in Mazzolà and Salieri's *La scuola dei gelosi* may be partly related to this phenomenon; here two characters pretend to be involved in solfège-practice while the others twitch in spasms of jealousy and fury. The richly orchestrated and rhythmically elaborate background serves to "restrain" the warring characters until the tension becomes intolerable and they lapse into homophonic patter and a final *Presto* stretta.

9-5: Gazzaniga, *La locanda,* from I, finale

Translation: What do I hear? What do I sense? Oh no, what a disgrace.

with a fast coda in which the deceiver explains the nature of the deception, leaving the audience in no doubt about the dramatic status of the lyrical moment. In "Di scrivermi" and the Wedding Quartet, the "grounding" function of this fast coda is taken over by the dissenting voices of Don Alfonso ("Io crepo se non rido") and Guglielmo ("Ah bevessero del tossico"). However, in making the comic distancing or ridicule simultaneous with the seduction of the audience, thus denying it "last word" status, as well as in avoiding a conventionally risible dupe, Mozart and Da Ponte complicate the conventional meaning of "beauty as trick": if the tricksters participate—even dissentingly—in the enchanted responses to the trick, the question of who exerts power over whom is remarkably difficult to answer. In contrast, while Don Alfonso's recitative comment immediately after "Soave sia il vento" ("I'm not a bad actor" [Io non sono cattivo comico]) surely also comes from the tradition of "last word" commentary, its dissociation from the "beautiful" number weakens its capacity to ironize the beauty, or to clarify Don Alfonso's participation in it.

Mozart and Da Ponte also complicate the meaning of the conventional use of "beautiful" music to indicate emotional seriousness or depth. This complication occurs not because Fiordiligi and Dorabella are mistaken about the doings of their lovers—indeed, pathetic climaxes and moments of self-revelation are usually the result of confusions or deceptions of which the audience (at least) is perfectly well aware—but because in all three ensembles both tricksters and dupes participate in the cantabile lines. If this beauty represents, as it must, the truth of the women's experience, it also represents the men's rhetorical powers. At the same time, if these moments are taken seriously as drama, the listener must believe that something about the manipulators' participation is also somehow authentic. Stefan Kunze, for example, reads the men's apparently heartfelt participation in "Di scrivermi" as a sort of farewell to the old order of innocent trust and unquestioning belief in their lovers' fidelity.[34] Whether or not one wants to reconcile the contradictions of these moments into a single overarching reading, the fact remains that the simultaneity of the emotions and the way the music draws the audience into the trick is, if not absolutely unique in the repertory, at least extremely unusual.[35]

The only comparable instance in the genre of which I am aware occurs in the first-act finale of Haydn's *Il mondo della luna* where the old dupe Buonafede thinks (on the basis of the assurance of the *finto astrologo* Ecclitico and a sleeping draught to help the illusion) that he is going to the moon. He and Ecclitico bid a touching farewell to the world (not shown in Example 9-6, below). His daughter and his maid come in as he is being "transported" and believe him to be dying. Fond farewells follow. The entire sequence uses the muted-strings accompanimental figure shown in Example 9-6. The mixture of knowing and ignorant characters involved in a fictive act of farewell is similar to that in the farewell sequence in *Così*, the texture and general affect of the music are remarkably like "Soave sia il vento," the common involvement of philosophy/astrology should not be ignored; and as in Mozart's trio, the cynical mastermind uses the same musical material as everyone else (though his words clearly betray his distance from the prevailing sentiment). Note the floating oboe and then full-wind lines in mm. 14–16, which parallel the nondoubling viola and wind lines in mm. 32ff. of "Soave sia il vento":

[34] Stefan Kunze, "Über das Verhältnis von musikalisch autonomer Struktur und Textbau in Mozarts Opern," *M-Jb* (1973–74) p. 218.

[35] Brown, *Così*, p. 110, correctly points out that numbers expressing conflicting emotions at moments of farewell are quite common in opera seria and quotes an aria from Metastasio's *Demetrio* as an example. Even here, however, the salient conflicting emotions are identified separately and are expressed in the same medium (words). The importance of what is never verbally articulated remains the extraordinary aspect of Mozart's farewell ensembles.

9-6: Haydn, *Il mondo della luna*, I, finale, mm. 13–16

9-6: *(Continued)*

Translation:
> **Clarice and Lisetta:** My master/Dear Father, what's going on?
> **Bonafede:**   I'm going, I'm going

In both these instances the beauty of the music lifts the dramatic moment above straightforward dramatic irony and puts the audience on the knife edge between empathy and ridicule.[36]

What is fascinating about these moments in both *Il mondo della luna* and *Così* is that beautiful music becomes a dramatic agent in its own right, and the cleverly deployed exhibition of "pure" compositional skill translates into dramatic acuity.[37] What Mozart has done in these three numbers in *Così* is to deploy his genius for absolute beauty precisely at the crucial joints in the drama, as the experiment begins and ends. The stillness and utter self-containedness of these moments is in strong tension with the contiguous actions that precipitate and end the trick, just as their harmony and almost unbearable sweetness is in tension with the different aims and

[36] Paisiello's setting of this moment treats it as a jolly march, with everyone (apparently) stepping out toward the extraterrestrial world.

[37] Comparable moments in other Haydn operas, such as the trio for Princess Rezia and her two slaves in *L'incontro improvviso* no. 12, have less dramatic power. This trio, for example, uses three characters whose interests essentially coincide, so that the indubitable beauty of the moment has no real edge; it is not fragile or liminal in the way that the segment from *Il mondo della luna* and the three ensembles from *Così* are.

desires of the characters involved. Their aura of suspended animation is dreamlike; in each case the dream is of perfect happiness and fidelity—it doesn't matter very much to whom. Although the C major hymn to the Count in the second-act finale of *Figaro* is in some ways comparable to these moments, it does not balance so tensely on the hinges of the action. The trio "Protegga il giusto ciel" sung by Donna Anna, Donna Elvira, and Don Ottavio in the first act of *Don Giovanni* occurs at a crucial juncture in the action, but there is no tension among the characters; none of the three is tricking or deceiving the others. The moment in *Il mondo della luna* is liminal (and literally dreamlike) in rather the same way as these three moments in *Così*, as it comes at the moment when the trick begins to take effect, and its participants are in tension with one another. Indeed, comparison with superficially similar ensembles in the other Mozart–Da Ponte operas suggests that the three ensembles in *Così* derive their extraordinary power not only from their beauty, but from the tensions that beauty both covers and throws into relief—among the characters who sing them, between the moments they occupy and their dramatic contexts, and between the conventions they rely on and the meanings they project.

CONCLUSION

It should be clear by now that textual, musical, and dramatic conventions pervade *Così* on every level, from intertextual references to particular works to the most general embodiment of the conventions of comedy; and that Mozart and Da Ponte use the conventional structures and devices of opera buffa in such a way that the habits of the repertory are both reinforced in principle and subverted in many of their particulars. The aesthetic effect of this is to suggest that however unsatisfactory some of these generic norms and conventions may be, convention itself is indispensable; it is the artist's job to make the best of what his chosen genre offers, whatever the inevitable contradictions and conflicts. The value of accepting a given or conventional situation while fully understanding its limitations is, of course, the manifest theme of Da Ponte's libretto; it is one way of embracing the Enlightened ethos of reconciling reason and desire. The original couples reunite not simply because dramatic conventions suggest that they should do so—indeed, as we have seen, the Viennese repertory of opera buffa repertory does not offer an exact parallel to the ending of *Così*, though it does allow the ending to be understood as dependent on the notion of convention. Rather, the original lovers reunite because there is, as Don Alfonso implies, a lesson in wisdom to be learned from clear-eyed acceptance of what is given; and pain is an inevitable part of wisdom. Thus the "opera about opera" (or, more generally, the "opera about art") aspect of *Così fan tutte* is not simply a playful surface masking a painful emotional truth.

Rather, it is, I think, a signal of the work's most pervasive social and emotional meanings; indeed, one of Mozart and Da Ponte's greatest achievements in *Così* is to have related art and life through their thematizing of convention.

Don Alfonso's lesson is not without potential for smug superiority, which seems to be reinforced by the movement from the first of his action-framing pronouncements—"O pazzo desire! / Cercar di scoprire / Quel mal che, trovato, / Meschini ci fa" (O insane desire to try and uncover the trouble that, when found, will make you miserable)—to the second: "V'ingannai, ma fu l'inganno / isinganno ai vostri amanti . . ." (I deceived you, but the deceit cured your lovers of misapprehension). The opera as a whole, however, suggests that these positions never really exclude one another but rather tremble in the balance: are the lovers really better off for having had a world of intense and beyond-the-norm feeling opened to them and then redirected? Perhaps so, in terms of knowledge of the human heart; perhaps not in terms of pursuing their own local, limited, and conventional happiness. The opera, then, communicates a gap between the bourgeois ideal of painful but bracing self-realization and the rococo acceptance of normative frameworks—a gap amusingly reified in the co-existence in the critical literature of assertions that *Così* represents a philosophy at the end of its currency, and that it was so far ahead of its time as to undermine the emergent foundations of bourgeois self-conception.[38]

Rather than trying to "fix" *Così*'s position in a particular temporal or philosophical framework, and rather than deciding whether Don Alfonso, Da Ponte, or Mozart speaks the "real" truth, however, I would suggest that on every level and in every dimension of this opera the heart of the matter lies in the negotiable spaces between unthinking acceptance and wanton undermining of both aesthetic and moral conventions.[39] One reason for the enduring significance of this work is precisely that those spaces *are* negotiable—for some listeners and performers the dream of perfect happiness and beauty offered by certain moments in the opera will outweigh the demands of convention, for others the power of convention will outweigh that dream, and for yet others (myself included) the extraordinary beauty of much of the opera stands as an ideal toward which artistic

[38] Brown, *Così*, p. 2 and Kunze, *Mozarts Opern*, p. 433.

[39] Bernard Williams, "Mozart's Comedies and the Sense of an Ending," *MT* 122 (1981) p. 453, also explicitly describes the end of *Così* as not only conventional but "about" convention: "The affirmation that convention is reality and that deeper sentiment will be over-ruled is exactly what the work means. Its bitterness will then be considerable, and it will be compressed into the end . . ." I do not read the ending of *Così* as bitter, which seems to me to suggest a rather romantic or idealist notion of human relations; it seems to me perhaps more "grown-up" than disillusioned. Frits Noske suggests something like this in his comment that the second-act finale shows "how persons are united in society" (*The Signifier and the Signified* [The Hague: Nijhoff, 1977] p. 119).

and behavioral conventions should strive even while acknowledging the futility of the attempt.[40]

Whatever one's decision in these matters, the way *Così fan tutte* sets up a clear opposition between acceptance and rejection of convention and then works between and around that opposition, suggesting the costs and benefits of each position, is entirely characteristic of every aspect of this work, as indeed of its reception. Indeed, it has to an extraordinary degree stimulated criticism that revels in binary oppositions. Text vs. music, rococo vs. bourgeois, surface vs. depth, playfulness vs. seriousness, mechanism vs. sentiment, appearance vs. essence, faith vs. reason, and love vs. marriage, are just a few of the conceptual pairs that appear with varying frequency in the literature. It is in the nature of binary oppositions that one pole is valued over—even to the exclusion of—the other, but despite the efforts of many critics to tip the balance in one direction or another (usually in the direction of music, depth, seriousness, essence, etc.), the work brilliantly maintains its precarious and delicate equilibrium—surely a moral as well as an aesthetic lesson. *Così*'s defiance of clear oppositions persists even (or especially) with respect to its place in the Viennese repertory of opera buffa. It *does* stand out from its context, it *has* transcended the contingencies of its function as "mere entertainment," it *is* probably more moving and profound than the operas by "the others" with which it shared the stage (though not more so than Mozart's other Da Ponte settings). At the same time, *Così*'s transcendence is both deeply and explicitly rooted in the habits of its genre and the particular stimuli provided by its immediate repertory; and its originality arises from its profound understanding of that repertory's conventions. It is a testament not only to Da Ponte and Mozart's genius, but to the richness of opera buffa as it developed in Vienna in the late Theresian and Josephine eras that such a work could emerge, not through defiance of, but through acceptance of, and generosity toward, the apparently mechanical habits of that merely entertaining and thoroughly conventional repertory.

---

[40] Cf. Scott Burnham, "Mozart's *felix culpa: Così fan tutte* and the Irony of Beauty," *MQ* 78(1994), pp. 77–98.

Appendix One

OPERAS CONSULTED[1]

Date of First Viennese Performance[2]	Composer/Librettist	Title	Original Place and Date
1764	Piccinni/Goldoni	*La buona figliuola* (The Good Girl)	Rome 1760
[1766	Haydn/Friberth	*La canterina* (The Singer)	Eisenstadt 1766]
1767[3]	Sacchini/Tassi	*La contadina in corte* (The Peasant-Girl at Court)	Rome 1765
1767[4]	Gassmann/Goldoni	*L'amore artigiano* (Love among the Artisans)	Vienna 1767
1768[5]	Guglielmi/Chiari	*La sposa fedele* (The Faithful Bride)	Venice 1767
[1768	Haydn/Goldoni	*Lo speziale* (The Apothecary)	Eszterháza 1768]
1769	Gassmann/Calzabigi	*L'opera seria* (The Opera Seria)	Vienna 1769
1770	Guglielmi/Cavalieri	*L'impresa dell'opera* (The Opera Commission)	Milan 1765
	*Salieri/Boccherini	*Don Chisciotte alle nozze di Gamace* (Don Quixote at the Wedding of Gamace)	Vienna 1770
	[Haydn/Goldoni	*Le pescatrici* (The Fisherfolk)	Eszterháza 1770]
1771	Piccinni/Petrosellini	*L'incognita perseguitata* (The Persecuted Foundling)	Venice 1764
	*Salieri/Cipretti	*La moda* (The Fashion)	Vienna 1771
1772	Gazzaniga/Bertati	*La locanda* (The Inn)	Venice 1771
	Salieri/Boccherini	*La fiera di Venezia*[6] (The Venetian Carnival)	Vienna 1772
	*Gassmann/Boccherini	*I rovinati* (The Destitutes)	Vienna 1772
	*Salieri/Petrosellini	*Il Barone di Rocca antica* (The Baron of Ancient Fortress)	Vienna 1772

Date of First Viennese Performance[2]	Composer/Librettist	Title	Original Place and Date
	*Piccinni/anonymous	L'americano (The American)	Rome 1772
1773	Felici/Tassi	L'amore soldato (Love in the Military)	Venice 1769
	Anfossi/Petrosellini	L'incognita perseguitata/ Metilde ritrovata (The Persecuted Foundling/ Matilda Rediscovered)	Rome 1773
	[Haydn/Coltellini(?)	L'infeldeltà delusa (False Infidelity)	Eszterháza 1773]
	Salieri/Poggi	La locandiera[7] (The Innkeeperess)	Vienna 1773
1774	Piccinni/Petrosellini	L'astratto (The Absent-Minded Man)	Venice 1772
	Anfossi/Bertati	Il geloso in cimento (The Jealous Man in Trouble)	Vienna 1774[8]
	Gazzaniga/Bertati	L'isola di Alcina (Alcina's Island)	Venice 1772
	*Salieri/De Gamerra	La calamità de' cuori (The Hearts' Magnet)	Vienna 1774
	Paisiello/Boccherini	Il tamburro notturno[9] (The Drum in the Night)	Venice 1773
1775	Paisiello/Livigni	L'innocente fortunata (The Lucky Ingenue)	Venice 1773
	Paisiello/Livigni	La frascatana (The Girl from Frascati)	Venice 1774
	[Haydn/Friberth	L'incontro improvviso (The Unexpected Meeting)	Eszterháza 1775]
	Anfossi/?Petrosellini	La finta giardiniera (The False Gardener-Girl)	Rome 1774
	[Mozart/?Petrosellini	La finta giardiniera	Munich 1775]
	*Paisiello/Lorenzi	Il duello (The Duel)	Naples 1774
	*Paisiello/Lorenzi	Don Anchise Campanone[10]	Venice 1773
1776[11]	Paisiello/Petrosellini	Le due contesse[12] (The Two Countesses)	Rome 1776
1777	Guglielmi?/Badini	Orlando paladino (Knight Roland)	London 1771[13]
	Anfossi/Puttini	La vera costanza (True Fidelity)	Rome 1776

Date of First Viennese Performance[2]	Composer/Librettist	Title	Original Place and Date
	Anfossi/Bertati	*Isabella e Rodrigo* (Isabella and Rodrigo)	Venice 1776
	Righini/Porta	*Il convitato di pietra* (The Stone Guest)	Prague 1776
	Sarti/Grandi	*Le gelosie villane*[14] (Boondock Jealousies)	Venice 1776
	[Haydn/Goldoni	*Il mondo della luna* (The Moon-World)	Eszterháza 1777]
1778	Righini/Porta	*La vedova scaltra*[15] (The Crafty Widow)	Prague 1778
1779[16]	Traetta/Bertati	*Il cavaliere errante* (The Wandering Knight)	Naples 1777[17]
	Naumann/Bertati	*Le nozze disturbate* (Disturbed Nuptials)	Venice 1773
	Anfossi/Bertati	*Lo sposo disperato* (The Desperate Husband)	Venice 1777
	Gazzaniga/Bertati	*La vendemmia/ La dama incognita*[18] (The Grape-Harvest/ The Lady in Disguise)	Florence 1778
	[Haydn/Puttini	*La vera costanza*[19] (True Fidelity)	Eszterháza 1779]
1780	[Haydn/Lorenzi	*La fedeltà premiata* (Fidelity Rewarded)	Eszterháza 1780]
1782	[Haydn/Porta	*Orlando paladino* (Knight Roland)	Eszterháza 1782]
1783	Salieri/Mazzolà	*La scuola dei gelosi* (The School for Jealous People)	Venice 1778
	Cimarosa/Petrosellini	*L'italiana in Londra* (The Italian Girl in London)	Rome 1779
	Sarti/anon., after Goldoni	*Fra i due litiganti il terzo gode* (Between Two Contenders, the Third Wins)	Milan 1782
	Anfossi/?Petrosellini[20]	*Il curioso indiscreto* (Unwise Curiosity)	Rome 1777
	Paisiello/Petrosellini	*Il barbiere di Siviglia* (The Barber of Seville)	St. P'sburg 1782
	Paisiello/Bertati	*I filosofi immaginari* (The Imaginary Astrologers)	St. P'sburg 1779
	Anfossi/Livigni	*I viaggiatori felici* (The Happy Travelers)	Venice 1780

Date of First Viennese Performance[2]	Composer/Librettist	Title	Original Place and Date
1784	Sarti/Porta	*I contratempi* (The Mishaps)	Venice 1778
	Guglielmi/Neri	*Le vicende d'amore* (What Love Entails)	Rome 1784
	Paisiello/Casti	*Il re Teodoro in Venezia* (King Theodore in Venice)	Vienna 1784
	Cimarosa/Livigni	*Giannina e Bernardone* (Giannina and Bernardone)	Venice 1781
1785	Paisiello/anonymous	*La contadina di spirito* (The Country-Girl Who Sticks Up for Herself)	St. P'sburg 1779
	Righini/Porta	*L'incontro inaspettato* (The Unexpected Meeting)	Vienna 1785
	Cimarosa/Petrosellini	*Il pittore parigino* (The Parisian Painter)	Rome 1781
	Paisiello/Abate F.B.A.F	*La discordia fortunata*[21] (The Lucky Disagreement)	Venice 1775
	Salieri/Casti	*La grotta di Trofonio* (Trofonio's Grotto)	Vienna 1785
	Bianchi/Bertati	*La villanella rapita* (The Abducted Country Girl)	Venice 1783
1786	Mozart/Da Ponte	*Le nozze di Figaro* (The Marriage of Figaro)	Vienna 1786
	Sarti/Bertati	*I finti eredi* (The False Heirs)	St. P'sburg 1785
	Paisiello/Palomba	*Le gare generose* (The Contests in Generosity)	Naples 1786
	Martìn y Soler/ Da Ponte	*Una cosa rara* (A Rare Thing)	Vienna 1786
1787	Martìn y Soler/ Da Ponte	*L'arbore di Diana* (The Tree of Diana)	Vienna 1787
1788	*Salieri/Da Ponte	*Axur, re di Ormus* (Axur, King of Hormuz)	Vienna 1788
	Mozart/Da Ponte	*Don Giovanni*	Prague 1787
	Anfossi/Livigni	*Le gelosie fortunate* (Lucky Jealousies)	Venice 1786
1789	Cimarosa/Anelli	*I due supposti conti* (The Two Supposed Counts)	Milan 1784
1790	Mozart/Da Ponte	*Così fan tutte* (Thus Do All Women)	Vienna 1790

Date of First Viennese Performance[2]	Composer/Librettist	Title	Original Place and Date
	Paisiello/Lorenzi /Da Ponte	*Nina ossia La pazza per amore* (Nina, or the Woman Driven Mad by Love)	Naples 1789
	*Guglielmi/Zini	*La pastorella nobile* (The Noble Shepherdess)	Naples 1788
	Guglielmi/Palomba /Da Ponte	*La quacquera spiritosa* (The Spirited Quakeress)	Naples 1783
	Paisiello/Palomba	*La molinara*[22] (The Milleress)	Naples 1788

[1]For operas noted with an asterisk I have consulted only a libretto. Haydn's *opere buffe* and Mozart's *La finta giardiniera* are included in the list in brackets even though they were not performed in Vienna; they provide easily accessible and useful comparisons to the more strictly Viennese repertory.

[2]This table includes only performances in Italian. Thus, Paisiello's *I filosofi immaginari,* which was performed in the Burgtheater in 1782 as *Die eingebildeten Philosophen* does not appear until its Italian debut in 1783; its German-language debut is indicated by a footnote to the Italian premiere. Second and other subsequent productions (often but not always indicated by a new printing of the libretto, and often but not always indicated in Michtner, *DAB,* or Zechmeister, *WT*) are also indicated in the footnotes. A full schedule of performances, based on contemporary *Theaterzetteln* (daily posters announcing the theatrical offerings) is provided in Franz Hadamowsky, *Die Wiener Hoftheater* (Vienna: Prachner, 1966) Part I.

[3]New libretto printed in 1770; also performed in 1782.

[4]Also performed in German in 1779, as *Die Liebe unter den Handwerksleuten.*

[5]Also performed in 1778 in German as *Robert und Kalliste.*

[6]Repeated in 1785.

[7]Repeated in 1782.

[8]See *NGO,* s.v. "Anfossi." Zechmeister, *WT* p. 549, dates the first performance April 25, 1774. However, the surviving Viennese libretto is dated 1775.

[9]Originally performed in Naples as *Il tamburro;* revised by Lorenzi as *Il tamburro notturno* for Venice, 1773.

[10]Originally written as *Gli amanti comici* (Naples 1772); revised for Venice 1773 as *Don Anchise Campanone.*

[11]The date from the libretto, corroborated by a listing in Hadamowsky, *Die Wiener Hoftheater* (Vienna: Prachner, 1966). This opera is not included in Zechmeister, *WT,* whose calendar of offerings stops in February 1776, before the April 8 opening of the Burgtheater as the Nationaltheater. Michtner lists only the Singspiels done between 1778 and 1783. He notes, however (*DAB,* pp. 23-24), that some of the singers from the officially dismissed buffa troupe tried to keep going under the direction first of Vincenzo Fanti, and then (after Fanti's death) of the dancing master Sacco; this effort lasted only until Carnival of 1777. Hadamowsky, however, lists nineteen operas done between 1776 and 1778: *L'amore artigiano,* Giovanni Amadeo Neumann [=Johann Gottlieb Naumann]'s *Armida, L'astratto,* Bertati and Anfossi's *L'avaro, La buona figliuola,* Sacchini's *La contadina ingentilita* [probably = *La contadina in corte*], Goldoni and Galuppi's *La contessina,* Bertati and Borghi's *La donna istabile, La frascatana, Le gelosie villane, Isabella e Rodrigo, La locanda, Il marchese villano,* Tozzi' s *Le nozze deluse , L'orfano perseguitata* [probably Anfossi's setting of *L'incognita perseguitata*], Goldoni and Galuppi's *Il re alla caccia,* [Piccinni's] *La schiava riconosciuta* [= *Gli*

stravaganti], *La sposa fedele*, and Martinelli and Guglielmi's *Il vecchio deluso* [probably = *Il ratto della sposa*]. Names of singers penciled into the score (Austrian National Library Mus. Hs. 17803) of *Le due contesse* suggest that this was one of the operas done by the "stragglers" from the old company; the fact that almost all the operas listed in Hadamowsky are repetitions of works done before 1776 also suggests that the performers were largely the same.

[12]Repeated in 1787.

[13]In London as *Le pazzie di Orlando*. Much of the music in the Viennese source is not by Guglielmi; Anfossi and Porta seem to have been involved with this production.

[14]Repeated in 1783 and 1790.

[15]The folder for the Eszterháza performance of this opera (in 1783) includes part of a poster for a Viennese production of *Il convitato di pietra*. Unfortunately the part that might indicate the date and the performers is torn off. However, the connection of this piece with *La vedova scaltra*, and the close correspondence between the Viennese repertory of 1777–79 and the Eszterháza repertory of the early 1780s suggests that Giuseppe Bustelli—some of whose repertory was sold to the Esterhazys in 1781—may have been responsible for some of the Viennese performances before 1779 as well as the ones whose libretti bear his name. See Bartha and Somfai, *Haydn als Opernkapellmeister* (Budapest: Akademiai Kiadó, 1960), pp. 252, 254.

[16]Hadamowsky, *Die Wiener Hoftheater* lists none of the operas from my 1779 set (and like the 1777 and 1778 operas, they are not in Michtner, *DAB* or in Zechmeister, *WT*). Their libretti indicate that they were directed by Giuseppe Bustelli, who was chiefly employed in Dresden and Prague, perhaps in conjunction with a traveling company of singers.

[17]First version, Parma 1760, as *Stordilano, Principe di Granata*.

[18]Repeated under the latter title in 1784.

[19]Revised in 1785.

[20]Some sources give Bertati as the librettist. R. Angermüller's article in *I vicini di Mozart*, strongly suggests Petrosellini.

[21]Also known as *L'avaro deluso*.

[22]Original title, *L'amor contrastato*.

MUSICAL FORMS IN OPERA
BUFFA ARIAS[1]

"Sonata-like" (ca. 30% of repertory)[2]

Theme:	A	B	(x)	A	B
Key:	I	V	(x)	I	I
Text:	a	b	(a/b)	a	b

Variations:
- with or without development;
- triple return—of initial text, opening vocal music, and tonic key—may be blurred
- in alternating tempi: e.g., A [slow] in I; B [fast] to V; A [slow] in I; B [fast] in I
- may have faster envoi[3]
- text through once or twice (occasionally more)

---

[1] This table is intended to give the principal formal "skeletons" for the ca. 800 arias in this repertory, to indicate the range of general formal practice. As the "variations" sections indicate, there are many versions of most of the forms in this repertory, and many arias approximate rather than embody these forms. I have indicated the essential features of each formal outline in the diagram immediately below its name.

[2] I use the term "sonata-like" not to indicate that composers had "sonata-form" in mind when they were writing these arias, but to sketch, in terms that encompass both tonal and thematic relations, the common elements of these arias. They share the presence of a more or less well-articulated expository paragraph with a cadence in the dominant (often, though by no means always confirmed by a ritornello), the return of all or most of the opening material in the tonic, and the "grounding" of the secondary-key material in the home key. Obviously, the force and clarity of the move to V, the degree of thematic contrast and "development," and the homecoming feel of the reprise vary enormously, depending on the text-content, the aria-type, and the proclivities of the composer.

[3] The envoi of an aria in a sonata-like or other closed form typically comes after a full (or nearly full) reprise of the expository paragraph. It is usually relatively brief; it normally sets new text in a faster tempo and often in a new meter. Among Mozart's Viennese operas the clearest example of an envoi is Osmin's "Erst geköpft, dann gehangen," at the end of "Solche hergelauf'ne Laffen," in *Die Entführung aus dem Serail,* though Cherubino's "E se non ho chi m'oda" at the end of "Non so più cosa son, cosa faccio," in *Le nozze di Figaro* would also "count" as a small example of the species despite its lack of thematic novelty. *La finta giardiniera* has a number of envoi-like endings, though most of them perform a more substantive formal function than the typical "tag."

Compressed da capo (ca. 15% of "sonata-like" forms)

A   B   : C :   A   B
I   V   : (x) :   I   I
a   a(b): b(c):   a   b

> Texts set to this form are almost always in two short (4–6 line) stanzas.

Binary (ca. 14% of repertory)

A B: (x)   B
I V: (x or V)   I
a b : a   b

Variations:
- may have envoi
- text-through once or twice
- may be almost through-composed
- includes ABCA forms

Reprise forms (ca. 3% of repertory)

A B A C
I V I I
a b a b

Variation:
- C may derive from B

Rondo (ca. 8% of repertory)[4]

A   B A C A B   *OR*   A   B   A   B   A
I   V I x I I   I   V   I   I   I

(text variable)

Variations:
- may have envoi
- may or may not use V as secondary key
- may be "sonata-like" form with 3rd use of A

---

[4] Expository paragraphs are often quite weakly articulated in rondo and rondo-like forms.

Through-composed (ca. 36% of repertory)

```
A   B   :   C   D . . .
I   (V) :   I . . . . . . .
```

Main variations:

- one, two, or many tempi in various relationships
- locally repetitive or discontinuous
- may begin with an expository paragraph

Rondò (ca. 12% of through-composed forms)

```
A   B   A   C  (D) C . . .
I   V   I   I  (?)  I
a   b   a   c . . .
```

Strophic (ca. 3% of repertory)

```
A   A   A
```

(harmonic plan variable)

```
a   b   c
```

Ternary (ca. 6% of repertory)

```
A   B   A
I   (x) I
a   b   a
```

Variations:

- A-section may be a single period, an exposition, or a complete I-V-I paragraph.
- B-section may contrast with or continue the material from A.

PLOT SUMMARIES FOR
I FINTI EREDI, LE GARE GENEROSE,
AND *L'INCOGNITA PERSEGUITATA*

(OPERAS MENTIONED FREQUENTLY
BUT NOT SUMMARIZED IN *NGO*)

I FINTI EREDI

The opera opens with quarrelsome couplings. The Cavaliere dall'Oca and Isabella, daughter of Don Griffagno, the local administrator, plainly detest each other, and the peasants Giannina and Pierotto quarrel. Both Don Griffagno and the Cavaliere show inappropriate interest in Giannina, which does not improve Pierotto's temper. The rumor circulates that the long-lost heir to the local marquisate has been found. Isabella takes a fancy to Pierotto and decides to pass him off as that heir, which will allow her to marry him. Giannina, meanwhile, imagines herself swept up by the incoming heir, and in any case, Pierotto thinks her in love with the Cavaliere. The first-act finale, which takes place at night, starts with Don Griffagno, the Cavaliere, and Pierotto all creeping out to woo Giannina; Giannina herself has come out to try and make amends with Pierotto, whom she has heard singing a serenade. Accusations and counter-accusations fly.

The second act begins as Don Griffagno plans to announce that Giannina is actually the true heir to the marquisate, which will allow him to marry her. His daughter Isabella is still determined to marry Pierotto in his guise as the new heir. Giannina and Pierotto meet in their new personae and quarrel about who should bow to whom. (Giannina insults Pierotto by assuming that his new clothes represent his future job as her cook—after all, he does make a great polenta.) In the midst of this, the real marquis appears. The locals take him for a lunatic impostor but are eventually convinced of the correctness of his claim and the falsity of their own. The Marquis decides to give a party to celebrate his return, in the course of which he will indicate his choice of wife by throwing her a handkerchief. He has, of course, chosen Giannina. The handkerchief is thrown and Pierotto picks it up, at first not understanding its implication. Once he understands what is going on, he excoriates the Marquis and pleads with the other characters to intercede on his behalf. Everyone (including Giannina) refuses. Finally

Giannina is moved to sympathy for her old lover, and the Marquis, unperturbed, throws the handkerchief to Isabella, who accepts it gladly.

LE GARE GENEROSE

Gelinda and Bastiano have eloped together from Naples to Halifax, but on the way their ship has been attacked by pirates. They escaped in total poverty, still not having paid the captain of the ship. They have been brought to Boston, where Mr. Dull has saved them from being hung and has bought them as slaves. Mr. Dull and his niece Meri plan to marry Gelinda (now "Dianina") and Bastiano (now "Bronton"), respectively; each is horrified at the other's lowly choice of spouse. The proposals are made, and the slaves are stupefied. Don Berlicco arrives from his travels abroad. He is a young man of poor origins who was raised by Mr. Dull, and who has just squandered the money he was supposed to invest. He notices that Bastiano is Neapolitan and announces that he carries a warrant for the arrest of such a person, who has eloped from Naples. (The warrant was actually given him by Gelinda's guardian, who has paid Berlicco to return her to Naples.) Gelinda and Bastiano try to make plans in the face of this disaster but are interrupted by Mr. Dull, who makes Bastiano do his accounts while he flirts with Gelinda, driving Bastiano into fits of jealousy. The first-act finale begins with the three men all planning to catch Gelinda, who has retired to her room to bewail her fate. Mr. Dull and Berlicco confront her (and the newly arrived Bastiano) with the descriptions of the eloped Neapolitans, and their identity is called into question. Gelinda and Bastiano deny the obvious, Bastiano wonders about an escape, and Gelinda accuses him to Berlicco and Dull of trying to abduct her. Bastiano is duly accused and led off to be punished.

   The second act opens with Mr. Dull reflecting on the trials to which his generosity will be put if "Dianina" really does turn out to be Gelinda. Bastiano is shown in prison, chained to an African. He is offered his freedom if he will cede "Dianina" to Mr. Dull (and Don Berlicco makes a similar offer). Gelinda's identity comes increasingly under suspicion, and finally Mr. Dull sends her and Bastiano into the garden together, so he can spy on them. Gelinda confesses to Mr. Dull, explains that she and Bastiano are married, and begs for mercy. Dull is moved and calls on his customary generosity. Bastiano, however, refuses to reveal his identity to Meri, who is still romantically interested in him. In the second act finale, Berlicco's mercenary interests in turning in the slaves are exposed, while Mr. Dull's generosity is demonstrated: he pays the dept to the ship's captain and arrests Berlicco for debt. Gelinda pays off Berlicco's debt with the inheritance that Mr. Dull has recovered from the ship's captain, and persuades Dull to let Meri marry Berlicco.

L'INCOGNITA PERSEGUITATA

Both the soldier Asdrubale and his father the Baron Tarpano declare their love to Giannetta, a foundling living in the Baron's house. Giannetta is also in love with Asdrubale but thinks the match socially impossible. She loves the Baron "like a father." The serving girls Carlotta and Nannina both love the servant Fabrizio, who also loves Giannetta, thinking her his social equal. The serving girls (especially Nannina) are spitefully jealous. The Baron's haughty daughter Clarice wants her lover Ernesto to have the Baron evict Giannetta because she is upset about her brother Asdrubale's love for the girl. Ernesto shows himself to be nobly compassionate and refuses to treat Giannetta this way. Asdrubale proposes an elopement; the Baron interrupts the tender scene, sends Asdrubale away, and Giannetta to her room. In the first-act finale Fabrizio goes to comfort Giannetta, which is misinterpreted by everyone else, and Giannetta is subject to general accusation.

The second act begins with Clarice asserting her distaste for a foundling relative, and with both the Baron and Asdrubale claiming that they do not love the poor girl. In the face of various insults and threats, Giannetta decides to run away. Eventually the other characters mobilize to look for her, and discover that she has found a new life among the local shepherds and shepherdesses. The second-act finale involves Giannetta's denial of her identity when the other characters find her, and the confusion attendant on this.

In the third act the servant Fabrizio threatens to kill himself if Giannetta will not let him join her in the countryside. However, Ernesto (who has defended Giannetta all along) has received a communication from his parents that reveals that Giannetta is his sister. This allows Asdrubale to marry her unproblematically; and Clarice can marry Ernesto in the knowledge that her family is untainted by unknown blood. Fabrizio and Nannina also plight their troth.

WORKS CITED

Abbate, Carolyn. *Unsung Voices: Opera and Musical Narrative in the Nineteenth Century.* Princeton: Princeton University Press, 1991.

Abbate, Carolyn, and Roger Parker. "Dismembering Mozart." *COJ* 2 (1990): 187–95.

Abert, Anna Amalie. "The Operas of Mozart." In *The New Oxford History of Music.* Vol. 7, *The Age of Enlightenment,* ed. Egon Wellesz and Frederick Sternfeld. Oxford: Oxford University Press, 1973, pp. 97–171.

Abert, Hermann. *W. A. Mozart: Neubearbeitete und erweiterte Ausgabe von Otto Jahns Mozart.* 6th ed. Leipzig: Breitkopf & Härtel, 1923–24.

———. "Paisiellos Buffokunst und ihre Beziehungen zu Mozart." In his *Gesammelte Schriften und Vorträge von Hermann Abert,* ed. Friedrich Blume. Halle: Niemeyer, 1929, pp. 365–96.

Abraham, Gerald. "The Operas." In *The Mozart Companion,* ed. H. C. Robbins Landon and Donald Mitchell. Corrected edition, New York: Norton, 1969, pp. 283–324.

Allanbrook, Wye J. *Rhythmic Gesture in Mozart: 'Le nozze di Figaro' and 'Don Giovanni.'* Chicago: University of Chicago Press, 1983.

———. "When the Fat Lady Sings." Unpublished typescript.

———. "Mozart's Happy Endings: A New Look at the 'Convention' of the 'Lieto Fine.'" *M-Jb* (1984–85): 1–5.

Allroggen, Gerhard. "Die Cavatine in der italienischen Oper des 18. Jahrhunderts." In *Festschrift Arno Forschert zum 60. Geburtstag am 29 Dezember 1985,* ed. Allroggen and Detlef Altenburg. Kassel: Bärenreiter, 1986, pp. 142–49.

Anderson, Emily, ed. *The Letters of Mozart and His Family.* 2d ed. prepared by A. Hyatt King and Monica Carolan. New York: St. Martin's Press, 1966.

Angermüller, Rudolph. *Antonio Salieri: Sein Leben und seine weltliche Werke unter besondere Berücksichtigung seiner "grossen" Opern.* 3 vols. Munich: Katzbichler, 1971.

———. "Zwei Selbstbiographien von Joseph Weigl (1766–1846)." *DJbM* 16 (1972): 46–85.

Armstrong, Nancy. *Desire and Domestic Fiction: A Political History of the Novel.* Oxford: Oxford University Press, 1987.

Attali, Jacques. *Noise: The Political Economy of Music.* Trans. Brian Massumi. Foreword by Fredric Jameson. Afterword by Susan McClary. Minneapolis: University of Minnesota Press, 1985.

Bakhtin, Mikhail. *Rabelais and His World.* Trans. Helen Iswolsky. Bloomington: Indiana University Press, 1984.

Balsano, Maria Antonella. "L'ottava di *Così fan tutte.*" In *Liedstudien: Wolfgang Osthoff zum 60. Geburtstag,* ed. Martin Just and Reinhard Wiesend. Tutzing: Schneider, 1989, pp. 279–91.

Bartha, Dénes, and László Somfai. *Haydn als Opernkapellmeister: Die Haydn-Dokumente der Esterházy-Opernsammlung.* Budapest: Akademiai Kiadó, 1960.

Bauman, Thomas. "German Opera from the National-Singspiel to *Die Zauber-flöte*." In *The Oxford Illustrated History of Opera*, ed. Roger Parker. Oxford: Oxford University Press, 1994, pp. 118–21.

Beales, Derek. *Joseph II*. Vol. 1, *In the Shadow of Maria Theresia*. Cambridge: Cambridge University Press, 1987.

———. "Court, Government and Society in Mozart's Vienna." In Sadie, *Wolfgang Amadè Mozart*, pp. 3–20.

Beckford, Peter. *Familiar Letters from Italy, to a Friend in England*. Salisbury: J. Easton, 1805.

Blanchetti, Francesco. "Tipologia musicale dei concertati nell'opera buffa di Giovanni Paisiello." *RIM* 19 (1984): 234–60.

Braunbehrens, Volkmar. *Mozart in Vienna 1781–91*. Trans. Timothy Bell. New York: Grove Weidenfeld, 1989.

Brown, Bruce Alan. *Gluck and the French Theatre in Vienna*. Oxford: Oxford University Press, 1991.

———. *W. A. Mozart: "Così fan tutte."* Cambridge: Cambridge University Press, 1995.

———. "Beaumarchais, Paisiello and the Genesis of *Così fan tutte*." In Sadie, *Wolfgang Amadè Mozart*, pp. 312–38.

———. "Lo Specchio Francese: Viennese Opera Buffa and the Legacy of French Theatre." In Hunter and Webster, *Opera Buffa in Mozart's Vienna*, pp. 50–81.

Brown, Bruce Alan, and John A. Rice. "Salieri's *Così fan tutte*." *COJ* 8 (1996): 17–44.

Brown, John. *Letters upon the Poetry and Music of the Italian Opera: Addressed to a Friend. By the Late Mr. John Brown, Painter*. Edinburgh: Bell and Bradfute, 1789.

Bruckmüller, Ernst. *Sozialgeschichte Österreichs*. Vienna and Munich: Herold, 1985.

Burney, Charles. *The Present State of Music in France and Italy*. 1773. Facsimile rpt., New York: Broude Brothers, 1969.

———. *The Present State of Music in Germany, The Netherlands, and United Provinces*. 1775. Facsimile rpt., New York: Broude Brothers, 1969.

Burnham, Scott. "Mozart's *felix culpa: Così fan tutte* and the Irony of Beauty." *Musical Quarterly* 78(1994): 77–98.

Bush, M. L. *The European Nobility*. Vol. 1, *Noble Privilege*. New York: Holmes and Meier, 1983.

Carter, Tim. *W.A. Mozart: "Le Nozze di Figaro."* Cambridge: Cambridge University Press, 1987.

Charlton, David. *Grétry and the Growth of Opéra-Comique*. Cambridge: Cambridge University Press, 1986.

Cone, Edward. "The World of Opera and Its Inhabitants." In his *Music: A View from Delft: Selected Essays*, ed. Robert P. Morgan. Chicago: University of Chicago Press, 1989, pp. 125–38.

Crampe-Casnabet, Michelle. "A Sampling of Eighteenth-Century Philosophy." In *A History of Women in the West*, ed. Georges Duby and Michelle Perrot. Vol. III, *Renaissance and Enlightenment Paradoxes*, ed. Natalie Zemon Davis and Arlette Farge. Cambridge, Mass: Harvard University Press, Belknap Press, 1993, pp. 315–48.

Crotti, Ilaria. "Percorsi della farsa tra romanzo e teatro." In Muraro, *I vicini*, pp. 489–547.

Da Ponte, Lorenzo. *Memorie*. Ed. Giuseppe Armani. 2d ed., Milan: Garzanti, 1980.

Degrada, Francesco. "Splendore e miseria della ragione: a proposito di *Così fan tutte*." In his *Il palazzo incantato: Studi sulla tradizione del melodramma dal barocco al romanticismo*. Fiesole: Discanto, 1979, vol. 2, pp. 3–18.

Della Corte, Andrea. *L'opera comica italiana nel '700: Studi ed appunti*. Bari: Laterza, 1923.

———. *Piccinni (settecento italiano): Con frammenti musicali inediti e due ritratti*. Bari: Laterza, 1928.

Dent, Edward J. "Ensembles and Finales in 18th Century Italian Opera," (part I) *SIMG* 11 (1909–10): 543–69, and (part II) 12 (1910–11): 112–38.

Dietrich, Margret, ed. *Das Burgtheater und sein Publikum*. Veröffentlichungen des Instituts für Publikumsforschung, no. 3. Vienna: Verlag der österreichischen Akademie der Wissenschaften, 1976.

———. "Dokumentation zur Uraufführung." In *Così fan tutte: Beiträge zur Wirkungsgeschichte von Mozarts Oper*, ed. Susanne Vill. Bayreuth: Mühl'scher Universitätsverlag, 1978, pp. 24–63.

Döhring, Sieghart. *Formgeschichte der Opernarien vom Ausgang des 18. bis zur Mitte des 19. Jahrhunderts*. Marburg-Lahn: Itzehoe, 1975.

Dyer, Richard. "Entertainment and Utopia." 1977. Rpt. in *Genre: The Musical*, ed. Rick Altman. London and New York: Routledge & Kegan Paul, 1981, pp. 175–89.

Eco, Umberto. "The Frames of Comic 'Freedom'." In *Carnival!* ed. Thomas A. Sebeok, pp. 1–10.

Edge, Dexter. "Mozart's Reception in Vienna, 1787–1791." In Sadie, *Wolfgang Amadè Mozart*, pp. 66–120.

Einstein, Alfred. *Mozart: His Character, His Work*. Trans. Arthur Mendel and Nathan Broder. London and New York: Oxford University Press, 1945.

Elias, Norbert. *The Court Society*. Trans. Edmund Jephcott. New York: Pantheon Books, 1983.

The Encyclopedia of Philosophy. New York: Macmillan/The Free Press, 1972.

Farnsworth, Rodney. "*Così fan tutte* as Parody and Burlesque." *OQ* 6 (1988–89): 50–68.

Feldman, Martha. "Magic Mirrors and the *Seria* Stage: Thoughts towards a Ritual View." *JAMS* 48 (1995): 423–84.

Finscher, Ludwig, ed. *Neues Handbuch der Musikwissenschaft*. Vol. 5, *Die Musik der 18. Jahrhunderts*. Laaber: Laaber-Verlag, 1985.

Flandrin, Jean-Louis. *Families in Former Times: Kinship, Household and Sexuality*. Trans. Richard Southern. Cambridge: Cambridge University Press, 1979.

Freud, Sigmund. *Beyond the Pleasure Principle*. Trans. and newly edited by James Strachey. Introduction by Gregory Zilboorg. New York: Norton, 1961.

Fried, Michael. *Absorption and Theatricality: Painting and Beholder in the Age of Diderot*. Berkeley: University of California Press, 1980.

Frye, Northrop. "The Mythos of Spring: Comedy." In his *Anatomy of Criticism*. Princeton: Princeton University Press, 1957, pp. 163–86.

Gallarati, Paolo. *La forza delle parole: Mozart drammaturgo*. Turin: Einaudi, 1993.

———. "Mozart and Eighteenth-Century Comedy." In Hunter and Webster, *Opera Buffa in Mozart's Vienna*, pp. 98–111.

Gay, Peter. *The Enlightenment: An Interpretation*. Vol. 2, *The Science of Freedom*. New York: Norton, 1977.

Gidwitz, Patricia Lewy. "Mozart's Fiordiligi: Adriana Ferrarese del Bene." *COJ* 8 (1996): 199–214.

Giller, Monika. "Die Sentimentalität im Spielplan und in der Darstellung des Burgtheaters am Ende des 18. Jahrhunderts (1776–1809)." Doctoral dissertation, University of Vienna, 1966.

Goehr, Lydia. *The Imaginary Museum of Musical Works: An Essay in the Philosophy of Music*. Oxford: Clarendon Press, 1992.

Goehring, Edmund J. "The Comic Vision of *Così Fan Tutte:* Literary and Operatic Traditions." Ph.D. dissertation, Columbia University, 1993.

———. "Despina, Cupid and the Pastoral Mode of *Così fan tutte*." *COJ* 7 (1995): 107–33.

———. "The Sentimental Muse of Opera Buffa." In Hunter and Webster, *Opera Buffa in Mozart's Vienna*, pp. 115–45.

Goethe, Johann Wolfgang von. *Italian Journey*. Ed. Thomas P. Saine and Jeffrey Sammons. Trans. Robert R. Heitner. Goethe's Collected Works, vol. 6. New York: Suhrkamp, 1989.

Goldin, Daniela. *La vera fenice: Librettisti e libretti tra Sette e Ottocento*. Turin: Einaudi, 1985.

Goldoni, Carlo. *Tutte le Opere di Carlo Goldoni*. Ed. Giuseppe Ortolani. 14 vols. Milan: Mondadori, 1935–.

———. *Memoirs of Carlo Goldoni, Written by Himself*. Trans. John Black. Edited with a preface by William A. Drake. 1926. Rpt. Westport, CT.: Greenwood, 1976.

Gombrich, E. H. "*Così fan tutte* (Procris included)." *Journal of the Warburg and Courtauld Institutes* 17 (1954): 372–74.

Gordon, Daniel. "Philosophy, Sociology, and Gender in the Enlightenment Conception of Public Opinion." *French Historical Studies* 17 (1992): 882–911.

Green, Rebecca Lee. "Power and Patriarchy in the Goldoni Operas of Joseph Haydn." Ph.D. dissertation, University of Toronto, 1995.

Grout, Donald Jay. *A Short History of Opera*. 3d ed., with Hermine Wiegel Williams. New York: Columbia University Press, 1988.

Gustafson, Susan E. *Absent Mothers and Orphaned Fathers: Narcissism and Abjection in Lessing's Aesthetic and Dramatic Production*. Detroit: Wayne State University Press, 1995.

Habermas, Jürgen. *The Structural Transformation of the Public Sphere: An Inquiry into a Category of Bourgeois Society*. Trans. Thomas Burger with Frederick Lawrence. Cambridge, MA: Harvard University Press, 1989.

Hadamowsky, Franz. *Die Wiener Hoftheater (Staatstheater) 1776–1966: Verzeichnis der aufgeführten Stücke mit Bestandnachweis und täglichem Spielplan*. Part I: 1776–1810. Vienna: Prachner, 1966.

Haider-Pregler, Hilde. *Des sittlichen Bürgers Abendschule: Bildungsanspruch und Bildungsauftrag des Burgtheaters im 18. Jahrhundert*. Vienna and Munich: Jugend und Volk, 1980.

Hart, Gail K. "Voyeuristic Star-Gazing: Authority, Instinct and the Women's World of Goethe's *Stella*." *Monatshefte* 82 (1990): 408–20.

Heartz, Daniel. *Mozart's Operas*. Edited, with contributing essays, by Thomas Bauman. Berkeley: University of California Press, 1990.

———. "From Beaumarchais to Da Ponte: The Metamorphosis of *Figaro*." In his *Mozart's Operas*, pp. 107–22.

———. "Citation, Reference, and Recall in *Così fan tutte*." In his *Mozart's Operas*, pp. 229–53.

———. "La Clemenza di Sarastro: Masonic Beneficence in the Last Operas." In his *Mozart's Operas*, pp. 255–76.

———. "Constructing *Le nozze di Figaro*. In his *Mozart's Operas*, pp. 133–56.

———. *Haydn, Mozart, and the Viennese School 1740–1780*. New York: Norton, 1995.

Henze-Döhring, Sabine. *Opera Seria, Opera Buffa und Mozarts 'Don Giovanni': Zur Gattungskonvergenz in der italienischen Oper des 18. Jahrhunderts*. Laaber: Laaber-Verlag, 1986.

———. "La tecnica del concertato in Paisiello e Rossini." *NRMI* 22 (1988): 1–23.

Herbert, Christopher. "Comedy: The World of Pleasure." *Genre* 17 (1984): 401–16.

Hill, Laura Callegari. Introduction to *La grotta di Trofonio*. 1785. Facsimile rpt., Bologna: Forni, 1984.

Hunter, G. K. "The Idea of Comedy in Some Seventeenth-Century Comedies." In *Poetry and Drama in the English Renaissance: Essays in Honor of Jiro Ozu*, ed. Koshi Nakanori and Yasuo Tamaizumi. Tokyo: Kinokuniya, 1980, pp. 71–91.

Hunter, Mary. "'Se Vuol Ballare' Quoted: A Moment in the Reception History of *Figaro*." *MT* 130 (1989): 464–67.

———. "*Così fan tutte* et les conventions musicales de son temps." In *L'Avant-scène opéra* 131–132, ed. Michel Noiray, pp. 158–64.

———. "Some Representations of Opera Seria in Opera Buffa." *COJ* 3 (1991): 89–108.

———. "Landscapes, Gardens and Gothic Settings in the *Opere Buffe* of Mozart and His Contemporaries." *CM* 51 (1993): 94–105.

———. "Bourgeois Values and Opera Buffa in 1780s Vienna." In Hunter and Webster, *Opera Buffa in Mozart's Vienna*, pp. 165–96.

———. "Rousseau, the Countess, and the Female Domain." In *Mozart Studies 2*, ed. Cliff Eisen. Oxford: Oxford University Press, 1997, pp. 1–26.

Hunter, Mary, and James Webster. *Opera Buffa in Mozart's Vienna*. Cambridge: Cambridge University Press, 1997.

Ingarden, Roman. *The Work of Music and the Problem of Its Identity*. Trans. Adam Czerniawsky. Ed. Jean Harrell. Berkeley: University of California Press, 1986.

Jagendorf, Zvi. *The Happy End of Comedy: Jonson, Molière and Shakespeare*. Newark: University of Delaware Press, 1984.

Jauss, Hans Robert. *Toward an Aesthetic of Reception*. Trans. Timothy Bahti. Introduction by Paul de Man. Minneapolis: University of Minnesota Press, 1982.

———. "Rousseau's *Nouvelle Héloise* and Goethe's *Werther* within the Shift of Horizons from the French Enlightenment to German Idealism." In his *Ques-*

tion and Answer: Forms of Dialogic Understanding, trans. Michael Hays. Minneapolis: University of Minnesota Press, 1988, pp. 151–97.

Kelly, Michael. *Reminiscences of Michael Kelly, of the King's Theatre, and Theatre Royal Drury Lane, including A Period of Nearly Half a Century with Original Anecdotes of Many Distinguished Persons, Political, Literary, and Musical.* 2 vols. London: Henry Colburn, 1826.

Kerman, Joseph. *Opera as Drama.* New and revised ed. Berkeley: University of California Press, 1988.

Kimbell, David. *Italian Opera.* Cambridge: Cambridge University Press, 1991.

Kindermann, Heinz. "Das Publikum und die Schauspielerrepublik." In Dietrich, *Das Burgtheater und sein Publikum,* pp. 97–122.

Kivy, Peter. "Opera Talk: A Philosophical Phantasie." *COJ* 3 (1991): 63–77.

Kritsch, Cornelia, and Herbert Zeman. "Rätsel eines genialen Opernentwurf—Da Ponte's Libretto zu 'Così fan tutte' und das literarische Umfeld." In *Die österreichische Literatur: Ihr Profil an der Wende vom 18. zum 19. Jahrhundert (1750–1830),* Part I, ed. Herbert Zeman. Graz: Akademische Druck- und Verlagsanstalt, 1979, pp. 355–77.

Kunze, Stefan. *Don Giovanni vor Mozart: Die Tradition der Don-Giovanni-Opern im italienischen Buffa-Theater des 18. Jahrhunderts.* Munich: Fink, 1972.

———. "Über das Verhältnis von musikalisch autonomer Struktur und Textbau in Mozarts Opern." *M-Jb* (1973–74): 217–32.

———. *Mozarts Opern.* Stuttgart: Reclam, 1984.

———. "Per una descrizione tipologica della *introduzione* nell'opera buffa del settecento e particolarmente nei drammi giocosi di Carlo Goldoni e Baldassare Galuppi." In *Galuppiana 1985: Studi e Ricerche: Atti del Convegno Internazionale, Venezia . . . 1985,* ed. Maria Teresa Muraro and Franco Rossi. Florence: Olschki, 1986, pp. 165–78.

Landes, Joan B. *Women and the Public Sphere in the Age of the French Revolution.* Ithaca: Cornell University Press, 1988.

Landon, H. C. Robbins. *Mozart and Vienna.* London: Thames and Hudson, 1991.

Lavagetto, Mario. *Quei più modesti romanzi.* Milan: Garzanti, 1979.

Link, Dorothea. "The Viennese Operatic Canon and Mozart's *Così fan tutte.*" *Mitteilungen der internationales Stiftung Mozarteum* 38 (1990): 111–21.

———. "The Da Ponte Operas of Martín y Soler." Ph. D. dissertation, University of Toronto, 1991.

———. "*Così fan tutte:* Dorabella and Amore." *M-Jb* (1991): 888–94.

———. "*L'arbore di Diana:* A Model for *Così fan tutte.*" In Sadie, *Wolfgang Amadè Mozart,* pp. 362–73.

Lippmann, Friedrich. "Il 'Grande Finale' nell'opera buffa e nell'opera seria: Paisiello e Rossini." *RIM* 27 (1992): 225–55.

Lühning, Helga. *Titus-Vertonungen im 18. Jahrhundert: Untersuchungen zur Tradition der Opera Seria von Hasse bis Mozart.* Cologne: Arno-Volk, Laaber-Verlag, 1983.

Mamczarz, Irène. *Les Intermèdes comiques italiens.* Paris: Editions du Centre National de la Recherche Scientifique, 1972.

Manfredini, Vincenzo. *Difesa della musica moderna e de' suoi celebri esecutori.* 1788. Facsimile rpt. Bologna: Forni, 1972.

Markley, Robert. "Sentimentality as Performance: Shaftesbury, Sterne, and the Theatrics of Virtue." In *The New Eighteenth Century: Theory, Politics, English Literature,* ed. Felicity Nussbaum and Laura Brown. New York and London: Routledge, 1987, pp. 210–30.

Marshall, David. *The Figure of Theater: Shaftesbury, Defoe, Adam Smith, and George Eliot.* New York: Columbia University Press, 1986.

Martinotti, Sergio. "Per un altro ritratto di Salieri." In Muraro, *I vicini,* pp. 273–96.

Mattern, Volker. *Das Dramma giocoso La finta giardiniera: Ein Vergleich der Vertonungen von Pasquale Anfossi und Wolfgang Amadeus Mozart.* Laaber: Laaber-Verlag, 1989.

Mayer, Hans. "*Così fan tutte* und die Endzeit des Ancien Régime." In his *Versuche über die Oper,* Frankfurt am Main: Suhrkamp, 1981, pp. 9–52.

Michtner, Otto. *Das Alte Burgtheater als Opernbühne: Von der Einführung des Deutschen Singspiels (1778) bis zum Tod Kaiser Leopolds II (1792).* Vienna: Böhlau, 1970.

Moindrot, Isabelle. "*Così fan tutte* ou les artifices de l'idéal." In *L'Avant-scène opéra* 131–132: *Così fan tutte,* ed. Michel Noiray, pp. 23–35.

Mozart: Briefe und Aufzeichnungen. Gesamtausgabe. Collected and annotated by Wilhelm Bauer and Otto Erich Deutsch. 7 vols. Kassel: Bärenreiter, 1962–75.

Mulvey, Laura. "Visual Pleasure and Narrative Cinema." *Screen* 16 (1975): 9–16.

Muraro, Maria Teresa, and David Bryant, eds. *I vicini di Mozart: Il teatro musicale tra Sette e Ottocento.* 2 vols. Florence: Olschki, 1989.

Noiray, Michel, ed. *L'Avant-scène opéra* 131–132: *Così fan tutte.* Paris: L'Avant-scène opéra, 1990.

Noske, Frits. *The Signifier and the Signified: Studies in the Operas of Mozart and Verdi.* The Hague: Nijhoff, 1977.

Nussbaum, Felicity. *Torrid Zones: Maternity, Sexuality, and Empire in Eighteenth-Century English Narratives.* Baltimore: The Johns Hopkins University Press, 1995.

Osthoff, Wolfgang. "Mozarts Cavatinen und ihrer Tradition." In *Frankfurter musikhistorische Studien: Helmuth Osthoff zu seinem siebzigsten Geburtstag: Überreicht von Kollegen, Mitarbeitern und Schülern,* ed. Wilhelm Stauder, Ursula Aarburg, and Peter Cahn. Tutzing: Schneider, 1969, pp. 139–77.

———. "Die Opera buffa." In *Gattungen der Musik in Einzeldarstellungen. Gedenkschrift Leo Schrade,* ed. Wulf Arlt, Ernst Lichtenhahn, and Hans Oesch. Vol. I. Berlin and Munich: Francke, 1973, pp. 678–743.

Payer von Thurn, Rudolf. *Joseph II als Theaterdirektor: Ungedruckte Briefe und Aktenstücke aus den Kinderjahren des Burgtheaters.* Vienna: Heidrich, 1920.

Pezzl, Johann. *Skizze von Wien.* 1786–90. Partially trans. in H. C. Robbins Landon, *Mozart and Vienna.* London: Thames and Hudson, 1991, pp. 54–191. See also *Skizze von Wien: Ein Kultur- und Sittenbild aus der josefinischen Zeit.* Ed. Gustav Gugitz and Anton Schlossar. Graz: Leykam, 1923.

Pichler, Karoline. *Denkwürdigkeiten aus meinem Leben.* Vienna: A. Pichlers Witwe, 1844.

Piozzi, Hester Lynch. *Observations and Reflections Made in the Course of a Jour-*

ney through France, Italy and Germany. Ed. Herbert Barrows. Ann Arbor: University of Michigan Press, 1967.

Pirani, Federico. "*Il curioso indiscreto*: Un'opera buffa tra Roma e la Vienna di Mozart." In *Mozart: Gli orientamenti della critica moderna. Atti del convegno internazionale, Cremona . . . 1991,* ed. Giacomo Fornari. Lucca: Libreria Musicale Italiana Editrice, 1994, pp. 47–67.

———. "Operatic Links between Rome and Vienna, 1776–1790." In Sadie, *Wolfgang Amadè Mozart,* pp. 395–402.

Platoff, John. "Music and Drama in the Opera Buffa Finale: Mozart and His Contemporaries in Vienna," Ph.D. dissertation, University of Pennsylvania, 1984.

———. "Musical and Dramatic Structure in the Opera Buffa Finale." *JM* 7 (1989): 191–230.

———. "The Buffa Aria in Mozart's Vienna." *COJ* 2 (1990): 99–120.

———. "Tonal Organization in 'Buffa' Finales and the Act II Finale of *Le nozze di Figaro.*" *M&L* 72 (1991): 387–403.

———. "How Original Was Mozart? The Evidence from Opera Buffa." *EM* 20 (1992): 105–17.

———. "A New History for Martín's *Una cosa rara.*" *JM* 12 (1994): 85–115.

———. "Catalogue Arias and the 'Catalogue Aria.'" In Sadie, *Wolfgang Amadè Mozart,* pp. 296–311.

Rabin, Ronald. "Mozart, Da Ponte, and the Dramaturgy of Opera Buffa." Ph.D. dissertation, Cornell University, 1996.

———. "Figaro as Misogynist." In Hunter and Webster, *Opera Buffa in Mozart's Vienna,* pp. 232–60.

Ratner, Leonard. *Classic Music: Expression, Form, and Style.* New York: Schirmer, 1980.

Reckford, Kenneth. *Aristophanes' Old-and-New Comedy.* Chapel Hill: University of North Carolina Press, 1987.

Rector, Monica. "The Code and Message of Carnival: 'Escolas-de-Samba.'" In *Carnival!* ed. Thomas Sebeok, pp. 37–165.

Rice, John A. "Emperor and Impresario: Leopold II and the Transformation of Viennese Musical Theater, 1790–92." Ph. D. dissertation, University of California, Berkeley, 1987.

———. "Rondò vocali di Salieri e Mozart per Adriana Ferrarese." In Muraro, *I vicini,* pp. 185–209.

Rice, John A., and Bruce Alan Brown. "Salieri's *Così fan tutte,*" *COJ* 8 (1996): 17–43.

Richter, Joseph. *Der Zuschauer in Wien, oder Gerade so sind die Wiener und Wienerinnen.* Vol. 5, *Ein Beytrag zum Patriotismus und Theatergeschmack der Wiener.* Vienna: Hochenleitter, 1790.

Riesbeck, Johann Kaspar. *Briefe eines reisenden Franzosen über Deutschland.* Ed. Jochen Golz. Berlin: Rütten & Loening, 1976.

Robinson, Michael F. "Paisiello, Mozart and Casti." In *Internationaler Musikwissenschaftlicher Kongress zum Mozartjahr 1791, Baden-Wien.* Tutzing: Schneider, 1993, pp. 71–79.

Rosand, Ellen. "Operatic Ambiguities and the Power of Music." *COJ* 4 (1992): 75–80.

Rosen, Charles. *The Classical Style: Haydn, Mozart, Beethoven.* London: Faber & Faber, 1971.

———. *Sonata Forms.* New York: Norton, 1980.

Rosen, David. "Cone's and Kivy's World of Opera." *COJ* 4 (1992): 61–74.

Rosselli, John. "Balanced on a Turning Point: *Così fan tutte*'s Difficult History." *Times Literary Supplement,* June 7, 1991, 15–16

———. *Singers of Italian Opera: The History of a Profession.* Cambridge: Cambridge University Press, 1992.

Sadie, Stanley, ed. *The New Grove Dictionary of Opera.* 4 vols. London: Macmillan, 1992.

———, ed. *Wolfgang Amadè Mozart: Essays on His Life and His Music.* Oxford: Clarendon Press, 1996.

Sartori, Claudio. *I libretti italiani a stampa dalle origini al 1800.* 7 vols. Milan: Bertola & Locatelli, 1990–94.

Schindler, Otto. "Das Publikum des Burgtheaters in der Josephinischen Ära: Versuch einer Strukturbestimmung." In Dietrich, *Das Burgtheater und sein Publikum,* pp. 11–96.

Schubart, Christoph Friedrich Daniel. *Ideen zu einer Aesthetik der Tonkunst.* Ed. Ludwig Schubart. Stuttgart: Scheible, 1839.

Sebeok, Thomas A., assisted by Marcia E. Erickson. *Carnival!* Berlin: Mouton, 1984.

Senici, Emanuele. "'Col Suono Orribile de' Miei Sospir': Rage Arias in Viennese Opera Buffa of the 1780's." Unpublished paper, Cornell University, 1994.

Sisman, Elaine. "Haydn's Theatre Symphonies." *JAMS* 63 (1990): 292–352.

Sonnenfels, Joseph von. *Briefe über die Wienerische Schaubühne.* 1768. Facsimile rpt. ed. Hilde Haider-Pregler. Graz: Akademische Druck- und Verlagsanstalt, 1988.

Sparshott, Francis. "Aesthetics of Music: Limits and Grounds." In *What Is Music,* ed. Philip Alperson. University Park, PA: Pennsylvania State University Press, 1987, pp. 33–100.

Splitt, Gerhard. "Gespielte Aufklärung: *Così fan tutte* oder die Umkehrung der Moral." *Freiburger Universitätsblätter* 27 (Sept. 1988): 47–71.

Steptoe, Andrew. *The Mozart–Da Ponte Operas.* Oxford: Clarendon Press, 1988.

Strohm, Reinhard. *Die italienische Oper im 18. Jahrhundert.* Wilhelmshaven: Heinrichshofen, 1979.

Tanzer, Gerhard. *Spectacle müssen seyn: Die Freizeit der Wiener im 18. Jahrhundert.* Vienna: Böhlau, 1992.

Taschenbuch des Wiener Theaters: Erstes Jahr. Vienna: Trattner, 1777.

Theatralalmanach von Wien für das Jahr 1773. Verfasset von einigen Liebhabern der deutschen Schaubühne. Ed. Christian Gottlob Klemm and Franz Heufeld. Vienna, Kurzböck, 1773.

Till, Nicholas. *Mozart and the Enlightenment: Truth, Virtue, and Beauty in Mozart's Operas.* New York: Norton, 1993.

Troy, Charles E. *The Comic Intermezzo: A Study in the History of Eighteenth-Century Italian Opera.* Ann Arbor: UMI Research Press, 1979.

Waldoff, Jessica. "Sentiment and Sensibility in *La vera costanza.*" In *Haydn Studies,* ed. Dean Sutcliffe. Oxford: Oxford University Press, forthcoming.

Wangermann, Ernst. *The Austrian Achievement 1700–1800*. London: Thames and Hudson, 1973.

Warburton, Ernest, ed. *The Librettos of Mozart's Operas*. 7 vols. New York: Garland, 1992.

Weber, Horst. "Der Serva-padrona-Topos in der Oper: Komik als Spiel mit musikalischen und sozialen Normen." *AfMw* 65 (1988): 87–110.

Webster, James. "The Analysis of Mozart's Arias." In *Mozart Studies,* ed. Cliff Eisen. Oxford: Clarendon Press, 1991, pp. 101–99.

———. "How 'Operatic' Are Mozart's Concertos?" In *Mozart's Piano Concertos: Text, Context, Interpretation,* ed. Neal Zaslaw. Ann Arbor: University of Michigan Press, 1996, pp. 107–37.

———, and Mary Hunter. *Opera Buffa in Mozart's Vienna*. Cambridge: Cambridge University Press, 1997.

———. "Understanding Opera Buffa: Analysis = Interpretation." In *Opera Buffa in Mozart's Vienna,* ed. Hunter and Webster, pp. 340–77.

Wiel, Taddeo. *I teatri musicali veneziani del settecento*. With afterword by Reinhard Strohm. Leipzig: Peters, 1979.

Wiennrischer Opernkalender mit Scenen aus den neuesten und beliebtesten Opern auf das Jahr 1796. Vienna: Mathias Ludwig, 1796.

Wienold, Hanns, and Eberhard Hüppe. "*Così fan tutte* oder die hohe Kunst der Konvention." In *Mozart: Die Da Ponte-Opern*. Special issue of *Musik-Konzepte* (Dec. 1991): 293–321.

Wiesend, Reinhard. "Le revisioni di Metastasio di alcuni suoi drammi e la situazione della musica per melodramma negli anni '50 del Settecento." In *Metastasio e il mondo musicale,* ed. Maria Teresa Muraro. Florence: Olschki, 1986, pp. 171–197.

Williams, Bernard. "Mozart's Comedies and the Sense of an Ending." *MT* 122 (1981): 451–54.

Wolff, Hellmuth Christian. *Geschichte der Komischen Oper*. Wilhelmshaven: Heinrichshofen, 1981.

Zechmeister, Gustav. *Die Wiener Theater nächst der Burg und nächst dem Kärntnerthor von 1747 bis 1776*. Vienna: Böhlau, 1971.

Zeman, Herbert, and Cornelia Kritsch. "Rätsel eines genialen Opernentwurf—Da Pontes Libretto zu 'Così fan tutte' und das literarische Umfeld." In *Die österreichische Literatur: Ihr Profil an der Wende vom 18. zum 19. Jahrhundert (1750–1830),* Part I, ed. Herbert Zeman. Graz: Akademische Druck- und Verlagsanstalt, 1979, pp. 355–77.

INDEX

PAGE NUMBERS in italics indicate musical or textual extract. Music examples are indicated by title as sub-subentries within the title of the opera.

PAGE REFERENCES for operas are listed by composer (librettist in parentheses), with cross-references back to the composer from individual opera titles and librettists (the latter in parentheses) listed alphabetically. Operas set to music by more than one composer are listed alphabetically by title (e.g., at *La finta giardiniera*), with page numbers, where the discussions refers to either or both settings, but by composer when the discussion touches a specific setting.

OPERAS INDICATED with asterisks were used for specific comparisons only and do not appear in Appendix One.

Abbate, Carolyn, 105, 225
Abert, Anna Amalie, 286–87
Abert, Hermann, 214n.24, 280n. 7
Abraham, Gerald, 287
Adamberger, Johann Valentin, 5
Allanbrook, Wye J., 6n.11, 29, 65n.37, 104, 111n.4, 145–46, 175n.32
Allroggen, Gerhard, 96n. 7
Americano, L'. See under Piccinni, Niccolò
Amore soldato, L'. See Felici, Alessandro
(Anelli, Angelo), *Griselda* (*see under* Piccinni, Niccolò); *I due supposti conti* (*see under* Cimarosa, Domenico)
Anfossi, Pasquale, *Il curioso indiscreto* (Bertati), 29, 32, 61, *47–48*, 124, *127–28*, 196n.2, 249–50, 257n.31, 301; ("Son Regina disperata"), *142–44*; *La finta giardiniera* (?Petrosellini), 300, ("Se l'augellin sen fugge"), *36–37*, ("Vorrei punirti"), *140–41*; *Le gelosie fortunate* (Livigni), 42, 157n.5, 302; *Il geloso in cimento* (Bertati), 34, 300; *L'incognita perseguitata* (Petrosellini), 33, 137n.18, 196n.1, 209, 211n.17, 300, ("Due pupillette amabili"), *149–50*, (*introduzione*), *199–200, 205–7*, (plot summary), 311; *Isabella e Rodrigo* (Bertati), 41, 301; *Lo sposo disperato* (Bertati), 61, 83n.23, 284, 301; *La vera costanza* (Puttini), 42, 300; *I viaggiatori felici* (Livigni), 62, 301
Angermüller, Rudolph, 268, 269n.68
Angiolini, Gasparo, 7

aria agitata, 280
arias, 95–155; buffa, 110–26; —, antifemale diatribes, 125; —, catalogues in, 124–25; —, formal fluidity in, 123–24; cavatinas, 96; compressed da capo form, 139; formal rhetoric, 102–3; —, in the *serva/contadina* aria, 135–36; and individuality, 100–101, 103–9; musical forms, 102–3, 305–7; and performance, 104–5; rondò, 96, 147, 151; seria, 137–46; social values, 22–23; type of, 95–102
Ariosto, Ludovico, *Orlando furioso*, 248, 259
Armstrong, Nancy, 154
Astarita, Gennaro, 32
Astratto, L'. See under Piccinni, Niccolò
Axur, re di Ormus. See under Salieri, Antonio

Badini, Carlo Francesco, *Orlando paladino* (orig. *Le pazzie di Orlando*). *See under* Guglielmi, Pietro
Baglioni, Costanza, 44
Bakhtin, Mikhail, 72–74
Balsano, Maria Antonella, 266
Barbier de Séville, Le. See under Beaumarchais, Pierre Augustin Caron de
Barbiere di Siviglia, Il. See under Paisiello, Giovanni
Barone di Rocca antica, II. See under Salieri, Antonio
Bauman, Thomas, 8

Beales, Derek, 9n.28, 12n.40, 78n.14

Beaumarchais, Pierre Augustin Caron de, 8; *Le barbier de Séville*, 31; *Le mariage de Figaro*, 3, 31, 53

Beckford, Peter, 27n. 2

Benucci, Francesco, 4, 5, 43, 126, 258, 270

(Bertati, Giovanni), 257; *Il cavaliere errante* (*see under* Traetta, Tommaso); *Il curioso indiscreto* (*see under* Anfossi, Pasquale); *Don Giovanni* (*see under* Gazzaniga, Giuseppe); *Le donne fanatiche* (*see under* Gazzaniga, Guiseppe); *I filosofi immaginari* (*see under* Paisiello, Giovanni); *I finti eredi* (*see under* Sarti, Giuseppe); *Il geloso in cimento* (*see under* Anfossi, Paquale); *Isabella e Rodrigo* (*see under* Anfossi, Pasquale); *L'isola di Alcina* (*see under* Gazzaniga, Guiseppe); *La locanda* (*see under* Gazzaniga, Guiseppe); *Il matrimonio segreto* (*see under* Cimarosa, Domenico); *Le nozze disturbate* (*see under* Naumann, Johann Gottlieb); *Lo sposo disperato* (*see under* Anfossi, Pasquale); *La vendemmia* (*see under* Gazzaniga, Guiseppe); *La villanella rapita* (*see under* Bianchi, Francesco)

Bianchi, Francesco, *La villanella rapita* (Bertati), 3, 18, 24, 41, 75, 78–79, 197, 284, 302; substitute finale, 75, 79

Boccaccio, Giovanni, *Decameron*, 248

(Boccherini, Giovanni Gastone), *La fiera di Venezia* (*see under* Salieri, Antonio); *Don Chisciotte alle nozze di Gamace* (*see under* Salieri, Antonio); *I rovinati* (*see under* Gassmann, Florian Leopold); *Il tamburro notturno* (*see under* Paisiello, Giovanni)

Borghi, Giovanni Battista, *L'amore in campagna*, 83n.23

Braunbehrens, Volkmar, 20n.62

Brown, Bruce Alan, 7n.17, 66n.39, 247–50, 257, 259, 265, 272n.74, 280n.6, 281n.13, 286, 293

Brown, John, 95–96, 139

Bruckmüller, Ernst, 53–54, 56, 174–75

buffa arias. *See under* arias

Buona figliuola, La. See under Piccinni, Niccolò

*Burbero di buon core, Il. See under Martín y Soler, Vicente

Burney, Charles, 43–44

Burnham, Scott, 298n.40

Bussani, Francesco, 258

Bustelli, Giuseppe, 304n. 16

Calamità de' cuori, La. See under Salieri, Antonio

Calvesi, Vincenzo, 252, 258

(Calzabigi, Ranieri de'), *Amiti e Ontario*, 66n.39; *L'opera seria* (*see under* Gassmann, Florian Leopold)

Canterina, La. See under Haydn, Joseph

Caribaldi, Giacomo, 18–19, 45

carnival (theory of), 21, 40–41, 72–73; "uncrowned king," 73–79

(Casti, Giambattista), 5, 257, 267, 268, 269; *La grotta di Trofonio* (*see under* Salieri, Antonio); *Prima la musica e poi le parole* (*see under* Salieri, Antonio); *Il re Teodoro in Venezia* (*see under* Paisiello, Giovanni)

Cavaliere errante, Il. See under Traetta, Tommaso

(Cavalieri, Bartolomeo), *L'impresa dell' opera* (*see under* Guglielmi, Pietro)

Cavalieri, Caterina, 8, 43, 257

Cervantes, Miguel de, *Don Quixote*, 32

Chardin, Pierre, 88

(Chiari, Pietro), *La contadina di spirito* (*see under* Paisiello, Giovanni); *La sposa fedele* (*see under* Guglielmi, Pietro)

Chi dell' altrui si veste. See under Cimarosa, Domenico

Christmann, Johann, 96

* *Cifra, La. See under* Salieri, Antonio

Cimarosa, Domenico, *Chi dell' altrui si veste* (Palomba), 43; *I due supposti conti* (Anelli), 59n.26, 302; *Giannina e Bernardone* (Livigni), 196n.1, 302; *L'italiana in Londra* (Petrosellini), 65, 200n.10, 265, 301; *Il matrimonio segreto* (Bertati), 61; *Il pittore parigino* (Petrosellini), *34*, 282, 302; ("Sul mio core invan presume"), *36–39*

(Cipretti, Pietro), *La moda. See under* Salieri, Antonio

Coltellini, Celeste, 43

comedy: and *Così fan tutte*, 286; endings

of, 29–30; and generational cycle, 67; social functions of endings of, 69–70; social reversals as characteristic of, 71–73; and ternary structures in *introduzioni*, 67, 209

Contadina in corte, La. See under Sacchini, Antonio

Contratempi, I. See under Sarti, Giuseppe

convention, 34–46; in arias, 95–103, 110–55; in *Così*, 273–98

Convitato di pietra, Il. See under Righini, Vincenzo

Cosa rara, Una. See under Martín y Soler, Vicente

Così fan tutte. See under Mozart, Wolfgang Amadeus

Crotti, Ilaria, 30n. 11

Curioso indiscreto, Il. See under Anfossi, Pasquale

(Da Ponte, Lorenzo), 3n.6, 5, 6, 29, 78, 215, 248, 249, 250n.18, 257, 258, 268, 269, 286, 298; *L'ape musicale,* 257; *L'arbore di Diana,* 54 (*see also* Martín y Soler, Vicente); *Axur, re di Ormus* (*see under* Salieri, Antonio); *Il burbero di buon core* (*see under* Martín y Soler, Vicente); *La cifra (see under* Salieri, Antonio); *Una cosa rara (see under* Martín y Soler, Vicente); *Così fan tutte (see under* Mozart, Wolfgang Amadeus); description of finale, 212; *Don Giovanni (see under* Mozart, Wolfgang Amadeus); *Gli equivoci (see under* Storace, Stephen); *Nina, o sia la pazza per amore (see under* Paisiello, Giovanni); *Le nozze di Figaro* (*see under* Mozart, Wolfgang Amadeus)

(De Gamerra, Giovanni), *La calamità de' cuori. See under* Salieri, Antonio

Degrada, Francesco, 285

Della Corte, Andrea, xi, 258

Dent, Edward J., 214n. 21, 267

Dietrich, Margret, xi, 57

Discordia fortunata, La. See under Paisiello, Giovanni

Dittersdorf, Carl Ditters von, 8

Don Anchise Campanone. See under Paisiello, Giovanni

Don Chisciotte alle nozze di Gamace. See under Salieri, Antonio

Don Chisciotte della Mancia. See under Paisiello, Giovanni

Don Giovanni. See under Gazzaniga, Giuseppe; Mozart, Wolfgang Amadeus

Donizetti, Gaetano, *Don Pasquale,* 83n.23

Donne fanatiche, Le. See under Gazzaniga, Giuseppe

Due contesse, Le. See under Paisiello, Giovanni

Duello, Il. See under Paisiello, Giovanni

Due supposti conti, I. See under Cimarosa, Domenico

Dyer, Richard, 52n.1

Eco, Umberto, 73

Edge, Dexter, 6n.14, 13n.46, 14, 254

Einstein, Alfred, 287

Elias, Norbert, 139n. 23

ensemble principle, 158

ensembles, 156–95; and gender, 160–61; and individuality, 156–57, 162; and instrumental music, 156; and musical form, 158–60, 162–63, 172–74, 211–14; dramatic functions of endings, 174, 177; opening choruses, 199; social implications of endings, 174–75, 179; social values, 23; substitutions and additions, 17–18

ensemble spirit, 156, 198

entertainment: defined for purpose of book, 4; poetics of, xi, 22; and notion of repertory, 15–16

Entführung aus dem Serail, Die. See under Mozart, Wolfgang Amadeus

Equivoci, Gli. See under Storace, Stephen

Fedeltà premiata, La. See under Haydn, Joseph

Feldman, Martha, 139

Felici, Alessandro, *L'amore soldato* (Tassi), 300

Ferrarese, Adriana del Bene, 17, 250, 257, 258n.34; Tarchi's arias for, in *L'arbore di Diana,* 252–54

Fiera di Venezia, La. See under Salieri, Antonio

Filosofi immaginari, I. See under Paisiello, Giovanni

finales, 210–43; and individuality, 216–23; and law of increase, 211–14; and musical form, 214

Finta giardiniera, La, 29, 42, 59n. 26, *68, 86, 137–38*, 199. *See also* Anfossi, Pasquale; and Mozart, Wolfgang Amadeus
Finti eredi, I. See under Sarti, Giuseppe
Fra i due litiganti il terzo gode. See under Sarti, Giuseppe
Frascatana, La. See under Paisiello, Giovanni
French theatrical tradition, 8
Freud, Sigmund, 31, 52
(Friberth Karl), *La canterina* (*see under* Haydn, Joseph); *L'incontro improvviso* (*see under* Haydn, Joseph)
Fried, Michael, 88
Frye, Northrop, 67–68, 81

Gare generose, Le. See under Paisiello, Giovanni
Gasparini, Giulia, 44n.37
Gassmann, Florian Leopold, *L'amore artigiano* (Goldoni), 19–20, 147–48, 198, 299; *introduzione, 200–203*; *L'opera seria* (Calzabigi), 160n.12, 299; *I rovinati* (Boccherini), 299
Gay, Peter, 174
Gazzaniga, Giuseppe, *Don Giovanni* (Bertati), 65n.35; *Le donne fanatiche* (Bertati), 44; *L'isola di Alcina* (Bertati), 200n.9, 211, 225n.32, 251n.23, 300; ("Sento un affanno in petto"), *140–42*; *La locanda* (Bertati), 299; (act I, finale), 291, *292*; *La vendemmia* (Bertati), *59, 87–88*, 301; ("Del destin invan mi lagno),*" 60*
Gebler, Tobias Philipp, 9, 52–53
Gelosie fortunate, Le. See under Anfossi, Pasquale
Gelosie villane, Le. See under Sarti, Giuseppe
Geloso in cimento, Il. See under Anfossi, Pasquale
gender: in *introduzioni*, 161; and lower-class characters, 110–40; and rage, 144–46; and sentiment, 146–55
Gerber, William, 265
German drama, 7–13, 63
Gherardi, Pietro, 137n.18
Giannetta, La. See Anfossi, Pasquale, *L'incognita persequita*
Giannetta persequita, La. See Anfossi, Pasquale, *L'incognita persequita*

Giannina e Bernardone. See Cimarosa, Domenico
Giller, Monika, 63
Ginguené, Pierre-Louis, 86–87
(Giovannini, Pietro), *Giulio Sabino. See under* Sarti, Giuseppe
*Giulio Sabino. See under Sarti, Giuseppe
Gluck, Christoph Willibald, 7, 150; *Don Juan*, 32; *Orfeo*, chorus of Furies in, 217–18, 260
Goethe, Johann Wolfgang von, 44
Goehring, Edmund J., 214n.26, 275n.3
(Goldoni, Carlo), 33, 63n.34, 65, 71; *L'amore artigiano* (*see under* Gassmann, Florian Leopold); *La buona figliuola* (*see under* Piccinni, Niccolò); *La calamità de' cuori* (*see under* Salieri, Antonio); ?*Fra i due litiganti il terzo gode* (*see under* Sarti, Giuseppe); *Il mondo della luna* (*see under* Haydn, Joseph; Paisiello, Giovanni); *Le nozze*, 34; *Le pescatrici* (*see under* Haydn, Joseph); *La scuola moderna*, 249; *Lo speziale* (*see under* Haydn, Joseph); *La vedova scaltra* (*see under* Righini, Vincenzo)
Gordon, Daniel, 91n.36
Grandi, Tommaso, *Le gelosie villane. See under* Sarti, Giuseppe
Green, Rebecca Lee, 72n.4, 145n.29
Greuze, Jean-Baptiste, 88
*Griselda, La. See under Piccinni, Niccolò
Grotta di Trofonio, La. See under Salieri, Antonio
Grout, Donald Jay, 214n. 21
Guglielmi, Pietro, *L'impresa dell'opera* (Cavalieri), 200n.9, 299; *Orlando paladino* (Badini), 300; *La pastorella nobile* (Zini), 303; *La quacquera spiritosa* (Palomba), 157n.5, 303; *La sposa fedele* (Chiari), 41, 299; *Le vicende d'amore* (Neri), 43, 59, 302

Handel, Georg Frideric, *Giulio Cesare*, 251n.23
Haydn, Joseph, 18n.60, 19, 33; *La canterina* (Friberth), 299; *La fedeltà premiata* (Lorenzi), 42, 80n.18, 301; *L'infedeltà delusa* (?Coltellini), 300; *L'incontro improvviso* (Friberth), 41, 110n.3, 295n.37, 300; *Il mondo della luna* (Goldoni), 61, 137n.18, 150n.39, 196n.2, 265, 301,

(act I finale), *293–96*; *Orlando paladino* (Porta), 301; *Le pescatrici* (Goldoni), 299; *Lo speziale* (Goldoni), 197n.4, 299; *La vera costanza* (Puttini), 291, 301

Heartz, Daniel, 3, 41n.25, 47n.43, 69, 201n.12, 247n.2, 249, 272n.74, 280nn.6, 7

Henze-Döhring, Sabine, 215n.30

Herbert, Christopher, 28

Heufeld, Franz, 8; *Theatral-almanach...1773*, 10, 22n.65, 43

Hunter, G. K., 69–70

Hüppe, Eberhard, 286n.24

Impresa dell'opera, L'. See under Guglielmi, Pietro

Incognita perseguitata, La, 42, 59n.26; plot summary, 311. *See also* Anfossi, Pasquale; Piccinni, Niccolò

Incontro inaspettato, L'. See under Righini, Vincenzo

Incontro improvviso, L'. See under Haydn, Joseph

Infedeltà delusa, L'. See under Haydn, Joseph

intertextuality, 30, 34

introduzioni: and comedy, 68–69, 196–209; definitions and designations, 197–98; gender in, 161; musical and dramatic form in, 198–209; tableaux and springboards, 209–10

Isabella e Rodrigo. See under Anfossi, Pasquale

Isola di Alcina, L'. See under Gazzaniga, Giuseppe

Italiana in Londra, L'. See under Cimarosa, Domenico

Jagendorf, Zvi, 29–30

Jauss, Hans Robert, xi

Joseph II, 5, 7, 12, 14, 17, 20, 21, 27, 42–43, 53, 67, 78, 79

Justi, J.H.G. von, 174

Kerman, Joseph, 267, 270

Khevenhüller, Count Johann Joseph, 27

Klemm, Christian Gottlob, *Theatral-almanach . . . 1773*, 10, 22n.65, 43

Koch, Johann Christoph, 146

Kunze, Stefan, 209, 265, 267, 278, 280, 285–86, 293

Laclos, Louis Choderlos de, *Les liaisons dangereuses*, 248

Landes, Joan B., 91n.36

Lavagetto, Mario, 31, 52

Leopold, Silke, xi, 272n.74, 285

Lessing, Gotthold Ephraim, 8

Link, Dorothea, 251nn.19, 22, 252n.24, 254, 256, 260n.41, 266

Lippmann, Friedrich, 211n.16

(Livigni, Filippo): *La frascatana* (*see under* Paisiello, Giovanni); *Le gelosie fortunate* (*see under* Anfossi, Pasquale); *Giannina e Bernardone* (*see under* Cimarosa, Domenico); *L' innocente fortunata* (*see under* Paisiello, Giovanni); *La locanda* (*see under* Gazzaniga, Giuseppe); *I viaggiatori felici* (*see under* Anfossi, Pasquale)

Locandiera, La. See under Salieri, Antonio

(Lorenzi, Giambattista): *Don Anchise Campanone* (*see under* Paisiello, Giovanni); *Don Chisciotte della Mancia* (*see under* Paisiello, Giovanni); *Il duello* (*see under* Paisiello, Giovanni); *La fedeltà premiata* (*see under* Haydn, Joseph); *Nina, o sia la pazza per amore* ([adapted by Da Ponte] *see under* Paisiello, Giovanni)

Mamczarz, Irène, xi

Mandini, Stefano, 43, 45

Manfredini, Vincenzo, 96

Marchesi, Luigi, 7, 43, 139

Maria Theresia, 67, 78

Mariage de Figaro, Le. See under Beaumarchais, Pierre Augustin Caron de

Marivaux, Pierre Carlet de Chamblain, 248

Markley, Robert, 155n.44

Marshall, David, 88n.33

Martinotti, Sergio, 269n.68

Martín y Soler, Vicente, 24, 150, 157; *L'arbore di Diana* (Da Ponte), 43, 139n.22, 158, 196n.2, 213, 250–56, 265, 283, 302, ("Pian, pianino"), *163–68*, ("Sento che Dea son io"), *137–38*, ("Teco porta"), 253; *Il burbero di buon core* (Da Ponte), 31n.15, 32; *Una cosa rara* (Da Ponte), 4, 6n.14, 45, *58–59*, 60, 62, *75–79*, 145, 158, 161, *175–76*, 196, 198, 199, 280, 302, (act I finale), *223–24*; (comment by Pezzl), 14,

Martín y Soler, Vicente (*cont.*)
   ("Non farmi più languire"), *47*, ("Per
   pietà non vi sdegnate"), *288–90*,
   ("Seguir degg'io chi fugge"), *77*
Matrimonio segreto, Il. See under
   Cimarosa, Domenico
Mayer, Hans, 267
Mazzolà, Caterino, *La scuola dei gelosi. See
   under* Salieri, Antonio
Metastasio, Pietro: *Demetrio,* 33, 142, 249;
   Demofoonte, 142; *L'olimpiade,* 33
Metilde ritrovata, La. See Anfossi, Pasquale,
   L'incognita perseguitata
Michtner, Otto, xi, 8
Moda, La. See under Salieri, Antonio
Moindrot, Isabelle, 267
Molinara, La. See under Paisiello,
   Giovanni
Mondo della luna, Il. See under Haydn,
   Joseph; Paisiello, Giovanni
Morichelli-Boselli, Anna, 250, 258n.34
Mozart, Wolfgang Amadeus, 5, 6, 19,
   35n.22, 155, 157; *Così fan tutte* (Da
   Ponte), 24, 42, 65, 81, 84, 98n.13, 104,
   125, 139, 147, 157, 161, 196n.2, 197,
   198–99, 223, 247–98, 302, (act II fi-
   nale), *264*, ("Come scoglio"), 275, *279*,
   ("Donne mie"), 48, 104, ("In uomini"),
   275–77, ("Prenderò quel brunettino"),
   277, *279*, ("Scioccherie di poeti"), *262*,
   ("Smanie implacabili"), 275, *278*; *Don
   Giovanni* (Da Ponte), 29, 30, 32, 65, 66,
   124, 158, 161, 162, 196n.3, 197,
   204n.13, 223, 270n.70, 296, 302; *Die
   Entführung aus dem Serail* (Stephanie),
   8, 41; *La finta giardiniera* (?Petrosellini),
   18n.60, 300; *Idomeneo* (Varesco),
   280n.6, insertion arias in *Il curioso indiscreto,* 250n.14; insertions in *La villanella
   rapita,* 157; *Le nozze di Figaro* (Da
   Ponte), 3–5, 23–24, 31n.15, 61, 66, 75,
   79, 81, 82, 88, 98n.13, 100, 104, 109,
   111, 125, 145–46, 147, 158, 161
   and n.15, 196n.1, 197, 198, 213, 214,
   223, 226, 247, 296, 302, ("Aprite un
   po'"), 48, ("Deh vieni non tardar"),
   47n.43, ("In quegl' anni"), 47, ("Voi
   che sapete"), 46; variations on "Salve tu
   Domine," from *I filosofi immaginari,* K.
   398/416e, 36

Naumann, Johann Gottlieb: *Le nozze dis-
   turbate* (Bertati), 291, 301, ("In quegl'
   ultimi momenti"), *49–51*
Neri (first name unknown), *Le vicende d'
   amore. See under* Guglielmi, Pietro
Nina, La. See under Paisiello, Giovanni
Noiray, Michel, 281n.8
Noske, Frits, 281n.10, 297n.39
Nozze di Figaro, Le. See under Mozart,
   Wolfgang Amadeus
Nozze disturbate, Le. See under Naumann,
   Johann Gottlieb
Novello, Mary, 257
Noverre, Jean-Georges, 7, 11

opera buffa: in contemporary Viennese
   writings, 10–13; conventions in *Così fan
   tutte,* 273–98; endings, 23–24, 28–30,
   283–85; gender-representation in casts
   of, 60n.12; general musical qualities of,
   19–20; and geographic location, 55;
   household setting of, 61–63, 268,
   282–83; names of characters in, 35;
   newly composed vs. imported, 15, 17;
   notion of "the work" in, 16–17; number
   of performances, 6; as a pan-European
   genre, 15; performative aspects, 21,
   42–51, 88–92, 103–9; rankings and
   arrangements of characters, 58–67; redundancy in, 21–22; representation of
   society as a whole, 199; *serva padrona* archetype, 83–84, 85; social configuration
   of theatres for, 57–58; between 1776
   and 1783, 303n.11; and sex, 44–45;
   ticket prices for, 14; title-changes in, 33;
   and topical references, 54; wives and
   mothers in, 62–63
opera seria, 30n.13, 146; in dialogue with
   opera buffa, 6–7
opera seria, L'. See under Gassmann, Florian
   Leopold
Orlando paladino. See under Guglielmi,
   Pietro; Haydn, Joseph
Osthoff, Wolfgang, xii, 96n.7, 156, 214
Ovid, *Metamorphoses,* 248

Paisiello, Giovanni: *Il barbiere di Siviglia*
   (Petrosellini), 3–4, 5, 6n.14, 24, 40, 43,
   61, 66, 74, 157, 158, 160n.12, 161,
   196n.2, 210n.15, 211n.17, 247, 280,

288, 301; ("Deh riede la primavera"), 46; *La contadina di spirito* (anon.), 83n.23, 302; *La discordia fortunata* (Abate F.B.A.F.), 302; *Don Anchise Campanone* (Lorenzi), 300; *Don Chisciotte della Mancia* (Lorenzi), 32; *Le due contesse* (Petrosellini), 31n.15, 83n.23, *125*, 157n.5, 300; *Il duello* (Lorenzi), 300; *I filosofi immaginari* (Bertati), 32, 36, 61, 196n.2, 199, 211n.17, 213, 223, *225*, 260, 265, 301, ("A voi darla in matrimonio"), *111–24*, 210, (act II finale), *216–19*, (—, text and translation), *227–33*; *La frascatana* (Livigni), *28, 64*, 157n.4, 196n.1, 197, 211n.17, 300; *Le gare generose* (Palomba), 41, 66, 196n.3, 200n.10, 211, 302, (plot summary), 310, (act I finale), *221–22*, ("Ola, dico"), *177–95*; *L'innocente fortunata* (Livigni), 300, ("Ben lo dicea mio Padre"), 17n.57; *La molinara* (Palomba), 157n.4, 303; *Il mondo della luna* (Goldoni), 295; *Nina, o sia la pazza per amore* (Lorenzi/Da Ponte), 303; *Il re Teodoro in Venezia* (Casti), 31n.15, 199, 302; *Il tamburro notturno* (Boccherini), 300

Palomba, Giuseppe: *Chi dell' altrui si veste* (*see under* Cimarosa, Domenico); *Le gare generose* (*see under* Paisiello, Giovanni); *La molinara* (*see under* Paisiello, Giovanni); *La quacquera spiritosa* (*see under* Guglielmi, Pietro)

Parker, Roger, 225–26

parody: in *Così fan tutte*, 280–82; in rage arias, 142–44

parti serie, 80, 137–40, 160

Passmore, John, 264–65

pastoral, 67–68, 76–78, 209–10, 260n.40, 266

Pastorella nobile, La. See under Guglielmi, Pietro

performative aspects. *See under* opera buffa

Pescatrici, Le. See under Haydn, Joseph

(Petrosellini, Giuseppe): *L'astratto* (*see under* Piccinni, Niccolò); *Il barbiere di Siviglia* (*see under* Paisiello, Giovanni); *Il barone di Rocca antica* (*see under* Salieri, Antonio); *Le due contesse* (*see under* Paisiello, Giovanni); *La finta giardiniera*

(uncertain attribution; *see under* Anfossi, Pasquale; Mozart, Wolfgang Amadeus); *L'incognita perseguitata* (*see under* Anfossi, Pasquale; Piccinni, Niccolò); *L'italiana in Londra* (*see under* Cimarosa, Domenico); *Il pittore parigino* (*see under* Cimarosa, Domenico)

Pezzl, Johann, 14, 56, 66, 91, 126, 137, 155

Piccinni, Niccolò: *L'americano* (anon.), 300; *L'astratto* (Petrosellini), 55, 59, 83n.23, 196n.2, 200n.10, 211n.17, 300, ("Io mi sento in mezzo al core"), *99–101*; *La buona figliuola* (Goldoni), 42, 61, 197n.4, 211n.17, 284, 299, ("Che piacer, che bel diletto"), *86–87*; *Griselda* (Anelli), 86; *L'incognita perseguitata* (Petrosellini), 33, 299

Piozzi, Hester Lynch, 56, 67

Pirani, Federico, 18

Piticchio, Francesco, 3n.6, insertion aria in *I finti eredi*, 3–4, 5, 17

Pittore parigino, Il. See under Cimarosa, Domenico

Platoff, John, 110n.2, 123nn.6 and 7, 124, 159, 166, 177, 211, 213, 214–15, 216, 225

Poggi, Domenico, *La locandiera. See under* Salieri, Antonio

(Porta, Nunziato): *I contratempi* (*see under* Sarti, Giuseppe); *Il convitato di pietra* (*see under* Righini, Vincenzo); *L'incontro inaspettato* (*see under* Righini, Vincenzo)

*Prima la musica e poi le parole. See under Salieri, Antonio

Puttini, Francesco, *La vera costanza. See under* Anfossi, Pasquale; Haydn, Joseph

Rabin, Ronald, 40n.24, 158n.7, 159, 162–63, 168n.23, 177n.33

Ratner, Leonard, 6n.11

Reckford, Kenneth, 69–70

Rector, Monica, 72n.3

Re Teodoro in Venezia, Il. See under Paisiello, Giovanni

Rice, John A., 15, 252n.25, 257

Richter, Joseph, 43

Riesbeck, Baron Johann Kaspar von, 13, 126, 155

Righini, Vincenzo: *Il convitato di pietra*

Righini, Vincenzo (*cont.*)
(Porta), 32, *64*, 196n. 3, 200n. 9, 301;
L'incontro inaspettato (Porta), 86, 212,
302; *La vedova scaltra* (Goldoni), *28*, 34,
301
Robinson, Michael F., xii
Rosen, Charles, 139n.20
Rosenberg-Orsini, Count Franz Xaver
Wolf, 12, 42–43
Rosselli, John, 272n.74, 282–83
Rossini, Gioachino, *Il barbiere di Siviglia*,
40
Rovinati, I. See under Gassmann, Florian
Leopold

Sacchini, Antonio, *La contadina in corte*
(Tassi), 31n.15, 83n.23, 299
Salieri, Antonio, 6, 8, 24, 157; *Axur, re di
Ormus* (Da Ponte), 199, 302; *Il barone
di Rocca antica* (Petroselllini), 43, 299;
La calamita de' cuori (De Gamerra),
58n.24, 300; *La cifra* (Da Ponte), 158;
and *Così fan tutte*, 257; *Les Danaïdes*
(Roullet), 268; "Deh se ti guida onore,"
in Anfossi's *L'incognita perseguitata*,
105–8, 149–50; *Don Chisciotte alle
nozze di Gamace* (Boccherini), 32, 299;
La fiera di Venezia (Boccherini), 31, 46,
55, 83, 144n.28, 160n.11, 161, 199,
284, 299; *La grotta di Trofonio* (Casti),
16, 32, 42, 55, 158, 161, 250, 302; —,
and *Così fan tutte*, 257–72, ("Amici,
a quel che veggio"), *261*, ("Spirti invisibili"), *263*, *271*; *La locandiera* (Poggi),
31, 300, ("Vo pensando e ripensando"),
151–54; *La moda* (Cipretti), 160n.12,
299; *Prima la musica e poi le parole*
(Casti), 46; *La scuola dei gelosi* (Mazzolà), 15n.54, 62n.29, 158, 301
Sarti, Giuseppe: *I contratempi* (Porta), 42,
55, 302; *I finti eredi* (Bertati), 3–5, 24,
41, 60–61, *67–68*, 111n.3, 283–84,
302, (plot summary), 309–10; *Fra i due
litiganti il terzo gode* (Goldoni/anon.),
3, *28*, 34, 45, 61, *81–82*, 196, 210, 213,
216, 225, 288, 301, (act II finale),
89–90, *219–21*, (—, text and translation), *234–43*, (—, *introduzione*),
203–4, 205, *207–9*, ("L'onda placida"),
148–49, ("Sono una fanciullina"),
128–36; *Le gelosie villane* (Grandi),

31n.15, 301, ("Deh, caro padre amato"),
168–74; *Giulio Sabino* (Giovannini),
7, 43
Sartori, Claudio, xi
Schindler, Otto G., xi, 14, 57
Schroeder, Friedrich Ludwig, 5
Schubart, Christoph Friedrich Daniel,
146n.32
Scuola dei gelosi, La. See under Salieri, Antonio
Sellars, Peter, 84n.25
sentiment: and the domestic sphere, 154;
and social class, 146–55
sentimental heroines, 41–42, 84–91
seria arias. *See under* arias
Shakespeare, William, 8, 32
Singspiel, 8–9
singer-classifications, 35
social class: and the buffa aria, 125–26; and
coloratura, 139–40; Habsburg stimu-
lation of bourgeois, 53; in Milan vs. Lon-
don, 56–57; of opera buffa audiences,
13–15; reflected in the seria aria,
137–40; and sentiment, 146–55; in the
serva/contadina aria, 126–27, 136–37.
See also under Vienna
Sonnenfels, Joseph von, 9, 18–19, 45
Speziale, Lo. See under Haydn, Joseph
Sposa fedele, La. See under Guglielmi, Pietro
Sposo disperato, Lo. See under Anfossi,
Pasquale
Steptoe, Andrew, 269n.68
Storace, Nancy, 4, 5, 17, 43, 45, 47n.43
Storace, Stephen, *Gli equivoci* (Da Ponte),
31n.15, 32, 158
Strohm, Reinhard, xii, 71–72, 156
Swieten, Baron van, 79

Tamburro notturno, Il. See under Paisiello,
Giovanni
Tarchi, Angelo, insertion arias in *L'arbore
di Diana*, 252, *254–56*
Tassi, Niccolò: *L'amore soldato* (*see under*
Felici, Alessandro); *La contadina in corte*
(*see under* Sacchini, Antonio)
Till, Nicholas, 285
Tomeoni-Dutilleu, Irene, 44n.37
Topoi, 6
Traetta, Tommaso, *Il cavaliere errante*
(Bertati), 301
Troy, Charles E., xii, 83n.23

Vedova scaltra, La. See under Righini, Vincenzo

Vélez de Guevara, Luis, 78

Vendemmia, La. See under Gazzaniga, Giuseppe

Vera costanza, La. 86, 200n.9. *See also* Anfossi, Pasquale; Haydn, Joseph

Verdi, Giuseppe, 31

Viaggiatori felici, I. See under Anfossi, Pasquale

Vicende d'amore, Le. See under Guglielmi, Pietro

Vienna: attitudes toward opera buffa, 7–13; Burgtheater, (audiences), 13–15, (description), 57–58; cicisbeism, 155; change in Joseph II's status, 78–79; contradictory social patterns, 54; Kärntnerthortheater, 7, 16–17, 18; literature about opera buffa, 10–12; marriage and social class, 91–92; relations between artisanal and upper classes, 66–67; sentiment and marriage, 155; suburban theatres, 8

Villanella rapita, La. See under Bianchi, Francesco

Villeneuve, Luisa, 234

Voltaire, François Marie Arouet de, 265

Wangermann, Ernst, 12, 20n.63

Weber, Horst, 85

Webster, James, 96–97, 108–9, 151–54

Weigl, Joseph, 18n.59; substitute finale in *La villanella rapita*, 75

Weiss, Piero, 55

Wiel, Taddeo, xi

Wienold, Hanns, 286n.24

Williams, Bernard, 297n.39

Wolff, Hellmuth Christian, xii, 286

women: absence of (wives and mothers), 62–63; lower-class, and sex, 136–37; and rage, 140–45; and the rondò, 147; and "to-be-looked-at" mode of expression, 127

Zanetti, Roberto, xii

Zechmeister, Gustav, xi

Zini, Francesco Saverio, *La pastorella nobile. See under* Guglielmi, Pietro

Zinzendorf, Count Franz Carl, 13, 36, 45, 158, 269, 270

About the Author

MARY HUNTER is Professor of Music at Bowdoin College.
She is the editor, with James Webster, of
Opera Buffa in Mosart's Vienna.